Praise for *Domain-Driven Design*

"This book belongs on the shelf of every thoughtful software developer."

—Kent Beck

"Eric Evans has written a fantastic book on how you can make the design of your software match your mental model of the problem domain you are addressing.

His book is very compatible with XP. It is not about drawing pictures of a domain; it is about how you think of it, the language you use to talk about it, and how you organize your software to reflect your improving understanding of it. Eric thinks that learning about your problem domain is as likely to happen at the end of your project as at the beginning, and so refactoring is a big part of his technique.

The book is a fun read. Eric has lots of interesting stories, and he has a way with words. I see this book as essential reading for software developers—it is a future classic."

—Ralph Johnson, author of *Design Patterns*

"If you don't think you are getting value from your investment in object-oriented programming, this book will tell you what you've forgotten to do."

—Ward Cunningham

"What Eric has managed to capture is a part of the design process that experienced object designers have always used, but that we have been singularly unsuccessful as a group in conveying to the rest of the industry. We've given away bits and pieces of this knowledge . . . but we've never organized and systematized the principles of building domain logic. This book is important."

—Kyle Brown, author of *Enterprise Java Programming with IBM WebSphere*

"Eric Evans convincingly argues for the importance of domain modeling as the central focus of development and provides a solid framework and set of techniques for accomplishing it. This is timeless wisdom, and will hold up long after the methodologies du jour have gone out of fashion."

—Dave Collins, author of *Designing Object-Oriented User Interfaces*

"Eric weaves real-world experience modeling—and building—business applications into a practical, useful book. Written from the perspective of a trusted practitioner, Eric's descriptions of ubiquitous language, the benefits of sharing models with users, object life-cycle management, logical and physical application structuring, and the process and results of deep refactoring are major contributions to our field."

—Luke Hohmann, author of *Beyond Software Architecture*

Domain-Driven Design

Domain-Driven Design

TACKLING COMPLEXITY IN THE HEART OF SOFTWARE

Eric Evans

✦✦Addison-Wesley

Upper Saddle River, NJ • Boston • Indianapolis • San Francisco
New York • Toronto • Montreal • London • Munich • Paris • Madrid
Capetown • Sydney • Tokyo • Singapore • Mexico City

See page 517 for photo credits.

The publisher offers discounts on this book when ordered in quantity for bulk purchases and special sales. For more information, please contact:

U.S. Corporate and Government Sales
(800) 382-3419
corpsales@pearsontechgroup.com

For sales outside of the U.S., please contact:

International Sales
international@pearsoned.com

Visit Addison-Wesley on the Web: www.awprofessional.com

Library of Congress Cataloging-in-Publication Data
Evans, Eric, 1962–
   Domain-driven design : tackling complexity in the heart of software / Eric
   Evans.
      p. cm.
   Includes bibliographical references and index.
   ISBN 0-321-12521-5
      1. Computer software—Development. 2. Object-oriented programming
      (Computer science)   I. Title.

QA76.76.D47E82 2003
005.1—dc21

2003050331

ISBN   0-321-12521-5

Text printed in the United States on recycled paper at Courier Westford in Westford, Massachusetts.

Eighteenth Printing V013 May 2012

To Mom and Dad

CONTENTS

FOREWORD

There are many things that make software development complex. But the heart of this complexity is the essential intricacy of the problem domain itself. If you're trying to add automation to complicated human enterprise, then your software cannot dodge this complexity—all it can do is control it.

The key to controlling complexity is a good domain model, a model that goes beyond a surface vision of a domain by introducing an underlying structure, which gives the software developers the leverage they need. A good domain model can be incredibly valuable, but it's not something that's easy to make. Few people can do it well, and it's very hard to teach.

Eric Evans is one of those few who can create domain models well. I discovered this by working with him—one of those wonderful times when you find a client who's more skilled than you are. Our collaboration was short but enormous fun. Since then we've stayed in touch, and I've watched this book gestate slowly.

gestate

It's been well worth the wait.

This book has evolved into one that satisfies a huge ambition: To describe and build a vocabulary about the very art of domain modeling. To provide a frame of reference through which we can explain this activity as well as teach this hard-to-learn skill. It's a book that's given me many new ideas as it has taken shape, and I'd be astonished if even old hands at conceptual modeling don't get a raft of new ideas from reading this book.

Eric also cements many of the things that we've learned over the years. First, in domain modeling, you shouldn't separate the concepts from the implementation. An effective domain modeler can not only use a whiteboard with an accountant, but also write Java with a programmer. Partly this is true because you cannot build a *useful* conceptual model without considering implementation issues. But the primary reason why concepts and implementation belong together is this: The greatest value of a domain model is that it provides a *ubiquitous language* that ties domain experts and technologists together.

Another lesson you'll learn from this book is that domain models aren't first modeled and then implemented. Like many people, I've come to reject the phased thinking of "design, then build." But the lesson of Eric's experience is that the really powerful domain models evolve over time, and even the most experienced modelers find that they gain their best ideas after the initial releases of a system.

I think, and hope, that this will be an enormously influential book. One that will add structure and cohesion to a very slippery field while it teaches a lot of people how to use a valuable tool. Domain models can have big consequences in controlling software development—in whatever language or environment they are implemented.

One final yet important thought. One of things I most respect about this book is that Eric is not afraid to talk about the times when he *hasn't* been successful. Most authors like to maintain an air of disinterested omnipotence. Eric makes it clear that like most of us, he's tasted both success and disappointment. The important thing is that he can learn from both—and more important for us is that he can pass on his lessons.

Martin Fowler
April 2003

PREFACE

Leading software designers have recognized domain modeling and design as critical topics for at least 20 years, yet surprisingly little has been written about what needs to be done or how to do it. Although it has never been formulated clearly, a philosophy has emerged as an undercurrent in the object community, a philosophy I call *domain-driven design*.

I have spent the past decade developing complex systems in several business and technical domains. In my work, I have tried best practices in design and development process as they have emerged from the leaders in object-oriented development. Some of my projects were very successful; a few failed. A feature common to the successes was a rich domain model that evolved through iterations of design and became part of the fabric of the project.

This book provides a framework for making design decisions and a technical vocabulary for discussing domain design. It is a synthesis of widely accepted best practices along with my own insights and experiences. Software development teams facing complex domains can use this framework to approach domain-driven design systematically.

Contrasting Three Projects

Three projects stand out in my memory as vivid examples of how dramatically domain design practice can affect development results. Although all three projects delivered useful software, only one achieved its ambitious objectives and produced complex software that continued to evolve to meet the ongoing needs of the organization.

I watched one project get out of the gate fast, by delivering a useful, simple Web-based trading system. Developers were flying by the seat of their pants, but this didn't hinder them because simple software can be written with little attention to design. As a result of this initial success, expectations for future development were sky-high. That is when I was asked to work on the second version. When I took a close look, I saw that they lacked a domain model, or even a common language on the project, and were saddled with an unstructured design. The project leaders did not agree with my assessment, and I declined the job. A year later, the team found itself bogged down and unable to deliver a second version. Although their use of technology was not exemplary, it was the business logic that overcame them. Their first release had ossified prematurely into a high-maintenance legacy.

Lifting this ceiling on complexity calls for a more serious approach to the design of domain logic. Early in my career, I was fortunate to end up on a project that did emphasize domain design. This project, in a domain at least as complex as the first one, also started with a modest initial success, delivering a simple application for institutional traders. But in this case, the initial delivery was followed up with successive accelerations of development. Each iteration opened exciting new options for integrating and elaborating the functionality of the previous release. The team was able to respond to the needs of the traders with flexibility and expanding capability. This upward trajectory was directly attributable to an incisive domain model, repeatedly refined and expressed in code. As the team gained new insight into the domain, the model deepened. The quality of communication improved not only among developers but also between developers and domain experts, and the design—far from imposing an ever-heavier maintenance burden—became easier to modify and extend.

Unfortunately, projects don't arrive at such a virtuous cycle just by taking models seriously. One project from my past started with lofty aspirations to build a global enterprise system based on a domain model, but after years of disappointment, it lowered its sights and settled into conventionality. The team had good tools and a good understanding of the business, and it gave careful attention to modeling. But a poorly chosen separation of developer roles disconnected modeling from implementation, so that the design did not reflect the deep analysis that was going on. In any case, the design of detailed business objects was not rigorous enough to support combining them in elaborate applications. Repeated iteration produced no improvement in the code, due to uneven skill levels among developers, who had no awareness of the informal body of style and technique for creating model-based objects that also function as practical, running software. As months rolled by, development work became mired in complexity and the team lost its cohesive vision of the system. After years of effort, the project did produce modest, useful software, but the team had given up its early ambitions along with the model focus.

The Challenge of Complexity

Many things can put a project off course: bureaucracy, unclear objectives, and lack of resources, to name a few. But it is the approach to design that largely determines how complex software can become. When complexity gets out of hand, developers can no longer understand the software well enough to change or extend it easily and safely. On the other hand, a good design can create opportunities to exploit those complex features.

Some design factors are technological. A great deal of effort has gone into the design of networks, databases, and other technical dimensions of software. Many books have been written about how to solve these problems. Legions of developers have cultivated their skills and followed each technical advancement.

Yet the most significant complexity of many applications is not technical. It is in the domain itself, the activity or business of the user. When this domain complexity is not handled in the design, it won't matter that the infrastructural technology is well conceived. A successful design must systematically deal with this central aspect of the software.

The premise of this book is twofold:

1. For most software projects, the primary focus should be on the domain and domain logic.

2. Complex domain designs should be based on a model.

Domain-driven design is both a way of thinking and a set of priorities, aimed at accelerating software projects that have to deal with complicated domains. To accomplish that goal, this book presents an extensive set of design practices, techniques, and principles.

Design Versus Development Process

Design books. Process books. They seldom even reference each other. Each topic is complex in its own right. This is a design book, but I believe that design and process are inextricable. Design concepts must be implemented successfully or else they will dry up into academic discussion.

When people learn design techniques, they feel excited by the possibilities. Then the messy realities of a real project descend on them. They can't fit the new design ideas with the technology they must use. Or they don't know when to let go of a particular design aspect in the interest of time and when to dig in their heels and find a clean solution. Developers can and do talk with each other abstractly about the application of design principles, but it is more natural to talk about how real things get done. So, although this is a design book, I'm going to barge right across that artificial boundary into process when I need to. This will help put design principles in context.

This book is not tied to a particular methodology, but it is oriented toward the new family of "Agile development processes." Specifically, it assumes that a couple of practices are in place on the project. These two practices are prerequisites for applying the approach in this book.

1. *Development is iterative.* Iterative development has been advocated and practiced for decades, and it is a cornerstone of Agile development methods. There are many good discussions in the literature of Agile development and Extreme Programming (or XP), among them, *Surviving Object-Oriented Projects* (Cockburn 1998) and *Extreme Programming Explained* (Beck 1999).

2. *Developers and domain experts have a close relationship.* Domain-driven design crunches a huge amount of knowledge into a model that reflects deep insight into the domain and a focus on the key concepts. This is a collaboration between those who know the domain and those who know how to build software.

Because development is iterative, this collaboration must continue throughout the project's life.

Extreme Programming, conceived by Kent Beck, Ward Cunningham, and others (see *Extreme Programming Explained* [Beck 2000]), is the most prominent of the Agile processes and the one I have worked with most. Throughout this book, to make explanations concrete, I will use XP as the basis for discussion of the interaction of design and process. The principles illustrated are easily adapted to other Agile processes.

In recent years there has been a rebellion against elaborate development methodologies that burden projects with useless, static documents and obsessive upfront planning and design. Instead, the Agile processes, such as XP, emphasize the ability to cope with change and uncertainty.

Extreme Programming recognizes the importance of design decisions, but it strongly resists upfront design. Instead, it puts an admirable effort into communication and improving the project's ability to change course rapidly. With that ability to react, developers can use the "simplest thing that could work" at any stage of a project and then continuously refactor, making many small design improvements, ultimately arriving at a design that fits the customer's true needs.

This minimalism has been a much-needed antidote to some of the excesses of design enthusiasts. Projects have been bogged down by cumbersome documents that provided little value. They have suffered from "analysis paralysis," with team members so afraid of an imperfect design that they made no progress at all. Something had to change.

Unfortunately, some of these process ideas can be misinterpreted. Each person has a different definition of "simplest." Continuous refactoring is a series of small redesigns; developers without solid design principles will produce a code base that is hard to understand or change—the opposite of agility. And although fear of unanticipated requirements often leads to overengineering, the attempt to avoid overengineering can develop into another fear: a fear of doing any deep design thinking at all.

In fact, XP works best for developers with a sharp design sense. The XP process assumes that you can improve a design by refactoring, and that you will do this often and rapidly. But past design choices make refactoring itself either easier or harder. The XP process attempts to increase team communication, but model and design choices clarify or confuse communication.

This book intertwines design and development practice and illustrates how domain-driven design and Agile development reinforce each other. A sophisticated approach to domain modeling within the context of an Agile development process will accelerate development. The interrelationship of process with domain development makes this approach more practical than any treatment of "pure" design in a vacuum.

The Structure of This Book

The book is divided into four major sections:

Part I: Putting the Domain Model to Work presents the basic goals of domain-driven development; these goals motivate the practices in later sections. Because there are so many approaches to software development, Part I defines terms and gives an overview of the implications of using the domain model to drive communication and design.

Part II: The Building Blocks of a Model-Driven Design condenses a core of best practices in object-oriented domain modeling into a set of basic building blocks. This section focuses on bridging the gap between models and practical, running software. Sharing these standard patterns brings order to the design. Team members more easily understand each other's work. Using standard patterns also contributes terminology to a common language, which all team members can use to discuss model and design decisions.

But the main point of this section is to focus on the kinds of decisions that keep the model and implementation aligned with each other, each reinforcing the other's effectiveness. This alignment requires attention to the detail of individual elements. Careful crafting at this small scale gives developers a steady foundation from which to apply the modeling approaches of Parts III and IV.

Part III: Refactoring Toward Deeper Insight goes beyond the building blocks to the challenge of assembling them into practical models that provide the payoff. Rather than jumping directly into esoteric design principles, this section emphasizes the discovery process. Valuable models do not emerge immediately; they require a deep understanding of the domain. That understanding comes from diving in, implementing an initial design based on a probably naive model, and then transforming it again and again. Each time the team gains insight, the model is transformed to reveal that richer knowledge, and the code is refactored to reflect the deeper model and make its potential available to the application. Then, once in a while, this onion peeling leads to an opportunity to break through to a much deeper model, attended by a rush of profound design changes.

Exploration is inherently open-ended, but it does not have to be random. Part III delves into modeling principles that can guide choices along the way, and techniques that help direct the search.

Part IV: Strategic Design deals with situations that arise in complex systems, larger organizations, and interactions with external systems and legacy systems. This section explores a triad of principles that apply to the system as a whole: context, distillation, and large-scale structure. Strategic design decisions are made by teams, or even among teams. Strategic design enables the goals of Part I to be realized on a larger scale, for a big system or an application that fits into a sprawling, enterprise-wide network.

Throughout the book, discussions are illustrated not with oversimplified, "toy" problems, but with realistic examples adapted from actual projects.

Much of the book is written as a set of "patterns." Readers should be able to understand the material without concern about this device, but those who are interested in the style and format of the patterns may want to read the appendix.

Supplemental materials can be found at http://domaindrivendesign.org, including additional example code and community discussion.

Who Should Read This Book

This book is written primarily for developers of object-oriented software. Most members of a software project team can benefit from some parts of the book. It will make the most sense to people who are currently involved with a project, trying to do some of these things as they go through, and to people who already have deep experience with such projects.

Some knowledge of object-oriented modeling is necessary to benefit from this book. The examples include UML diagrams and Java code, so the ability to read those languages at a basic level is important, but it is unnecessary to have mastered the details of either. Knowledge of Extreme Programming will add perspective to the discussions of development process, but the material should be understandable to those without background knowledge.

For intermediate software developers—readers who already know something of object-oriented design and may have read one or two software design books—this book will fill in gaps and provide perspective on how object modeling fits into real life on a software project. The book will help intermediate developers learn to apply sophisticated modeling and design skills to practical problems.

Advanced or expert software developers will be interested in the book's comprehensive framework for dealing with the domain. This systematic approach to design will help technical leaders guide their teams down this path. Also, the coherent terminology used throughout the book will help advanced developers communicate with their peers.

This book is a narrative, and it can be read from beginning to end, or from the beginning of any chapter. Readers of various backgrounds may wish to take different paths through the book, but I do recommend that all readers start with the introduction to Part I, as well as

Chapter 1. Beyond that, the core is probably Chapters 2, 3, 9, and 14. A skimmer who already has some grasp of a topic should be able to pick up the main points by reading headings and bold text. A very advanced reader may want to skim Parts I and II and will probably be most interested in Parts III and IV.

In addition to this core readership, analysts and relatively technical project managers will also benefit from reading the book. Analysts can draw on the connection between model and design to make more effective contributions in the context of an Agile project. Analysts may also use some of the principles of strategic design to better focus and organize their work.

Project managers should be interested in the emphasis on making a team more effective and more focused on designing software meaningful to business experts and users. And because strategic design decisions are interrelated with team organization and work styles, these design decisions necessarily involve the leadership of the project and have a major impact on the project's trajectory.

A Domain-Driven Team

Although an individual developer who understands domain-driven design will gain valuable design techniques and perspective, the biggest gains come when a team joins together to apply a domain-driven design approach and to move the domain model to the project's center of discourse. By doing so, the team members will share a language that enriches their communication and keeps it connected to the software. They will produce a lucid implementation in step with a model, giving leverage to application development. They will share a map of how the design work of different teams relates, and they will systematically focus attention on the features that are most distinctive and valuable to the organization.

Domain-driven design is a difficult technical challenge that can pay off big, opening opportunities just when most software projects begin to ossify into legacy.

ACKNOWLEDGMENTS

I have been working on this book, in one form or another, for more than four years, and many people have helped and supported me along the way.

I thank those people who have read manuscripts and commented. This book would simply not have been possible without that feedback. A few have given their reviews especially generous attention. The Silicon Valley Patterns Group, led by Russ Rufer and Tracy Bialek, spent seven weeks scrutinizing the first complete draft of the book. The University of Illinois reading group led by Ralph Johnson also spent several weeks reviewing a later draft. Listening to the long, lively discussions of these groups had a profound effect. Kyle Brown and Martin Fowler contributed detailed feedback, valuable insights, and invaluable moral support (while sitting on a fish). Ward Cunningham's comments helped me shore up some important weak points. Alistair Cockburn encouraged me early on and helped me find my way through the publication process, as did Hilary Evans. David Siegel and Eugene Wallingford have helped me avoid embarrassing myself in the more technical parts. Vibhu Mohindra and Vladimir Gitlevich painstakingly checked all the code examples.

Rob Mee read some of my earliest explorations of the material, and brainstormed ideas with me when I was groping for some way to communicate this style of design. He then pored over a much later draft with me.

Josh Kerievsky is responsible for one of the major turning points in the book's development: He persuaded me to try out the "Alexandrian" pattern format, which became so central to the book's organization. He also helped me to bring together some of the material now in Part II into a coherent form for the first time, during the intensive "shepherding" process preceding the PLoP conference in 1999. This became a seed around which much of the rest of the book formed.

Also I thank Awad Faddoul for the hundreds of hours I sat writing in his wonderful café. That retreat, along with a lot of windsurfing, helped me keep going.

And I'm very grateful to Martine Jousset, Richard Paselk, and Ross Venables for creating some beautiful photographs to illustrate a few key concepts (see photo credits on page 517).

Before I could have conceived of this book, I had to form my view and understanding of software development. That formation owed a lot to the generosity of a few brilliant people who acted as informal mentors to me, as well as friends. David Siegel, Eric Gold, and Iseult White, each in a different way, helped me develop my way of thinking about software design. Meanwhile, Bruce Gordon, Richard Freyberg, and Dr. Judith Segal, also in very different ways, helped me find my way in the world of successful project work.

My own notions naturally grew out of a body of ideas in the air at that time. Some of those contributions will be clear in the main text and referenced where possible. Others are so fundamental that I don't even realize their influence on me.

My master's thesis advisor, Dr. Bala Subramanium, turned me on to mathematical modeling, which we applied to chemical reaction kinetics. Modeling is modeling, and that work was part of the path that led to this book.

Even before that, my way of thinking was shaped by my parents, Carol and Gary Evans. And a few special teachers awakened my interest or helped me lay foundations, especially Dale Currier (a high school math teacher), Mary Brown (a high school English composition teacher), and Josephine McGlamery (a sixth-grade science teacher).

Finally, I thank my friends and family, and Fernando De Leon, for their encouragement all along the way.

I

Putting the Domain Model to Work

This eighteenth-century Chinese map represents the whole world. In the center and taking up most of the space is China, surrounded by perfunctory representations of other countries. This was a model of the world appropriate to that society, which had intentionally turned inward. The worldview that the map represents must not have been helpful in dealing with foreigners. Certainly it would not serve modern China at all. Maps are models, and every model represents some aspect of reality or an idea that is of interest. A model is a simplification. It is an interpretation of reality that abstracts the aspects relevant to solving the problem at hand and ignores extraneous detail.

Every software program relates to some activity or interest of its user. That subject area to which the user applies the program is the *domain* of the software. Some domains involve the physical world: The domain of an airline-booking program involves real people getting on real aircraft. Some domains are intangible: The domain of an accounting program is money and finance. Software domains usually have little to do with computers, though there are exceptions: The domain of a source-code control system is software development itself.

To create software that is valuably involved in users' activities, a development team must bring to bear a body of knowledge related to those activities. The breadth of knowledge required can be daunting. The volume and complexity of information can be overwhelming. Models are tools for grappling with this overload. A model is a selectively simplified and consciously structured form of knowledge. An appropriate model makes sense of information and focuses it on a problem.

A domain model is not a particular diagram; it is the idea that the diagram is intended to convey. It is not just the knowledge in a domain expert's head; *it is a rigorously organized and selective abstraction of that knowledge.* A diagram can represent and communicate a model, as can carefully written code, as can an English sentence.

Domain modeling is not a matter of making as "realistic" a model as possible. Even in a domain of tangible real-world things, our model is an artificial creation. Nor is it just the construction of a software mechanism that gives the necessary results. It is more like moviemaking, loosely representing reality to a particular purpose. Even a documentary film does not show unedited real life. Just as a moviemaker selects aspects of experience and presents them in an idiosyncratic way to tell a story or make a point, a domain modeler chooses a particular model for its utility.

The Utility of a Model in Domain-Driven Design

In domain-driven design, three basic uses determine the choice of a model.

1. *The model and the heart of the design shape each other.* It is the intimate link between the model and the implementation that makes the model relevant and ensures that the analysis that went into it applies to the final product, a running program. This binding of model and implementation also helps during maintenance and continuing development, because the code can be interpreted based on understanding the model. (See Chapter 3.)

2. *The model is the backbone of a language used by all team members.* Because of the binding of model and implementation, developers can talk about the program in this language. They can communicate with domain experts without translation. And because the language is based on the model, our natural linguistic abilities can be turned to refining the model itself. (See Chapter 2.)

3. *The model is distilled knowledge.* The model is the team's agreed-upon way of structuring domain knowledge and distinguishing the elements of most interest. A model captures how we choose to think about the domain as we select terms, break down concepts, and relate them. The shared language allows developers and domain experts to collaborate effectively as they wrestle information into this form. The binding of model and implementation makes experience with early versions of the software applicable as feedback into the modeling process. (See Chapter 1.)

The next three chapters set out to examine the meaning and value of each of these contributions in turn, and the ways they are intertwined. Using a model in these ways can support the development of software with rich functionality that would otherwise take a massive investment of ad hoc development.

The Heart of Software

The heart of software is its ability to solve domain-related problems for its user. All other features, vital though they may be, support this basic purpose. When the domain is complex, this is a difficult task, calling for the concentrated effort of talented and skilled people. Developers have to steep themselves in the domain to build up knowledge of the business. They must hone their modeling skills and master domain design.

steep

Yet these are not the priorities on most software projects. Most talented developers do not have much interest in learning about the specific domain in which they are working, much less making a major commitment to expand their domain-modeling skills. Technical people enjoy quantifiable problems that exercise their technical skills. Domain work is messy and demands a lot of complicated new knowledge that doesn't seem to add to a computer scientist's capabilities.

Instead, the technical talent goes to work on elaborate frameworks, trying to solve domain problems with technology. Learning about and modeling the domain is left to others. Complexity in the heart of software has to be tackled head-on. To do otherwise is to risk irrelevance.

In a TV talk show interview, comedian John Cleese told a story of an event during the filming of *Monty Python and the Holy Grail*. They had been shooting a particular scene over and over, but somehow it wasn't funny. Finally, he took a break and consulted with fellow comedian Michael Palin (the other actor in the scene), and they came up with a slight variation. They shot one more take, and it turned out funny, so they called it a day.

The next morning, Cleese was looking at the rough cut the film editor had put together of the previous day's work. Coming to the scene they had struggled with, Cleese found that it wasn't funny; one of the earlier takes had been used.

He asked the film editor why he hadn't used the last take, as directed. "Couldn't use it. Someone walked in-shot," the editor replied. Cleese watched the scene again, and then again. Still he could see nothing wrong. Finally, the editor stopped the film and pointed out a coat sleeve that was visible for a moment at the edge of the picture.

The film editor was focused on the precise execution of his own specialty. He was concerned that other film editors who saw the movie would judge his work based on its technical perfection. In the process, the heart of the scene had been lost ("The Late Late Show with Craig Kilborn," CBS, September 2001).

Fortunately, the funny scene was restored by a director who understood comedy. In just the same way, leaders within a team who understand the centrality of the domain can put their software project back on course when development of a model that reflects deep understanding gets lost in the shuffle.

This book will show that domain development holds opportunities to cultivate very sophisticated design skills. The messiness of most software domains is actually an interesting technical challenge. In fact, in many scientific disciplines, "complexity" is one of the most exciting current topics, as researchers attempt to tackle the messiness of the real world. A software developer has that same prospect when facing a complicated domain that has never been formalized. Creating a lucid model that cuts through that complexity is exciting.

There are systematic ways of thinking that developers can employ to search for insight and produce effective models. There are design techniques that can bring order to a sprawling software application. Cultivation of these skills makes a developer much more valuable, even in an initially unfamiliar domain.

ONE

Crunching Knowledge

A few years ago, I set out to design a specialized software tool for printed-circuit board (PCB) design. One catch: I didn't know anything about electronic hardware. I had access to some PCB designers, of course, but they typically got my head spinning in three minutes. How was I going to understand enough to write this software? I certainly wasn't going to become an electrical engineer before the delivery deadline!

We tried having the PCB designers tell me exactly what the software should do. Bad idea. They were great circuit designers, but their software ideas usually involved reading in an ASCII file, sorting it, writing it back out with some annotation, and producing a report. This was clearly not going to lead to the leap forward in productivity that they were looking for.

The first few meetings were discouraging, but there was a glimmer of hope in the reports they asked for. They always involved "nets" and various details about them. A net, in this domain, is essentially a wire conductor that can connect any number of components on a PCB and carry an electrical signal to everything it is connected to. We had the first element of the domain model.

Figure 1.1

I started drawing diagrams for them as we discussed the things they wanted the software to do. I used an informal variant of object interaction diagrams to walk through scenarios.

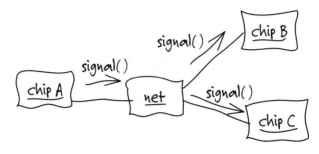

Figure 1.2

PCB Expert 1: The components wouldn't have to be chips.

Developer (Me): So I should just call them "components"?

Expert 1: We call them "component instances." There could be many of the same component.

Expert 2: The "net" box looks just like a component instance.

Expert 1: He's not using our notation. Everything is a box for them, I guess.

Developer: Sorry to say, yes. I guess I'd better explain this notation a little more.

They constantly corrected me, and as they did I started to learn. We ironed out collisions and ambiguities in their terminology and differences between their technical opinions, and they learned. They began to explain things more precisely and consistently, and we started to develop a model together.

Expert 1: It isn't enough to say a signal arrives at a ref-des, we have to know the pin.

Developer: Ref-des?

Expert 2: Same thing as a component instance. Ref-des is what it's called in a particular tool we use.

Expert 1: Anyhow, a net connects a particular pin of one instance to a particular pin of another.

Developer: Are you saying that a pin belongs to only one component instance and connects to only one net?

Expert 1: Yes, that's right.

Expert 2: Also, every net has a topology, an arrangement that determines the way the elements of the net connect.

Developer: OK, how about this?

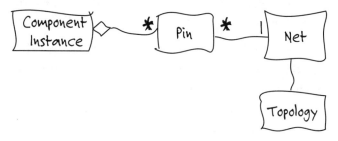

Figure 1.3

To focus our exploration, we limited ourselves, for a while, to studying one particular feature. A "probe simulation" would trace the propagation of a signal to detect likely sites of certain kinds of problems in the design.

Developer: I understand how the signal gets carried by the **Net** to all the **Pins** attached, but how does it go any further than that? Does the **Topology** have something to do with it?

Expert 2: No. The component pushes the signal through.

Developer: We certainly can't model the internal behavior of a chip. That's way too complicated.

Expert 2: We don't have to. We can use a simplification. Just a list of pushes through the component from certain **Pins** to certain others.

Developer: Something like this?

[With considerable trial-and-error, together we sketched out a scenario.]

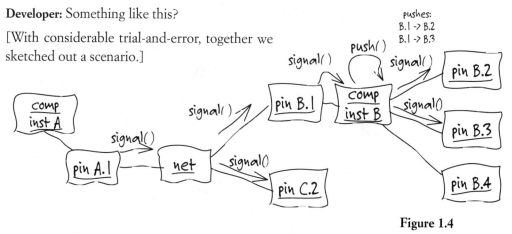

Figure 1.4

Developer: But what exactly do you need to know from this computation?

Expert 2: We'd be looking for long signal delays—say, any signal path that was more than two or three hops. It's a rule of thumb. If the path is too long, the signal may not arrive during the clock cycle.

Developer: More than three hops. . . . So we need to calculate the path lengths. And what counts as a hop?

Expert 2: Each time the signal goes over a **Net**, that's one hop.

Developer: So we could pass the number of hops along, and a **Net** could increment it, like this.

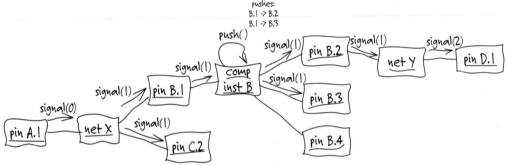

Figure 1.5

Developer: The only part that isn't clear to me is where the "pushes" come from. Do we store that data for every **Component Instance**?

Expert 2: The pushes would be the same for all the instances of a component.

Developer: So the type of component determines the pushes. They'll be the same for every instance?

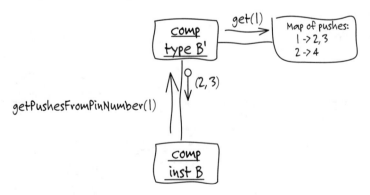

Figure 1.6

CHAPTER 1: CRUNCHING KNOWLEDGE

Expert 2: I'm not sure exactly what some of this means, but I would imagine storing push-throughs for each component would look something like that.

Developer: Sorry, I got a little too detailed there. I was just thinking it through. . . . So, now, where does the **Topology** come into it?

Expert 1: That's not used for the probe simulation.

Developer: Then I'm going to drop it out for now, OK? We can bring it back when we get to those features.

And so it went (with much more stumbling than is shown here). Brainstorming and refining; questioning and explaining. The model developed along with my understanding of the domain and their understanding of how the model would play into the solution. A class diagram representing that early model looks something like this.

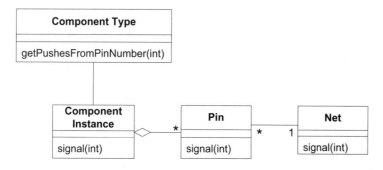

Figure 1.7

After a couple more part-time days of this, I felt I understood enough to attempt some code. I wrote a very simple prototype, driven by an automated test framework. I avoided all infrastructure. There was no persistence, and no user interface (UI). This allowed me to concentrate on the behavior. I was able to demonstrate a simple probe simulation in just a few more days. Although it used dummy data and wrote raw text to the console, it was nonetheless doing the actual computation of path lengths using Java objects. Those Java objects reflected a model shared by the domain experts and myself.

The concreteness of this prototype made clearer to the domain experts what the model meant and how it related to the functioning software. From that point, our model discussions became more interactive, as they could see how I incorporated my newly acquired knowledge into the model and then into the software. And they had concrete feedback from the prototype to evaluate their own thoughts.

Embedded in that model, which naturally became much more complicated than the one shown here, was knowledge about the domain of PCB relevant to the problems we were solving. It consolidated many synonyms and slight variations in descriptions. It excluded hundreds of facts that the engineers understood but that were not directly relevant, such as the actual digital features of the components. A software specialist like me could look at the diagrams and in minutes start to get a grip on what the software was about. He or she would have a framework to organize new information and learn faster, to make better guesses about what was important and what was not, and to communicate better with the PCB engineers.

As the engineers described new features they needed, I made them walk me through scenarios of how the objects interacted. When the model objects couldn't carry us through an important scenario, we brainstormed new ones or changed old ones, crunching their knowledge. We refined the model; the code coevolved. A few months later the PCB engineers had a rich tool that exceeded their expectations.

Ingredients of Effective Modeling

Certain things we did led to the success I just described.

1. *Binding the model and the implementation.* That crude prototype forged the essential link early, and it was maintained through all subsequent iterations.

2. *Cultivating a language based on the model.* At first, the engineers had to explain elementary PCB issues to me, and I had to explain what a class diagram meant. But as the project proceeded, any of us could take terms straight out of the model, organize them into sentences consistent with the structure of the model, and be unambiguously understood without translation.

3. *Developing a knowledge-rich model.* The objects had behavior and enforced rules. The model wasn't just a data schema; it was

integral to solving a complex problem. It captured knowledge of various kinds.

4. *Distilling the model.* Important concepts were added to the model as it became more complete, but equally important, concepts were dropped when they didn't prove useful or central. When an unneeded concept was tied to one that was needed, a new model was found that distinguished the essential concept so that the other could be dropped.

5. *Brainstorming and experimenting.* The language, combined with sketches and a brainstorming attitude, turned our discussions into laboratories of the model, in which hundreds of experimental variations could be exercised, tried, and judged. As the team went through scenarios, the spoken expressions themselves provided a quick viability test of a proposed model, as the ear could quickly detect either the clarity and ease or the awkwardness of expression.

It is the creativity of brainstorming and massive experimentation, leveraged through a model-based language and disciplined by the feedback loop through implementation, that makes it possible to find a knowledge-rich model and distill it. This kind of *knowledge crunching* turns the knowledge of the team into valuable models.

Knowledge Crunching

Financial analysts crunch numbers. They sift through reams of detailed figures, combining and recombining them looking for the underlying meaning, searching for a simple presentation that brings out what is really important—an understanding that can be the basis of a financial decision.

Effective domain modelers are knowledge crunchers. They take a torrent of information and probe for the relevant trickle. They try one organizing idea after another, searching for the simple view that makes sense of the mass. Many models are tried and rejected or transformed. Success comes in an emerging set of abstract concepts that makes sense of all the detail. This distillation is a rigorous expression of the particular knowledge that has been found most relevant.

Knowledge crunching is not a solitary activity. A team of developers and domain experts collaborate, typically led by developers. Together they draw in information and crunch it into a useful form. The raw material comes from the minds of domain experts, from users of existing systems, from the prior experience of the technical team with a related legacy system or another project in the same domain. It comes in the form of documents written for the project or used in the business, and lots and lots of talk. Early versions or prototypes feed experience back into the team and change interpretations.

In the old waterfall method, the business experts talk to the analysts, and analysts digest and abstract and pass the result along to the programmers, who code the software. This approach fails because it completely lacks feedback. The analysts have full responsibility for creating the model, based only on input from the business experts. They have no opportunity to learn from the programmers or gain experience with early versions of software. Knowledge trickles in one direction, but does not accumulate.

Other projects use an iterative process, but they fail to build up knowledge because they don't abstract. Developers get the experts to describe a desired feature and then they go build it. They show the experts the result and ask what to do next. If the programmers practice refactoring, they can keep the software clean enough to continue extending it, but if programmers are not interested in the domain, they learn only what the application should do, not the principles behind it. Useful software can be built that way, but the project will never arrive at a point where powerful new features unfold as corollaries to older features.

Good programmers will naturally start to abstract and develop a model that can do more work. But when this happens only in a technical setting, without collaboration with domain experts, the concepts are naive. That shallowness of knowledge produces software that does a basic job but lacks a deep connection to the domain expert's way of thinking.

The interaction between team members changes as all members crunch the model together. The constant refinement of the domain model forces the developers to learn the important principles of the business they are assisting, rather than to produce functions mechanically. The domain experts often refine their own understanding by being forced to distill what they know to essentials, and they come to understand the conceptual rigor that software projects require.

All this makes the team members more competent knowledge crunchers. They winnow out the extraneous. They recast the model into an ever more useful form. Because analysts and programmers are feeding into it, it is cleanly organized and abstracted, so it can provide leverage for the implementation. Because the domain experts are feeding into it, the model reflects deep knowledge of the business. The abstractions are true business principles.

As the model improves, it becomes a tool for organizing the information that continues to flow through the project. The model focuses requirements analysis. It intimately interacts with programming and design. And in a virtuous cycle, it deepens team members' insight into the domain, letting them see more clearly and leading to further refinement of the model. These models are never perfect; they evolve. They must be practical and useful in making sense of the domain. They must be rigorous enough to make the application simple to implement and understand.

Continuous Learning

When we set out to write software, we never know enough. Knowledge on the project is fragmented, scattered among many people and documents, and it's mixed with other information so that we don't even know which bits of knowledge we really need. Domains that seem less technically daunting can be deceiving: we don't realize how much we don't know. This ignorance leads us to make false assumptions.

Meanwhile, all projects leak knowledge. People who have learned something move on. Reorganization scatters the team, and the knowledge is fragmented again. Crucial subsystems are outsourced in such a way that code is delivered but knowledge isn't. And with typical design approaches, the code and documents don't express this hard-earned knowledge in a usable form, so when the oral tradition is interrupted for any reason, the knowledge is lost.

Highly productive teams grow their knowledge consciously, practicing *continuous learning* (Kerievsky 2003). For developers, this means improving technical knowledge, along with general domain-modeling skills (such as those in this book). But it also includes serious learning about the specific domain they are working in.

These self-educated team members form a stable core of people to focus on the development tasks that involve the most critical areas. (For more on this, see Chapter 15.) The accumulated knowledge in the minds of this core team makes them more effective knowledge crunchers.

At this point, stop and ask yourself a question. Did you learn something about the PCB design process? Although this example has been a superficial treatment of that domain, there should be some learning when a domain model is discussed. I learned an enormous amount. I did not learn how to be a PCB engineer. That was not the goal. I learned to talk to PCB experts, understand the major concepts relevant to the application, and sanity-check what we were building.

In fact, our team eventually discovered that the probe simulation was a low priority for development, and the feature was eventually dropped altogether. With it went the parts of the model that captured understanding of pushing signals through components and counting hops. The core of the application turned out to lie elsewhere, and the model changed to bring those aspects onto center stage. The domain experts had learned more and had clarified the goal of the application. (Chapter 15 discusses these issues in depth.)

Even so, the early work was essential. Key model elements were retained, but more important, that work set in motion the process of knowledge crunching that made all subsequent work effective: the knowledge gained by team members, developers, and domain experts alike; the beginnings of a shared language; and the closing of a feedback loop through implementation. A voyage of discovery has to start somewhere.

Knowledge-Rich Design

The kind of knowledge captured in a model such as the PCB example goes beyond "find the nouns." Business activities and rules are as central to a domain as are the entities involved; any domain will have various categories of concepts. Knowledge crunching yields models that reflect this kind of insight. In parallel with model changes, developers refactor the implementation to express the model, giving the application use of that knowledge.

It is with this move beyond entities and values that knowledge crunching can get intense, because there may be actual inconsistency among business rules. Domain experts are usually not aware of how complex their mental processes are as, in the course of their work, they navigate all these rules, reconcile contradictions, and fill in gaps with common sense. Software can't do this. It is through knowledge crunching in close collaboration with software experts that the rules are clarified, fleshed out, reconciled, or placed out of scope.

Example

Extracting a Hidden Concept

Let's start with a very simple domain model that could be the basis of an application for booking cargos onto a voyage of a ship.

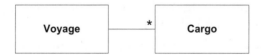

Figure 1.8

We can state that the booking application's responsibility is to associate each **Cargo** with a **Voyage**, recording and tracking that relationship. So far so good. Somewhere in the application code there could be a method like this:

```
public int makeBooking(Cargo cargo, Voyage voyage) {
    int confirmation = orderConfirmationSequence.next();
    voyage.addCargo(cargo, confirmation);
    return confirmation;
}
```

Because there are always last-minute cancellations, standard practice in the shipping industry is to accept more cargo than a particular vessel can carry on a voyage. This is called "overbooking."

Sometimes a simple percentage of capacity is used, such as booking 110 percent of capacity. In other cases complex rules are applied, favoring major customers or certain kinds of cargo.

This is a basic strategy in the shipping domain that would be known to any businessperson in the shipping industry, but it might not be understood by all technical people on a software team.

The requirements document contains this line:

Allow 10% overbooking.

The class diagram and code now look like this:

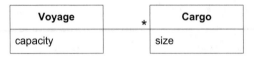

Figure 1.9

```
public int makeBooking(Cargo cargo, Voyage voyage) {
    double maxBooking = voyage.capacity() * 1.1;
    if ((voyage.bookedCargoSize() + cargo.size()) > maxBooking)
        return -1;
    int confirmation = orderConfirmationSequence.next();
    voyage.addCargo(cargo, confirmation);
    return confirmation;
}
```

Now an important business rule is hidden as a guard clause in an application method. Later, in Chapter 4, we'll look at the principle of LAYERED ARCHITECTURE, which would guide us to move the overbooking rule into a domain object, but for now let's concentrate on how we could make this knowledge more explicit and accessible to everyone on the project. This will bring us to a similar solution.

1. As written, it is unlikely that any business expert could read this code to verify the rule, even with the guidance of a developer.

2. It would be difficult for a technical, non-businessperson to connect the requirement text with the code.

If the rule were more complex, that much more would be at stake.

We can change the design to better capture this knowledge. The overbooking rule is a policy. *Policy* is another name for the design pattern known as STRATEGY (Gamma et al. 1995). It is usually motivated by the need to substitute different rules, which is not needed here, as far as we know. But the concept we are trying to capture does fit the *meaning* of a policy, which is an equally important motivation in domain-driven design. (See Chapter 12, "Relating Design Patterns to the Model.")

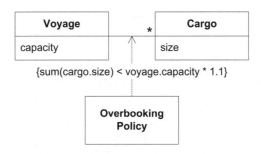

Figure 1.10

The code is now:

```
public int makeBooking(Cargo cargo, Voyage voyage) {
    if (!overbookingPolicy.isAllowed(cargo, voyage)) return -1;
    int confirmation = orderConfirmationSequence.next();
    voyage.addCargo(cargo, confirmation);
    return confirmation;
}
```

The new **Overbooking Policy** class contains this method:

```
public boolean isAllowed(Cargo cargo, Voyage voyage) {
    return (cargo.size() + voyage.bookedCargoSize()) <=
        (voyage.capacity() * 1.1);
}
```

It will be clear to all that overbooking is a distinct policy, and the implementation of that rule is explicit and separate.

Now, *I am not recommending that such an elaborate design be applied to every detail of the domain.* Chapter 15, "Distillation," goes into depth on how to focus on the important and minimize or separate everything else. This example is meant to show that a domain model and corresponding design can be used to secure and share knowledge. The more explicit design has these advantages:

1. In order to bring the design to this stage, the programmers and everyone else involved will have come to understand the nature

of overbooking as a distinct and important business rule, not just an obscure calculation.

2. Programmers can show business experts technical artifacts, even code, that should be intelligible to domain experts (with guidance), thereby closing the feedback loop.

Deep Models

Useful models seldom lie on the surface. As we come to understand the domain and the needs of the application, we usually discard superficial model elements that seemed important in the beginning, or we shift their perspective. Subtle abstractions emerge that would not have occurred to us at the outset but that pierce to the heart of the matter.

The preceding example is loosely based on one of the projects that I'll be drawing on for several examples throughout the book: a container shipping system. The examples in this book will be kept accessible to non-shipping experts. But on a real project, where continuous learning prepares the team members, models of utility and clarity often call for sophistication both in the domain and in modeling technique.

On that project, because a shipment begins with the act of booking cargo, we developed a model that allowed us to describe the cargo, its itinerary, and so on. This was all necessary and useful, yet the domain experts felt dissatisfied. There was a way they looked at their business that we were missing.

Eventually, after months of knowledge crunching, we realized that the handling of cargo, the physical loading and unloading, the movements from place to place, was largely carried out by subcontractors or by operational people in the company. In the view of our shipping experts, there was a series of transfers of responsibility between parties. A process governed that transfer of legal and practical responsibility, from the shipper to some local carrier, from one carrier to another, and finally to the consignee. Often, the cargo would sit in a warehouse while important steps were being taken. At other times, the cargo would move through complex physical steps that were not relevant to the shipping company's business decisions. Rather than the logistics of the itinerary, what came to the fore were legal documents such as the bill of lading, and processes leading to the release of payments.

This deeper view of the shipping business did not lead to the removal of the Itinerary object, but the model changed profoundly. Our view of shipping changed from moving containers from place to place, to transferring responsibility for cargo from entity to entity. Features for handling these transfers of responsibility were no longer awkwardly attached to loading operations, but were supported by a model that came out of an understanding of the significant relationship between those operations and those responsibilities.

Knowledge crunching is an exploration, and you can't know where you will end up.

Communication and the Use of Language

A domain model can be the core of a common language for a software project. The model is a set of concepts built up in the heads of people on the project, with terms and relationships that reflect domain insight. These terms and interrelationships provide the semantics of a language that is tailored to the domain while being precise enough for technical development. This is a crucial cord that weaves the model into development activity and binds it with the code.

This model-based communication is not limited to diagrams in Unified Modeling Language (UML). To make most effective use of a model, it needs to pervade every medium of communication. It increases the utility of written text documents, as well as the informal diagrams and casual conversation reemphasized in Agile processes. It improves communication through the code itself and through the tests for that code.

The use of language on a project is subtle but all-important. . . .

Ubiquitous Language

For first you write a sentence,
And then you chop it small;
Then mix the bits, and sort them out
Just as they chance to fall:
The order of the phrases makes
No difference at all.
—*Lewis Carroll, "Poeta Fit, Non Nascitur"*

To create a supple, knowledge-rich design calls for a versatile, shared team language, and a lively experimentation with language that seldom happens on software projects.

❋ ❋ ❋

Domain experts have limited understanding of the technical jargon of software development, but they use the jargon of their field —probably in various flavors. Developers, on the other hand, may understand and discuss the system in descriptive, functional terms, devoid of the meaning carried by the experts' language. Or developers may create abstractions that support their design but are not understood by the domain experts. Developers working on different parts of the problem work out their own design concepts and ways of describing the domain.

Across this linguistic divide, the domain experts vaguely describe what they want. Developers, struggling to understand a domain new to them, vaguely understand. A few members of the team manage to become bilingual, but they become bottlenecks of information flow, and their translations are inexact.

On a project without a common language, developers have to translate for domain experts. Domain experts translate between developers and still other domain experts. Developers even translate for each other. Translation muddles model concepts, which leads to destructive refactoring of code. The indirectness of communication conceals the formation of schisms—different team members use terms differently but don't realize it. This leads to unreliable software that doesn't fit together (see Chapter 14). The effort of translation prevents the interplay of knowledge and ideas that lead to deep model insights.

A project faces serious problems when its language is fractured. Domain experts use their jargon while technical team members have their own language tuned for discussing the domain in terms of design.

The terminology of day-to-day discussions is disconnected from the terminology embedded in the code (ultimately the most important product of a software project). And even the same person uses different language in speech and in writing, so that the most incisive expressions of the domain often emerge in a transient form that is never captured in the code or even in writing.

Translation blunts communication and makes knowledge crunching anemic.

Yet none of these dialects can be a common language because none serves all needs.

The overhead cost of all the translation, plus the risk of misunderstanding, is just too high. A project needs a common language that is more robust than the lowest common denominator. With a conscious effort by the team, the domain model can provide the backbone for that common language, while connecting team communication to the software implementation. That language can be ubiquitous in the team's work.

The vocabulary of that UBIQUITOUS LANGUAGE includes the names of classes and prominent operations. The LANGUAGE includes terms to discuss rules that have been made explicit in the model. It is supplemented with terms from high-level organizing principles imposed on the model (such as CONTEXT MAPS and large-scale structures, which will be discussed in Chapters 14 and 16). Finally, this language is enriched with the names of patterns the team commonly applies to the domain model.

The model relationships become the combinatory rules all languages have. The meanings of words and phrases echo the semantics of the model.

The model-based language should be used among developers to describe not only artifacts in the system, but tasks and functionality. This same model should supply the language for the developers and domain experts to communicate with each other, and for the domain experts to communicate among themselves about requirements, development planning, and features. The more pervasively the language is used, the more smoothly understanding will flow.

At least, this is where we need to go. But initially the model may simply not be good enough to fill these roles. It may lack the semantic richness of the specialized jargons of the field. But those jargons can't be used unadulterated because they contain ambiguities and contradictions. It may lack the more subtle and active features the developers have created in the code, either because they do not think of those as part of a model, or because the coding style is procedural and only implicitly carries those concepts of the domain.

But although the sequence seems circular, the knowledge crunching process that can produce a more useful kind of model depends on the team's commitment to model-based language. Persistent use of the UBIQUITOUS LANGUAGE will force the model's weaknesses into the open. The team will experiment and find alternatives to awkward terms or combinations. As gaps are found in the language, new words will enter the discussion. *These changes to the language will be recognized as changes in the domain model* and will lead the team to update class diagrams and rename classes and methods in the code, or even change behavior, when the meaning of a term changes.

Committed to using this language in the context of implementation, the developers will point out imprecision or contradictions, engaging the domain experts in discovering workable alternatives.

Of course, domain experts will speak outside the scope of the UBIQUITOUS LANGUAGE, to explain and give broader context. But within the scope the model addresses, they should use LANGUAGE and raise concerns when they find it awkward or incomplete—or wrong. By using the model-based language pervasively and not being satisfied until it flows, we approach a model that is complete and comprehensible, made up of simple elements that combine to express complex ideas.

Therefore:

Use the model as the backbone of a language. Commit the team to exercising that language relentlessly in all communication within the team and in the code. Use the same language in diagrams, writing, and especially speech.

Iron out difficulties by experimenting with alternative expressions, which reflect alternative models. Then refactor the code, renaming classes, methods, and modules to conform to the new

model. Resolve confusion over terms in conversation, in just the way we come to agree on the meaning of ordinary words.

Recognize that a change in the UBIQUITOUS LANGUAGE is a change to the model.

Domain experts should object to terms or structures that are awkward or inadequate to convey domain understanding; developers should watch for ambiguity or inconsistency that will trip up design.

With a UBIQUITOUS LANGUAGE, the model is not just a design artifact. It becomes integral to everything the developers and domain experts do together. The LANGUAGE carries knowledge in a dynamic form. Discussion in the LANGUAGE brings to life the meaning behind the diagrams and code.

✳ ✳ ✳

This discussion of UBIQUITOUS LANGUAGE assumes that there is just one model in play. Chapter 14, "Maintaining Model Integrity," deals with the coexistence of different models (and LANGUAGES) and how to keep a model from splintering.

The UBIQUITOUS LANGUAGE is the primary carrier of the aspects of design that don't appear in code—large-scale structures that organize the whole system (see Chapter 16), BOUNDED CONTEXTS that define the relationships of different systems and models (see Chapter 14), and other patterns applied to the model and design.

Example

Working Out a Cargo Router

The following two dialogs have subtle, but important, differences. In each scenario, watch for how much the speakers talk about what the software means to the business versus how it works technically. Are the user and developer speaking the same language? Is that language rich enough to carry the discussion of what the application must do?

Scenario 1: Minimal Abstraction of the Domain

Database table: cargo_bookings

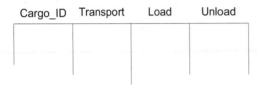

Figure 2.1

User: So when we change the customs clearance point, we need to redo the whole routing plan.

Developer: Right. We'll delete all the rows in the shipment table with that cargo id, then we'll pass the origin, destination, and the new customs clearance point into the **Routing Service,** and it will re-populate the table. We'll have to have a Boolean in the **Cargo** so we'll know there is data in the shipment table.

User: Delete the rows? OK, whatever. Anyway, if we didn't have a customs clearance point at all before, we'll have to do the same thing.

Developer: Sure, anytime you change the origin, destination, or customs clearance point (or enter one for the first time), we'll check to see if we have shipment data and then we'll delete it and then let the **Routing Service** regenerate it.

User: Of course, if the old customs clearance just happened to be the right one, we wouldn't want to do that.

Developer: Oh, no problem. It's easier to just make the **Routing Service** redo the loads and unloads every time.

User: Yes, but it's extra work for us to make all the supporting plans for a new itinerary, so we don't want to reroute unless the change necessitates it.

Developer: *Ugh.* Well, then, if you are entering a customs clearance point for the first time, we'll have to query the table to find the old derived customs clearance point, and then compare it to the new one. Then we'll know if we need to redo it.

User: You won't have to worry about this on origin or destination, since the itinerary would always change then.

Developer: Good. We won't.

Scenario 2: Domain Model Enriched to Support Discussion

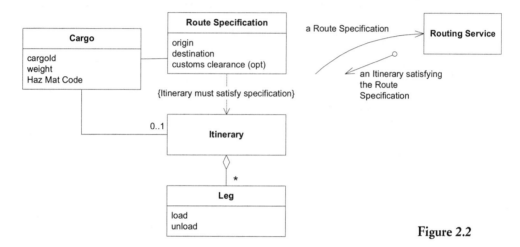

Figure 2.2

User: So when we change the customs clearance point, we need to redo the whole routing plan.

Developer: Right. When you change any of the attributes in the **Route Specification**, we'll delete the old **Itinerary** and ask the **Routing Service** to generate a new one based on the new **Route Specification**.

User: If we hadn't specified a customs clearance point at all before, we'll have to do that at the same time.

Developer: Sure, anytime you change anything in the **Route Spec**, we'll regenerate the **Itinerary**. That includes entering something for the first time.

User: Of course, if the old customs clearance just happened to be the right one, we wouldn't want to do that.

Developer: Oh, no problem. It's easier to just make the **Routing Service** redo the **Itinerary** every time.

User: Yes, but it's extra work for us to make all the supporting plans for a new **Itinerary**, so we don't want to reroute unless the change necessitates it.

Developer: Oh. Then we'll have to add some functionality to the **Route Specification**. Then, whenever you change anything in the **Spec**, we'll see if the **Itinerary** still satisfies the **Specification**. If it doesn't, we'll have the **Routing Service** regenerate the **Itinerary**.

User: You won't have to worry about this on origin or destination, since the **Itinerary** would always change then.

Developer: Fine, but it will be simpler for us to just do the comparison every time. The **Itinerary** will only be generated when the **Route Specification** is no longer satisfied.

The second dialog conveys more of the intent of the domain expert. The user employed the word "itinerary" in both dialogs, but in the second it was an object the two could discuss precisely, concretely. They discussed the "route specification" explicitly, instead of describing it each time in terms of attributes and procedures.

These two dialogs were deliberately constructed to closely parallel each other. Realistically, the first would have been more verbose, bloated with explanations of application features and miscommunications. The domain-model-based terminology of the second design makes the second dialog more concise.

Modeling Out Loud

The detachment of speech from other forms of communication is a particularly great loss because we humans have a genius for spoken language. Unfortunately, when people speak, they usually don't use the language of the domain model.

That statement may not ring true for you initially, and indeed there are exceptions. But the next time you attend a requirements or design discussion, really listen. You'll hear descriptions of features in business jargon or layman's versions of the jargon. You'll hear talk about technical artifacts and concrete functionality. Sure, you'll hear terms from the domain model; obvious nouns in the common language from the business jargon will typically be coded as objects, and so those terms will tend to be mentioned. But do you hear phrases that could even remotely be described in terms of relationships and interactions in your current domain model?

One of the best ways to refine a model is to explore with speech, trying out loud various constructs from possible model variations. Rough edges are easy to hear.

> "If we give the **Routing Service** an origin, destination, and arrival time, it can look up the stops the cargo will have to make and, well . . . stick them in the database." (*vague and technical*)

> "The origin, destination, and so on . . . it all feeds into the **Routing Service**, and we get back an **Itinerary** that has everything we need in it." (*more complete, but verbose*)

> "A **Routing Service** finds an **Itinerary** that satisfies a **Route Specification**." (*concise*)

It is vital that we play around with words and phrases, harnessing our linguistic abilities to the modeling effort, just as it is vital to engage our visual/spatial reasoning by sketching diagrams. Just as we employ our analytical abilities with methodical analysis and design, and that mysterious "feel" of the code. These ways of thinking complement each other, and it takes all of them to find useful models and designs. Of all of these, experimenting with language is most often overlooked. (Part III of this book will delve into this discovery process and show this interplay in several dialogs.)

In fact, our brains seem to be somewhat specialized for dealing with complexity in spoken language (one good treatment for laymen, like myself, is *The Language Instinct,* by Steven Pinker [Pinker 1994]). For example, when people of different language backgrounds come together for commerce, if they don't have a common language they invent one, called a *pidgin*. The pidgin is not as comprehensive as the speakers' original languages, but it is suited to the task at hand. When people are talking, they naturally discover differences in interpretation and the meaning of their words, and they naturally resolve those differences. They find rough spots in the language and smooth them out.

Once I took an intensive Spanish class in college. The rule in the classroom was that not a word of English could be spoken. At first, it was frustrating. It felt very unnatural, and required a lot of self-discipline. But eventually my classmates and I broke through to a level of fluency that we could never have reached through exercises on paper.

As we use the UBIQUITOUS LANGUAGE of the domain model in discussions—especially discussions in which developers and domain experts hash out scenarios and requirements—we become more fluent in the language and teach each other its nuances. We naturally come to share the language that we speak in a way that never happens with diagrams and documents.

Bringing about a UBIQUITOUS LANGUAGE on a software project is easier said than done, and we have to fully employ our natural talents to pull it off. Just as humans' visual and spatial capabilities let us convey and process information rapidly in graphical overviews, we can exploit our innate talent for grammatical, meaningful language to drive model development.

Therefore, as an addendum to the UBIQUITOUS LANGUAGE pattern:

Play with the model as you talk about the system. Describe scenarios out loud using the elements and interactions of the model, combining concepts in ways allowed by the model. Find easier ways to say what you need to say, and then take those new ideas back down to the diagrams and code.

One Team, One Language

Technical people often feel the need to "shield" the business experts from the domain model. They say:

"Too abstract for them."

"They don't understand objects."

"We have to collect requirements in their terminology."

These are just a few of the reasons I've heard for having two languages on the team. Forget them.

Of course there are technical components of the design that may not concern the domain experts, but the core of the model had better interest them. Too abstract? Then how do you know the abstractions are sound? Do you understand the domain as deeply as they do? Sometimes specific requirements are collected from lower-level users, and a subset of the more concrete terminology may be needed for them, but a domain expert is assumed to be capable of thinking somewhat deeply about his or her field. *If sophisticated domain experts don't understand the model, there is something wrong with the model.*

Now at the beginning, when the users are discussing future capabilities of the system that haven't been modeled yet, there is no model for them to use. But as soon as they begin to work through these new ideas with the developers, the process of groping toward a shared model begins. It may start out awkward and incomplete, but it will gradually get refined. As the new language evolves, the domain experts must make the extra effort to adopt it, and to retrofit any old documents that are still important.

When domain experts use this LANGUAGE in discussions with developers or among themselves, they quickly discover areas where the model is inadequate for their needs or seems wrong to them. The domain experts (with the help of the developers) will also find areas where the precision of the model-based language exposes contradictions or vagueness in their thinking.

The developers and domain experts can informally test the model by walking through scenarios, using the model objects step-by-step. Almost every discussion is an opportunity for the developers and user experts to play with the model together, deepening each other's understanding and refining concepts as they go.

The domain experts can use the language of the model in writing use cases, and can work even more directly with the model by specifying acceptance tests.

Objections are sometimes raised to the idea of using the language of the model to collect requirements. After all, shouldn't requirements be independent of the design that fulfills them? This overlooks the reality that all language is based on some model. The meanings of words are slippery things. The domain model will typically derive from the domain experts' own jargon but will have been "cleaned up," to have sharper, narrower definitions. Of course, the domain experts should object if these definitions diverge from the meanings accepted in the field. In an Agile process, requirements evolve as a project goes along because hardly ever does the knowledge exist up front to specify an application adequately. Part of this evolution should be the reframing of the requirements in the refined UBIQUITOUS LANGUAGE.

Multiplicity of languages is often necessary, but the linguistic division should never be between the domain experts and the developers. (Chapter 12, "Maintaining Model Integrity," deals with the coexistence of models on the same project.)

Of course, developers do use technical terminology that a domain expert wouldn't understand. Developers have an extensive jargon that they need to discuss the technical aspects of a system. Almost certainly, the users will also have specialized jargon that goes well beyond the narrow scope of the application and the understanding of the developers. But these are *extensions* to the language. These dialects should not contain alternative vocabularies for the same domain that reflect distinct models.

Figure 2.3
UBIQUITOUS LANGUAGE is cultivated in the intersection of jargons.

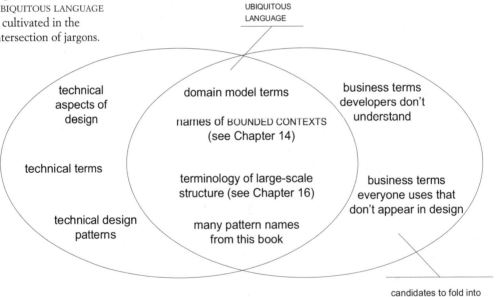

UBIQUITOUS
LANGUAGE

technical aspects of design

technical terms

technical design patterns

domain model terms

names of BOUNDED CONTEXTS (see Chapter 14)

terminology of large-scale structure (see Chapter 16)

many pattern names from this book

business terms developers don't understand

business terms everyone uses that don't appear in design

candidates to fold into model (see Chapter 10)

With a UBIQUITOUS LANGUAGE, conversations among developers, discussions among domain experts, and expressions in the code itself are all based on the same language, derived from a shared domain model.

Documents and Diagrams

Whenever I'm in a meeting discussing a software design, I can hardly function without drawing on a whiteboard or sketchpad. A good part of what I draw is UML diagrams, mostly class diagrams or object-interactions.

Some people are naturally visual, and diagrams help people grasp certain kinds of information. UML diagrams are pretty good at communicating relationships between objects, and they are fair at showing interactions. But they do not convey the conceptual definitions of those objects. In a meeting, I would flesh out those meanings in speech as I sketched the diagram, or they would emerge in a dialog with other participants.

Simple, informal UML diagrams can anchor a discussion. Sketch a diagram of three to five objects central to the issue at hand, and everyone can stay focused. Everyone will share a view of the relationships between the objects and, significantly, the objects' names. The spoken discussion can be more effective with this aid. A diagram can be changed as people try different thought experiments, and the sketch will take on some of the fluidity of spoken words, a true part of the discussion. After all, UML stands for Unified Modeling *Language*.

The trouble comes when people feel compelled to convey the whole model or design through UML. A lot of object model diagrams are too complete and, simultaneously, leave too much out. They are too complete because people feel they have to put all the objects that they are going to code into a modeling tool. With all that detail, no one can see the forest for the trees.

Yet in spite of all that detail, the attributes and relationships are only half the story of an object model. The behavior of those objects and the constraints on them are not so easily illustrated. Object interaction diagrams can illustrate some tricky hotspots in the design, but the bulk of the interactions can't be shown that way. It is just too much work, both to create the diagrams and to read them. And an interaction diagram can still only imply the purpose behind the model. To include constraints and assertions, UML falls back on text, placed in little brackets, inserted into the diagram.

The behavioral responsibilities of an object can be hinted at through operation names, and they can be implicitly demonstrated with object interaction (or sequence) diagrams, but they cannot be *stated*. So, this task falls to supplemental text or conversation. In other words, a UML diagram cannot convey two of the most important aspects of a model: the meaning of the concepts it represents, and what the objects are meant to do. This needn't trouble us, though, because careful use of English (or Spanish, or whatever) can fill this role pretty well.

Nor is UML a very satisfying programming language. Every attempt I've seen to use the code-generation capabilities of the modeling tools has been counterproductive. If you are constrained by the capabilities of UML, you will often have to leave out the most crucial part of the model because it is some rule that doesn't fit into a box-and-line diagram. And, of course, a code generator cannot make use of those textual annotations. If you do use some technology that allows executable programs to be written in a UML-like diagramming language, then the UML diagram is reduced to merely another way to view the program itself, and the very meaning of "model" is lost. If you use UML as your implementation language, you will still need other means of communicating the uncluttered model.

 Diagrams are a means of communication and explanation, and they facilitate brainstorming. They serve these ends best if they are minimal. Comprehensive diagrams of the entire object model fail to communicate or explain; they overwhelm the reader with detail and they lack meaning. This leads us away from the all-encompassing object model diagram, or even the all-encompassing database repository of UML. It leads us toward simplified diagrams of conceptually important parts of the object model that are essential to understanding the design. The diagrams in this book are typical of those I use on projects. They simplify, they explain, and they even incorporate a bit of nonstandard notation when it clarifies their point. They show design constraints, but they are not design specifications in every detail. They represent the skeletons of ideas.

The vital detail about the design is captured in the code. A well-written implementation should be transparent, revealing the model underlying it. (Making sure that this happens is the subject of the next chapter and much of the rest of this book.) Supplemental diagrams and documents can guide people's attention to the central points. Natural language discussion can fill in the nuances of meaning. This is why I prefer to turn things inside out from the way a typical UML diagram handles them. Rather than a diagram annotated with text, I write a text document illustrated with selective and simplified diagrams.

Always remember that *the model is not the diagram.* The diagram's purpose is to help communicate and explain the model. The code can serve as a repository of the details of the design. Well-written Java is as expressive as UML in its way. Carefully selected and constructed diagrams can serve to focus attention and aid navigation if they are not obscured by a compulsion to represent the model or design completely.

Written Design Documents

Spoken communication supplements the code's rigor and detail with meaning. But although talking is critical to connecting everyone to the model, a group of any size will probably need the stability and shareability of some written documents. But making written documents that actually help the team produce good software is a challenge.

Once a document takes on a persistent form, it often loses its connection with the flow of the project. It is left behind by the evolution of the code, or by the evolution of the language of the project.

Many approaches can work. A few specific documents will be suggested much later, in Part IV of this book, which address particular needs, but I make no attempt to prescribe a set of documents a project should use. Instead, I will offer two general guidelines for evaluating a document.

Documents Should Complement Code and Speech

Each Agile process has its own philosophy about documents. Extreme Programming advocates using no extra design documents at all and letting the code speak for itself. Running code doesn't lie, as any other document might. The behavior of running code is unambiguous.

Extreme Programming concentrates exclusively on the *active* elements of a program and executable tests. Even comments added to the code do not affect program behavior, so they always fall out of sync with the active code and its driving model. External documents and diagrams do not affect the behavior of the program, so they fall out of sync. On the other hand, spoken communication and ephemeral diagrams on whiteboards do not linger to create confusion. This dependence on the code as communication medium motivates developers to keep the code clean and transparent.

But code as a design document does have its limits. It can overwhelm the reader with detail. Although its behavior is unambiguous, that doesn't mean it is obvious. And the meaning behind a behavior can be hard to convey. In other words, documenting exclusively through code has some of the same basic problems as using comprehensive UML diagrams. Of course, massive spoken communication within the team gives context and guidance around the code, but it is ephemeral and localized. And developers are not the only people who need to understand the model.

A document shouldn't try to do what the code already does well. The code already supplies the detail. It is an exact specification of program behavior.

Other documents need to illuminate meaning, to give insight into large-scale structures, and to focus attention on core elements. Documents can clarify design intent when the programming language does not support a straightforward implementation of a concept. Written documents should complement the code and the talking.

Documents Should Work for a Living and Stay Current

When I document a model in writing, I diagram small, carefully selected subsets of the model and surround them with text. I define the classes and their responsibilities in words and frame them in a context of meaning as only a natural language can. But the diagram shows some of the choices that have been made in formalizing and paring down the concepts into an object model. These diagrams can be somewhat casual—even hand-drawn. In addition to saving labor, hand-drawn diagrams have the advantage of *feeling* casual and temporary. These are good things to communicate because they are generally true of our model ideas.

The greatest value of a design document is to explain the concepts of the model, help in navigating the detail of the code, and perhaps give some insight into the model's intended style of use. Depending on the philosophy of the team, the whole design document could be as simple as a set of sketches posted on the walls, or it could be substantial.

A document must be involved in project activities. The easiest way to judge this is to observe the document's interaction with the UBIQUITOUS LANGUAGE. Is the document written in the language people speak on the project (now)? Is it written in the language embedded in the code?

Listen to the UBIQUITOUS LANGUAGE and how it is changing. If the terms explained in a design document don't start showing up in conversations and code, the document is not fulfilling its purpose. Maybe the document is too big or complicated. Maybe it is not focused on a sufficiently important topic. People are either not reading it or not finding it compelling. If it is having no impact on the UBIQUITOUS LANGUAGE, something is wrong.

Conversely, you may hear the UBIQUITOUS LANGUAGE changing naturally while a document is being left behind. Evidently the document does not seem relevant to people or does not seem important enough to update. It could safely be archived as history, but left active it could create confusion and hurt the project. And if a document isn't playing an important role, keeping it up to date through sheer will and discipline wastes effort.

The UBIQUITOUS LANGUAGE allows other documents, such as requirements specifications, to be more concise and less ambiguous. As the domain model comes to reflect the most relevant knowledge of the business, application requirements become scenarios within that model, and the UBIQUITOUS LANGUAGE can be used to describe such a scenario in terms that directly connect to the MODEL-DRIVEN DESIGN (see Chapter 3). As a result, specifications can be written more simply, because they do not have to convey the business knowledge that lies behind the model.

By keeping documents minimal and focusing them on *complementing* code and conversation, documents can stay connected to the project. Let the UBIQUITOUS LANGUAGE and its evolution be your guide to choosing documents that live and get woven into the project's activity.

Executable Bedrock

Now let's examine the choice of the XP community and some others, to rely almost exclusively on the executable code and its tests. Much of this book discusses ways to make the code convey meaning through a MODEL-DRIVEN DESIGN (see Chapter 3). Well-written code can be very communicative, but the message it communicates is not guaranteed to be accurate. Oh, the reality of the *behavior* caused by a section of code is inescapable. But a method name can be ambiguous, misleading, or out of date compared to the internals of the method. The assertions in a test are rigorous, but the story told by variable names and the organization of the code is not. Good programming style keeps this connection as direct as possible, but it is still an exercise in self-discipline. It takes fastidiousness to write code that doesn't just *do* the right thing but also *says* the right thing.

Elimination of those discrepancies is a major selling point of approaches such as declarative design (discussed in Chapter 10), in which a statement of the purpose of a program element determines its actual behavior in the program. The drive to generate programs from UML is partly motivated by this, though it generally hasn't worked out well so far.

Still, while even code can mislead, it is closer to the ground than other documents. Aligning the behavior, intent, and message of code using current standard technology requires discipline and a certain way of thinking about design (discussed at length in Part III). To communicate effectively, the code must be based on the same language used to write the requirements—the same language that the developers speak with each other and with domain experts.

Explanatory Models

The thrust of this book is that one model should underlie implementation, design, and team communication. Having separate models for these separate purposes poses a hazard.

Models can also be valuable as education aids to teach about the domain. The model that drives the design is one view of the domain, but it may aid learning to have other views, used only as educational tools, to communicate general knowledge of the domain. For this purpose, people can use pictures or words that convey other kinds of models unrelated to software design.

One particular reason that other models are needed is scope. The technical model that drives the software development process must be strictly pared down to the necessary minimum to fulfill its functions. An explanatory model can include aspects of the domain that provide context that clarifies the more narrowly scoped model.

Explanatory models offer the freedom to create much more communicative styles tailored to a particular topic. Visual metaphors used by the domain experts in a field often present clearer explanations, educating developers and harmonizing experts. Explanatory models also present the domain in a way that is simply different, and multiple, diverse explanations help people learn.

There is no need for explanatory models to be object models, and it is generally best if they are not. It is actually helpful to avoid UML in these models, to avoid any false impression of correspondence with the software design. Even though the explanatory model and the model that drives design do often correspond, the similarities will seldom be exact. To avoid confusion, everyone must be conscious of the distinction.

Example

Shipping Operations and Routes

Consider an application that tracks cargos for a shipping company. The model includes a detailed view of how port operations and vessel voyages are assembled into an operational plan for a cargo (a "route"). But to the uninitiated, a class diagram may not be very illuminating.

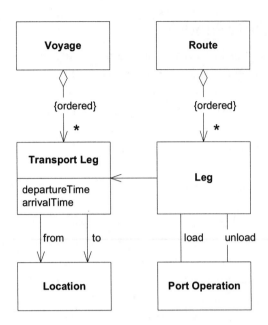

Figure 2.4
A class diagram for a
shipping route

In such a case, an explanatory model can help team members understand what the class diagram actually means. Here is another way of looking at the same concepts:

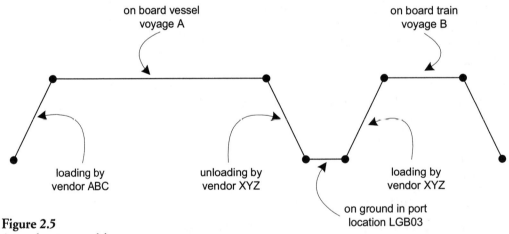

Figure 2.5
An explanatory model
for a shipping route

Each line in Figure 2.5 represents either a port operation (loading or unloading the cargo), or cargo sitting in storage on the ground, or cargo sitting on a ship en route. This does not correspond in detail with the class diagram, but it reinforces key points from the domain.

This sort of diagram, along with natural language explanations of the model it represents, can help developers and domain experts alike understand the more rigorous software model diagrams. Together they are easier to understand than either view alone.

THREE

Binding Model and Implementation

The first thing I saw as I walked through the door was a complete class diagram printed on large sheets of paper that covered a large wall. It was my first day on a project in which smart people had spent months carefully researching and developing a detailed model of the domain. The typical object in the model had intricate associations with three or four other objects, and this web of associations had few natural borders. In this respect, the analysts had been true to the nature of the domain.

As overwhelming as the wall-size diagram was, the model did capture some knowledge. After a moderate amount of study, I learned quite a bit (though that learning was hard to direct—much like randomly browsing the Web). I was more troubled to find that my study gave no insight into the application's code and design.

When the developers had begun implementing the application, they had quickly discovered that the tangle of associations, although navigable by a human analyst, didn't translate into storable, retrievable units that could be manipulated with transactional integrity. Mind you, this project was using an object database, so the developers didn't even have to face the challenges of mapping objects into relational tables. At a fundamental level, the model did not provide a guide to implementation.

Because the model was "correct," the result of extensive collaboration between technical analysts and business experts, the developers reached the conclusion that conceptually based objects could not be the foundation of their design. So they proceeded to develop an ad hoc design. Their design did use a few of the same class names and attributes for data storage, but it was not based on the existing, or any, model.

The project had a domain model, but what good is a model on paper unless it directly aids the development of running software?

A few years later, I saw the same end result come from a completely different process. This project was to replace an existing C++ application with a new design implemented in Java. The old application had been hacked together without any regard for object modeling. The design of the old application, if there was one, had accreted as one capability after another had been laid on top of the existing code, without any noticeable generalization or abstraction.

The eerie thing was that the end products of the two processes were very similar! Both had functionality, but were bloated, very hard to understand, and eventually unmaintainable. Though the implementations had, in places, a kind of directness, you couldn't gain much insight about the purpose of the system by reading the code. Neither process took any advantage of the object paradigm available in their development environment, except as fancy data structures.

Models come in many varieties and serve many roles, even those restricted to the context of a software development project. Domain-driven design calls for a model that doesn't just aid early analysis but is the very foundation of the design. This approach has some important implications for the code. What is less obvious is that domain-driven design requires a different approach to modeling. . . .

MODEL-DRIVEN DESIGN

The astrolabe, used to compute star positions, is a mechanical implementation of a model of the sky.

Tightly relating the code to an underlying model gives the code meaning and makes the model relevant.

✳ ✳ ✳

Projects that have no domain model at all, but just write code to fulfill one function after another, gain few of the advantages of knowledge crunching and communication discussed in the previous two chapters. A complex domain will swamp them.

On the other hand, many complex projects do attempt some sort of domain model, but they don't maintain a tight connection between the model and the code. The model they develop, possibly useful as an exploratory tool at the outset, becomes increasingly irrelevant and even misleading. All the care lavished on the model provides little reassurance that the design is correct, because the two are different.

This connection can break down in many ways, but the detachment is often a conscious choice. Many design methodologies advocate an *analysis model*, quite distinct from the design and usually developed by different people. It is called an analysis model because it is the product of analyzing the business domain to organize its concepts without any consideration of the part it will play in a software system. An analysis model is meant as a tool for understanding only;

A Medieval Sky Computer
Ancient Greek astronomers devised the astrolabe, which was perfected by medieval Islamic scientists. A rotating web (called a *rete*) represented the positions of the fixed stars on the celestial sphere. Interchangeable plates engraved with a local spherical coordinate system represented the views from different latitudes. Rotating the rete against the plate enabled a calculation of celestial positions for any time and day of the year. Conversely, given a stellar or solar position, the time could be calculated. The astrolabe was a mechanical implementation of an object-oriented model of the sky.

mixing in implementation concerns is thought to muddy the waters. Later, a design is created that may have only a loose correspondence to the analysis model. The analysis model is not created with design issues in mind, and therefore it is likely to be quite impractical for those needs.

Some knowledge crunching happens during such an analysis, but most of it is lost when coding begins, when the developers are forced to come up with new abstractions for the design. Then there is no guarantee that the insights gained by the analysts and embedded in the model will be retained or rediscovered. At this point, maintaining any mapping between the design and the loosely connected model is not cost-effective.

The pure analysis model even falls short of its primary goal of understanding the domain, because crucial discoveries always emerge during the design/implementation effort. Very specific, unanticipated problems always arise. An up-front model will go into depth about some irrelevant subjects, while it overlooks some important subjects. Other subjects will be represented in ways that are not useful to the application. The result is that pure analysis models get abandoned soon after coding starts, and most of the ground has to be covered again. But the second time around, if the developers perceive analysis to be a separate process, modeling happens in a less disciplined way. If the managers perceive analysis to be a separate process, the development team may not be given adequate access to domain experts.

Whatever the cause, software that lacks a concept at the foundation of its design is, at best, a mechanism that does useful things without explaining its actions.

If the design, or some central part of it, does not map to the domain model, that model is of little value, and the correctness of the software is suspect. At the same time, complex mappings between models and design functions are difficult to understand and, in practice, impossible to maintain as the design changes. A deadly divide opens between analysis and design so that insight gained in each of those activities does not feed into the other.

An analysis must capture fundamental concepts from the domain in a comprehensible, expressive way. The design has to specify a set of components that can be constructed with the programming tools in use on the project that will perform efficiently in the target deployment environment and will correctly solve the problems posed for the application.

MODEL-DRIVEN DESIGN discards the dichotomy of analysis model and design to search out a single model that serves both purposes. Setting aside purely technical issues, each object in the design plays a conceptual role described in the model. This requires us to be more demanding of the chosen model, since it must fulfill two quite different objectives.

There are always many ways of abstracting a domain, and there are always many designs that can solve an application problem. This is what makes it practical to bind the model and design. This binding mustn't come at the cost of a weakened analysis, fatally compromised by technical considerations. Nor can we accept clumsy designs, reflecting domain ideas but eschewing software design principles. This approach demands a model that works well as both analysis and design. When a model doesn't seem to be practical for implementation, we must search for a new one. When a model doesn't faithfully express the key concepts of the domain, we must search for a new one. The modeling and design process then becomes a single iterative loop.

The imperative to relate the domain model closely to the design adds one more criterion for choosing the more useful models out of the universe of possible models. It calls for hard thinking and usually takes multiple iterations and a lot of refactoring, but it makes the model *relevant*.

Therefore:

Design a portion of the software system to reflect the domain model in a very literal way, so that mapping is obvious. Revisit the model and modify it to be implemented more naturally in software, even as you seek to make it reflect deeper insight into the domain. Demand a single model that serves both purposes well, in addition to supporting a robust UBIQUITOUS LANGUAGE.

Draw from the model the terminology used in the design and the basic assignment of responsibilities. The code becomes an expression of the model, so a change to the code may be a change to the model. Its effect must ripple through the rest of the project's activities accordingly.

To tie the implementation slavishly to a model usually requires software development tools and languages that support a modeling paradigm, such as object-oriented programming.

Sometimes there will be different models for different subsystems (see Chapter 14), but only one model should apply to a particular part of the system, throughout all aspects of the development effort, from the code to requirements analysis.

The single model reduces the chances of error, because the design is now a direct outgrowth of the carefully considered model. The design, and even the code itself, has the communicativeness of a model.

❄ ❄ ❄

Developing a single model that captures the problem and provides a practical design is easier said than done. You can't just take any model and turn it into a workable design. The model has to be carefully crafted to make for a practical implementation. Design and implementation techniques have to be employed that allow code to express a model effectively (see Part II). Knowledge crunchers explore model options and refine them into practical software elements. Development becomes an iterative process of refining the model, the design, and the code as a single activity (see Part III).

Modeling Paradigms and Tool Support

To make a MODEL-DRIVEN DESIGN pay off, the correspondence must be literal, exact within bounds of human error. To make such a close correspondence of model and design possible, it is almost essential to work within a modeling paradigm supported by software tools that allow you to create direct analogs to the concepts in the model.

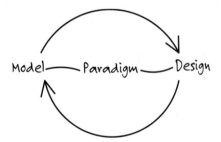

Figure 3.1

Object-oriented programming is powerful because it is based on a modeling paradigm, and it provides implementations of the model constructs. As far as the programmer is concerned, objects really exist in memory, they have associations with other objects, they are organized into classes, and they provide behavior available by messaging. Although many developers benefit from just applying the technical capabilities of objects to organize program code, the real breakthrough of object design comes when the code expresses the concepts of a model. Java and many other tools allow the creation of objects and relationships directly analogous to conceptual object models.

Although it has never reached the mass usage that object-oriented languages have, the Prolog language is a natural fit for MODEL-DRIVEN DESIGN. In this case, the paradigm is logic, and the model is a set of logical rules and facts they operate on.

MODEL-DRIVEN DESIGN has limited applicability using languages such as C, because there is no modeling paradigm that corresponds to a purely *procedural* language. Those languages are procedural in the sense that the programmer tells the computer a series of steps to follow. Although the programmer may be thinking about the concepts of the domain, the program itself is a series of technical manipulations of data. The result may be useful, but the program doesn't capture much of the meaning. Procedural languages often support complex data types that begin to correspond to more natural conceptions of the domain, but these complex types are only organized data, and they don't capture the active aspects of the domain. The result is that software written in procedural languages has complicated functions linked together based on anticipated paths of execution, rather than by conceptual connections in the domain model.

Before I ever heard of object-oriented programming, I wrote FORTRAN programs to solve mathematical models, which is just the sort of domain in which FORTRAN excels. Mathematical functions are the main conceptual component of such a model and can be cleanly expressed in FORTRAN. Even so, there is no way to capture higher level meaning beyond the functions. Most non-mathematical domains don't lend themselves to MODEL-DRIVEN DESIGN in procedural languages because the domains are not conceptualized as math functions or as steps in a procedure.

Object-oriented design, the paradigm that currently dominates the majority of ambitious projects, is the approach used primarily in this book.

Example

From Procedural to MODEL-DRIVEN

As discussed in Chapter 1, a printed circuit board (PCB) can be viewed as a collection of electrical conductors (called *nets*) connecting the pins of various components. There are often tens of thousands of nets. Special software, called a PCB layout tool, finds a physical arrangement for all the nets so that they don't cross or interfere with each other. It does this by optimizing their paths while satisfying an enormous number of constraints placed by the human designers that restrict the way they can be laid out. Although PCB layout tools are very sophisticated, they still have some shortcomings.

One problem is that each of these thousands of nets has its own set of layout rules. PCB engineers see many nets as belonging to natural groupings that should share the same rules. For example, some nets form *buses*.

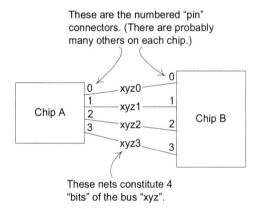

Figure 3.2
An explanatory diagram
of buses and nets

By lumping nets into a bus, perhaps 8 or 16 or 256 at a time, the engineer cuts the job down to a more manageable size, improving productivity and reducing errors. The trouble is, the layout tool has no such concept as a bus. Rules have to be assigned to tens of thousands of nets, one net at a time.

A Mechanistic Design

Desperate engineers worked around this limitation in the layout tool by writing scripts that parse the layout tool's data files and insert rules directly into the file, applying them to an entire bus at a time.

The layout tool stores each circuit connection in a *net list* file, which looks something like this:

```
Net Name      Component.Pin
--------      -------------
Xyz0          A.0, B.0
Xyz1          A.1, B.1
Xyz2          A.2, B.2
. . .
```

It stores the layout rules in a file format something like this:

```
Net Name      Rule Type        Parameters
--------      ---------        ----------
Xyz1          min_linewidth    5
Xyz1          max_delay        15
Xyz2          min_linewidth    5
Xyz2          max_delay        15
. . .
```

The engineers carefully use a naming convention for the nets so that an alphabetical sort of the data file will place the nets of a bus together in a sorted file. Then their script can parse the file and modify each net based on its bus. Actual code to parse, manipulate, and write the files is just too verbose and opaque to serve this example, so I'll just list the steps in the procedure.

```
1. Sort net list file by net name.
2. Read each line in file, seeking first one that starts with bus
   name pattern.
3. For each line with matching name, parse line to get net name.
4. Append net name with rule text to rules file.
5. Repeat from 3 until left of line no longer matches bus name.
```

So the input of a bus rule such as this:

Bus Name	Rule Type	Parameters
Xyz	max_vias	3

would result in adding net rules to the file like these:

Net Name	Rule Type	Parameters
. . .		
Xyz0	max_vias	3
Xyz1	max_vias	3
Xyz2	max_vias	3
. . .		

I imagine that the person who first wrote such a script had only this simple need, and if this were the only requirement, a script like this would make a lot of sense. But in practice, there are now dozens of scripts. They could, of course, be refactored to share sorting and string matching functions, and if the language supported function calls to encapsulate the details, the scripts could begin to read almost like the summary steps above. But still, they are just file manipulations. A different file format (and there are several) would require starting from scratch, even though the concept of grouping buses and applying rules to them is the same. If you wanted richer functionality or interactivity, you would have to pay for every inch.

What the script writers were trying to do was to supplement the tool's domain model with the concept of "bus." Their implementation infers the bus's existence through sorts and string matches, but it does not explicitly deal with the concept.

A MODEL-DRIVEN DESIGN

The preceding discussion has already described the concepts the domain experts use to think about their problems. Now we need to organize those concepts explicitly into a model we can base software on.

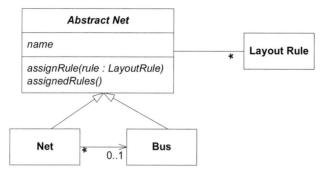

Figure 3.3
A class diagram oriented toward efficient assignment of layout rules

With these objects implemented in an object-oriented language, the core functionality becomes almost trivial.

The `assignRule()` method can be implemented on **Abstract Net.** The `assignedRules()` method on **Net** takes its own rules and its **Bus**'s rules.

```
abstract class AbstractNet {
    private Set rules;

    void assignRule(LayoutRule rule) {
        rules.add(rule);
    }

    Set assignedRules() {
        return rules;
    }
}

class Net extends AbstractNet {
    private Bus bus;

    Set assignedRules() {
        Set result = new HashSet();
        result.addAll(super.assignedRules());
        result.addAll(bus.assignedRules());
        return result;
    }
}
```

Of course, there would be a great deal of supporting code, but this covers the basic functionality of the script.

The application requires import/export logic, which we'll encapsulate into some simple services.

Service	Responsibility
Net List import	Reads Net List file, creates instance of Net for each entry
Net Rule export	Given a collection of Nets, writes all attached rules into the Rules File

We'll also need a few utilities:

Class	Responsibility
Net Repository	Provides access to Nets by name
Inferred Bus Factory	Given a collection of Nets, uses naming conventions to infer Buses, creates instances
Bus Repository	Provides access to Buses by name

Now, starting the application is a matter of initializing the repositories with imported data:

```
Collection nets = NetListImportService.read(aFile);
NetRepository.addAll(nets);
Collection buses = InferredBusFactory.groupIntoBuses(nets);
BusRepository.addAll(buses);
```

Each of the services and repositories can be unit-tested. Even more important, the core domain logic can be tested. Here is a unit test of the most central behavior (using the JUnit test framework):

```
public void testBusRuleAssignment() {
    Net a0 = new Net("a0");
    Net a1 = new Net("a1");
    Bus a = new Bus("a"); //Bus is not conceptually dependent
    a.addNet(a0);          //on name-based recognition, and so
    a.addNet(a1);          //its tests should not be either.

    NetRule minWidth4 = NetRule.create(MIN_WIDTH, 4);
    a.assignRule(minWidth4);

    assertTrue(a0.assignedRules().contains(minWidth4));
    assertEquals(minWidth4, a0.getRule(MIN_WIDTH));
    assertEquals(minWidth4, a1.getRule(MIN_WIDTH));
}
```

An interactive user interface could present a list of buses, allowing the user to assign rules to each, or it could read from a file of rules for backward compatibility. A façade makes access simple for either interface. Its implementation echoes the test:

```
public void assignBusRule(String busName, String ruleType,
        double parameter){
    Bus bus = BusRepository.getByName(busName);
    bus.assignRule(NetRule.create(ruleType, parameter));
}
```

Finishing:

```
NetRuleExport.write(aFileName, NetRepository.allNets());
```

(The service asks each **Net** for `assignedRules()`, and then writes them fully expanded.)

Of course, if there were only one operation (as in the example), the script-based approach might be just as practical. But in reality, there were 20 or more. The MODEL-DRIVEN DESIGN scales easily and can include constraints on combining rules and other enhancements.

The second design also accommodates testing. Its components have well-defined interfaces that can be unit-tested. The only way to test the script is to do an end-to-end file-in/file-out comparison.

Keep in mind that such a design does not emerge in a single step. It would take several iterations of refactoring and knowledge crunching to distill the important concepts of the domain into a simple, incisive model.

Letting the Bones Show: Why Models Matter to Users

In theory, perhaps, you could present a user with any view of a system, regardless of what lies beneath. But in practice, a mismatch causes confusion at best—bugs at worst. Consider a very simple example of how users are misled by superimposed models of bookmarks for Web sites in current releases of Microsoft Internet Explorer.[1]

---

1. Brian Marick mentioned this example to me.

A user of Internet Explorer thinks of "Favorites" as a list of names of Web sites that persist from session to session. But the implementation treats a Favorite as a file containing a URL, and whose filename is put in the Favorites list. That's a problem if the Web page title contains characters that are illegal in Windows filenames. Suppose a user tries to store a Favorite and types the following name for it: "Laziness: The Secret to Happiness". An error message will say: "A filename cannot contain any of the following characters: \ / : * ? " < > | ". What filename? On the other hand, if the Web page title already contains an illegal character, Internet Explorer will just quietly strip it out. The loss of data may be benign in this case, but not what the user would have expected. Quietly changing data is completely unacceptable in most applications.

MODEL-DRIVEN DESIGN calls for working with only one model (within any single context, as will be discussed in Chapter 14). Most of the advice and examples go to the problems of having separate analysis models and design models, but here we have a problem arising from a different pair of models: the user model and the design/implementation model.

Of course, an unadorned view of the domain model would definitely not be convenient for the user in most cases. But trying to create in the UI an illusion of a model other than the domain model will cause confusion unless the illusion is perfect. If Web Favorites are actually just a collection of shortcut files, then expose this fact to the user and eliminate the confusing alternative model. Not only will the feature be less confusing, but the user can then leverage what he knows about the file system to deal with Web Favorites. He can reorganize them with the File Explorer, for example, rather than use awkward tools built into the Web browser. Informed users would be more able to exploit the flexibility of storing Web shortcuts anywhere in the file system. Just by removing the misleading extra model, the power of the application would increase and become clearer. Why make the user learn a new model when the programmers felt the old model was good enough?

Alternatively, store the Favorites in a different way, say in a data file, so that they can be subject to their own rules. Those rules would presumably be the naming rules that apply to Web pages. That would again provide a single model. This one tells the user that everything he knows about naming Web sites applies to Favorites.

When a design is based on a model that reflects the basic concerns of the users and domain experts, the bones of the design can be revealed to the user to a greater extent than with other design approaches. Revealing the model gives the user more access to the potential of the software and yields consistent, predictable behavior.

Hands-On Modelers

Manufacturing is a popular metaphor for software development. One inference from this metaphor: highly skilled engineers design; less skilled laborers assemble the products. This metaphor has messed up a lot of projects for one simple reason—software development is *all* design. All teams have specialized roles for members, but overseparation of responsibility for analysis, modeling, design, and programming interferes with MODEL-DRIVEN DESIGN.

On one project, my job was to coordinate different application teams and help develop the domain model that would drive the design. But the management thought that modelers should be modeling, and that coding was a waste of those skills, so I was in effect forbidden to program or work on details with programmers.

Things seemed to be OK for a while. Working with domain experts and the development leads of the different teams, we crunched knowledge and refined a nice core model. But that model was never put to work, for two reasons.

First, some of the model's intent was lost in the handoff. The overall effect of a model can be very sensitive to details (as will be discussed in Parts II and III), and those details don't always come across in a UML diagram or a general discussion. If I could have rolled up my sleeves and worked with the other developers directly, providing some code to follow as examples, and providing some close support, the team could have taken up the abstractions of the model and run with them.

The other problem was the indirectness of feedback from the interaction of the model with the implementation and the technology. For example, certain aspects of the model turned out to be wildly inefficient on our technology platform, but the full implications didn't trickle back to me for months. Relatively minor changes could have fixed the problem, but by then it didn't matter. The developers were well on their way to writing software that did work—without the model, which had been reduced to a mere data structure, wherever it was still used at all. The developers had thrown the baby out with the bathwater, but what choice did they have? They could no longer risk being saddled with the dictates of the architect in the ivory tower.

The initial circumstances of this project were about as favorable to a hands-off modeler as they ever are. I already had extensive hands-on experience with most of the technology used on the project. I had even led a small development team on the same project before my role changed, so I was familiar with the project's development process and programming environment. Even those factors were not enough to make me effective, given the separation of modeler from implementation.

If the people who write the code do not feel responsible for the **model, or don't understand how to make the model work for an application, then the model has nothing to do with the software. If developers don't realize that changing code changes the model, then their refactoring will weaken the model rather than strengthen it. Meanwhile, when a modeler is separated from the implementation process, he or she never acquires, or quickly loses, a feel for the constraints of implementation. The basic constraint of MODEL-DRIVEN DESIGN—that the model supports an effective implementation and abstracts key domain knowledge—is half-gone, and the resulting models will be impractical. Finally, the knowledge and skills of experienced designers won't be transferred to other developers if the division of labor prevents the kind of collaboration that conveys the subtleties of coding a MODEL-DRIVEN DESIGN.**

The need for HANDS-ON MODELERS does not mean that team members cannot have specialized roles. Every Agile process, including Extreme Programming, defines roles for team members, and other informal specializations tend to emerge naturally. The problem arises from separating two tasks that are coupled in a MODEL-DRIVEN DESIGN, modeling and implementation.

The effectiveness of an overall design is very sensitive to the quality and consistency of fine-grained design and implementation decisions. With a MODEL-DRIVEN DESIGN, a portion of the code is an expression of the model; changing that code changes the model. Programmers are modelers, whether anyone likes it or not. So it is better to set up the project so that the programmers do good modeling work.

Therefore:

Any technical person contributing to the model must spend some time touching the code, whatever primary role he or she plays

on the project. **Anyone responsible for changing code must learn to express a model through the code. Every developer must be involved in some level of discussion about the model and have contact with domain experts. Those who contribute in different ways must consciously engage those who touch the code in a dynamic exchange of model ideas through the** UBIQUITOUS LANGUAGE.

❋ ❋ ❋

The sharp separation of modeling and programming doesn't work, yet large projects still need technical leaders who coordinate high-level design and modeling and help work out the most difficult or most critical decisions. Part IV, "Strategic Design," deals with such decisions and should stimulate ideas for more productive ways to define the roles and responsibilities of high-level technical people.

Domain-driven design puts a model to work to solve problems for an application. Through knowledge crunching, a team distills a torrent of chaotic information into a practical model. A MODEL-DRIVEN DESIGN intimately connects the model and the implementation. The UBIQUITOUS LANGUAGE is the channel for all that information to flow between developers, domain experts, and the software.

The result is software that provides rich functionality based on a fundamental understanding of the core domain.

As mentioned, success with MODEL-DRIVEN DESIGN is sensitive to detailed design decisions, which is the subject of the next several chapters.

II

The Building Blocks of a Model-Driven Design

To keep a software implementation crisp and in lockstep with a model, in spite of messy realities, you must apply the best practices of modeling and design. This book is not an introduction to object-oriented design, nor does it propose radical design fundamentals. Domain-driven design shifts the emphasis of certain conventional ideas.

Certain kinds of decisions keep the model and implementation aligned with each other, each reinforcing the other's effectiveness. This alignment requires attention to the details of individual elements. Careful crafting at this small scale gives developers a steady platform from which to apply the modeling approaches of Parts III and IV.

The design style in this book largely follows the principle of "responsibility-driven design," put forward in Wirfs-Brock et al. 1990 and updated in Wirfs-Brock 2003. It also draws heavily (especially in Part III) on the ideas of "design by contract" described in Meyer 1988. It is consistent with the general background of other widely held best practices of object-oriented design, which are described in such books as Larman 1998.

As a project hits bumps, large or small, developers may find themselves in situations that make those principles seem inapplicable. To make the domain-driven design process resilient, developers need to understand *how* the well-known fundamentals support MODEL-DRIVEN DESIGN, so they can compromise without derailing.

The material in the following three chapters is organized as a "pattern language" (see Appendix A), which will show how subtle model distinctions and design decisions affect the domain-driven design process.

The diagram on the top of the next page is a *navigation map*. It shows the patterns that will be presented in this section and a few of the ways they relate to each other.

Sharing these standard patterns brings order to the design and makes it easier for team members to understand each other's work. Using standard patterns also adds to the UBIQUITOUS LANGUAGE, which all team members can use to discuss model and design decisions.

Developing a good domain model is an art. But the practical design and implementation of a model's individual elements can be relatively systematic. Isolating the domain design from the mass of other concerns

application services

domain services

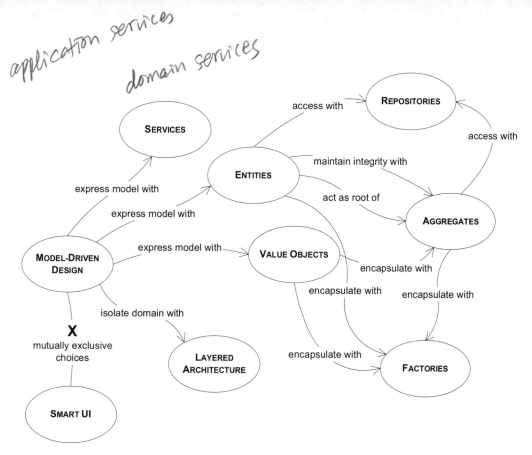

A navigation map of the language of MODEL-DRIVEN DESIGN

in the software system will greatly clarify the design's connection to the model. Defining model elements according to certain distinctions sharpens their meanings. Following proven patterns for individual elements helps produce a model that is practical to implement.

Elaborate models can cut through complexity only if care is taken with the fundamentals, resulting in detailed elements that the team can confidently combine.

FOUR

Isolating the Domain

The part of the software that specifically solves problems from the domain usually constitutes only a small portion of the entire software system, although its importance is disproportionate to its size. To apply our best thinking, we need to be able to look at the elements of our model and see them as a system. We must not be forced to pick them out of a much larger mix of objects, like trying to identify constellations in the night sky. We need to decouple the domain objects from other functions of the system, so we can avoid confusing the domain concepts with other concepts related only to software technology or losing sight of the domain altogether in the mass of the system.

Sophisticated techniques for this isolation have emerged. This is well-trodden ground, but it is so critical to the successful application of domain-modeling principles that it must be reviewed briefly, from a domain-driven point of view. . . .

LAYERED ARCHITECTURE

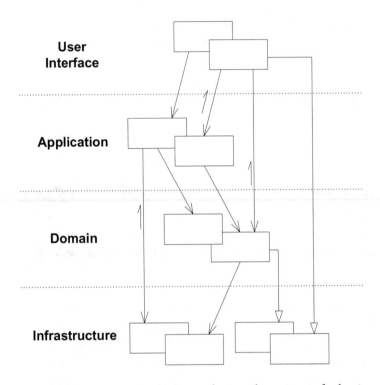

For a shipping application to support the simple user act of selecting a cargo's destination from a list of cities, there must be program code that (1) draws a widget on the screen, (2) queries the database for all the possible cities, (3) interprets the user's input and validates it, (4) associates the selected city with the cargo, and (5) commits the change to the database. All of this code is part of the same program, but only a little of it is related to the business of shipping.

Software programs involve design and code to carry out many different kinds of tasks. They accept user input, carry out business logic, access databases, communicate over networks, display information to users, and so on. So the code involved in each program function can be substantial.

In an object-oriented program, UI, database, and other support code often gets written directly into the business objects. Additional business logic is embedded in the behavior of UI widgets and database scripts. This happens because it is the easiest way to make things work, in the short run.

When the domain-related code is diffused through such a large amount of other code, it becomes extremely difficult to see and to reason about. Superficial changes to the UI can actually change business logic. To change a business rule may require meticulous tracing of UI code, database code, or other program elements. Implementing coherent, model-driven objects becomes impractical. Automated testing is awkward. With all the technologies and logic involved in each activity, a program must be kept very simple or it becomes impossible to understand.

Creating programs that can handle very complex tasks calls for separation of concerns, allowing concentration on different parts of the design in isolation. At the same time, the intricate interactions within the system must be maintained in spite of the separation.

There are all sorts of ways a software system might be divided, but through experience and convention, the industry has converged on LAYERED ARCHITECTURES, and specifically a few fairly standard layers. The metaphor of layering is so widely used that it feels intuitive to most developers. Many good discussions of layering are available in the literature, sometimes in the format of a pattern (as in Buschmann et al. 1996, pp. 31–51). The essential principle is that any element of a layer depends only on other elements in the same layer or on elements of the layers "beneath" it. Communication upward must pass through some indirect mechanism, which I'll discuss a little later.

The value of layers is that each specializes in a particular aspect of a computer program. This specialization allows more cohesive designs of each aspect, and it makes these designs much easier to interpret. Of course, it is vital to choose layers that isolate the most important cohesive design aspects. Again, experience and convention have led to some convergence. Although there are many variations, most successful architectures use some version of these four conceptual layers:

User Interface (or Presentation Layer)	Responsible for showing information to the user and interpreting the user's commands. The external actor might sometimes be another computer system rather than a human user.
Application Layer	Defines the jobs the software is supposed to do and directs the expressive domain objects to work out problems. The tasks this layer is responsible for are meaningful to the business or necessary for interaction with the application layers of other systems. This layer is kept thin. It does not contain business rules or knowledge, but only coordinates tasks and delegates work to collaborations of domain objects in the next layer down. It does not have state reflecting the business situation, but it can have state that reflects the progress of a task for the user or the program.
Domain Layer (or Model Layer)	Responsible for representing concepts of the business, information about the business situation, and business rules. State that reflects the business situation is controlled and used here, even though the technical details of storing it are delegated to the infrastructure. *This layer is the heart of business software.*
Infrastructure Layer	Provides generic technical capabilities that support the higher layers: message sending for the application, persistence for the domain, drawing widgets for the UI, and so on. The infrastructure layer may also support the pattern of interactions between the four layers through an architectural framework.

Some projects don't make a sharp distinction between the user interface and application layers. Others have multiple infrastructure layers. But it is the crucial separation of the *domain layer* that enables MODEL-DRIVEN DESIGN.

Therefore:

Partition a complex program into layers. Develop a design within each layer that is cohesive and that depends only on the layers below. Follow standard architectural patterns to provide loose coupling to the layers above. Concentrate all the code related to the domain model in one layer and isolate it from the user interface, application, and infrastructure code. The domain objects, free of the responsibility of displaying themselves, storing themselves, managing application tasks, and so forth, can be focused on expressing the

domain model. This allows a model to evolve to be rich enough and clear enough to capture essential business knowledge and put it to work.

Separating the domain layer from the infrastructure and user interface layers allows a much cleaner design of each layer. Isolated layers are much less expensive to maintain, because they tend to evolve at different rates and respond to different needs. The separation also helps with deployment in a distributed system, by allowing different layers to be placed flexibly in different servers or clients, in order to minimize communication overhead and improve performance (Fowler 1996).

Example

Partitioning Online Banking Functionality into Layers

An application provides various capabilities for maintaining bank accounts. One feature is funds transfer, in which the user enters or chooses two account numbers and an amount of money and then initiates a transfer.

To make this example manageable, I've omitted major technical features, most notably security. The domain design is also oversimplified. (Realistic complexity would only increase the need for layered architecture.) Furthermore, the particular infrastructure implied here is meant to be simple and obvious to make the example clear—it is not a suggested design. The responsibilities of the remaining functionality would be layered as shown in Figure 4.1.

Note that the domain layer, *not the application layer*, is responsible for fundamental business rules—in this case, the rule is "Every credit has a matching debit."

The application also makes no assumptions about the source of the transfer request. The program presumably includes a UI with entry fields for account numbers and amounts and with buttons for commands. But that user interface could be replaced by a wire request in XML without affecting the application layer or any of the lower layers. This decoupling is important not because projects frequently need to replace user interfaces with wire requests but because a clean separation of concerns keeps the design of each layer easy to understand and maintain.

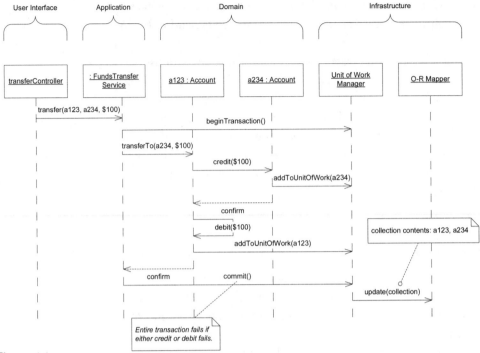

Figure 4.1

Objects carry out responsibilities consistent with their layer and are more coupled to other objects in their layer.

In fact, Figure 4.1 itself mildly illustrates the problem of not isolating the domain. Because everything from the request to transaction control had to be included, the domain layer had to be dumbed down to keep the overall interaction simple enough to follow. If we were focused on the design of the isolated domain layer, we would have space on the page and in our heads for a model that better represented the domain's rules, perhaps including ledgers, credit and debit objects, or monetary transaction objects.

Relating the Layers

So far the discussion has focused on the separation of layers and the way in which that partitioning improves the design of each aspect of the program, particularly the domain layer. But of course, the layers have to be connected. To do this without losing the benefit of the separation is the motivation behind a number of patterns.

Layers are meant to be loosely coupled, with design dependencies in only one direction. Upper layers can use or manipulate elements of lower ones straightforwardly by calling their public interfaces, holding references to them (at least temporarily), and generally using conventional means of interaction. But when an object of a lower level needs to communicate upward (beyond answering a direct query), we need another mechanism, drawing on architectural patterns for relating layers such as callbacks or OBSERVERS (Gamma et al. 1995).

The grandfather of patterns for connecting the UI to the application and domain layers is MODEL-VIEW-CONTROLLER (MVC). It was pioneered in the Smalltalk world back in the 1970s and has inspired many of the UI architectures that followed. Fowler (2003) discusses this pattern and several useful variations on the theme. Larman (1998) explores these concerns in the MODEL-VIEW SEPARATION PATTERN, and his APPLICATION COORDINATOR is one approach to connecting the application layer.

There are other styles of connecting the UI and the application. For our purposes, all approaches are fine as long as they maintain the isolation of the domain layer, allowing domain objects to be designed without simultaneously thinking about the user interface that might interact with them.

The infrastructure layer usually does not initiate action in the domain layer. Being "below" the domain layer, it should have no specific knowledge of the domain it is serving. Indeed, such technical capabilities are most often offered as SERVICES. For example, if an application needs to send an e-mail, some message-sending interface can be located in the infrastructure layer and the application layer elements can request the transmission of the message. This decoupling gives some extra versatility. The message-sending interface might be connected to an e-mail sender, a fax sender, or whatever else is available. But the main benefit is simplifying the application layer, keeping it narrowly focused on its job: knowing *when* to send a message, but not burdened with *how*.

The application and domain layers call on the SERVICES provided by the infrastructure layer. When the scope of a SERVICE has been well chosen and its interface well designed, the caller can remain loosely coupled and uncomplicated by the elaborate behavior the SERVICE interface encapsulates.

But not all infrastructure comes in the form of SERVICES callable from the higher layers. Some technical components are designed to directly support the basic functions of other layers (such as providing an abstract base class for all domain objects) and provide the mechanisms for them to relate (such as implementations of MVC and the like). Such an "architectural framework" has much more impact on the design of the other parts of the program.

Architectural Frameworks

When infrastructure is provided in the form of SERVICES called on through interfaces, it is fairly intuitive how the layering works and how to keep the layers loosely coupled. But some technical problems call for more intrusive forms of infrastructure. Frameworks that integrate many infrastructure needs often require the other layers to be implemented in very particular ways, for example as a subclass of a framework class or with structured method signatures. (It may seem counterintuitive for a subclass to be in a layer higher than that of the parent class, but keep in mind which class reflects more knowledge of the other.) The best architectural frameworks solve complex technical problems while allowing the domain developer to concentrate on expressing a model. But frameworks can easily get in the way, either by making too many assumptions that constrain domain design choices or by making the implementation so heavyweight that development slows down.

Some form of architectural framework usually is needed (though sometimes teams choose frameworks that don't serve them well). When applying a framework, the team needs to focus on its goal: building an implementation that expresses a domain model and uses it to solve important problems. The team must seek ways of employing the framework to those ends, even if it means not using all of the framework's features. For example, early J2EE applications often implemented all domain objects as "entity beans." This approach bogged down both performance and the pace of development. Instead, current best practice is to use the J2EE framework for larger grain objects, implementing most business logic with generic Java objects. A lot of the downside of frameworks can be avoided by applying them selectively to solve difficult problems without looking for a one-size-fits-all solution. Judiciously applying only the most valuable of framework features reduces the coupling of the implementation and the framework, allowing more flexibility in later design decisions. More important, given how very complicated many of the current frameworks are to use, this minimalism helps keep the business objects readable and expressive.

Architectural frameworks and other tools will continue to evolve. Newer frameworks will automate or prefabricate more and more of the technical aspects of an application. If this is done right, application developers will increasingly concentrate their time on modeling the core business problems, greatly improving productivity and quality. But as we move in this direction, we must guard against our enthusiasm for technical solutions; elaborate frameworks can also straitjacket application developers.

The Domain Layer Is Where the Model Lives

LAYERED ARCHITECTURE is used in most systems today, under various layering schemes. Many styles of development can also benefit from layering. However, domain-driven design requires only one particular layer to exist.

The domain model is a set of concepts. The "domain layer" is the manifestation of that model and all directly related design elements. The design and implementation of business logic constitute the domain layer. In a MODEL-DRIVEN DESIGN, the software constructs of the domain layer mirror the model concepts.

It is not practical to achieve that correspondence when the domain logic is mixed with other concerns of the program. Isolating the domain implementation is a prerequisite for domain-driven design.

The Smart UI "Anti-Pattern"

. . . That sums up the widely accepted LAYERED ARCHITECTURE pattern for object applications. But this separation of UI, application, and domain is so often attempted and so seldom accomplished that its negation deserves a discussion in its own right.

Many software projects do take and should continue to take a much less sophisticated design approach that I call the SMART UI. But SMART UI is an alternate, mutually exclusive fork in the road, incompatible with the approach of domain-driven design. If that road is taken, most of what is in this book is not applicable. My interest is in the situations where the SMART UI does not apply, which is why I call it, with tongue in cheek, an "anti-pattern." Discussing it here provides a useful contrast and will help clarify the circumstances that justify the more difficult path taken in the rest of the book.

❊   ❊   ❊

A project needs to deliver simple functionality, dominated by data entry and display, with few business rules. Staff is not composed of advanced object modelers.

If an unsophisticated team with a simple project decides to try a MODEL-DRIVEN DESIGN with LAYERED ARCHITECTURE, it will face a difficult learning curve. Team members will have to master complex new technologies and stumble through the process of learning object modeling (which is challenging, even with the help of this book!). The overhead of managing infrastructure and layers makes very simple tasks take longer. Simple projects come with short time lines and modest expectations. Long before the team completes the assigned task, much less demonstrates the exciting possibilities of its approach, the project will have been canceled.

Even if the team is given more time, the team members are likely to fail to master the techniques without expert help. And in the end, if they do surmount these challenges, they will have produced a simple system. Rich capabilities were never requested.

A more experienced team would not face the same trade-offs. Seasoned developers could flatten the learning curve and compress the time needed to manage the layers. Domain-driven design pays off best for ambitious projects, and it does require strong skills. Not all projects are ambitious. Not all project teams can muster those skills.

Therefore, when circumstances warrant:

Put all the business logic into the user interface. Chop the application into small functions and implement them as separate user interfaces, embedding the business rules into them. Use a relational database as a shared repository of the data. Use the most automated UI building and visual programming tools available.

Heresy! The gospel (as advocated everywhere, including elsewhere in this book) is that domain and UI should be separate. In fact, it is difficult to apply any of the methods discussed later in this book without that separation, and so this SMART UI can be considered an "anti-pattern" in the context of domain-driven design. Yet it is a legitimate pattern in some other contexts. In truth, there are advantages to the SMART UI, and there are situations where it works best—which partially accounts for why it is so common. Considering it here helps us understand why we need to separate application from domain and, importantly, when we might not want to.

Advantages

- Productivity is high and immediate for simple applications.

- Less capable developers can work this way with little training.

- Even deficiencies in requirements analysis can be overcome by releasing a prototype to users and then quickly changing the product to fit their requests.

- Applications are decoupled from each other, so that delivery schedules of small modules can be planned relatively accurately. Expanding the system with additional, simple behavior can be easy.

- Relational databases work well and provide integration at the data level.

- 4GL tools work well.

- When applications are handed off, maintenance programmers will be able to quickly redo portions they can't figure out, because the effects of the changes should be localized to each particular UI.

Disadvantages

- Integration of applications is difficult except through the database.

- There is no reuse of behavior and no abstraction of the business problem. Business rules have to be duplicated in each operation to which they apply.

- Rapid prototyping and iteration reach a natural limit because the lack of abstraction limits refactoring options.

- Complexity buries you quickly, so the growth path is strictly toward additional simple applications. There is no graceful path to richer behavior.

If this pattern is applied consciously, a team can avoid taking on a great deal of overhead required by other approaches. It is a common mistake to undertake a sophisticated design approach that the team isn't committed to carrying all the way through. Another common, costly mistake is to build a complex infrastructure and use industrial-strength tools for a project that doesn't need them.

Most flexible languages (such as Java) are overkill for these applications and will cost dearly. A 4GL-style tool is the way to go.

Remember, one of the consequences of this pattern is that you can't migrate to another design approach except by replacing entire applications. Just using a general-purpose language such as Java won't really put you in a position to later abandon the SMART UI, so if you've chosen that path, you should choose development tools geared to it. Don't bother hedging your bet. Just using a flexible language doesn't create a flexible system, but it may well produce an expensive one.

By the same token, a team committed to a MODEL-DRIVEN DESIGN needs to design that way from the outset. Of course, even experienced project teams with big ambitions have to start with simple functionality and work their way up through successive iterations. But those first tentative steps will be MODEL-DRIVEN with an isolated domain layer, or the project will most likely be stuck with a SMART UI.

✳ ✳ ✳

The SMART UI is discussed only to clarify why and when a pattern such as LAYERED ARCHITECTURE is needed in order to isolate a domain layer.

There are other solutions in between SMART UI and LAYERED ARCHITECTURE. For example, Fowler (2003) describes the TRANSACTION SCRIPT, which separates UI from application but does not provide for an object model. The bottom line is this: *If the architecture isolates the domain-related code in a way that allows a cohesive domain design loosely coupled to the rest of the system, then that architecture can probably support domain-driven design.*

Other development styles have their place, but you must accept varying limits on complexity and flexibility. Failing to decouple the domain design can really be disastrous in certain settings. If you have a complex application and are committing to MODEL-DRIVEN DESIGN, bite the bullet, get the necessary experts, and *avoid* the SMART UI.

Other Kinds of Isolation

Unfortunately, there are influences other than infrastructure and user interfaces that can corrupt your delicate domain model. You must deal with other domain components that are not fully integrated into your model. You have to cope with other development teams who use different models of the same domain. These and other factors can blur your model and rob it of its utility. Chapter 14, "Maintaining Model Integrity," deals with this topic, introducing such patterns as BOUNDED CONTEXT and ANTICORRUPTION LAYER. A really complicated domain model can become unwieldy all by itself. Chapter 15, "Distillation," discusses how to make distinctions within the domain layer that can unencumber the essential concepts of the domain from peripheral detail.

unencumber

But all that comes later. Next, we'll look at the nuts and bolts of co-evolving an effective domain model and an expressive implementation. After all, the best part of isolating the domain is getting all that other stuff out of the way so that we can really focus on the domain design.

A Model Expressed in Software

To compromise in implementation without losing the punch of a MODEL-DRIVEN DESIGN requires a reframing of the basics. Connecting model and implementation has to be done at the detail level. This chapter focuses on those individual model elements, getting them in shape to support the activities in later chapters.

This discussion will start with the issues of designing and streamlining associations. Associations between objects are simple to conceive and to draw, but implementing them is a potential quagmire. Associations illustrate how crucial detailed implementation decisions are to the viability of a MODEL-DRIVEN DESIGN.

quagmire

Turning to the objects themselves, but continuing to scrutinize the relationship between detailed model choices and implementation concerns, we'll focus on making distinctions among the three patterns of model elements that express the model: ENTITIES, VALUE OBJECTS, and SERVICES.

Defining objects that capture concepts of the domain seems very intuitive on the surface, but serious challenges are lurking in the shades of meaning. Certain distinctions have emerged that clarify the meaning of model elements and tie into a body of design practices for carving out specific kinds of objects.

Does an object represent something with continuity and identity—something that is tracked through different states or even across different implementations? Or is it an attribute that describes the state of something else? This is the basic distinction between an

ENTITY and a VALUE OBJECT. Defining objects that clearly follow one pattern or the other makes the objects less ambiguous and lays out the path toward specific choices for robust design.

Then there are those aspects of the domain that are more clearly expressed as actions or operations, rather than as objects. Although it is a slight departure from object-oriented modeling tradition, it is often best to express these as SERVICES, rather than forcing responsibility for an operation onto some ENTITY or VALUE OBJECT. A SERVICE is something that is done for a client on request. In the technical layers of the software, there are many SERVICES. They emerge in the domain also, when some activity is modeled that corresponds to something the software must do, but does not correspond with state.

There are inevitable situations in which the purity of the object model must be compromised, such as for storage in a relational database. This chapter will lay out some guidelines for staying on course when you are forced to deal with these messy realities.

Finally, a discussion of MODULES will drive home the point that every design decision should be motivated by some insight into the domain. The ideas of high cohesion and low coupling, often thought of as technical metrics, can be applied to the concepts themselves. In a MODEL-DRIVEN DESIGN, MODULES are part of the model, and they should reflect concepts in the domain.

This chapter brings together all of these building blocks, which embody the model in software. These ideas are conventional, and the modeling and design biases that follow from them have been written about before. But framing them in this context will help developers create detailed components that will serve the priorities of domain-driven design when tackling the larger model and design issues. Also, a sense of the basic principles will help developers stay on course through the inevitable compromises.

Associations

The interaction between modeling and implementation is particularly tricky with the associations between objects.

For every traversable association in the model, there is a mechanism in the software with the same properties.

A model that shows an association between a customer and a sales representative corresponds to two things. On one hand, it abstracts a relationship developers deemed relevant between two real people. On the other hand, it corresponds to an object pointer between two Java objects, or an encapsulation of a database lookup, or some comparable implementation.

For example, a one-to-many association might be implemented as a collection in an instance variable. But the design is not necessarily so direct. There may be no collection; an accessor method may query a database to find the appropriate records and instantiate objects based on them. Both of these designs would reflect the same model. The design has to specify a particular traversal mechanism whose behavior is consistent with the association in the model.

In real life, there are lots of many-to-many associations, and a great number are naturally bidirectional. The same tends to be true of early forms of a model as we brainstorm and explore the domain. But these general associations complicate implementation and maintenance. Furthermore, they communicate very little about the nature of the relationship.

There are at least three ways of making associations more tractable.

1. Imposing a traversal direction

2. Adding a qualifier, effectively reducing multiplicity

3. Eliminating nonessential associations

It is important to constrain relationships as much as possible. A bidirectional association means that both objects can be understood only together. When application requirements do not call for traversal in both directions, adding a traversal direction reduces interdependence and simplifies the design. Understanding the domain may reveal a natural directional bias.

The United States has had many presidents, as have many other countries. This is a bidirectional, one-to-many relationship. Yet we seldom would start out with the name "George Washington" and ask, "Of which country was he president?" Pragmatically, we can reduce the relationship to a unidirectional association, traversable from country to president. This refinement actually reflects insight into the domain, as well as making a more practical design. It captures the understanding that one direction of the association is much more meaningful and important than the other. It keeps the "Person" class independent of the far less fundamental concept of "President."

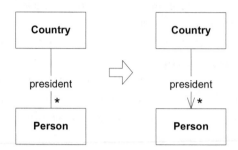

Figure 5.1
Some traversal directions reflect a natural bias in the domain.

Very often, deeper understanding leads to a "qualified" relationship. Looking deeper into presidents, we realize that (except in a civil war, perhaps) a country has only one president at a time. This qualifier reduces the multiplicity to one-to-one, and explicitly embeds an important rule into the model. Who was president of the United States in 1790? George Washington.

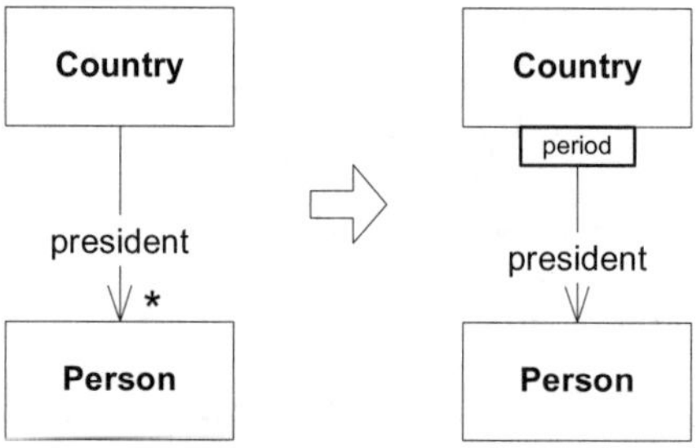

Figure 5.2
Constrained associations communicate more knowledge and are more practical designs.

Constraining the traversal direction of a many-to-many association effectively reduces its implementation to one-to-many—a *much* easier design.

Consistently constraining associations in ways that reflect the bias of the domain not only makes those associations more communicative and simpler to implement, it also gives significance to the remaining bidirectional associations. When the bidirectionality of a relationship is a semantic characteristic of the domain, when it's needed for application functionality, the retention of both traversal directions conveys that.

Of course, the ultimate simplification is to eliminate an association altogether, if it is not essential to the job at hand or the fundamental meaning of the model objects.

Example

Associations in a Brokerage Account

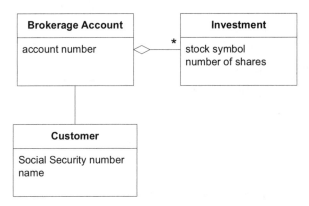

Figure 5.3

One Java implementation of **Brokerage Account** in this model would be

```java
public class BrokerageAccount {
    String accountNumber;
    Customer customer;
    Set investments;
  // Constructors, etc. omitted

    public Customer getCustomer() {
      return customer;
    }
    public Set getInvestments() {
      return investments;
    }
}
```

But if we need to fetch the data from a relational database, another implementation, equally consistent with the model, would be the following:

Table: BROKERAGE_ACCOUNT

ACCOUNT_NUMBER	CUSTOMER_SS_NUMBER

Table: CUSTOMER

SS_NUMBER	NAME

Table: INVESTMENT

ACCOUNT_NUMBER	STOCK_SYMBOL	AMOUNT

```
public class BrokerageAccount {
  String accountNumber;
  String customerSocialSecurityNumber;

  // Omit constructors, etc.

  public Customer getCustomer() {
    String sqlQuery =
      "SELECT * FROM CUSTOMER WHERE" +
      "SS_NUMBER='"+customerSocialSecurityNumber+"'";
    return QueryService.findSingleCustomerFor(sqlQuery);
  }
  public Set getInvestments() {
    String sqlQuery =
      "SELECT * FROM INVESTMENT WHERE" +
      "BROKERAGE_ACCOUNT='"+accountNumber+"'";
    return QueryService.findInvestmentsFor(sqlQuery);
  }
}
```

(*Note:* The QueryService, a utility for fetching rows from the database and creating objects, is simple for explaining examples, but it's not necessarily a good design for a real project.)

Let's refine the model by qualifying the association between **Brokerage Account** and **Investment**, reducing its multiplicity. This says there can be only one investment per stock.

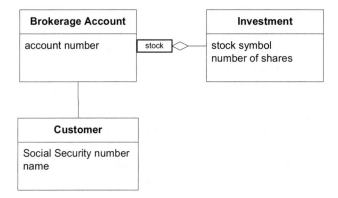

Figure 5.4

This wouldn't be true of all business situations (for example, if the lots need to be tracked), but whatever the particular rules, as constraints on associations are discovered they should be included in the model and implementation. They make the model more precise and the implementation easier to maintain.

The Java implementation could become:

```java
public class BrokerageAccount {
   String accountNumber;
   Customer customer;
   Map investments;

   // Omitting constructors, etc.

   public Customer getCustomer() {
     return customer;
   }
   public Investment getInvestment(String stockSymbol) {
     return (Investment)investments.get(stockSymbol);
   }
}
```

And an SQL-based implementation would be:

```java
public class BrokerageAccount {
   String accountNumber;
   String customerSocialSecurityNumber;

   //Omitting constructors, etc.
```

```java
public Customer getCustomer() {
    String sqlQuery = "SELECT * FROM CUSTOMER WHERE SS_NUMBER='"
        + customerSocialSecurityNumber + "'";
    return QueryService.findSingleCustomerFor(sqlQuery);
}
public Investment getInvestment(String stockSymbol) {
    String sqlQuery = "SELECT * FROM INVESTMENT "
        + "WHERE BROKERAGE_ACCOUNT='" + accountNumber + "'"
        + "AND STOCK_SYMBOL='" + stockSymbol +"'";
    return QueryService.findInvestmentFor(sqlQuery);


}
}
```

Carefully distilling and constraining the model's associations will take you a long way toward a MODEL-DRIVEN DESIGN. Now let's turn to the objects themselves. Certain distinctions clarify the model while making for a more practical implementation. . . .

Entities (a.k.a. Reference Objects)

Many objects are not fundamentally defined by their attributes, but rather by a thread of continuity and identity.

 A landlady sued me, claiming major damages to her property. The papers I was served described an apartment with holes in the walls, stains on the carpet, and a noxious liquid in the sink that gave off caustic fumes that had made the kitchen wallpaper peel. The court documents named me as the tenant responsible for the damages, identifying me by name and by my then-current address. This was confusing to me, because I had never even visited that ruined place.

 After a moment, I realized that it must be a case of mistaken identity. I called the plaintiff and told her this, but she didn't believe me. The former tenant had been eluding her for months. How could I prove that I was not the same person who had cost her so much money? I was the only Eric Evans in the phone book.

 Well, the phone book turned out to be my salvation. Because I had been living in the same apartment for two years, I asked her if she still had the previous year's book. After she found it and verified that my listing was the same (right next to my namesake's listing), she realized that I was not the person she wanted to sue, apologized, and promised to drop the case.

Computers are not that resourceful. A case of mistaken identity in a software system leads to data corruption and program errors.

There are special technical challenges here, which I'll discuss in a bit, but first let's look at the fundamental issue: Many things are defined by their identity, and not by any attribute. In our typical conception, a person (to continue with the nontechnical example) has an identity that stretches from birth to death and even beyond. That person's physical attributes transform and ultimately disappear. The name may change. Financial relationships come and go. There is not a single attribute of a person that cannot change; yet the identity persists. Am I the same person I was at age five? This kind of metaphysical question is important in the search for effective domain models. Slightly rephrased: Does the user of the application *care* if I am the same person I was at age five?

In a software system for tracking accounts due, that modest "customer" object may have a more colorful side. It accumulates status by prompt payment or is turned over to a bill-collection agency for failure to pay. It may lead a double life in another system altogether when the sales force extracts customer data into its contact management software. In any case, it is unceremoniously squashed flat to be stored in a database table. When new business stops flowing from that source, the customer object will be retired to an archive, a shadow of its former self.

Each of these forms of the customer is a different implementation based on a different programming language and technology. But when a phone call comes in with an order, it is important to know: Is this the customer who has the delinquent account? Is this the customer that Jack (a particular sales representative) has been working with for weeks? Is this a completely new customer?

A conceptual identity has to be matched between multiple implementations of the objects, its stored forms, and real-world actors such as the phone caller. Attributes may not match. A sales representative may have entered an address update into the contact software, which is just being propagated to accounts due. Two customer contacts may have the same name. In distributed software, multiple users could be entering data from different sources, causing update transactions to propagate through the system to be reconciled in different databases asynchronously.

Object modeling tends to lead us to focus on the attributes of an object, but the fundamental concept of an ENTITY is an abstract continuity threading through a life cycle and even passing through multiple forms.

Some objects are not defined primarily by their attributes. They represent a thread of identity that runs through time and often across distinct representations. Sometimes such an object must be matched with another object even though attributes differ. An object must be distinguished from other objects even though they might have the same attributes. Mistaken identity can lead to data corruption.

An object defined primarily by its identity is called an ENTITY.[1] ENTITIES have special modeling and design considerations. They have life cycles that can radically change their form and content, but a thread of continuity must be maintained. Their identities must be defined so that they can be effectively tracked. Their class definitions, responsibilities, attributes, and associations should revolve around who they are, rather than the particular attributes they carry. Even for ENTITIES that don't transform so radically or have such complicated life cycles, placing them in the semantic category leads to more lucid models and more robust implementations.

Of course, most "ENTITIES" in a software system are not people or entities in the usual sense of the word. An ENTITY is anything that has continuity through a life cycle and distinctions independent of attributes that are important to the application's user. It could be a person, a city, a car, a lottery ticket, or a bank transaction.

On the other hand, not all objects in the model are ENTITIES, with meaningful identities. This issue is confused by the fact that object-oriented languages build "identity" operations into every object (for example, the "==" operator in Java). These operations determine if two references point to the same object by comparing their location in memory or by some other mechanism. In this sense, every object instance has identity. In the domain of, say, creating a Java runtime environment or a technical framework for caching remote objects locally, every object instance may indeed be an ENTITY. But this identity

---

1. A model ENTITY is not the same thing as a Java "entity bean." Entity beans were meant as a framework for implementing ENTITIES, more or less, but it hasn't worked out that way. Most ENTITIES are implemented as ordinary objects. Regardless of how they are implemented, ENTITIES are a fundamental distinction in a domain model.

mechanism means very little in other application domains. Identity is a subtle and meaningful attribute of ENTITIES, which can't be turned over to the automatic features of the language.

Consider transactions in a banking application. Two deposits of the same amount to the same account on the same day are still distinct transactions, so they have identity and are ENTITIES. On the other hand, the amount attributes of those two transactions are probably instances of some money object. These values have no identity, since there is no usefulness in distinguishing them. In fact, two objects can have the same identity without having the same attributes or even, necessarily, being of the same class. When the bank customer is reconciling the transactions of the bank statement with the transactions of the check registry, the task is, specifically, to match transactions that have the same identity, even though they were recorded by different people on different dates (the bank clearing date being later than the date on the check). The purpose of the check number is to serve as a unique identifier for this purpose, whether the problem is being handled by a computer program or by hand. Deposits and cash withdrawals, which don't have an identifying number, can be trickier, but the same principle applies: each transaction is an ENTITY, which appears in at least two forms.

It is common for identity to be significant outside a particular software system, as is the case with the banking transactions and the apartment tenants. But sometimes the identity is important only in the context of the system, such as the identity of a computer process.

Therefore:

When an object is distinguished by its identity, rather than its attributes, make this primary to its definition in the model. Keep the class definition simple and focused on life cycle continuity and identity. Define a means of distinguishing each object regardless of its form or history. Be alert to requirements that call for matching objects by attributes. Define an operation that is guaranteed to produce a unique result for each object, possibly by attaching a symbol that is guaranteed unique. This means of identification may come from the outside, or it may be an arbitrary identifier created by and for the system, but it must correspond to the identity distinctions in the model. The model must define what it *means* to be the same thing.

Identity is not intrinsic to a thing in the world; it is a meaning superimposed because it is useful. In fact, the same real-world thing might or might not be represented as an ENTITY in a domain model.

An application for booking seats in a stadium might treat seats and attendees as ENTITIES. In the case of assigned seating, in which each ticket has a seat number on it, the seat is an ENTITY. Its identifier is the seat number, which is unique within the stadium. The seat may have many other attributes, such as its location, whether the view is obstructed, and the price, but only the seat number, or a unique row and position, is used to identify and distinguish seats.

On the other hand, if the event is "general admission," meaning that ticket holders sit wherever they find an empty seat, there is no need to distinguish individual seats. Only the total number of seats is important. Although the seat numbers are still engraved on the physical seats, there is no need for the software to track them. In fact, it would be erroneous for the model to associate specific seat numbers with tickets, because there is no such constraint at a general admission event. In such a case, seats are *not* ENTITIES, and no identifier is needed.

✳   ✳   ✳

Modeling ENTITIES

It is natural to think about the attributes when modeling an object, and it is quite important to think about its behavior. But the most basic responsibility of ENTITIES is to establish continuity so that behavior can be clear and predictable. They do this best if they are kept spare. Rather than focusing on the attributes or even the behavior, strip the ENTITY object's definition down to the most intrinsic characteristics, particularly those that identify it or are commonly used to find or match it. Add only behavior that is essential to the concept and attributes that are required by that behavior. Beyond that, look to remove behavior and attributes into other objects associated with the core ENTITY. Some of these will be other ENTITIES. Some will be VALUE OBJECTS, which is the next pattern in this chapter. Beyond identity issues, ENTITIES tend to fulfill their responsibilities by coordinating the operations of objects they own.

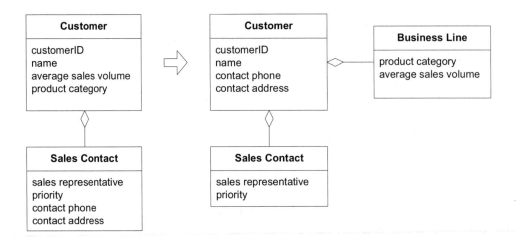

Figure 5.5

Attributes associated
with identity stay with
the ENTITY.

The customerID is the one and only identifier of the **Customer**
ENTITY in Figure 5.5, but the phone number and address would
often be used to find or match a **Customer**. The name does not *define*
a person's identity, but it is often used as part of the means of determining it. In this example, the phone and address attributes moved
into **Customer**, but on a real project, that choice would depend on
how the domain's customers are typically matched or distinguished.
For example, if a **Customer** has many contact phone numbers for different purposes, then the phone number is not associated with identity and should stay with the **Sales Contact**.

Designing the Identity Operation

Each ENTITY must have an operational way of establishing its identity
with another object—distinguishable even from another object with
the same descriptive attributes. An identifying attribute must be guaranteed to be unique within the system however that system is defined—even if distributed, even when objects are archived.

As mentioned earlier, object-oriented languages have "identity"
operations that determine if two references point to the same object
by comparing the objects' locations in memory. This kind of identity
tracking is too fragile for our purposes. In most technologies for persistent storage of objects, every time an object is retrieved from a
database, a new instance is created, and so the initial identity is lost.
Every time an object is transmitted across a network, a new instance
is created on the destination, and once again the identity is lost. The

problem can be even worse when multiple versions of the same object exist in the system, such as when updates propagate through a distributed database.

Even with frameworks that simplify these technical problems, the fundamental issue exists: How do you know that two objects represent the same conceptual ENTITY? The definition of identity emerges from the model. Defining identity demands understanding of the domain.

Sometimes certain data attributes, or combinations of attributes, can be guaranteed or simply constrained to be unique within the system. This approach provides a unique key for the ENTITY. Daily newspapers, for example, might be identified by the name of the newspaper, the city, and the date of publication. (But watch out for extra editions and name changes!)

When there is no true unique key made up of the attributes of an object, another common solution is to attach to each instance a symbol (such as a number or a string) that is unique within the class. Once this ID symbol is created and stored as an attribute of the ENTITY, it is designated immutable. It must never change, even if the development system is unable to directly enforce this rule. For example, the ID attribute is preserved as the object gets flattened into a database and reconstructed. Sometimes a technical framework helps with this process, but otherwise it just takes engineering discipline.

Often the ID is generated automatically by the system. The generation algorithm must guarantee uniqueness within the system, which can be a challenge with concurrent processing and in distributed systems. Generating such an ID may require techniques that are beyond the scope of this book. The goal here is to point out when the considerations arise, so that developers are aware they have a problem to solve and know how to narrow down their concerns to the critical areas. The key is to recognize that identity concerns hinge on specific aspects of the model. Often, the means of identification demand a careful study of the domain, as well.

When the ID is automatically generated, the user may never need to see it. The ID may be needed only internally, such as in a contact management application that lets the user find records by a person's name. The program needs to be able to distinguish two contacts with exactly the same name in a simple, unambiguous way. The unique, internal IDs let the system do just that. After retrieving the two distinct items, the system will show two separate contacts to the user, but the IDs may not be shown. The user will distinguish them on the basis of their company, their location, and so on.

Finally, there are cases in which a generated ID *is* of interest to the user. When I ship a package through a parcel delivery service, I'm given a tracking number, generated by the shipping company's software, which I can use to identify and follow up on my package. When I book airline tickets or reserve a hotel, I'm given confirmation numbers that are unique identifiers for the transaction.

In some cases, the uniqueness of the ID must apply beyond the computer system's boundaries. For example, if medical records are being exchanged between two hospitals that have separate computer systems, ideally each system will use the same patient ID, but this is difficult if they generate their own symbol. Such systems often use an identifier issued by some other institution, typically a government agency. In the United States, the Social Security number is often used by hospitals as an identifier for a person. Such methods are not foolproof. Not everyone has a Social Security number (children and non-residents of the United States, especially), and many people object to its use, for privacy reasons.

In less formal situations (say, video rental), telephone numbers are used as identifiers. But a telephone can be shared. The number can change. An old number can even be reassigned to a different person.

For these reasons, specially assigned identifiers are often used (such as frequent flier numbers), and other attributes, such as phone numbers and Social Security numbers, are used to match and verify. In any case, when the application requires an external ID, the users of the system become responsible for supplying IDs that are unique, and the system must give them adequate tools to handle exceptions that arise.

Given all these technical problems, it is easy to lose sight of the underlying conceptual problem: What does it mean for two objects to be the same thing? It is easy enough to stamp each object with an ID, or to write an operation that compares two instances, but if these IDs or operations don't correspond to some meaningful distinction in the domain, they just confuse matters more. This is why identity-assigning operations often involve human input. Checkbook reconciliation software, for instance, may offer likely matches, but the user is expected to make the final determination.

VALUE OBJECTS

Many objects have no conceptual identity. These objects describe some characteristic of a thing.

* * *

When a child is drawing, he cares about the color of the marker he chooses, and he may care about the sharpness of the tip. But if there are two markers of the same color and shape, he probably won't care which one he uses. If a marker is lost and replaced by another of the same color from a new pack, he can resume his work unconcerned about the switch.

Ask the child about the various drawings on the refrigerator, and he will quickly distinguish those he made from those his sister made. He and his sister have useful identities, as do their completed drawings. But imagine how complicated it would be if he had to track which lines in a drawing were made by each marker. Drawing would no longer be child's play.

Because the most conspicuous objects in a model are usually EN-TITIES, and because it is so important to track each ENTITY's identity, it is natural to consider assigning an identity to all domain objects. Indeed, some frameworks assign a unique ID to every object.

The system has to cope with all that tracking, and many possible performance optimizations are ruled out. Analytical effort is required to define meaningful identities and work out foolproof ways to track

**Is "Address" a
VALUE OBJECT?
Who's Asking?**
In software for a mail-
order company, an
address is needed to
confirm the credit card,
and to address the parcel.
But if a roommate also
orders from the same
company, it is not impor-
tant to realize they are in
the same location. Ad-
dress is a VALUE OBJECT.

In software for the
postal service, intended
to organize delivery
routes, the country could
be formed into a hier-
archy of regions, cities,
postal zones, and blocks,
terminating in individual
addresses. These address
objects would derive
their zip code from their
parent in the hierarchy,
and if the postal service
decided to reassign postal
zones, all the addresses
within would go along
for the ride. Here,
Address is an ENTITY.

In software for an
electric utility company,
an address corresponds
to a destination for the
company's lines and ser-
vice. If roommates each
called to order electrical
service, the company
would need to realize it.
Address is an ENTITY.
Alternatively, the model
could associate utility
service with a "dwelling,"
an ENTITY with an
attribute of address. Then
Address would be a
VALUE OBJECT.

objects across distributed systems or in database storage. Equally important, taking on artificial identities is misleading. It muddles the
model, forcing all objects into the same mold.

**Tracking the identity of ENTITIES is essential, but attaching
identity to other objects can hurt system performance, add analytical
work, and muddle the model by making all objects look the same.**

**Software design is a constant battle with complexity. We must
make distinctions so that special handling is applied only where
necessary.**

**However, if we think of this category of object as just the ab-
sence of identity, we haven't added much to our toolbox or vocabulary. In fact, these objects have characteristics of their own and their
own significance to the model.** *These are the objects that describe things.*

An object that represents a descriptive aspect of the domain with
no conceptual identity is called a VALUE OBJECT. VALUE OBJECTS are
instantiated to represent elements of the design that we care about
only for *what* they are, not *who* or *which* they are.

Colors are an example of VALUE OBJECTS that are provided in
the base libraries of many modern development systems; so are
strings and numbers. (You don't care which "4" you have or which
"Q".) These basic examples are simple, but VALUE OBJECTS are not
necessarily simple. For example, a color-mixing program might have
a rich model in which enhanced color objects could be combined to
produce other colors. These colors could have complex algorithms
for collaborating to derive the new resulting VALUE OBJECT.

A VALUE OBJECT can be an assemblage of other objects. In software for designing house plans, an object could be created for each
window style. This "window style" could be incorporated into a
"window" object, along with height and width, as well as rules governing how these attributes can be changed and combined. These
windows are intricate VALUE OBJECTS made up of other VALUE OB-
JECTS. They in turn would be incorporated into larger elements of a
plan, such as "wall" objects.

VALUE OBJECTS can even reference ENTITIES. For example, if I
ask an online map service for a scenic driving route from San Francisco to Los Angeles, it might derive a Route object linking L.A. and
San Francisco via the Pacific Coast Highway. That Route object

would be a VALUE, even though the three objects it references (two cities and a highway) are all ENTITIES.

VALUE OBJECTS are often passed as parameters in messages between objects. They are frequently transient, created for an operation and then discarded. VALUE OBJECTS are used as attributes of ENTITIES (and other VALUES). A person may be modeled as an ENTITY with an identity, but that person's *name* is a VALUE.

When you care only about the attributes of an element of the model, classify it as a VALUE OBJECT. Make it express the meaning of the attributes it conveys and give it related functionality. Treat the VALUE OBJECT as immutable. Don't give it any identity and avoid the design complexities necessary to maintain ENTITIES.

The attributes that make up a VALUE OBJECT should form a conceptual whole.[2] For example, street, city, and postal code shouldn't be separate attributes of a Person object. They are part of a single, whole address, which makes a simpler Person, and a more coherent VALUE OBJECT.

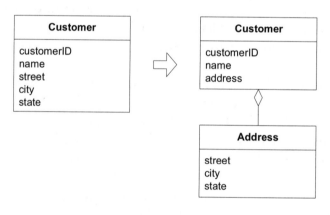

Figure 5.6
A VALUE OBJECT can give information about an ENTITY. It should be conceptually whole.

❋   ❋   ❋

Designing VALUE OBJECTS

We don't care which instance we have of a VALUE OBJECT. This lack of constraints gives us design freedom we can use to simplify the design or optimize performance. This involves making choices about copying, sharing, and immutability.

---

2. The WHOLE VALUE pattern, by Ward Cunningham.

If two people have the same name, that does not make them the same person, or make them interchangeable. But the object representing the name is interchangeable, because only the spelling of the name matters. A Name object can be *copied* from the first Person object to the second.

In fact, the two Person objects might not need their own name instances. The same Name object could be *shared* between the two Person objects (each with a pointer to the same name instance) with no change in their behavior or identity. That is, their behavior will be correct until some change is made to the name of one person. Then the other person's name would change also! To protect against this, in order for an object to be shared safely, it must be *immutable*: it cannot be changed except by full replacement.

The same issues arise when an object passes one of its attributes to another object as an argument or return value. Anything could happen to the wandering object while it is out of control of its owner. The VALUE could be changed in a way that corrupts the owner, by violating the owner's invariants. This problem is avoided either by making the passed object immutable, or by passing a copy.

Creating extra options for performance tuning can be important because VALUE OBJECTS tend to be numerous. The example of the house design software hints at this. If each electrical outlet is a separate VALUE OBJECT, there might be a hundred of them in a single version of a single house plan. But if all outlets are considered interchangeable, we could share just one instance of an outlet and point to it a hundred times (an example of FLYWEIGHT [Gamma et al. 1995]). In large systems, this kind of effect can be multiplied by thousands, and such an optimization can make the difference between a usable system and one that slows to a crawl, choked on millions of redundant objects. This is just one example of an optimization trick that is not available for ENTITIES.

The economy of copying versus sharing depends on the implementation environment. Although copies may clog the system with huge numbers of objects, sharing can slow down a distributed system. When a copy is passed between two machines, a single message is sent and the copy lives independently on the receiving machine. But if a single instance is being shared, only a reference is passed, requiring a message back to the object for each interaction.

　　　　　CHAPTER 5: A MODEL EXPRESSED IN SOFTWARE

Sharing is best restricted to those cases in which it is most valuable and least troublesome:

- When saving space or object count in the database is critical

- When communication overhead is low (such as in a centralized server)

- When the shared object is strictly immutable

Immutability of an attribute or an object can be declared in some languages and environments but not in others. Such features help communicate the design decision, but they are not essential. Many of the distinctions we are making in the model cannot be explicitly declared in the implementation with most current tools and programming languages. You can't declare ENTITIES, for example, and then have an identity operation automatically enforced. But the lack of direct language support for a conceptual distinction does not mean that the distinction is not useful. It just means that more discipline is needed to maintain the rules that will be only implicit in the implementation. This can be reinforced with naming conventions, selective documentation, and *lots of discussion*.

As long as a VALUE OBJECT is immutable, change management is simple—there isn't any change except full replacement. Immutable objects can be freely shared, as in the electrical outlet example. If garbage collection is reliable, deletion is just a matter of dropping all references to the object. When a VALUE OBJECT is designated immutable in the design, developers are free to make decisions about issues such as copying and sharing on a purely technical basis, secure in the knowledge that the application does not rely on particular instances of the objects.

Defining VALUE OBJECTS and designating them as immutable is a case of following a general rule: Avoiding unnecessary constraints in a model leaves developers free to do purely technical performance tuning. Explicitly defining the essential constraints lets developers tweak the design while keeping safe from changing meaningful behavior. Such design tweaks are often very specific to the technology in use on a particular project.

Special Cases: When to Allow Mutability

Immutability is a great simplifier in an implementation, making sharing and reference passing safe. It is also consistent with the meaning of a value. If the value of an attribute changes, you use a different VALUE OBJECT, rather than modifying the existing one. Even so, there are cases when performance considerations will favor allowing a VALUE OBJECT to be mutable. These factors would weigh in favor of a mutable implementation:

- If the VALUE changes frequently

- If object creation or deletion is expensive

- If replacement (rather than modification) will disturb clustering (as discussed in the previous example)

- If there is not much sharing of VALUES, or if such sharing is forgone to improve clustering or for some other technical reason

Just to reiterate: If a VALUE's implementation is to be mutable, then it *must not* be shared. Whether you will be sharing or not, design VALUE OBJECTS as immutable when you can.

Tuning a Database with VALUE OBJECTS

Databases, at the lowest level, have to place data in a physical location on a disk, and it takes time for physical parts to move around and read that data. Sophisticated databases attempt to cluster these physical addresses so that related data can be fetched from the disk in a single physical operation.

If an object is referenced by many other objects, some of those objects will not be located nearby (on the same page), requiring an additional physical operation to get the data. By making a copy, rather than sharing a reference to the same instance, a VALUE OBJECT that is acting as an attribute of many ENTITIES can be stored on the same page as each ENTITY that uses it. This technique of storing multiple copies of the same data is called *denormalization* and is often used when access time is more critical than storage space or simplicity of maintenance.

In a relational database, you might want to put a particular VALUE in the table of the ENTITY that owns it, rather than creating an association to a separate table. In a distributed system, holding a reference to a VALUE OBJECT on another server will probably make for slow responses to messages; instead, a copy of the whole object should be passed to the other server. We can freely make these copies because we are dealing with VALUE OBJECTS.

Designing Associations That Involve VALUE OBJECTS

Most of the earlier discussion of associations applies to ENTITIES and VALUE OBJECTS alike. The fewer and simpler the associations in the model, the better.

But, while bidirectional associations between ENTITIES may be hard to maintain, bidirectional associations between two VALUE OBJECTS just make no sense. Without identity, it is meaningless to say that an object points back to the same VALUE OBJECT that points to it. The most you could say is that it points to an object that is *equal* to the one pointing to it, but you would have to enforce that invariant somewhere. And although you could do so, and set up pointers going both ways, it is hard to think of examples where such an arrangement would be useful. Try to completely eliminate bidirectional associations between VALUE OBJECTS. If in the end such associations seem necessary in your model, rethink the decision to declare the object a VALUE OBJECT in the first place. Maybe it has an identity that hasn't been explicitly recognized yet.

ENTITIES and VALUE OBJECTS are the main elements of conventional object models, but pragmatic designers have come to use one other element, SERVICES. . . .

SERVICES

Sometimes, it just isn't a thing.

In some cases, the clearest and most pragmatic design includes operations that do not conceptually belong to any object. Rather than force the issue, we can follow the natural contours of the problem space and include SERVICES explicitly in the model.

✳ ✳ ✳

There are important domain operations that can't find a natural home in an ENTITY or VALUE OBJECT. Some of these are intrinsically activities or actions, not things, but since our modeling paradigm is objects, we try to fit them into objects anyway.

Now, the more common mistake is to give up too easily on fitting the behavior into an appropriate object, gradually slipping toward procedural programming. But when we force an operation into an object that doesn't fit the object's definition, the object loses its conceptual clarity and becomes hard to understand or refactor. Complex operations can easily swamp a simple object, obscuring its role. And because these operations often draw together many domain objects, coordinating them and putting them into action, the added responsibility will create dependencies on all those objects, tangling concepts that could be understood independently.

Sometimes services masquerade as model objects, appearing as objects with no meaning beyond doing some operation. These "doers" end up with names ending in "Manager" and the like. They have no state of their own nor any meaning in the domain beyond the operation they host. Still, at least this solution gives these distinct behaviors a home without messing up a real model object.

Some concepts from the domain aren't natural to model as objects. Forcing the required domain functionality to be the responsibility of an ENTITY or VALUE either distorts the definition of a model-based object or adds meaningless artificial objects.

A SERVICE is an operation offered as an interface that stands alone in the model, without encapsulating state, as ENTITIES and VALUE OBJECTS do. SERVICES are a common pattern in technical frameworks, but they can also apply in the domain layer.

The name *service* emphasizes the relationship with other objects. Unlike ENTITIES and VALUE OBJECTS, it is defined purely in terms of what it can do for a client. A SERVICE tends to be named for an activity, rather than an entity—a verb rather than a noun. A SERVICE can still have an abstract, intentional definition; it just has a different flavor than the definition of an object. A SERVICE should still have a defined responsibility, and that responsibility and the interface fulfilling it should be defined as part of the domain model. Operation names should come from the UBIQUITOUS LANGUAGE or be introduced into it. Parameters and results should be domain objects.

SERVICES should be used judiciously and not allowed to strip the ENTITIES and VALUE OBJECTS of all their behavior. But when an operation is actually an important domain concept, a SERVICE forms a natural part of a MODEL-DRIVEN DESIGN. Declared in the model as a SERVICE, rather than as a phony object that doesn't actually represent anything, the standalone operation will not mislead anyone.

A good SERVICE has three characteristics.

1. The operation relates to a domain concept that is not a natural part of an ENTITY or VALUE OBJECT.

2. The interface is defined in terms of other elements of the domain model.

3. The operation is stateless.

Statelessness here means that any client can use any instance of a particular SERVICE without regard to the instance's individual history. The execution of a SERVICE will use information that is accessible globally, and may even change that global information (that is, it may have side effects). But the SERVICE does not hold state of its own that affects its own behavior, as most domain objects do.

When a significant process or transformation in the domain is not a natural responsibility of an ENTITY or VALUE OBJECT, add an operation to the model as a standalone interface declared as a SERVICE. Define the interface in terms of the language of the model and make sure the operation name is part of the UBIQUITOUS LANGUAGE. Make the SERVICE stateless.

❊ ❊ ❊

SERVICES and the Isolated Domain Layer

This pattern is focused on those SERVICES that have an important meaning in the domain in their own right, but of course SERVICES are not used only in the domain layer. It takes care to distinguish SERVICES that belong to the domain layer from those of other layers, and to factor responsibilities to keep that distinction sharp.

Most SERVICES discussed in the literature are purely technical and belong in the infrastructure layer. Domain and application SERVICES collaborate with these infrastructure SERVICES. For example, a bank might have an application that sends an e-mail to a customer when an account balance falls below a specific threshold. The interface that encapsulates the e-mail system, and perhaps alternate means of notification, is a SERVICE in the infrastructure layer.

It can be harder to distinguish application SERVICES from domain SERVICES. The application layer is responsible for ordering the notification. The domain layer is responsible for determining if a threshold was met—though this task probably does not call for a SERVICE, because it would fit the responsibility of an "account" object. That banking application could be responsible for funds transfers. If a SERVICE were devised to make appropriate debits and credits for a funds transfer, that capability would belong in the domain layer. Funds transfer has a meaning in the banking domain language, and it involves fundamental business logic. Technical SERVICES should lack any business meaning at all.

Many domain or application SERVICES are built on top of the populations of ENTITIES and VALUES, behaving like scripts that organize the potential of the domain to actually get something done.

ENTITIES and VALUE OBJECTS are often too fine-grained to provide a convenient access to the capabilities of the domain layer. Here we encounter a very fine line between the domain layer and the application layer. For example, if the banking application can convert and export our transactions into a spreadsheet file for us to analyze, that export is an application SERVICE. There is no meaning of "file formats" in the domain of banking, and there are no business rules involved.

On the other hand, a feature that can transfer funds from one account to another is a domain SERVICE because it embeds significant business rules (crediting and debiting the appropriate accounts, for example) and because a "funds transfer" is a meaningful banking term. In this case, the SERVICE does not do much on its own; it would ask the two Account objects to do most of the work. But to put the "transfer" operation on the Account object would be awkward, because the operation involves two accounts and some global rules.

We might like to create a Funds Transfer object to represent the two entries plus the rules and history around the transfer. But we are still left with calls to SERVICES in the interbank networks. What's more, in most development systems, it is awkward to make a direct interface between a domain object and external resources. We can dress up such external SERVICES with a FACADE that takes inputs in terms of the model, perhaps returning a Funds Transfer object as its result. But whatever intermediaries we might have, and even though they don't belong to us, those SERVICES are carrying out the domain responsibility of funds transfer.

Partitioning Services into Layers

Application	*Funds Transfer App Service* • Digests input (such as an XML request). • Sends message to domain service for fulfillment. • Listens for confirmation. • Decides to send notification using infrastructure service.
Domain	*Funds Transfer Domain Service* • Interacts with necessary Account and Ledger objects, making appropriate debits and credits. • Supplies confirmation of result (transfer allowed or not, and so on).
Infrastructure	*Send Notification Service* • Sends e-mails, letters, and other communications as directed by the application.

Granularity

Although this pattern discussion has emphasized the expressiveness of modeling a concept as a SERVICE, the pattern is also valuable as a means of controlling granularity in the interfaces of the domain layer, as well as decoupling clients from the ENTITIES and VALUE OBJECTS.

Medium-grained, stateless SERVICES can be easier to reuse in large systems because they encapsulate significant functionality behind a simple interface. Also, fine-grained objects can lead to inefficient messaging in a distributed system.

As previously discussed, fine-grained domain objects can contribute to knowledge leaks from the domain into the application layer, where the domain object's behavior is coordinated. The complexity of a highly detailed interaction ends up being handled in the application layer, allowing domain knowledge to creep into the application or user interface code, where it is lost from the domain layer. The judicious introduction of domain services can help maintain the bright line between layers.

This pattern favors interface simplicity over client control and versatility. It provides a medium grain of functionality very useful in packaging components of large or distributed systems. And sometimes a SERVICE is the most natural way to express a domain concept.

Access to SERVICES

Distributed system architectures, such as J2EE and CORBA, provide special publishing mechanisms for SERVICES, with conventions for their use, and they add distribution and access capabilities. But such frameworks are not always in use on a project, and even when they are, they are likely to be overkill when the motivation is just a logical separation of concerns.

The means of providing access to a SERVICE is not as important as the design decision to carve off specific responsibilities. A "doer" object may be satisfactory as an implementation of a SERVICE's interface. A simple SINGLETON (Gamma et al. 1995) can be written easily to provide access. Coding conventions can make it clear that these objects are just delivery mechanisms for SERVICE interfaces, and not meaningful domain objects. Elaborate architectures should be used only when there is a real need to distribute the system or otherwise draw on the framework's capabilities.

MODULES (A.K.A. PACKAGES)

MODULES are an old, established design element. There are technical considerations, but cognitive overload is the primary motivation for modularity. MODULES give people two views of the model: They can look at detail within a MODULE without being overwhelmed by the whole, or they can look at relationships between MODULES in views that exclude interior detail.

The MODULES in the domain layer should emerge as a meaningful part of the model, telling the story of the domain on a larger scale.

✳ ✳ ✳

Everyone uses MODULES, but few treat them as a full-fledged part of the model. Code gets broken down into all sorts of categories, from aspects of the technical architecture to developers' work assignments. Even developers who refactor a lot tend to content themselves with MODULES conceived early in the project.

It is a truism that there should be low coupling between MODULES and high cohesion within them. Explanations of coupling and cohesion tend to make them sound like technical metrics, to be judged mechanically based on the distributions of associations and interactions. Yet it isn't just code being divided into MODULES, but concepts. There is a limit to how many things a person can think about at once (hence low coupling). Incoherent fragments of ideas are as hard to understand as an undifferentiated soup of ideas (hence high cohesion).

Low coupling and high cohesion are general design principles that apply as much to individual objects as to MODULES, but they are particularly important at this larger grain of modeling and design. These terms have been around for a long time; one patterns-style explanation can be found in Larman 1998.

Whenever two model elements are separated into different modules, the relationships between them become less direct than they were, which increases the overhead of understanding their place in the design. Low coupling between MODULES minimizes this cost, and makes it possible to analyze the contents of one MODULE with a minimum of reference to others that interact.

At the same time, the elements of a good model have synergy, and well-chosen MODULES bring together elements of the model with particularly rich conceptual relationships. This high cohesion of objects with related responsibilities allows modeling and design work to concentrate within a single MODULE, a scale of complexity a human mind can easily handle.

MODULES and the smaller elements should coevolve, but typically they do not. MODULES are chosen to organize an early form of the objects. After that, the objects tend to change in ways that keep them in the bounds of the existing MODULE definition. Refactoring MODULES is more work and more disruptive than refactoring classes, and probably can't be as frequent. But just as model objects tend to start out naive and concrete and then gradually transform to reveal deeper insight, MODULES can become subtle and abstract. Letting the MODULES reflect changing understanding of the domain will also allow more freedom for the objects within them to evolve.

Like everything else in a domain-driven design, MODULES are a *communications mechanism*. The *meaning* of the objects being partitioned needs to drive the choice of MODULES. When you place some classes together in a MODULE, you are telling the next developer who looks at your design to think about them together. If your model is telling a story, the MODULES are chapters. The name of the MODULE conveys its meaning. These names enter the UBIQUITOUS LANGUAGE. "Now let's talk about the 'customer' module," you might say to a business expert, and the context is set for your conversation.

Therefore:

Choose MODULES that tell the story of the system and contain a cohesive set of concepts. This often yields low coupling between MODULES, but if it doesn't, look for a way to change the model to disentangle the concepts, or search for an overlooked concept that might be the basis of a MODULE that would bring the elements together in a meaningful way. Seek low coupling in the sense of concepts that can be understood and reasoned about independently of each other. Refine the model until it partitions according to high-level domain concepts and the corresponding code is decoupled as well.

Give the MODULES names that become part of the UBIQUITOUS LANGUAGE. MODULES and their names should reflect insight into the domain.

Looking at conceptual relationships is not an alternative to technical measures. They are different levels of the same issue, and both have to be accomplished. But model-focused thinking produces a deeper solution, rather than an incidental one. And when there has to be a trade-off, it is best to go with the conceptual clarity, even if it means more references between MODULES or occasional ripple effects when changes are made to a MODULE. Developers can handle these problems if they understand the story the model is telling them.

✳ ✳ ✳

Agile MODULES

MODULES need to coevolve with the rest of the model. This means refactoring MODULES right along with the model and code. But this refactoring often doesn't happen. Changing MODULES tends to require widespread updates to the code. Such changes can be disruptive to team communication and can even throw a monkey wrench into development tools, such as source code control systems. As a result, MODULE structures and names often reflect much earlier forms of the model than the classes do.

Inevitable early mistakes in MODULE choices lead to high coupling, which makes it hard to refactor. The lack of refactoring just keeps increasing the inertia. It can only be overcome by biting the bullet and reorganizing MODULES based on experience of where the trouble spots lie.

Some development tools and programming systems exacerbate the problem. Whatever development technology the implementation will be based on, we need to look for ways of minimizing the work of refactoring MODULES, and minimizing clutter in communicating to other developers.

Example

Package Coding Conventions in Java

In Java, imports (dependencies) must be declared in some individual class. A modeler probably thinks of packages as depending on other packages, but this can't be stated in Java. Common coding conventions encourage the import of specific classes, resulting in code like this:

```
ClassA1
import packageB.ClassB1;
import packageB.ClassB2;
import packageB.ClassB3;
import packageC.ClassC1;
import packageC.ClassC2;
import packageC.ClassC3;

. . .
```

In Java, unfortunately, there is no escape from importing *into* individual classes, but you can at least import entire packages at a time, reflecting the intention that packages are highly cohesive units while simultaneously reducing the effort of changing package names.

```
ClassA1
import packageB.*;
import packageC.*;

. . .
```

True, this technique means mixing two scales (classes depend on packages), but it communicates more than the previous voluminous list of classes—it conveys the intent to create a dependency on particular MODULES.

If an individual class really does depend on a specific class in another package, and the local MODULE doesn't seem to have a conceptual dependency on the other MODULE, then maybe a class should be moved, or the MODULES themselves should be reconsidered.

The Pitfalls of Infrastructure-Driven Packaging

Strong forces on our packaging decisions come from technical frameworks. Some of these are helpful, while others need to be resisted.

An example of a very useful framework standard is the enforcement of LAYERED ARCHITECTURE by placing infrastructure and user interface code into separate groups of packages, leaving the domain layer physically separated into its own set of packages.

On the other hand, tiered architectures can fragment the implementation of the model objects. Some frameworks create tiers by spreading the responsibilities of a single domain object across multiple objects and then placing those objects in separate packages. For example, with J2EE a common practice is to place data and data access into an "entity bean" while placing associated business logic into a "session bean." In addition to the increased implementation complexity of each component, the separation immediately robs an object model of cohesion. One of the most fundamental concepts of objects is to encapsulate data with the logic that operates on that data. This kind of tiered implementation is not fatal, because both components can be viewed as together constituting the implementation of a single model element, but to make matters worse, the entity and session beans are often separated into different packages. At that point, viewing the various objects and mentally fitting them back together as a single conceptual ENTITY is just too much effort. We lose the connection between the model and design. Best practice is to use EJBs at a larger grain than ENTITY objects, reducing the downside of separating tiers. But fine-grain objects are often split into tiers also.

For example, I encountered these problems on a rather intelligently run project in which each conceptual object was actually broken into four tiers. Each division had a good rationale. The first tier was a data persistence layer, handling mapping and access to the relational database. Then came a layer that handled behavior intrinsic to the object in all situations. Next was a layer for superimposing application-specific functionality. The fourth tier was meant as a public interface, decoupled from all the implementation below. This scheme was a bit too complicated, but the layers were well defined and there was some tidiness to the separation of concerns. We could have lived with mentally connecting all the physical objects making up one conceptual object. The separation of aspects even helped at times. In particular, having the persistence code moved out removed a lot of clutter.

But on top of all this, the framework required each tier to be in a separate set of packages, named according to a convention that identified the tier. This took up all the mental room for partitioning. As a result, domain developers tended to avoid making too many MODULES (each of which was multiplied by four) and hardly ever changed one, because the effort of refactoring a MODULE was prohibitive.

Worse, hunting down all the data and behavior that defined a single conceptual class was so difficult (combined with the indirectness of the layering) that developers didn't have much mental space left to think about models. The application was delivered, but with an anemic domain model that basically fulfilled the database access requirements of the application, with behavior supplied by a few SERVICES. The leverage that should have derived from MODEL-DRIVEN DESIGN was limited because the code did not transparently reveal the model and allow a developer to work with it.

This kind of framework design is attempting to address two legitimate issues. One is the logical division of concerns: One object has responsibility for database access, another for business logic, and so on. Such divisions make it easier to understand the functioning of each tier (on a technical level) and make it easier to switch out layers. The trouble is that the cost to application development is not recognized. This is not a book on framework design, so I won't go into alternative solutions to that problem, but they do exist. And even if there were no options, it would be better to trade off these benefits for a more cohesive domain layer.

The other motivation for these packaging schemes is the distribution of tiers. This could be a strong argument if the code actually got deployed on different servers. Usually it does not. The flexibility is sought just in case it is needed. On a project that hopes to get leverage from MODEL-DRIVEN DESIGN, this sacrifice is too great unless it solves an immediate and pressing problem.

Elaborate technically driven packaging schemes impose two costs.

- If the framework's partitioning conventions pull apart the elements implementing the conceptual objects, the code no longer reveals the model.

- There is only so much partitioning a mind can stitch back together, and if the framework uses it all up, the domain developers lose their ability to chunk the model into meaningful pieces.

It is best to keep things simple. Choose a minimum of technical partitioning rules that are essential to the technical environment or actually aid development. For example, decoupling complicated data persistence code from the behavioral aspects of the objects may make refactoring easier.

Unless there is a real intention to distribute code on different servers, keep all the code that implements a single conceptual object in the same MODULE, if not the same object.

We could have come to the same conclusion by drawing on the old standard, "high cohesion/low coupling." The connections between an "object" implementing the business logic and the one responsible for database access are so extensive that the coupling is very high.

There are other pitfalls where framework design or just conventions of a company or project can undermine MODEL-DRIVEN DESIGN by obscuring the natural cohesion of the domain objects, but the bottom line is the same. The restrictions, or just the large number of required packages, rules out the use of other packaging schemes that are tailored to the needs of the domain model.

Use packaging to separate the domain layer from other code. Otherwise, leave as much freedom as possible to the domain developers to package the domain objects in ways that support their model and design choices.

One exception arises when code is generated based on a declarative design (discussed in Chapter 10). In that case, the developers do not need to read the code, and it is better to put it into a separate package so that it is out of the way, not cluttering up the design elements developers actually have to work with.

Modularity becomes more critical as the design gets bigger and more complex. This section presents the basic considerations. Much of Part IV, "Strategic Design," provides approaches to packaging and breaking down big models and designs, and ways to give people focal points to guide understanding.

Each concept from the domain model should be reflected in an element of implementation. The ENTITIES, VALUE OBJECTS, and their associations, along with a few domain SERVICES and the organizing MODULES, are points of direct correspondence between the implementation and the model. The objects, pointers, and retrieval mechanisms in the implementation must map to model elements straightforwardly, obviously. If they do not, clean up the code, go back and change the model, or both.

Resist the temptation to add anything to the domain objects that does not closely relate to the concepts they represent. These design elements have their job to do: they express the model. There are other domain-related responsibilities that must be carried out and other data that must be managed in order to make the system work, but they don't belong in these objects. In Chapter 6, I will discuss some supporting objects that fulfill the technical responsibilities of the domain layer, such as defining database searches and encapsulating complex object creation.

The four patterns in this chapter provide the building blocks for an object model. But MODEL-DRIVEN DESIGN does not necessarily mean forcing everything into an object mold. There are also other model paradigms supported by tools, such as rules engines. Projects have to make pragmatic trade-offs between them. These other tools and techniques are means to the end of a MODEL-DRIVEN DESIGN, not alternatives to it.

Modeling Paradigms

MODEL-DRIVEN DESIGN calls for an implementation technology in tune with the particular modeling paradigm being applied. Many such paradigms have been experimented with, but only a few have been widely used in practice. At present, the dominant paradigm is object-oriented design, and most complex projects these days set out to use objects. This predominance has come about for a variety of reasons: some factors are intrinsic to objects, some are circumstantial, and others derive from the advantages that come from wide usage itself.

Why the Object Paradigm Predominates

Many of the reasons teams choose the object paradigm are not technical, or even intrinsic to objects. But right out of the gate, object modeling does strike a nice balance of simplicity and sophistication.

If a modeling paradigm is too esoteric, not enough developers will master it, and they will use it badly. If the nontechnical members of the team can't grasp at least the rudiments of the paradigm, they will not understand the model, and the UBIQUITOUS LANGUAGE will be lost. The fundamentals of object-oriented design seem to come naturally to most people. Although some developers miss the subtleties of modeling, even nontechnologists can follow a diagram of an object model.

Yet, simple as the concept of object modeling is, it has proven rich enough to capture important domain knowledge. And it has been supported from the outset by development tools that allowed a model to be expressed in software.

Today, the object paradigm also has some significant circumstantial advantages deriving from maturity and widespread adoption. Without mature infrastructure and tool support, a project can get sidetracked into technological R&D, delaying and diverting resources away from application development and introducing technical risks. Some technologies don't play well with others, and it may not be possible to integrate them with industry-standard solutions, forcing the team to reinvent common utilities. But over the years, many of these problems have been solved for objects, or made irrelevant by widespread adoption. (Now it falls on other approaches to integrate with mainstream object technology.) Most new technologies provide the means to integrate with the popular object-oriented platforms. This makes integration easier and even leaves open the option of mixing in subsystems based on other modeling paradigms (which we will discuss later in this chapter).

Equally important is the maturity of the *developer community and the design culture itself*. A project that adopts a novel paradigm may be unable to find developers with expertise in the technology, or with the experience to create effective models in the chosen paradigm. It may not be feasible to educate developers in a reasonable amount of time because the patterns for making the most of the paradigm and technology haven't gelled yet. Perhaps the pioneers of the field are effective but haven't yet published their insights in an accessible form.

Objects are already understood by a community of thousands of developers, project managers, and all the other specialists involved in project work.

A story from an object-oriented project of only a decade ago illustrates the risks of working in an immature paradigm. In the early 1990s, this project committed itself to several cutting-edge technologies, including use of an object-oriented database on a large scale. It was exciting. People on the team would proudly tell visitors that we were deploying the biggest database this technology had ever supported. When I joined the project, different teams were spinning out object-oriented designs and storing their objects in the database effortlessly. But gradually the realization crept upon us that we were beginning to absorb a significant fraction of the database's capacity—with test data! The actual database would be dozens of times larger. The actual transaction volume would be dozens of times higher. Was it impossible to use this technology for this application? Had we used it improperly? We were out of our depth.

Fortunately, we were able to bring onto the team one of a handful of people in the world with the skills to extricate us from the problem. He named his price and we paid it. There were three sources of the problem. First, the off-the-shelf infrastructure provided with the database simply didn't scale up to our needs. Second, storage of fine-grained objects turned out to be much more costly than we had realized. Third, parts of the object model had such a tangle of interdependencies that contention became a problem with a relatively small number of concurrent transactions.

With the help of this hired expert, we enhanced the infrastructure. The team, now aware of the impact of fine-grained objects, began to find models that worked better with this technology. All of us deepened our thinking about the importance of limiting the web of relationships in a model, and we began applying this new understanding to making better models with more decoupling between closely interrelated aggregates.

Several months were lost in this recovery, in addition to the earlier months spent going down a failed path. And this had not been the team's first setback resulting from the immaturity of the chosen technologies and our own lack of experience with the associated learning curve. Sadly, this project eventually retrenched and became quite conservative. To this day they use the exotic technologies, but for cautiously scoped applications that probably don't really benefit from them.

A decade later, object-oriented technology is relatively mature. Most common infrastructure needs can be met with off-the-shelf solutions that have been used in the field. Mission-critical tools come from major vendors, often multiple vendors, or from stable open-source projects. Many of these infrastructure pieces themselves are used widely enough that there is a base of people who already understand them, as well as books explaining them, and so forth. The limitations of these established technologies are fairly well understood, so that knowledgeable teams are less likely to overreach.

Other interesting modeling paradigms just don't have this maturity. Some are too hard to master and will never be used outside small specialties. Others have potential, but the technical infrastructure is still patchy or shaky, and few people understand the subtleties of creating good models for them. These may come of age, but they are not ready for most projects.

This is why, for the present, most projects attempting MODEL-DRIVEN DESIGN are wise to use object-oriented technology as the core of their system. They will not be locked into an object-only system—because objects have become the mainstream of the industry, integration tools are available to connect with almost any other technology in current use.

Yet this doesn't mean that people should restrict themselves to objects forever. Traveling with the crowd provides some safety, but it isn't always the way to go. Object models address a large number of practical software problems, but there are domains that are not natural to model as discrete packets of encapsulated behavior. For example, domains that are intensely mathematical or that are dominated by global logical reasoning do not fit well into the object-oriented paradigm.

Nonobjects in an Object World

A domain model does not have to be an object model. There are MODEL-DRIVEN DESIGNS implemented in Prolog, for example, with a model made up of logical rules and facts. Model paradigms have been conceived to address certain ways people like to think about domains. Then the models of those domains are shaped by the paradigm. The result is a model that conforms to the paradigm so that it can be effectively implemented in the tools that support that modeling style.

Whatever the dominant model paradigm may be on a project, there are bound to be parts of the domain that would be much easier to express in some other paradigm. When there are just a few anomalous elements of a domain that otherwise works well in a paradigm, developers can live with a few awkward objects in an otherwise consistent model. (Or, on the other extreme, if the greater part of the problem domain is more naturally expressed in a particular other paradigm, it may make sense to switch paradigms altogether and choose a different implementation platform.) But when major parts of the domain seem to belong to different paradigms, it is intellectually appealing to model each part in a paradigm that fits, using a mixture of tool sets to support implementation. When the interdependence is small, a subsystem in the other paradigm can be encapsulated, such as a complex math calculation that simply needs to be called by an object. Other times the different aspects are more intertwined, such as when the interaction of the objects depends on some mathematical relationships.

This is what motivates the integration into object systems of such nonobject components as business rules engines and workflow engines. Mixing paradigms allows developers to model particular concepts in the style that fits best. Furthermore, most systems must use some nonobject technical infrastructure, most commonly relational databases. But making a coherent model that spans paradigms is hard, and making the supporting tools coexist is complicated. When developers can't clearly see a coherent model embodied in the software, MODEL-DRIVEN DESIGN can go out the window, even as this mixture increases the need for it.

Sticking with MODEL-DRIVEN DESIGN When Mixing Paradigms

Rules engines will serve as an example of a technology sometimes mixed into an object-oriented application development project. A knowledge-rich domain model probably contains explicit rules, yet the object paradigm lacks specific semantics for stating rules and their interactions. Although rules can be modeled as objects, and often are successfully, object encapsulation makes it awkward to apply global rules that cross the whole system. Rules engine technology is appealing because it promises to provide a more natural and declarative way to define rules, effectively allowing the rules paradigm to be mixed into the object paradigm. The logic paradigm is well developed and powerful, and it seems like a good complement to the strengths and weaknesses of objects.

But people don't always get what they hope for out of rules engines. Some products just don't work very well. Some lack a seamless view that can show the relatedness of model concepts that run between the two implementation environments. One common outcome is an application fractured in two: a static data storage system using objects, and an ad hoc rules processing application that has lost almost all connection with the object model.

It is important to continue to think in terms of models while working with rules. The team has to find a single model that can work with both implementation paradigms. This is not easy, but it should be possible if the rules engine allows expressive implementation. Otherwise, the data and the rules become unconnected. The rules in the engine end up more like little programs than conceptual rules in the domain model. With tight, clear relationships between the rules and the objects, the meaning of both pieces is retained.

Without a seamless environment, it falls on the developers to distill a model made up of clear, fundamental concepts to hold the whole design together.

The most effective tool for holding the parts together is a robust UBIQUITOUS LANGUAGE that underlies the whole heterogeneous model. Consistently applying names in the two environments and exercising those names in the UBIQUITOUS LANGUAGE can help bridge the gap.

This is a topic that deserves a book of its own. The goal of this section is merely to show that it isn't necessary to give up MODEL-DRIVEN DESIGN, and that it is worth the effort to keep it.

Although a MODEL-DRIVEN DESIGN does not have to be object oriented, it *does* depend on having an expressive implementation of the model constructs, be they objects, rules, or workflows. If the available tool does not facilitate that expressiveness, reconsider the choice of tools. An unexpressive implementation negates the advantage of the extra paradigm.

Here are four rules of thumb for mixing nonobject elements into a predominantly object-oriented system:

- *Don't fight the implementation paradigm.* There's always another way to think about a domain. Find model concepts that fit the paradigm.

- *Lean on the ubiquitous language.* Even when there is no rigorous connection between tools, very consistent use of language can keep parts of the design from diverging.

- *Don't get hung up on UML.* Sometimes the fixation on a tool, such as UML diagramming, leads people to distort the model to make it fit what can easily be drawn. For example, UML does have some features for representing constraints, but they are not always sufficient. Some other style of drawing (perhaps conventional for the other paradigm), or simple English descriptions, are better than tortuous adaptation of a drawing style intended for a certain view of objects.

- *Be skeptical.* Is the tool really pulling its weight? Just because you have some rules, that doesn't necessarily mean you need the overhead of a rules engine. Rules can be expressed as objects, perhaps a little less neatly; multiple paradigms complicate matters enormously.

Before taking on the burden of mixed paradigms, the options within the dominant paradigm should be exhausted. Even though some domain concepts don't present themselves as obvious objects, they often can be modeled within the paradigm. Chapter 9 will discuss the modeling of unconventional types of concepts using object technology.

The relational paradigm is a special case of paradigm mixing. The most common nonobject technology, the relational database is also more intimately related to the object model than other components, because it acts as the persistent store of the data that makes up the objects themselves. Storing object data in relational databases will be discussed in Chapter 6, along with the many other challenges of the object life cycle.

SIX

The Life Cycle of a Domain Object

Every object has a life cycle. An object is born, it likely goes through various states, and it eventually dies—being either archived or deleted. Of course, many of these are simple, transient objects, created with an easy call to their constructor, used in some computation, and then abandoned to the garbage collector. There is no need to complicate such objects. But other objects have longer lives, not all of which are spent in active memory. They have complex interdependencies with other objects. They go through changes of state to which invariants apply. Managing these objects presents challenges that can easily derail an attempt at MODEL-DRIVEN DESIGN.

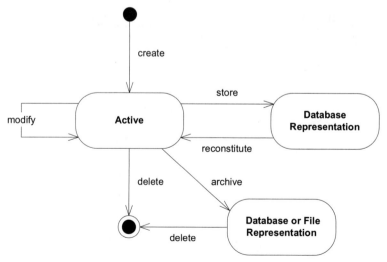

Figure 6.1
The life cycle of a domain object

The challenges fall into two categories.

1. Maintaining integrity throughout the life cycle

2. Preventing the model from getting swamped by the complexity of managing the life cycle

This chapter will address these issues through three patterns. First, AGGREGATES tighten up the model itself by defining clear ownership and boundaries, avoiding a chaotic, tangled web of objects. This pattern is crucial to maintaining integrity in all phases of the life cycle.

Next, the focus turns to the beginning of the life cycle, using FACTORIES to create and reconstitute complex objects and AGGREGATES, keeping their internal structure encapsulated. Finally, REPOSITORIES address the middle and end of the life cycle, providing the means of finding and retrieving persistent objects while encapsulating the immense infrastructure involved.

Although REPOSITORIES and FACTORIES do not themselves come from the domain, they have meaningful roles in the domain design. These constructs complete the MODEL-DRIVEN DESIGN by giving us accessible handles on the model objects.

Modeling AGGREGATES and adding FACTORIES and REPOSITORIES to the design gives us the ability to manipulate the model objects systematically and in meaningful units throughout their life cycle. AGGREGATES mark off the scope within which invariants have to be maintained at every stage of the life cycle. FACTORIES and REPOSITORIES operate on AGGREGATES, encapsulating the complexity of specific life cycle transitions.

AGGREGATES

Minimalist design of associations helps simplify traversal and limit the explosion of relationships somewhat, but most business domains are so interconnected that we still end up tracing long, deep paths through object references. In a way, this tangle reflects the realities of the world, which seldom obliges us with sharp boundaries. It is a problem in a software design.

Say you were deleting a Person object from a database. Along with the person go a name, birth date, and job description. But what about the address? There could be other people at the same address. If you delete the address, those Person objects will have references to a deleted object. If you leave it, you accumulate junk addresses in the database. Automatic garbage collection could eliminate the junk addresses, but that technical fix, even if available in your database system, ignores a basic modeling issue.

Even when considering an isolated transaction, the web of relationships in a typical object model gives no clear limit to the potential effect of a change. It is not practical to refresh every object in the system, just in case there is some dependency.

The problem is acute in a system with concurrent access to the same objects by multiple clients. With many users consulting and updating different objects in the system, we have to prevent simultaneous changes to interdependent objects. Getting the scope wrong has serious consequences.

It is difficult to guarantee the consistency of changes to objects in a model with complex associations. Invariants need to be maintained that apply to closely related groups of objects, not just discrete objects. Yet cautious locking schemes cause multiple users to interfere pointlessly with each other and make a system unusable.

Put another way, how do we know where an object made up of other objects begins and ends? In any system with persistent storage of data, there must be a scope for a transaction that changes data, and a way of maintaining the consistency of the data (that is, maintaining its invariants). Databases allow various locking schemes, and tests can be programmed. But these ad hoc solutions divert attention away from the model, and soon you are back to hacking and hoping.

In fact, finding a balanced solution to these kinds of problems calls for deeper understanding of the domain, this time extending to factors such as the frequency of change between the instances of certain classes. We need to find a model that leaves high-contention points looser and strict invariants tighter.

Although this problem surfaces as technical difficulties in database transactions, it is rooted in the model—in its lack of defined boundaries. A solution driven from the model will make the model easier to understand and make the design easier to communicate. As the model is revised, it will guide our changes to the implementation.

Schemes have been developed for defining ownership relationships in the model. The following simple but rigorous system, distilled from those concepts, includes a set of rules for implementing transactions that modify the objects and their owners.[1]

First we need an abstraction for encapsulating references within the model. An AGGREGATE is a cluster of associated objects that we treat as a unit for the purpose of data changes. Each AGGREGATE has a root and a boundary. The boundary defines what is inside the AGGREGATE. The root is a single, specific ENTITY contained in the

---

1. David Siegel devised and used this system on projects in the 1990s but has not published it.

AGGREGATE. The root is the only member of the AGGREGATE that outside objects are allowed to hold references to, although objects within the boundary may hold references to each other. ENTITIES other than the root have local identity, but that identity needs to be distinguishable only within the AGGREGATE, because no outside object can ever see it out of the context of the root ENTITY.

A model of a car might be used in software for an auto repair shop. The car is an ENTITY with global identity: we want to distinguish that car from all other cars in the world, even very similar ones. We can use the vehicle identification number for this, a unique identifier assigned to each new car. We might want to track the rotation history of the tires through the four wheel positions. We might want to know the mileage and tread wear of each tire. To know which tire is which, the tires must be identified ENTITIES also. But it is very unlikely that we care about the identity of those tires outside of the context of that particular car. If we replace the tires and send the old ones to a recycling plant, either our software will no longer track them at all, or they will become anonymous members of a heap of tires. No one will care about their rotation histories. More to the point, even while they are attached to the car, no one will try to query the system to find a particular tire and then see which car it is on. They will query the database to find a car and then ask it for a transient reference to the tires. Therefore, the car is the root ENTITY of the AGGREGATE whose boundary encloses the tires also. On the other hand, engine blocks have serial numbers engraved on them and are sometimes tracked independently of the car. In some applications, the engine might be the root of its own AGGREGATE.

Figure 6.2
Local versus global identity and object references

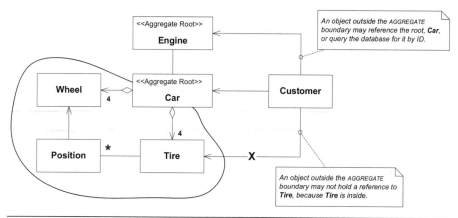

Invariants, which are consistency rules that must be maintained whenever data changes, will involve relationships between members of the AGGREGATE. Any rule that spans AGGREGATES will not be expected to be up-to-date at all times. Through event processing, batch processing, or other update mechanisms, other dependencies can be resolved within some specified time. But the invariants applied within an AGGREGATE will be enforced with the completion of each transaction.

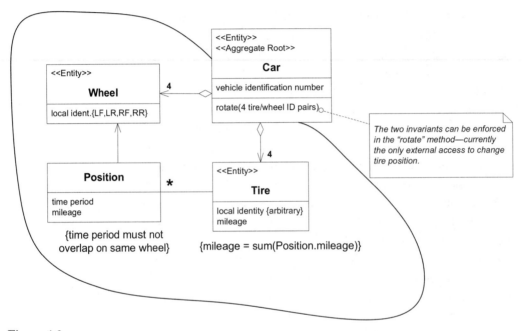

Figure 6.3

AGGREGATE invariants

Now, to translate that conceptual AGGREGATE into the implementation, we need a set of rules to apply to all transactions.

- The root ENTITY has global identity and is ultimately responsible for checking invariants.

- Root ENTITIES have global identity. ENTITIES inside the boundary have local identity, unique only within the AGGREGATE.

- Nothing outside the AGGREGATE boundary can hold a reference to anything inside, except to the root ENTITY. The root ENTITY can hand references to the internal ENTITIES to other objects, but those objects can use them only transiently, and they may not hold on to the reference. The root may hand a copy of a VALUE OBJECT to another object, and it doesn't matter what happens to it, because it's just a VALUE and no longer will have any association with the AGGREGATE.

- As a corollary to the previous rule, only AGGREGATE roots can be obtained directly with database queries. All other objects must be found by traversal of associations.

- Objects within the AGGREGATE can hold references to other AGGREGATE roots.

- A delete operation must remove everything within the AGGREGATE boundary at once. (With garbage collection, this is easy. Because there are no outside references to anything but the root, delete the root and everything else will be collected.)

- When a change to any object within the AGGREGATE boundary is committed, all invariants of the whole AGGREGATE must be satisfied.

Cluster the ENTITIES and VALUE OBJECTS into AGGREGATES and define boundaries around each. Choose one ENTITY to be the root of each AGGREGATE, and control all access to the objects inside the boundary through the root. Allow external objects to hold references to the root only. Transient references to internal members can be passed out for use within a single operation only. Because the root controls access, it cannot be blindsided by changes to the internals. This arrangement makes it practical to enforce all invariants for objects in the AGGREGATE and for the AGGREGATE as a whole in any state change.

It can be very helpful to have a technical framework that allows you to declare AGGREGATES and then automatically carries out the locking scheme and so forth. Without that assistance, the team must have the self-discipline to agree on the AGGREGATES and code consistently with them.

Purchase Order Integrity

Consider the complications possible in a simplified purchase order system.

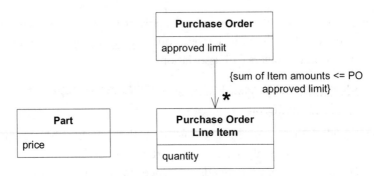

Figure 6.4
A model for a purchase order system

This diagram presents a pretty conventional view of a purchase order (PO), broken down into line items, with an invariant rule that the sum of the line items can't exceed the limit for the PO as a whole. The existing implementation has three interrelated problems.

1. *Invariant enforcement.* When a new line item is added, the PO checks the total and marks itself invalid if an item pushes it over the limit. As we'll see, this is not adequate protection.

2. *Change management.* When the PO is deleted or archived, the line items are taken along, but the model gives no guidance on where to stop following the relationships. There is also confusion about the impact of changing the part price at different times.

3. *Sharing the database.* Multiple users are creating contention problems in the database.

Multiple users will be entering and updating various POs concurrently, and we have to prevent them from messing up each other's work. Let's start with a very simple strategy, in which we lock any object a user begins to edit until that user commits the transaction. So, when George is editing line item 001, Amanda cannot access it. She can edit any other line item on any other PO (including other items in the PO George is working on).

PO #0012946	Approved Limit: $1,000.00			
Item #	Quantity	Part	Price	Amount
001	3	Guitars	@ 100.00	300.00
002	2	Trombones	@ 200.00	400.00
			Total:	700.00

Figure 6.5
The initial condition of the PO stored in the database

Objects will be read from the database and instantiated in each user's memory space. There they can be viewed and edited. Database locks will be requested only when an edit begins. So both George and Amanda can work concurrently, as long as they stay away from each other's items. All is well . . . until both George and Amanda start working on separate line items in the same PO.

George adds guitars in his view

PO #0012946	Approved Limit: $1000.00			
Item #	Quantity	Part	Price	Amount
001	**5**	Guitars	@ 100.00	**500.00**
002	2	Trombones	@ 200.00	400.00
			Total:	900.00

Amanda adds a trombone in her view

PO #0012946	Approved Limit: $1,000.00			
Item #	Quantity	Part	Price	Amount
001	3	Guitars	@ 100.00	300.00
002	**3**	Trombones	@ 200.00	**600.00**
			Total:	900.00

Everything looks fine to both users and to their software because they ignore changes to other parts of the database that happen during the transaction, and neither locked line item is involved in the other user's change.

Figure 6.6
Simultaneous edits in distinct transactions

PO #0012946	Approved Limit: **$1,000.00**			
Item #	Quantity	Part	Price	Amount
001	5	Guitars	@ 100.00	500.00
002	3	Trombones	@ 200.00	600.00
			Total:	**1,100.00**

Figure 6.7
The resulting PO violates the approval limit (broken invariant).

After both users have saved their changes, a PO is stored in the database that violates the invariant of the domain model. An important business rule has been broken. And nobody even knows.

Clearly, locking a single line item isn't an adequate safeguard. If instead we had locked an entire PO at a time, the problem would have been prevented.

George edits his view

PO #0012946	Approved Limit: $1000.00			
Item #	Quantity	Part	Price	Amount
001	5	Guitars	@ 100.00	**500.00**
002	2	Trombones	@ 200.00	400.00
			Total:	900.00

Amanda is locked out of PO #0012946

George's changes have been committed

Amanda gets access; George's change shows

PO #0012946	Approved Limit: $1000.00			
Item #	Quantity	Part	Price	Amount
001	5	Guitars	@ 100.00	500.00
002	3	Trombones	@ 200.00	**600.00**
	Limit exceeded →		Total:	1,100.00

Figure 6.8
Locking the entire PO allows the invariant to be enforced.

The program will not allow this transaction to be saved until Amanda has resolved the problem, perhaps by raising the limit or by eliminating a guitar. This mechanism prevents the problem, and it may be a fine solution if work is mostly spread widely across many POs. But if multiple people typically work simultaneously on different line items of a large PO, then this locking will get cumbersome.

Even assuming many small POs, there are other ways to violate the assertion. Consider that "part." If someone changed the price of a trombone while Amanda was adding to her order, wouldn't that violate the invariant too?

CHAPTER 6: THE LIFE CYCLE OF A DOMAIN OBJECT

Let's try locking the part in addition to the entire PO. Here's what happens when George, Amanda, and Sam are working on *different* POs:

George editing PO

Guitars and trombones locked

PO #0012946	Approved Limit: $1,000.00			
Item #	Quantity	Part	Price	Amount
001	**2**	Guitars	@ 100.00	**200.00**
002	**2**	Trombones	@ 200.00	400.00
			Total:	600.00

Amanda adds trombones; must wait on George

Violins locked

PO #0012932	Approved Limit: $1,850.00			
Item #	Quantity	Part	Price	Amount
001	3	Violins	@ 400.00	1,200.00
002	**2**	**Trombones**	**@ 200.00**	**400.00**
			Total:	1,600.00

Sam adds trombones; must wait on George

PO #0013003	Approved Limit: $15,000.00			
Item #	Quantity	Part	Price	Amount
001	1	Piano	@ 1,000.00	1,000.00
002	**2**	**Trombones**	**@ 200.00**	**400.00**
			Total:	1,400.00

Figure 6.9
Over-cautious locking is interfering with people's work.

The inconvenience is mounting, because there is a lot of contention for the instruments (the "parts"). And then:

George adds violins; must wait on Amanda (!)

PO #0012946	Approved Limit: $1,000.00			
Item #	Quantity	Part	Price	Amount
001	**2**	Guitars	@ 100.00	**200.00**
002	2	Trombones	@ 200.00	400.00
003	**1**	**Violins**	**@ 400.00**	**400.00**
			Total:	1,000.00

Figure 6.10
Deadlock

Those three will be waiting a while.

At this point we can begin to improve the model by incorporating the following knowledge of the business:

1. Parts are used in many POs (high contention).

2. There are fewer changes to parts than there are to POs.

3. Changes to part prices do not necessarily propagate to existing POs. It depends on the time of a price change relative to the status of the PO.

Point 3 is particularly obvious when we consider archived POs that have already been delivered. They should, of course, show the prices as of the time they were filled, rather than current prices.

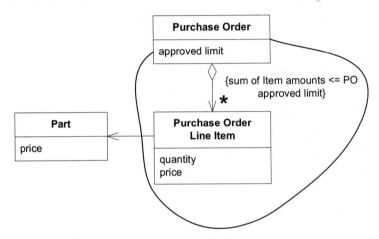

Figure 6.11
Price is copied into
Line Item. AGGREGATE
invariant can now be
enforced.

An implementation consistent with this model would guarantee the invariant relating PO and its items, while changes to the price of a part would not have to immediately affect the items that reference it. Broader consistency rules could be addressed in other ways. For example, the system could present a queue of items with outdated prices to the users each day, so they could update or exempt each one. But this is not an invariant that must be enforced at all times. By making the dependency of line items on parts looser, we avoid contention and reflect the realities of the business better. At the same time, tightening the relationship of the PO and its line items guarantees that an important business rule will be followed.

The AGGREGATE imposes an ownership of the PO and its items that is consistent with business practice. The creation and deletion of a PO and items are naturally tied together, while the creation and deletion of parts is independent.

✳   ✳   ✳

AGGREGATES mark off the scope within which invariants have to be maintained at every stage of the life cycle. The following patterns, FACTORIES and REPOSITORIES, operate on AGGREGATES, encapsulating the complexity of specific life cycle transitions. . . .

FACTORIES

When creation of an object, or an entire AGGREGATE, becomes complicated or reveals too much of the internal structure, FACTORIES provide encapsulation.

✳ ✳ ✳

Much of the power of objects rests in the intricate configuration of their internals and their associations. An object should be distilled until nothing remains that does not relate to its meaning or support its role in interactions. This mid-life cycle responsibility is plenty. Problems arise from overloading a complex object with responsibility for its own creation.

A car engine is an intricate piece of machinery, with dozens of parts collaborating to perform the engine's responsibility: to turn a shaft. One could imagine trying to design an engine block that could grab on to a set of pistons and insert them into its cylinders, spark plugs that would find their sockets and screw themselves in. But it seems unlikely that such a complicated machine would be as reliable or as efficient as our typical engines are. Instead, we accept that something else will assemble the pieces. Perhaps it will be a human mechanic or perhaps it will be an industrial robot. Both the robot and the human are actually more complex than the engine they assemble. The job of assembling parts is completely unrelated to the job of spinning a shaft. The assemblers function only during the creation of the car—you don't need a robot or a mechanic with you when you're driving. Because cars are never assembled and driven at the same time, there is no value in combining both of these functions into the same mechanism. Likewise, assembling a complex compound object is a job that is best separated from whatever job that object will have to do when it is finished.

But shifting responsibility to the other interested party, the client object in the application, leads to even worse problems. The client knows what job needs to be done and relies on the domain objects to carry out the necessary computations. If the client is expected to assemble the domain objects it needs, it must know something about the internal structure of the object. In order to enforce all the invariants that apply to the relationship of parts in the domain object, the client must know some of the object's rules. Even calling constructors couples the client to the concrete classes of the objects it is building. No change to the implementation of the domain objects can be made without changing the client, making refactoring harder.

A client taking on object creation becomes unnecessarily complicated and blurs its responsibility. It breaches the encapsulation of the domain objects and the AGGREGATES being created. Even worse, if the client is part of the application layer, then responsibilities have leaked out of the domain layer altogether. This tight coupling of the application to the specifics of the implementation strips away most of the benefits of abstraction in the domain layer and makes continuing changes ever more expensive.

Creation of an object can be a major operation in itself, but complex assembly operations do not fit the responsibility of the created objects. Combining such responsibilities can produce ungainly designs that are hard to understand. Making the client direct construction muddies the design of the client, breaches encapsulation of the assembled object or AGGREGATE, and overly couples the client to the implementation of the created object.

Complex object creation is a responsibility of the domain layer, yet that task does not belong to the objects that express the model. There are some cases in which an object creation and assembly corresponds to a milestone significant in the domain, such as "open a bank account." But object creation and assembly usually have no meaning in the domain; they are a necessity of the implementation. To solve this problem, we have to add constructs to the domain design that are not ENTITIES, VALUE OBJECTS, or SERVICES. This is a departure from the previous chapter, and it is important to make the point clear: We are adding elements to the design that do not correspond to anything in the model, but they are nonetheless part of the domain layer's responsibility.

Every object-oriented language provides a mechanism for creating objects (constructors in Java and C++, instance creation class methods in Smalltalk, for example), but there is a need for more abstract construction mechanisms that are decoupled from the other objects. A program element whose responsibility is the creation of other objects is called a FACTORY.

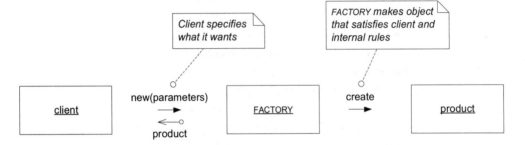

Figure 6.12
Basic interactions with a
FACTORY

Just as the interface of an object should encapsulate its implementation, thus allowing a client to use the object's behavior without knowing how it works, a FACTORY encapsulates the knowledge needed to create a complex object or AGGREGATE. It provides an interface that reflects the goals of the client and an abstract view of the created object.

Therefore:

Shift the responsibility for creating instances of complex objects and AGGREGATES to a separate object, which may itself have no responsibility in the domain model but is still part of the domain design. Provide an interface that encapsulates all complex assembly and that does not require the client to reference the concrete classes of the objects being instantiated. Create entire AGGREGATES as a piece, enforcing their invariants.

❊ ❊ ❊

There are many ways to design FACTORIES. Several special-purpose creation patterns—FACTORY METHOD, ABSTRACT FACTORY, and BUILDER—were thoroughly treated in Gamma et al. 1995. That book mostly explored patterns for the most difficult object construction problems. The point here is not to delve deeply into designing FACTORIES, but rather to show the place of FACTORIES as important components of a domain design. Proper use of FACTORIES can help keep a MODEL-DRIVEN DESIGN on track.

The two basic requirements for any good FACTORY are

1. Each creation method is atomic and enforces all invariants of the created object or AGGREGATE. A FACTORY should only be able to produce an object in a consistent state. For an ENTITY, this means the creation of the entire AGGREGATE, with all invariants satisfied, but probably with optional elements still to be added. For an immutable VALUE OBJECT, this means that all attributes are initialized to their correct final state. If the interface makes it possible to request an object that can't be created correctly, then an exception should be raised or some other mechanism should be invoked that will ensure that no improper return value is possible.

2. The FACTORY should be abstracted to the type desired, rather than the concrete class(es) created. The sophisticated FACTORY patterns in Gamma et al. 1995 help with this.

Choosing FACTORIES and Their Sites

Generally speaking, you create a factory to build something whose details you want to hide, and you place the FACTORY where you want the control to be. These decisions usually revolve around AGGREGATES.

For example, if you needed to add elements inside a preexisting AGGREGATE, you might create a FACTORY METHOD on the root of the AGGREGATE. This hides the implementation of the interior of the AGGREGATE from any external client, while giving the root responsibility for ensuring the integrity of the AGGREGATE as elements are added, as shown in Figure 6.13 on the next page.

Another example would be to place a FACTORY METHOD on an object that is closely involved in spawning another object, although it doesn't own the product once it is created. When the data and possibly the rules of one object are very dominant in the creation of an

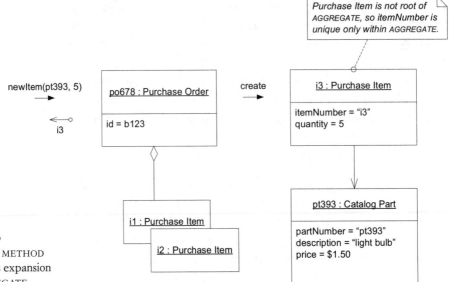

Figure 6.13
A FACTORY METHOD encapsulates expansion of an AGGREGATE.

object, this saves pulling information out of the spawner to be used elsewhere to create the object. It also communicates the special relationship between the spawner and the product.

In Figure 6.14, the **Trade Order** is not part of the same AGGREGATE as the **Brokerage Account** because, for a start, it will go on to interact with the trade execution application, where the **Brokerage Account** would only be in the way. Even so, it seems natural to give the **Brokerage Account** control over the creation of **Trade Orders**. The **Brokerage Account** contains information that will be embedded in the **Trade Order** (starting with its own identity), and it contains rules that govern what trades are allowed. We might also benefit from hiding the implementation of **Trade Order**. For example, it might be refactored into a hierarchy, with separate subclasses for **Buy Order** and **Sell Order**. The FACTORY keeps the client from being coupled to the concrete classes.

Figure 6.14
A FACTORY METHOD spawns an ENTITY that is not part of the same AGGREGATE.

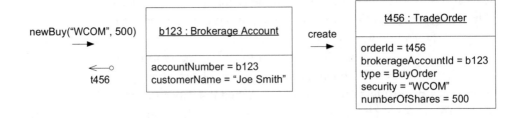

A FACTORY is very tightly coupled to its product, so a FACTORY should be attached only to an object that has a close natural relationship with the product. When there is something we want to hide—either the concrete implementation or the sheer complexity of construction—yet there doesn't seem to be a natural host, we must create a dedicated FACTORY object or SERVICE. A standalone FACTORY usually produces an entire AGGREGATE, handing out a reference to the root, and ensuring that the product AGGREGATE'S invariants are enforced. If an object interior to an AGGREGATE needs a FACTORY, and the AGGREGATE root is not a reasonable home for it, then go ahead and make a standalone FACTORY. But respect the rules limiting access within an AGGREGATE, and make sure there are only transient references to the product from outside the AGGREGATE.

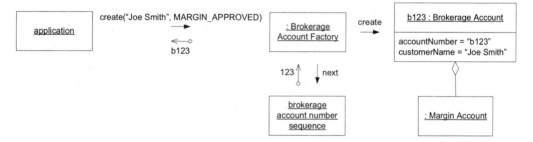

Figure 6.15
A standalone FACTORY builds AGGREGATE.

When a Constructor Is All You Need

I've seen far too much code in which *all* instances are created by directly calling class constructors, or whatever the primitive level of instance creation is for the programming language. The introduction of FACTORIES has great advantages, and is generally underused. Yet there are times when the directness of a constructor makes it the best choice. FACTORIES can actually obscure simple objects that don't use polymorphism.

The trade-offs favor a bare, public constructor in the following circumstances.

- The class is the type. It is not part of any interesting hierarchy, and it isn't used polymorphically by implementing an interface.

- The client cares about the implementation, perhaps as a way of choosing a STRATEGY.

- All of the attributes of the object are available to the client, so that no object creation gets nested inside the constructor exposed to the client.

- The construction is not complicated.

- A public constructor must follow the same rules as a FACTORY: It must be an atomic operation that satisfies all invariants of the created object.

Avoid calling constructors within constructors of other classes. Constructors should be dead simple. Complex assemblies, especially of AGGREGATES, call for FACTORIES. The threshold for choosing to use a little FACTORY METHOD isn't high.

The Java class library offers interesting examples. All collections implement interfaces that decouple the client from the concrete implementation. Yet they are all created by direct calls to constructors. A FACTORY could have encapsulated the collection hierarchy. The FACTORY's methods could have allowed a client to ask for the features it needed, with the FACTORY selecting the appropriate class to instantiate. Code that created collections would be more expressive, and new collection classes could be installed without breaking every Java program.

But there is a case in favor of the concrete constructors. First, the choice of implementation can be performance sensitive for many applications, so an application might want control. (Even so, a really smart FACTORY could accommodate such factors.) Anyway, there aren't very many collection classes, so it isn't that complicated to choose.

The abstract collection types preserve some value in spite of the lack of a FACTORY because of their usage patterns. Collections are very often created in one place and used in another. This means that the client that ultimately uses the collection—adding, removing, and retrieving its contents—can still talk to the interface and be decoupled from the implementation. The selection of a collection class typically falls to the object that owns the collection, or to the owning object's FACTORY.

Designing the Interface

When designing the method signature of a FACTORY, whether stand-alone or FACTORY METHOD, keep in mind these two points.

- *Each operation must be atomic.* You have to pass in everything needed to create a complete product in a single interaction with the FACTORY. You also have to decide what will happen if creation fails, in the event that some invariant isn't satisfied. You could throw an exception or just return a null. To be consistent, consider adopting a coding standard for failures in FACTORIES.

- *The FACTORY will be coupled to its arguments.* If you are not careful in your selection of input parameters, you can create a rat's nest of dependencies. The degree of coupling will depend on what you do with the argument. If it is simply plugged into the product, you've created a modest dependency. If you are picking parts out of the argument to use in the construction, the coupling gets tighter.

The safest parameters are those from a lower design layer. Even within a layer, there tend to be natural strata with more basic objects that are used by higher level objects. (Such layering will be discussed in different ways in Chapter 10, "Supple Design," and again in Chapter 16, "Large-Scale Structure.")

Another good choice of parameter is an object that is closely related to the product in the model, so that no new dependency is being added. In the earlier example of a **Purchase Order Item**, the FACTORY METHOD takes a **Catalog Part** as an argument, which is an essential association for the **Item**. This adds a direct dependency between the **Purchase Order** class and the **Part**. But these three objects form a close conceptual group. The **Purchase Order's** AGGREGATE already referenced the **Part**, anyway. So giving control to the AGGREGATE root and encapsulating the AGGREGATE's internal structure is a good trade-off.

Use the abstract type of the arguments, not their concrete classes. The FACTORY is coupled to the concrete class of the products; it does not need to be coupled to concrete parameters also.

Where Does Invariant Logic Go?

A FACTORY is responsible for ensuring that all invariants are met for the object or AGGREGATE it creates; yet you should always think twice before removing the rules applying to an object outside that object. The FACTORY can delegate invariant checking to the product, and this is often best.

But FACTORIES have a special relationship with their products. They already know their product's internal structure, and their entire reason for being involves the implementation of their product. Under some circumstances, there are advantages to placing invariant logic in the FACTORY and reducing clutter in the product. This is especially appealing with AGGREGATE rules (which span many objects). It is especially *unappealing* with FACTORY METHODS attached to other domain objects.

Although in principle invariants apply at the end of every operation, often the transformations allowed to the object can never bring them into play. There might be a rule that applies to the assignment of the identity attributes of an ENTITY. But after creation that identity is immutable. VALUE OBJECTS are completely immutable. An object doesn't need to carry around logic that will never be applied in its active lifetime. In such cases, the FACTORY is a logical place to put invariants, keeping the product simpler.

ENTITY FACTORIES Versus VALUE OBJECT FACTORIES

ENTITY FACTORIES differ from VALUE OBJECT FACTORIES in two ways. VALUE OBJECTS are immutable; the product comes out complete in its final form. So the FACTORY operations have to allow for a full description of the product. ENTITY FACTORIES tend to take just the essential attributes required to make a valid AGGREGATE. Details can be added later if they are not required by an invariant.

Then there are the issues involved in assigning identity to an ENTITY—irrelevant to a VALUE OBJECT. As pointed out in Chapter 5, an identifier can either be assigned automatically by the program or supplied from the outside, typically by the user. If a customer's identity is to be tracked by the telephone number, then that telephone number must obviously be passed in as an argument to the FACTORY. When the program is assigning an identifier, the FACTORY is a good place to control it. Although the actual generation of a unique tracking ID is typically done by a database "sequence" or other infrastructure mechanism, the FACTORY knows what to ask for and where to put it.

Reconstituting Stored Objects

Up to this point, the FACTORY has played its part in the very beginning of an object's life cycle. At some point, most objects get stored in databases or transmitted through a network, and few current database technologies retain the object character of their contents. Most transmission methods flatten an object into an even more limited presentation. Therefore, retrieval requires a potentially complex process of reassembling the parts into a live object.

A FACTORY used for reconstitution is very similar to one used for creation, with two major differences.

1. *An ENTITY FACTORY used for reconstitution does not assign a new tracking ID.* To do so would lose the continuity with the object's previous incarnation. So identifying attributes must be part of the input parameters in a FACTORY reconstituting a stored object.

2. *A FACTORY reconstituting an object will handle violation of an invariant differently.* During creation of a new object, a FACTORY should simply balk when an invariant isn't met, but a more flexible response may be necessary in reconstitution. If an object already exists somewhere in the system (such as in the database), this fact cannot be ignored. Yet we also can't ignore the rule violation. There has to be some strategy for repairing such inconsistencies, which can make reconstitution more challenging than the creation of new objects.

Figures 6.16 and 6.17 (on the next page) show two kinds of reconstitution. Object-mapping technologies may provide some or all of these services in the case of database reconstitution, which is convenient. Whenever there is exposed complexity in reconstituting an object from another medium, the FACTORY is a good option.

To sum up, the access points for creation of instances must be identified, and their scope must be defined explicitly. They may simply be constructors, but often there is a need for a more abstract or elaborate instance creation mechanism. This need introduces new constructs into the design: FACTORIES. FACTORIES usually do not express any part of the model, yet they are a part of the domain design that helps keep the model-expressing objects sharp.

A FACTORY encapsulates the life cycle transitions of creation and reconstitution. Another transition that exposes technical complexity that can swamp the domain design is the transition to and from storage. This transition is the responsibility of another domain design construct, the REPOSITORY.

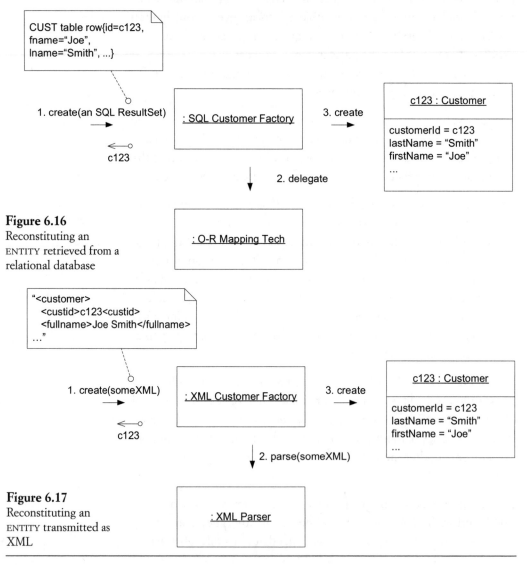

Figure 6.16
Reconstituting an ENTITY retrieved from a relational database

Figure 6.17
Reconstituting an ENTITY transmitted as XML

Repositories

Associations allow us to find an object based on its relationship to another. But we must have a starting point for a traversal to an ENTITY or VALUE in the middle of its life cycle.

✳ ✳ ✳

To do anything with an object, you have to hold a reference to it. How do you get that reference? One way is to create the object, as the creation operation will return a reference to the new object. A second way is to traverse an association. You start with an object you already know and ask it for an associated object. Any object-oriented program is going to do a lot of this, and these links give object models much of their expressive power. But you have to get that first object.

I actually encountered a project once in which the team was attempting, in an enthusiastic embrace of MODEL-DRIVEN DESIGN, to do *all* object access by creation or traversal! Their objects resided in an object database, and they reasoned that existing conceptual relationships would provide all necessary associations. They needed only to analyze them enough, making their entire domain model cohesive. This self-imposed limitation forced them to create just the kind of endless tangle that we have been trying to avert over the last few chapters, with careful implementation of ENTITIES and application of AGGREGATES. The team members didn't stick with this strategy long, but they never replaced it with another coherent approach. They cobbled together ad hoc solutions and became less ambitious.

Few would even think of this approach, much less be tempted by it, because they store most of their objects in relational databases. This storage technology makes it natural to use the third way of getting a reference: Execute a query to find the object in a database based on its attributes, or find the constituents of an object and then reconstitute it.

A database search is globally accessible and makes it possible to go directly to any object. There is no need for all objects to be interconnected, which allows us to keep the web of objects manageable. Whether to provide a traversal or depend on a search becomes a design decision, trading off the decoupling of the search against the cohesiveness of the association. Should the Customer object hold a collection of all the Orders placed? Or should the Orders be found in the database, with a search on the Customer ID field? The right combination of search and association makes the design comprehensible.

Unfortunately, developers don't usually get to think much about such design subtleties, because they are swimming in the sea of mechanisms needed to pull off the trick of storing an object and bringing it back—and eventually removing it from storage.

Now from a technical point of view, retrieval of a stored object is really a subset of creation, because the data from the database is used to assemble new objects. Indeed, the code that usually has to be written makes it hard to forget this reality. But conceptually, this is the *middle* of the life cycle of an ENTITY. A Customer object does not represent a new customer just because we stored it in a database and retrieved it. To keep this distinction in mind, I refer to the creation of an instance from stored data as *reconstitution*.

The goal of domain-driven design is to create better software by focusing on a model of the domain rather than the technology. By the time a developer has constructed an SQL query, passed it to a query service in the infrastructure layer, obtained a result set of table rows, pulled the necessary information out, and passed it to a constructor or FACTORY, the model focus is gone. It becomes natural to think of the objects as containers for the data that the queries provide, and the whole design shifts toward a data-processing style. The details of the technology vary, but the problem remains that the client is dealing with technology, rather than model concepts. Infrastructure such as METADATA MAPPING LAYERS (Fowler 2003) help a great deal, by making easier the conversion of the query result into objects, but the developer is still thinking about technical mechanisms, not the domain. Worse, as client code uses the database directly, developers are tempted to bypass model features such as AGGREGATES, or even object encapsulation, instead directly taking and manipulating the data they need. More and more domain rules become embedded in query code or simply lost. Object databases do eliminate the conversion problem, but search mechanisms are usually still mechanistic, and developers are still tempted to grab whatever objects they want.

A client needs a practical means of acquiring references to preexisting domain objects. If the infrastructure makes it easy to do so, the developers of the client may add more traversable associations, muddling the model. On the other hand, they may use queries to pull the exact data they need from the database, or to pull a few specific objects rather than navigating from AGGREGATE roots. Domain logic moves into queries and client code, and the ENTITIES and VALUE OBJECTS become mere data containers. The sheer technical complexity of applying most database access infrastructure quickly swamps the client code, which leads developers to dumb down the domain layer, which makes the model irrelevant.

Drawing on the design principles discussed so far, we can reduce the scope of the object access problem somewhat, assuming that we find a method of access that keeps the model focus sharp enough to employ those principles. For starters, we need not concern ourselves with transient objects. Transients (typically VALUE OBJECTS) live brief lives, used in the client operation that created them and then discarded. We also need no query access for persistent objects that are more convenient to find by traversal. For example, the address of a person could be requested from the Person object. And most important, *any object internal to an AGGREGATE is prohibited from access except by traversal from the root.*

Persistent VALUE OBJECTS are usually found by traversal from some ENTITY that acts as the root of the AGGREGATE that encapsulates them. In fact, a global search access to a VALUE is often meaningless, because finding a VALUE by its properties would be equivalent to creating a new instance with those properties. There are exceptions, though. For example, when I am planning travel online, I sometimes save a few prospective itineraries and return later to select one to book. Those itineraries are VALUES (if there were two made up of the same flights, I would not care which was which), but they have been associated with my user name and retrieved for me intact. Another case would be an "enumeration," when a type has a strictly limited, predetermined set of possible values. Global access to VALUE OBJECTS is much less common than for ENTITIES, though, and if you find you need to search the database for a preexisting VALUE, it is worth considering the possibility that you've really got an ENTITY whose identity you haven't recognized.

From this discussion, it is clear that most objects should not be accessed by a global search. It would be nice for the design to communicate those that do.

Now the problem can be restated more precisely.

A subset of persistent objects must be globally accessible through a search based on object attributes. Such access is needed for the roots of AGGREGATES that are not convenient to reach by traversal. They are usually ENTITIES, sometimes VALUE OBJECTS with complex internal structure, and sometimes enumerated VALUES. Providing access to other objects muddies important distinctions. Free database queries can actually breach the encapsulation of domain objects and AGGREGATES. Exposure of technical infrastructure and database access mechanisms complicates the client and obscures the MODEL-DRIVEN DESIGN.

There is a raft of techniques for dealing with the technical challenges of database access. Examples include encapsulating SQL into QUERY OBJECTS or translating between objects and tables with METADATA MAPPING LAYERS (Fowler 2003). FACTORIES can help reconstitute stored objects (as discussed later in this chapter). These and many other techniques help keep a lid on complexity.

But even so, take note of what has been lost. We are no longer thinking about concepts in our domain model. Our code will not be communicating about the business; it will be manipulating the technology of data retrieval. The REPOSITORY pattern is a simple conceptual framework to encapsulate those solutions and bring back our model focus.

A REPOSITORY represents all objects of a certain type as a conceptual set (usually emulated). It acts like a collection, except with more elaborate querying capability. Objects of the appropriate type are added and removed, and the machinery behind the REPOSITORY inserts them or deletes them from the database. This definition gathers a cohesive set of responsibilities for providing access to the roots of AGGREGATES from early life cycle through the end.

Clients request objects from the REPOSITORY using query methods that select objects based on criteria specified by the client, typically the value of certain attributes. The REPOSITORY retrieves the requested object, encapsulating the machinery of database queries and metadata mapping. REPOSITORIES can implement a variety of queries that select objects based on whatever criteria the client requires. They can also return summary information, such as a count of how many instances meet some criteria. They can even return summary calculations, such as the total across all matching objects of some numerical attribute.

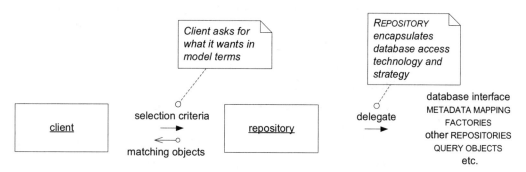

A REPOSITORY lifts a huge burden from the client, which can now talk to a simple, intention-revealing interface, and ask for what it needs in terms of the model. To support all this requires a lot of complex technical infrastructure, but the interface is simple and conceptually connected to the domain model.

Figure 6.18
A REPOSITORY doing a search for a client

Therefore:

For each type of object that needs global access, create an object that can provide the illusion of an in-memory collection of all objects of that type. Set up access through a well-known global interface.

Provide methods to add and remove objects, which will encapsulate the actual insertion or removal of data in the data store. Provide methods that select objects based on some criteria and return fully instantiated objects or collections of objects whose attribute values meet the criteria, thereby encapsulating the actual storage and query technology. Provide REPOSITORIES only for AGGREGATE roots that actually need direct access. Keep the client focused on the model, delegating all object storage and access to the REPOSITORIES.

❋ ❋ ❋

REPOSITORIES have many advantages, including the following:

- They present clients with a simple model for obtaining persistent objects and managing their life cycle.

- They decouple application and domain design from persistence technology, multiple database strategies, or even multiple data sources.

- They communicate design decisions about object access.

- They allow easy substitution of a dummy implementation, for use in testing (typically using an in-memory collection).

Querying a REPOSITORY

All repositories provide methods that allow a client to request objects matching some criteria, but there is a range of options of how to design this interface.

The easiest REPOSITORY to build has hard-coded queries with specific parameters. These queries can be various: retrieving an ENTITY by its identity (provided by almost all REPOSITORIES); requesting a collection of objects with a particular attribute value or a complex combination of parameters; selecting objects based on value ranges (such as date ranges); and even performing some calculations that fall within the general responsibility of a REPOSITORY (especially drawing on operations supported by the underlying database).

Although most queries return an object or a collection of objects, it also fits within the concept to return some types of summary calculations, such as an object count, or a sum of a numerical attribute that was intended by the model to be tallied.

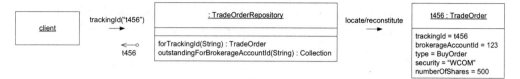

Hard-coded queries can be built on top of any infrastructure and without a lot of investment, because they do just what some client would have had to do anyway.

Figure 6.19
Hard-coded queries in a simple REPOSITORY

On projects with a lot of querying, a REPOSITORY framework can be built that allows more flexible queries. This calls for a staff familiar with the necessary technology and is greatly aided by a supportive infrastructure.

One particularly apt approach to generalizing REPOSITORIES through a framework is to use SPECIFICATION-based queries. A SPECIFICATION allows a client to describe (that is, specify) what it wants without concern for how it will be obtained. In the process, an object that can actually carry out the selection is created. This pattern will be discussed in depth in Chapter 9.

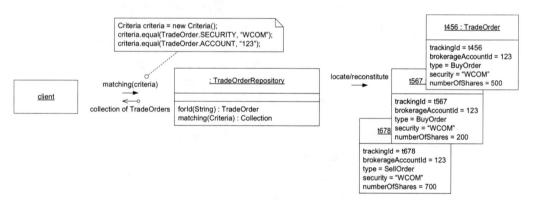

The SPECIFICATION-based query is elegant and flexible. Depending on the infrastructure available, it may be a modest framework or it may be prohibitively difficult. Rob Mee and Edward Hieatt discuss more of the technical issues involved in designing such REPOSITORIES in Fowler 2003.

Figure 6.20
A flexible, declarative SPECIFICATION of search criteria in a sophisticated REPOSITORY

Even a REPOSITORY design with flexible queries should allow for the addition of specialized hard-coded queries. They might be convenience methods that encapsulate an often-used query or a query that doesn't return the objects themselves, such as a mathematical summary of selected objects. Frameworks that don't allow for such contingencies tend to distort the domain design or get bypassed by developers.

Client Code Ignores REPOSITORY Implementation; Developers Do Not

Encapsulation of the persistence technology allows the client to be very simple, completely decoupled from the implementation of the REPOSITORY. But as is often the case with encapsulation, the developer must understand what is happening under the hood. The performance implications can be extreme when REPOSITORIES are used in different ways or work in different ways.

Kyle Brown told me the story of getting called in on a manufacturing application based on WebSphere that was being rolled out to production. The system was mysteriously running out of memory after a few hours of use. Kyle browsed through the code and found the reason: At one point, they were summarizing some information about every item in the plant. The developers had done this using a query called "all objects," which instantiated each of the objects and then selected the bits they needed. This code had the effect of bringing the entire database into memory at once! The problem hadn't shown up in testing because of the small amount of test data.

This is an obvious no-no, but much more subtle oversights can present equally serious problems. Developers need to understand the implications of using encapsulated behavior. That does not have to mean detailed familiarity with the implementation. Well-designed components can be characterized. (This is one of the main points of Chapter 10, "Supple Design.")

As was discussed in Chapter 5, the underlying technology may constrain your modeling choices. For example, a relational database can place a practical limit on deep compositional object structures. In just the same way, there must be feedback to developers in both directions between the use of the REPOSITORY and the implementation of its queries.

Implementing a REPOSITORY

Implementation will vary greatly, depending on the technology being used for persistence and the infrastructure you have. The ideal is to hide all the inner workings from the client (although not from the developer of the client), so that client code will be the same whether the data is stored in an object database, stored in a relational database, or simply held in memory. The REPOSITORY will delegate to the appropriate infrastructure services to get the job done. Encapsulating the mechanisms of storage, retrieval, and query is the most basic feature of a REPOSITORY implementation.

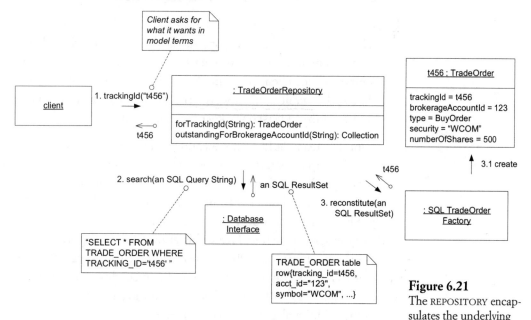

Figure 6.21
The REPOSITORY encapsulates the underlying data store.

The REPOSITORY concept is adaptable to many situations. The possibilities of implementation are so diverse that I can only list some concerns to keep in mind.

- *Abstract the type.* A REPOSITORY "contains" all instances of a specific type, but this does not mean that you need one REPOSITORY for each class. The type could be an abstract superclass of a hierarchy (for example, a **TradeOrder** could be a **BuyOrder** or a **SellOrder**). The type could be an interface whose implementers are not even hierarchically related. Or it could be a specific concrete class. Keep in mind that you may well face constraints imposed by the lack of such polymorphism in your database technology.

- *Take advantage of the decoupling from the client.* You have more freedom to change the implementation of a REPOSITORY than you would if the client were calling the mechanisms directly. You can take advantage of this to optimize for performance, by varying the query technique or by caching objects in memory, freely switching persistence strategies at any time. You can facilitate testing of the client code and the domain objects by providing an easily manipulated, dummy in-memory strategy.

 - *Leave transaction control to the client.* Although the REPOSITORY will insert into and delete from the database, it will ordinarily not commit anything. It is tempting to commit after saving, for example, but the client presumably has the context to correctly initiate and commit units of work. Transaction management will be simpler if the REPOSITORY keeps its hands off.

Typically teams add a framework to the infrastructure layer to support the implementation of REPOSITORIES. In addition to the collaboration with the lower level infrastructure components, the REPOSITORY superclass might implement some basic queries, especially when a flexible query is being implemented. Unfortunately, with a type system such as Java's, this approach would force you to type returned objects as "Object," leaving the client to cast them to the REPOSITORY'S contained type. But of course, this will have to be done with queries that return collections anyway in Java.

Some additional guidance on implementing REPOSITORIES and some of their supporting technical patterns such as QUERY OBJECT can be found in Fowler (2003).

Working Within Your Frameworks

Before implementing something like a REPOSITORY, you need to think carefully about the infrastructure you are committed to, especially any architectural frameworks. You may find that the framework provides services you can use to easily create a REPOSITORY, or you may find that the framework fights you all the way. You may discover that the architectural framework has already defined an equivalent pattern of getting persistent objects. Or you may discover that it has defined a pattern that is not like a REPOSITORY at all.

For example, your project might be committed to J2EE. Looking for conceptual affinities between the framework and the patterns of MODEL-DRIVEN DESIGN (and keeping in mind that an entity bean is *not* the same thing as an ENTITY), you may have chosen to use entity beans to correspond to AGGREGATE roots. The construct within the architectural framework of J2EE that is responsible for providing access to these objects is the "EJB Home." Trying to dress up the EJB Home to look like a REPOSITORY could lead to other problems.

In general, don't fight your frameworks. Seek ways to keep the fundamentals of domain-driven design and let go of the specifics when the framework is antagonistic. Look for affinities between the concepts of domain-driven design and the concepts in the framework. This is assuming that you have no choice but to use the framework. Many J2EE projects don't use entity beans at all. If you have the freedom, choose frameworks, or parts of frameworks, that are harmonious with the style of design you want to use.

The Relationship with FACTORIES

A FACTORY handles the beginning of an object's life; a REPOSITORY helps manage the middle and the end. When objects are being held in memory, or stored in an object database, this is straightforward. But typically there is at least some object storage in relational databases, files, or other, non-object-oriented systems. In such cases, the retrieved data must be reconstituted into object form.

Because the REPOSITORY is, in this case, creating objects based on data, many people consider the REPOSITORY to *be* a FACTORY— indeed it is, from a technical point of view. But it is more useful to keep the model in the forefront, and as mentioned before, the reconstitution of a stored object is not the creation of a new conceptual object. In this domain-driven view of the design, FACTORIES and REPOSITORIES have distinct responsibilities. The FACTORY makes new objects; the REPOSITORY finds old objects. The client of a REPOSITORY should be given the illusion that the objects are in memory. The object may have to be reconstituted (yes, a new instance may be created), but it is the same conceptual object, still in the middle of its life cycle.

These two views can be reconciled by making the REPOSITORY *delegate* object creation to a FACTORY, which (in theory, though seldom in practice) could also be used to create objects from scratch.

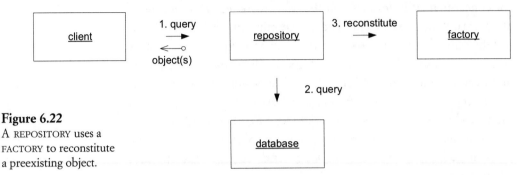

Figure 6.22
A REPOSITORY uses a FACTORY to reconstitute a preexisting object.

This clear separation also helps by unloading all responsibility for persistence from the FACTORIES. A FACTORY's job is to instantiate a potentially complex object from data. If the product is a new object, the client will know this and can add it to the REPOSITORY, which will encapsulate the storage of the object in the database.

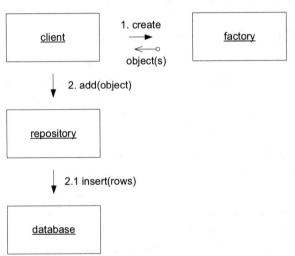

Figure 6.23
A client uses a REPOSITORY to store a new object.

One other case that drives people to combine FACTORY and REPOSITORY is the desire for "find or create" functionality, in which a client can describe an object it wants and, if no such object is found, will be given a newly created one. This function should be avoided. It is a minor convenience at best. A lot of cases in which it seems useful go away when ENTITIES and VALUE OBJECTS are distinguished. A client that wants a VALUE OBJECT can go straight to a FACTORY and ask for a new one. Usually, the distinction between a new object and an existing object is important in the domain, and a framework that transparently combines them will actually muddle the situation.

Designing Objects for Relational Databases

The most common nonobject component of primarily object-oriented software systems is the relational database. This reality presents the usual problems of a mixture of paradigms (see Chapter 5). But the database is more intimately related to the object model than are most other components. The database is not just interacting with the objects; it is storing the persistent form of the data that makes up the objects themselves. A good deal has been written about the technical challenges of mapping objects to relational tables and effectively storing and retrieving them. A recent discussion can be found in Fowler 2003. There are reasonably refined tools for creating and managing mappings between the two. Apart from the technical concerns, this mismatch can have a significant impact on the object model.

There are three common cases:

1. The database is primarily a repository for the objects.

2. The database was designed for another system.

3. The database is designed for this system but serves in roles other than object store.

When the database schema is being created specifically as a store for the objects, it is worth accepting some model limitations in order to keep the mapping very simple. Without other demands on schema design, the database can be structured to make aggregate integrity safer and more efficient as updates are made. Technically, the relational table design does not have to reflect the domain model. Mapping tools are sophisticated enough to bridge significant differences. The trouble is, multiple overlapping models are just too complicated. Many of the same arguments presented for MODEL-DRIVEN DESIGN— avoiding separate analysis and design models—apply to this mismatch. This does entail some sacrifice in the richness of the object model, and sometimes compromises have to be made in the database design (such as selective denormalization), but to do otherwise is to risk losing the tight coupling of model and implementation. This approach doesn't require a simplistic one-object/one-table mapping. Depending on the power of the mapping tool, some aggregation or composition of objects may be possible. But it is crucial that the mappings be transparent, easily understandable by inspecting the code or reading entries in the mapping tool.

- When the database is being viewed as an object store, don't let the data model and the object model diverge far, regardless of the powers of the mapping tools. Sacrifice some richness of object relationships to keep close to the relational model. Compromise some formal relational standards, such as normalization, if it helps simplify the object mapping.

- Processes outside the object system should not access such an object store. They could violate the invariants enforced by the objects. Also, their access will lock in the data model so that it is hard to change when the objects are refactored.

On the other hand, there are many cases in which the data comes from a legacy or external system that was never intended as a store of objects. In this situation, there are, in reality, two domain models coexisting in the same system. Chapter 14, "Maintaining Model Integrity," deals with this issue in depth. It may make sense to conform to the model implicit in the other system, or it may be better to make the model completely distinct.

Another reason for exceptions is performance. Quirky design changes may have to be introduced to solve execution speed problems.

But for the important common case of a relational database acting as the persistent form of an object-oriented domain, simple directness is best. A table row should contain an object, perhaps along with subsidiaries in an AGGREGATE. A foreign key in the table should translate to a reference to another ENTITY object. The necessity of sometimes deviating from this simple directness should not lead to total abandonment of the principle of simple mappings.

The UBIQUITOUS LANGUAGE can help tie the object and relational components together to a single model. The names and associations of elements in the objects should correspond meticulously to those of the relational tables. Although the power of some mapping tools may make this seem unnecessary, subtle differences in relationships will cause a lot of confusion.

The tradition of refactoring that has increasingly taken hold in the object world has not really affected relational database design much. What's more, serious data migration issues discourage frequent change. This may create a drag on the refactoring of the object model, but if the object model and the database model start to diverge, transparency can be lost quickly.

Finally, there are some reasons to go with a schema that is quite distinct from the object model, even when the database is being created specifically for your system. The database may also be used by other software that will not instantiate objects. The database may require little change, even while the behavior of the objects changes or evolves rapidly. Cutting the two loose from each other is a seductive path. It is often taken unintentionally, when the team fails to keep the database current with the model. If the separation is chosen consciously, it can result in a clean database schema—not an awkward one full of compromises conforming to last year's object model.

Using the Language: An Extended Example

The preceding three chapters introduced a pattern language for honing the fine detail of a model and maintaining a tight MODEL-DRIVEN DESIGN. In the earlier examples, the patterns were mostly applied one at a time, but on a real project you have to combine them. This chapter presents one elaborate example (still drastically simpler than a real project, of course). The example will step through a succession of model and design refinements as a hypothetical team deals with requirements and implementation issues and develops a MODEL-DRIVEN DESIGN, showing the forces that apply and how the patterns of Part II can resolve them.

Introducing the Cargo Shipping System

We're developing new software for a cargo shipping company. The initial requirements are three basic functions.

1. Track key handling of customer cargo

2. Book cargo in advance

3. Send invoices to customers automatically when the cargo reaches some point in its handling

In a real project, it would take some time and iteration to get to the clarity of this model. Part III of this book will go into the discovery process in depth. But here we'll start with a model that has the needed concepts in a reasonable form, and we'll focus on fine-tuning the details to support design.

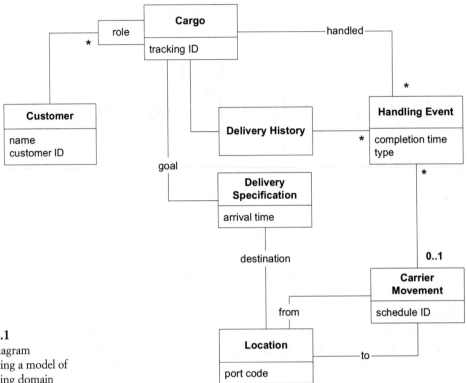

Figure 7.1
A class diagram representing a model of the shipping domain

This model organizes domain knowledge and provides a language for the team. We can make statements like this:

"Multiple **Customers** are involved with a **Cargo**, each playing a different *role*."

"The **Cargo** delivery *goal* is *specified*."

"A series of **Carrier Movements** satisfying the **Specification** will fulfill the delivery *goal*."

Each object in the model has a clear meaning:

A **Handling Event** is a discrete action taken with the **Cargo**, such as loading it onto a ship or clearing it through customs. This class would probably be elaborated into a hierarchy of different kinds of incidents, such as loading, unloading, or being claimed by the receiver.

Delivery Specification defines a delivery goal, which at minimum would include a destination and an arrival date, but it can be more complex. This class follows the SPECIFICATION pattern (see Chapter 9).

This responsibility could have been taken on by the **Cargo** object, but the abstraction of **Delivery Specification** gives at least three advantages.

1. Without **Delivery Specification**, the **Cargo** object would be responsible for the detailed meaning of all those attributes and associations for specifying the delivery goal. This would clutter up **Cargo** and make it harder to understand or change.

2. This abstraction makes it easy and safe to suppress detail when explaining the model as a whole. For example, there could be other criteria encapsulated in the **Delivery Specification**, but a diagram at this level of detail would not have to expose it. The diagram is telling the reader that there is a SPECIFICATION of delivery, and the details of that are not important to think about (and, in fact, could be easily changed later).

3. This model is more expressive. Adding **Delivery Specification** says explicitly that the exact means of delivery of the **Cargo** is undetermined, but that it must accomplish the goal set out in the **Delivery Specification**.

A *role* distinguishes the different parts played by **Customers** in a shipment. One is the "shipper," one the "receiver," one the "payer," and so on. Because only one **Customer** can play a given role for a particular **Cargo**, the association becomes a qualified many-to-one instead of many-to-many. *Role* might be implemented as simply a string, or it could be a class if other behavior is needed.

Carrier Movement represents one particular trip by a particular **Carrier** (such as a truck or a ship) from one **Location** to another. **Cargoes** can ride from place to place by being loaded onto **Carriers** for the duration of one or more **Carrier Movements**.

Delivery History reflects what has actually happened to a **Cargo**, as opposed to the **Delivery Specification**, which describes goals. A **Delivery History** object can compute the current **Location** of the **Cargo** by analyzing the last load or unload and the destination of the corresponding **Carrier Movement**. A successful delivery would end with a **Delivery History** that satisfied the goals of the **Delivery Specification**.

All the concepts needed to work through the requirements just described are present in this model, assuming appropriate mechanisms to persist the objects, find the relevant objects, and so on. Such implementation issues are not dealt with in the model, but they must be in the design.

In order to frame up a solid implementation, this model still needs some clarification and tightening.

Remember, ordinarily, model refinement, design, and implementation should go hand-in-hand in an iterative development process. But in this chapter, for clarity of explanation, we are starting with a relatively mature model, and changes will be motivated strictly by the need to connect that model with a practical implementation, employing the building block patterns.

Ordinarily, as the model is being refined to support the design better, it should also be refined to reflect new insight into the domain. But in this chapter, for clarity of explanation, changes will be strictly motivated by the need to connect with a practical implementation, employing the building block patterns.

Isolating the Domain: Introducing the Applications

To prevent domain responsibilities from being mixed with those of other parts of the system, let's apply LAYERED ARCHITECTURE to mark off a domain layer.

Without going into deep analysis, we can identify three user-level application functions, which we can assign to three application layer classes.

1. A **Tracking Query** that can access past and present handling of a particular **Cargo**

2. A **Booking Application** that allows a new **Cargo** to be registered and prepares the system for it

3. An **Incident Logging Application** that can record each handling of the **Cargo** (providing the information that is found by the **Tracking Query**)

These application classes are coordinators. They should not work out the answers to the questions they ask. That is the domain layer's job.

Distinguishing ENTITIES and VALUE OBJECTS

Considering each object in turn, we'll look for identity that must be tracked or a basic value that is represented. First we'll go through the clear-cut cases and then consider the more ambiguous ones.

Customer

Let's start with an easy one. A **Customer** object represents a person or a company, an entity in the usual sense of the word. The **Customer** object clearly has identity that matters to the user, so it is an ENTITY in the model. How to track it? Tax ID might be appropriate in some cases, but an international company could not use that. This question calls for consultation with a domain expert. We discuss the problem with a businessperson in the shipping company, and we discover that the company already has a customer database in which each **Customer** is assigned an ID number at first sales contact. This ID is already used throughout the company; using the number in our software will establish continuity of identity between those systems. It will initially be a manual entry.

Cargo

Two identical crates must be distinguishable, so **Cargo** objects are ENTITIES. In practice, all shipping companies assign tracking IDs to each piece of cargo. This ID will be automatically generated, visible to the user, and in this case, probably conveyed to the customer at booking time.

Handling Event and Carrier Movement

We care about such individual incidents because they allow us to keep track of what is going on. They reflect real-world events, which are not usually interchangeable, so they are ENTITIES. Each **Carrier Movement** will be identified by a code obtained from a shipping schedule.

Another discussion with a domain expert reveals that **Handling Events** can be uniquely identified by the combination of **Cargo** ID, completion time, and type. For example, the same **Cargo** cannot be both loaded and unloaded at the same time.

Location

Two places with the same name are not the same. Latitude and longitude could provide a unique key, but probably not a very practical one, since those measurements are not of interest to most purposes of this system, and they would be fairly complicated. More likely, the **Location** will be part of a geographical model of some kind that will relate places according to shipping lanes and other domain-specific concerns. So an arbitrary, internal, automatically generated identifier will suffice.

Delivery History

This is a tricky one. **Delivery Histories** are not interchangeable, so they are ENTITIES. But a **Delivery History** has a one-to-one relationship with its **Cargo**, so it doesn't really have an identity of its own. Its identity is borrowed from the **Cargo** that owns it. This will become clearer when we model the AGGREGATES.

Delivery Specification

Although it represents the goal of a **Cargo**, this abstraction does not depend on **Cargo**. It really expresses a hypothetical state of some **Delivery History**. We hope that the **Delivery History** attached to our **Cargo** will eventually satisfy the **Delivery Specification** attached to our **Cargo**. If we had two **Cargoes** going to the same place, they could share the same **Delivery Specification**, but they could not share the same **Delivery History**, even though the histories start out the same (empty). **Delivery Specifications** are VALUE OBJECTS.

Role and Other Attributes

Role says something about the association it qualifies, but it has no history or continuity. It is a VALUE OBJECT, and it could be shared among different **Cargo/Customer** associations.

Other attributes such as time stamps or names are VALUE OBJECTS.

Designing Associations in the Shipping Domain

None of the associations in the original diagram specified a traversal direction, but bidirectional associations are problematic in a design. Also, traversal direction often captures insight into the domain, deepening the model itself.

If the **Customer** has a direct reference to every **Cargo** it has shipped, it will become cumbersome for long-term, repeat **Customers**. Also, the concept of a **Customer** is not specific to **Cargo**. In a large system, the **Customer** may have roles to play with many objects. Best to keep it free of such specific responsibilities. If we need the ability to find **Cargoes** by **Customer**, this can be done through a database query. We'll return to this issue later in this chapter, in the section on REPOSITORIES.

If our application were tracking the inventory of ships, traversal from **Carrier Movement** to **Handling Event** would be important. But our business needs to track only the **Cargo**. Making the association traversable only from **Handling Event** to **Carrier Movement** captures that understanding of our business. This also reduces the implementation to a simple object reference, because the direction with multiplicity was disallowed.

The rationale behind the remaining decisions is explained in Figure 7.2, on the next page.

There is one circular reference in our model: **Cargo** knows its **Delivery History**, which holds a series of **Handling Events**, which in turn point back to the **Cargo**. Circular references logically exist in many domains and are sometimes necessary in design as well, but they are tricky to maintain. Implementation choices can help by avoiding holding the same information in two places that must be kept synchronized. In this case, we can make a simple but fragile implementation (in Java) in an initial prototype, by giving **Delivery History** a **List** object containing **Handling Events**. But at some point we'll probably want to drop the collection in favor of a database lookup with **Cargo** as the key. This discussion will be taken up again when choosing REPOSITORIES. If the query to see the history is relatively infrequent, this should give good performance, simplify maintenance, and reduce the overhead of adding **Handling Events**. If this query is very frequent, then it is better to go ahead and maintain the direct pointer. These design trade-offs balance simplicity of implementation against

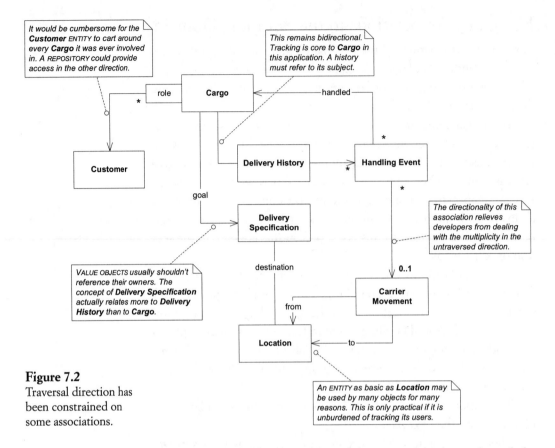

Figure 7.2
Traversal direction has
been constrained on
some associations.

Text in diagram boxes:

It would be cumbersome for the **Customer** ENTITY to cart around every **Cargo** it was ever involved in. A REPOSITORY could provide access in the other direction.

This remains bidirectional. Tracking is core to **Cargo** in this application. A history must refer to its subject.

The directionality of this association relieves developers from dealing with the multiplicity in the untraversed direction.

VALUE OBJECTS usually shouldn't reference their owners. The concept of **Delivery Specification** actually relates more to **Delivery History** than to **Cargo**.

An ENTITY as basic as **Location** may be used by many objects for many reasons. This is only practical if it is unburdened of tracking its users.

Diagram labels: role, Cargo, handled, Customer, Delivery History, Handling Event, goal, Delivery Specification, destination, from, Carrier Movement, 0..1, to, Location

performance. The model is the same; it contains the cycle and the bidirectional association.

AGGREGATE Boundaries

Customer, **Location**, and **Carrier Movement** have their own identities and are shared by many **Cargoes**, so they must be the roots of their own AGGREGATES, which contain their attributes and possibly other objects below the level of detail of this discussion. **Cargo** is also an obvious AGGREGATE root, but where to draw the boundary takes some thought.

The **Cargo** AGGREGATE could sweep in everything that would not exist but for the particular **Cargo**, which would include the **Delivery History**, the **Delivery Specification**, and the **Handling Events**. This fits for **Delivery History.** No one would look up a **Delivery History** directly without wanting the **Cargo** itself. With no need for direct global access, and with an identity that is really just derived from the **Cargo**, the **Delivery History** fits nicely inside **Cargo's** boundary, and it does not need to be a root. The **Delivery Specification** is a VALUE OBJECT, so there are no complications from including it in the **Cargo** AGGREGATE.

The **Handling Event** is another matter. Previously we have considered two possible database queries that would search for these: one, to find the **Handling Events** for a **Delivery History** as a possible alternative to the collection, would be local within the **Cargo** AGGREGATE; the other would be used to find all the operations to load and prepare for a particular **Carrier Movement**. In the second case, it seems that the activity of *handling* the **Cargo** has some meaning even when considered apart from the **Cargo** itself. So the **Handling Event** should be the root of its own AGGREGATE.

Figure 7.3

AGGREGATE boundaries imposed on the model. (Note: An ENTITY outside a drawn boundary is implied to be the root of its own AGGREGATE.)

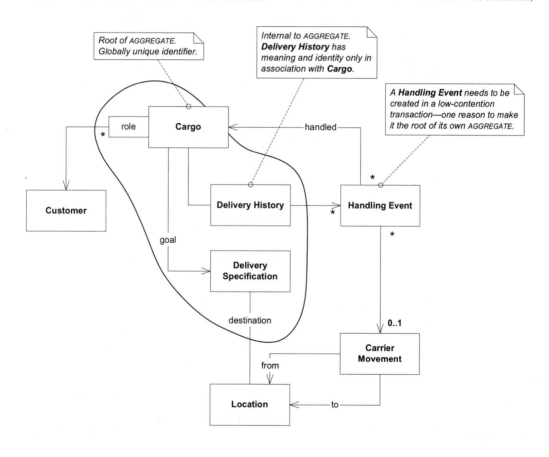

Selecting REPOSITORIES

There are five ENTITIES in the design that are roots of AGGREGATES, so we can limit our consideration to these, since none of the other objects is allowed to have REPOSITORIES.

To decide which of these candidates should actually have a REPOSITORY, we must go back to the application requirements. In order to take a booking through the **Booking Application**, the user needs to select the **Customer(s)** playing the various roles (shipper, receiver, and so on). So we need a **Customer Repository**. We also need to find a **Location** to specify as the destination for the **Cargo**, so we create a **Location Repository**.

The **Activity Logging Application** needs to allow the user to look up the **Carrier Movement** that a **Cargo** is being loaded onto, so we need a **Carrier Movement Repository**. This user must also tell the system which **Cargo** has been loaded, so we need a **Cargo Repository**.

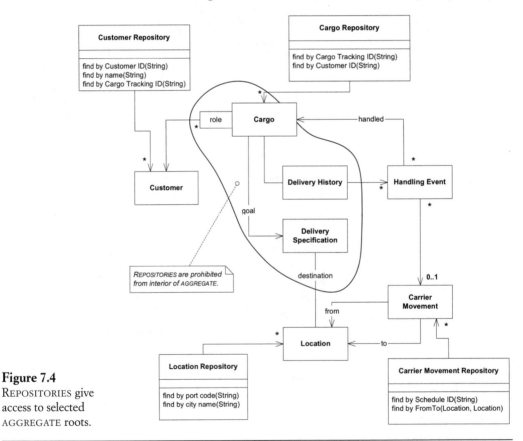

Figure 7.4
REPOSITORIES give access to selected AGGREGATE roots.

For now there is no **Handling Event Repository**, because we decided to implement the association with **Delivery History** as a collection in the first iteration, and we have no application requirement to find out what has been loaded onto a **Carrier Movement**. Either of these reasons could change; if they did, then we would add a REPOSITORY.

Walking Through Scenarios

To cross-check all these decisions, we have to constantly step through scenarios to confirm that we can solve application problems effectively.

Sample Application Feature: Changing the Destination of a **Cargo**

Occasionally a **Customer** calls up and says, "Oh no! We said to send our cargo to Hackensack, but we really need it in Hoboken." We are here to serve, so the system is required to provide for this change.

Delivery Specification is a VALUE OBJECT, so it would be simplest to just to throw it away and get a new one, then use a setter method on **Cargo** to replace the old one with the new one.

Sample Application Feature: Repeat Business

The users say that repeated bookings from the same **Customers** tend to be similar, so they want to use old **Cargoes** as prototypes for new ones. The application will allow them to find a **Cargo** in the REPOSITORY and then select a command to create a new **Cargo** based on the selected one. We'll design this using the PROTOTYPE pattern (Gamma et al. 1995).

Cargo is an ENTITY and is the root of an AGGREGATE. Therefore, it must be copied carefully; we need to consider what should happen to each object or attribute enclosed by its AGGREGATE boundary. Let's go over each one:

- **Delivery History:** We should create a new, empty one, because the history of the old one doesn't apply. This is the usual case with ENTITIES inside the AGGREGATE boundary.

- **Customer Roles:** We should copy the **Map** (or other collection) that holds the keyed references to **Customers**, including the keys, because they are likely to play the same roles in the new shipment. But we have to be careful *not* to copy the **Customer** objects themselves. We must end up with references to the same **Customer** objects as the old **Cargo** object referenced, because they are ENTITIES outside the AGGREGATE boundary.

- **Tracking ID:** We must provide a new **Tracking ID** from the same source as we would when creating a new **Cargo** from scratch.

Notice that we have copied everything inside the **Cargo** AGGREGATE boundary, we have made some modifications to the copy, but we have *affected nothing outside the AGGREGATE boundary* at all.

Object Creation

FACTORIES and Constructors for **Cargo**

Even if we have a fancy FACTORY for **Cargo**, or use another **Cargo** as the FACTORY, as in the "Repeat Business" scenario, we still have to have a primitive constructor. We would like the constructor to produce an object that fulfills its invariants or at least, in the case of an ENTITY, has its identity intact.

Given these decisions, we might create a FACTORY method on **Cargo** such as this:

```
public Cargo copyPrototype(String newTrackingID)
```

Or we might make a method on a standalone FACTORY such as this:

```
public Cargo newCargo(Cargo prototype, String newTrackingID)
```

A standalone FACTORY could also encapsulate the process of obtaining a new (automatically generated) ID for a new **Cargo**, in which case it would need only one argument:

```
public Cargo newCargo(Cargo prototype)
```

The result returned from any of these FACTORIES would be the same: a **Cargo** with an empty **Delivery History**, and a null **Delivery Specification**.

The two-way association between **Cargo** and **Delivery History** means that neither **Cargo** nor **Delivery History** is complete without pointing to its counterpart, so they must be created together. Remember that **Cargo** is the root of the AGGREGATE that includes **Delivery**

History. Therefore, we can allow **Cargo's** constructor or FACTORY to create a **Delivery History**. The **Delivery History** constructor will take a **Cargo** as an argument. The result would be something like this:

```
public Cargo(String id) {
    trackingID = id;
    deliveryHistory = new DeliveryHistory(this);
    customerRoles = new HashMap();
}
```

The result is a new **Cargo** with a new **Delivery History** that points back to the **Cargo**. The **Delivery History** constructor is used exclusively by its AGGREGATE root, namely **Cargo**, so that the composition of **Cargo** is encapsulated.

Adding a **Handling Event**

Each time the cargo is handled in the real world, some user will enter a **Handling Event** using the **Incident Logging Application**.

Every class must have primitive constructors. Because the **Handling Event** is an ENTITY, all attributes that define its identity must be passed to the constructor. As discussed previously, the **Handling Event** is uniquely identified by the combination of the ID of its **Cargo**, the completion time, and the event type. The only other attribute of **Handling Event** is the association to a **Carrier Movement**, which some types of **Handling Events** don't even have. A basic constructor that creates a valid **Handling Event** would be:

```
public HandlingEvent(Cargo c, String eventType, Date timeStamp) {
    handled = c;
    type = eventType;
    completionTime = timeStamp;
}
```

Nonidentifying attributes of an ENTITY can usually be added later. In this case, all attributes of the **Handling Event** are going to be set in the initial transaction and never altered (except possibly for correcting a data-entry error), so it could be convenient, and make client code more expressive, to add a simple FACTORY METHOD to **Handling Event** for each event type, taking all the necessary arguments. For example, a "loading event" does involve a **Carrier Movement**:

```
public static HandlingEvent newLoading(
    Cargo c, CarrierMovement loadedOnto, Date timeStamp) {
    HandlingEvent result =
        new HandlingEvent(c, LOADING_EVENT, timeStamp);
    result.setCarrierMovement(loadedOnto);
    return result;
}
```

The **Handling Event** in the model is an abstraction that might encapsulate a variety of specialized **Handling Event** classes, ranging from loading and unloading to sealing, storing, and other activities not related to **Carriers**. They might be implemented as multiple subclasses or have complicated initialization—or both. By adding FACTORY METHODS to the base class (**Handling Event**) for each type, instance creation is abstracted, freeing the client from knowledge of the implementation. The FACTORY is responsible for knowing what class was to be instantiated and how it should be initialized.

Unfortunately, the story isn't quite that simple. The cycle of references, from **Cargo** to **Delivery History** to **History Event** and back to **Cargo**, complicates instance creation. The **Delivery History** holds a collection of **Handling Events** relevant to its **Cargo**, and the new object must be added to this collection as part of the transaction. If this back-pointer were not created, the objects would be inconsistent.

Figure 7.5
Adding a **Handling Event** requires inserting it into a **Delivery History**.

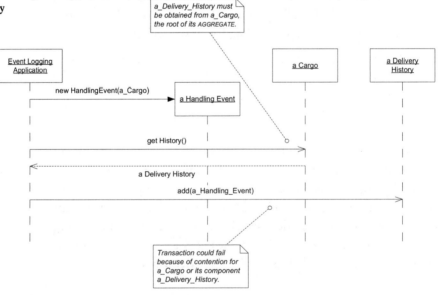

CHAPTER 7: USING THE LANGUAGE

Creation of the back-pointer could be encapsulated in the FAC-
TORY (and kept in the domain layer where it belongs), but now we'll
look at an alternative design that eliminates this awkward interaction
altogether.

Pause for Refactoring: An Alternative Design of the **Cargo** AGGREGATE

Modeling and design is not a constant forward process. It will grind
to a halt unless there is frequent refactoring to take advantage of new
insights to improve the model and the design.

By now, there are a couple of cumbersome aspects to this design,
although it does work and it does reflect the model. Problems that
didn't seem important when starting the design are beginning to be
annoying. Let's go back to one of them and, with the benefit of hind-
sight, stack the design deck in our favor.

The need to update **Delivery History** when adding a **Handling
Event** gets the **Cargo** AGGREGATE involved in the transaction. If some
other user was modifying **Cargo** at the same time, the **Handling Event**
transaction could fail or be delayed. Entering a **Handling Event** is an
operational activity that needs to be quick and simple, so an important application requirement is the ability to enter **Handling Events**
without contention. This pushes us to consider a different design.

Replacing the **Delivery History's** collection of **Handling Events**
with a query would allow **Handling Events** to be added without raising any integrity issues outside its own AGGREGATE. This change
would enable such transactions to complete without interference. If
there are a lot of **Handling Events** being entered and relatively few
queries, this design is more efficient. In fact, if a relational database is
the underlying technology, a query was probably being used under
the covers anyway to emulate the collection. Using a query rather
than a collection would also reduce the difficulty of maintaining consistency in the cyclical reference between **Cargo** and **Handling Event**.

To take responsibility for the queries, we'll add a REPOSITORY for
Handling Events. The **Handling Event Repository** will support a
query for the **Events** related to a certain **Cargo**. In addition, the REPOS-
ITORY can provide queries optimized to answer specific questions efficiently. For example, if a frequent access path is the **Delivery History**

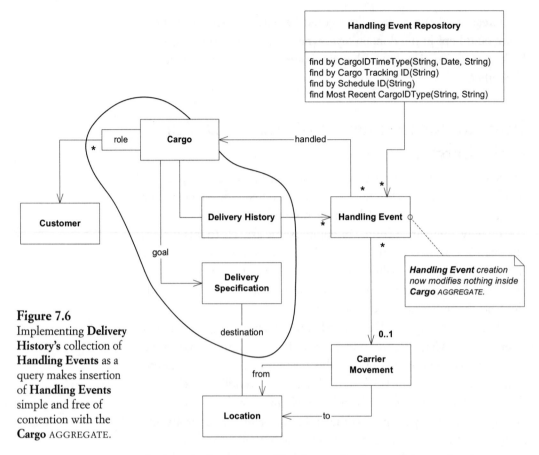

Figure 7.6
Implementing **Delivery History's** collection of **Handling Events** as a query makes insertion of **Handling Events** simple and free of contention with the **Cargo** AGGREGATE.

finding the last reported load or unload, in order to infer the current status of the **Cargo**, a query could be devised to return just that relevant **Handling Event**. And if we wanted a query to find all **Cargoes** loaded on a particular **Carrier Movement**, we could easily add it.

This leaves the **Delivery History** with no persistent state. At this point, there is no real need to keep it around. We could derive **Delivery History** itself whenever it is needed to answer some question. We can derive this object because, although the ENTITY will be repeatedly recreated, the association with the same **Cargo** object maintains the thread of continuity between incarnations.

The circular reference is no longer tricky to create and maintain. The **Cargo Factory** will be simplified to no longer attach an empty **Delivery History** to new instances. Database space can be reduced slightly, and the actual number of persistent objects might be reduced considerably, which is a limited resource in some object databases. If the common usage pattern is that the user seldom queries for the status of a **Cargo** until it arrives, then a lot of unneeded work will be avoided altogether.

On the other hand, if we are using an object database, traversing an association or an explicit collection is probably much faster than a REPOSITORY query. If the access pattern includes frequent listing of the full history, rather than the occasional targeted query of last position, the performance trade-off might favor the explicit collection. And remember that the added feature ("What is on this **Carrier Movement**?") hasn't been requested yet, and may never be, so we don't want to pay much for that option.

These kinds of alternatives and design trade-offs are everywhere, and I could come up with lots of examples just in this little simplified system. But the important point is that these are degrees of freedom within the same model. By modeling VALUES, ENTITIES, and their AGGREGATES as we have, we have reduced the impact of such design changes. For example, in this case all changes are encapsulated within the **Cargo's** AGGREGATE boundary. It also required the addition of the **Handling Event Repository**, but it did not call for any redesign of the **Handling Event** itself (although some implementation changes might be involved, depending on the details of the REPOSITORY framework).

MODULES in the Shipping Model

So far we've been looking at so few objects that modularity is not an issue. Now let's look at a little bigger part of a shipping model (though still simplified, of course) to see its organization into MODULES that will affect the model.

Figure 7.7 shows a model neatly partitioned by a hypothetical enthusiastic reader of this book. This diagram is a variation on the infrastructure-driven packaging problem raised in Chapter 5. In this case, the objects have been grouped according to the pattern each follows. The result is that objects that conceptually have little relationship (low cohesion) are crammed together, and associations run willy-nilly between all the MODULES (high coupling). The packages tell a story, but it is not the story of shipping; it is the story of what the developer was reading at the time.

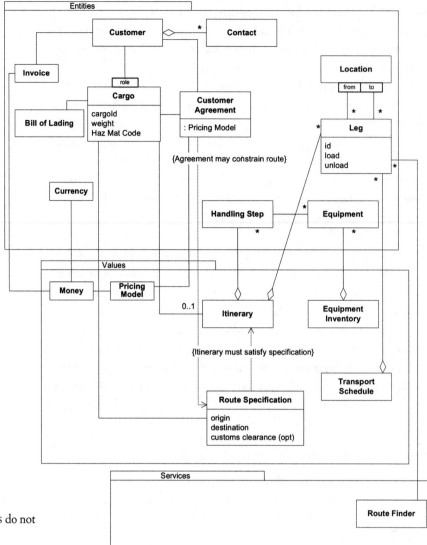

Figure 7.7
These MODULES do not convey domain knowledge.

Partitioning by pattern may seem like an obvious error, but it is not really any less sensible than separating persistent objects from transient ones or any other methodical scheme that is not grounded in the meaning of the objects.

Instead, we should be looking for the cohesive concepts and focusing on what we want to communicate to others on the project. As with smaller scale modeling decisions, there are many ways to do it. Figure 7.8 shows a straightforward one.

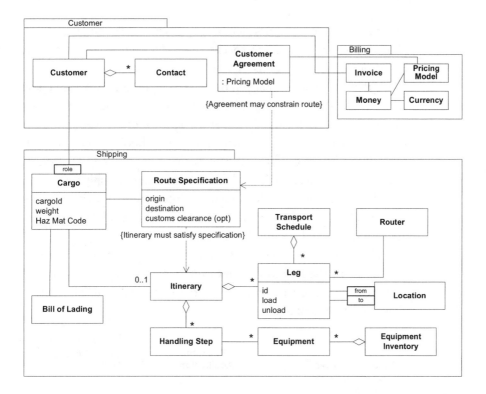

The MODULE names in Figure 7.8 contribute to the team's language. Our company does *shipping* for *customers* so that we can *bill* them. Our sales and marketing people deal with *customers*, and make agreements with them. The operations people do the *shipping*, getting the cargo to its specified destination. The back office takes care of *billing*, submitting invoices according to the pricing in the *customer's* agreement. That's one story I can tell with this set of MODULES.

This intuitive breakdown could be refined, certainly, in successive iterations, or even replaced entirely, but it is now aiding MODEL-DRIVEN DESIGN and contributing to the UBIQUITOUS LANGUAGE.

Figure 7.8
MODULES based on broad domain concepts

Introducing a New Feature: Allocation Checking

Up to this point, we've been working off the initial requirements and model. Now the first major new functions are going to be added.

The sales division of the imaginary shipping company uses other software to manage client relationships, sales projections, and so forth. One feature supports yield management by allowing the firm to allocate how much cargo of specific types they will attempt to book based on the type of goods, the origin and destination, or any other factor they may choose that can be entered as a category name. These constitute goals of how much will be sold of each type, so that more profitable types of business will not be crowded out by less profitable cargoes, while at the same time avoiding underbooking (not fully utilizing their shipping capacity) or excessive overbooking (resulting in bumping cargo so often that it hurts customer relationships).

Now they want this feature to be integrated with the booking system. When a booking comes in, they want it checked against these allocations to see if it should be accepted.

The information needed resides in two places, which will have to be queried by the **Booking Application** so that it can either accept or reject the requested booking. A sketch of the general information flows looks something like this.

Figure 7.9
Our **Booking Application** must use information from the **Sales Management System** and from our own domain REPOSITORIES.

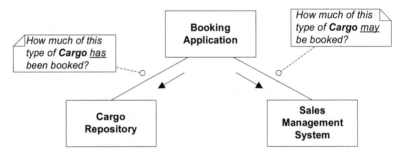

Connecting the Two Systems

The **Sales Management System** was not written with the same model in mind that we are working with here. If the **Booking Application** interacts with it directly, our application will have to accommodate the other system's design, which will make it harder to keep a clear MODEL-DRIVEN DESIGN and will confuse the UBIQUITOUS LANGUAGE. Instead, let's create another class whose job it will be to translate between our model and the language of the **Sales Management System**. It will not be a general translation mechanism. It will expose just the features our application needs, and it will reabstract them in terms of our domain model. This class will act as an ANTI-CORRUPTION LAYER (discussed in Chapter 14).

This is an interface to the **Sales Management System**, so we might first think of calling it something like "**Sales Management Interface**." But we would be missing an opportunity to use language to recast the problem along lines more useful to us. Instead, let's define a SERVICE for each of the allocation functions we need to get from the other system. We'll implement the SERVICES with a class whose name reflects its responsibility in our system: "**Allocation Checker**."

If some other integration is needed (for example, using the **Sales Management System's** customer database instead of our own **Customer** REPOSITORY), another translator can be created with SERVICES fulfilling that responsibility. It might still be useful to have a lower level class like **Sales Management System Interface** to handle the machinery of talking to the other program, but it wouldn't be responsible for translation. Also, it would be hidden behind the **Allocation Checker**, so it wouldn't show up in the domain design.

Enhancing the Model: Segmenting the Business

Now that we have outlined the interaction of the two systems, what kind of interface are we going to supply that can answer the question "How much of this type of **Cargo** may be booked?" The tricky issue is to define what the "type" of a **Cargo** is, because our domain model does not categorize **Cargoes** yet. In the **Sales Management System**, **Cargo** types are just a set of category keywords, and we could conform our types to that list. We could pass in a collection of strings as an argument. But we would be passing up another opportunity: this time, to reabstract the domain of the other system. We need to enrich our domain model to accommodate the knowledge that there are categories of cargo. We should brainstorm with a domain expert to work out the new concept.

Sometimes (as will be discussed in Chapter 11) an analysis pattern can give us an idea for a modeling solution. The book *Analysis Patterns* (Fowler 1996) describes a pattern that addresses this kind of problem: the ENTERPRISE SEGMENT. An ENTERPRISE SEGMENT is a set of dimensions that define a way of breaking down a business. These dimensions could include all those mentioned already for the shipping business, as well as time dimensions, such as month to date. Using this concept in our model of allocation makes the model more expressive and simplifies the interfaces. A class called "**Enterprise**

Segment" will appear in our domain model and design as an additional VALUE OBJECT, which will have to be derived for each **Cargo**.

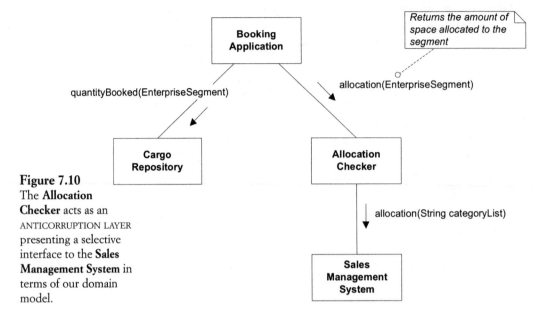

Figure 7.10
The **Allocation Checker** acts as an ANTICORRUPTION LAYER presenting a selective interface to the **Sales Management System** in terms of our domain model.

The **Allocation Checker** will translate between **Enterprise Segments** and the category names of the external system. The **Cargo Repository** must also provide a query based on the **Enterprise Segment**. In both cases, collaboration with the **Enterprise Segment** object can be used to perform the operations without breaching the **Segment's** encapsulation and complicating their own implementations. (Notice that the **Cargo Repository** is answering a query with a count, rather than a collection of instances.)

There are still a few problems with this design.

1. We have given the **Booking Application** the job of applying this rule: "A **Cargo** is accepted if the space allocated for its **Enterprise Segment** is greater than the quantity already booked plus the size of the new **Cargo**." Enforcing a business rule is domain responsibility and shouldn't be performed in the application layer.

2. It isn't clear how the **Booking Application** derives the **Enterprise Segment**.

Both of these responsibilities seem to belong to the **Allocation Checker**. Changing its interface can separate these two SERVICES and make the interaction clear and explicit.

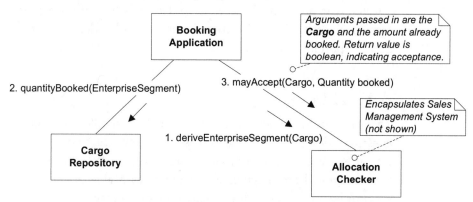

The only serious constraint imposed by this integration will be that the **Sales Management System** mustn't use dimensions that the **Allocation Checker** can't turn into **Enterprise Segments**. (Without applying the ENTERPRISE SEGMENT pattern, the same constraint would force the sales system to use only dimensions that can be used in a query to the **Cargo Repository**. This approach is feasible, but the sales system spills into other parts of the domain. In this design, the **Cargo Repository** need only be designed to handle **Enterprise Segment**, and changes in the sales system ripple only as far as the **Allocation Checker**, which was conceived as a FACADE in the first place.)

Figure 7.11
Domain responsibilities shifted from **Booking Application** to **Allocation Checker**

Performance Tuning

Although the **Allocation Checker's** interface is the only part that concerns the rest of the domain design, its internal implementation can present opportunities to solve performance problems, if they arise. For example, if the **Sales Management System** is running on another server, perhaps at another location, the communications overhead could be significant, and there are two message exchanges for each allocation check. There is no alternative to the second message, which invokes the **Sales Management System** to answer the basic question of whether a certain cargo should be accepted. But the first message, which derives the **Enterprise Segment** for a cargo, is based on relatively static data and behavior compared to the allocation decisions themselves. One design option would be to cache this information so that it could be relocated on the server with the **Allocation Checker**, reducing messaging overhead by half. There is a price for this flexibility. The design is more complicated and the duplicated data must now be kept up to date somehow. But when performance is critical in a distributed system, flexible deployment can be an important design goal.

A Final Look

That's it. This integration could have turned our simple, conceptually consistent design into a tangled mess, but now, using an ANTICORRUPTION LAYER, a SERVICE, and some ENTERPRISE SEGMENTS, we have integrated the functionality of the **Sales Management System** into our booking system cleanly, enriching the domain.

A final design question: Why not give **Cargo** the responsibility of deriving the **Enterprise Segment**? At first glance it seems elegant, if all the data the derivation is based on is in the **Cargo**, to make it a derived attribute of **Cargo**. Unfortunately, it is not that simple. **Enterprise Segments** are defined arbitrarily to divide along lines useful for business strategy. The same ENTITIES could be segmented differently for different purposes. We are deriving the segment for a particular **Cargo** for *booking allocation* purposes, but it could have a completely different **Enterprise Segment** for tax accounting purposes. Even the allocation **Enterprise Segment** could change if the **Sales Management System** is reconfigured because of a new sales strategy. So the **Cargo** would have to know about the **Allocation Checker**, which is well outside its conceptual responsibility, and it would be laden with methods for deriving specific types of **Enterprise Segment**. Therefore, the responsibility for deriving this value lies properly with the object that knows the rules for segmentation, rather than the object that has the data to which those rules apply. Those rules could be split out into a separate "**Strategy**" object, which could be passed to a **Cargo** to allow it to derive an **Enterprise Segment**. That solution seems to go beyond the requirements we have here, but it would be an option for a later design and shouldn't be a very disruptive change.

III

Refactoring Toward Deeper Insight

Part II of this book laid a foundation for maintaining the correspondence between model and implementation. Using a proven set of basic building blocks along with consistent language brings some sanity to the development effort.

Of course, the real challenge is to actually *find* an incisive model, one that captures subtle concerns of the domain experts and can drive a practical design. Ultimately, we hope to develop a model that captures a deep understanding of the domain. This should make the software more in tune with the way the domain experts think and more responsive to the user's needs. This part of the book will clarify that goal, describe the process by which it can be approached, and explain some design principles and patterns to apply to make the design accommodate the needs of the application as well as the developers themselves.

Success developing useful models comes down to three points.

1. Sophisticated domain models are achievable and worth the trouble.

2. They are seldom developed except through an iterative process of refactoring, including close involvement of the domain experts with developers interested in learning about the domain.

3. They may call for sophisticated design skills to implement and to use effectively.

Levels of Refactoring

Refactoring is the redesign of software in ways that do not change its functionality. Rather than making elaborate up-front design decisions, developers take code through a continuous series of small, discrete design changes, each leaving existing functionality unchanged while making the design more flexible or easier to understand. A suite of automated unit tests allows relatively safe experimentation with the code. The process frees the developers from the need to look far ahead.

But nearly all the literature on how to refactor focuses on mechanical changes to the code that make it easier to read or to enhance at a very detailed level. The approach of "refactoring to patterns"[1]

---

1. Patterns as targets for refactoring were briefly mentioned in Gamma et al. (1995). Joshua Kerievsky has developed refactoring to patterns into a more mature and useful form (Kerievsky 2003).

can give a higher-level target to the refactoring process when a developer recognizes an opportunity to apply an established design pattern. Still, it is a primarily technical view of the quality of a design.

The refactorings that have the greatest impact on the viability of the system are those motivated by new insights into the domain or those that clarify the model's expression through the code. This type of refactoring does not in any way replace the refactorings to design patterns or the micro-refactorings, which should proceed continuously. It superimposes another level: refactoring to a deeper model. Executing a refactoring based on domain insight often involves a series of micro-refactorings, but the motivation is not just the state of the code. Rather, the micro-refactorings provide convenient units of change toward a more insightful model. The goal is that not only can a developer understand what the code does; he or she can also understand *why* it does what it does and can relate that to the ongoing communication with the domain experts.

The catalog in *Refactoring* (Fowler 1999) covers most of the micro-refactorings that come up regularly. Each is motivated primarily by some problem that can be observed in the code itself. By contrast, domain models are transformed in such a range of ways as new insights emerge that a comprehensive catalog would be impossible to compile.

Modeling is as inherently unstructured as any exploration. Refactoring to deeper insight should follow wherever learning and deep thinking lead. Published collections of successful models can be helpful, as discussed in Chapter 11, but we shouldn't get sidetracked trying to reduce domain modeling to a cookbook or a toolkit. Modeling and design call for creativity. The next six chapters will suggest some specific approaches to thinking about improving a domain model, along with the design that brings it to life.

Deep Models

The traditional way of explaining object analysis involves identifying nouns and verbs in the requirements documents and using them as the initial objects and methods. This explanation is recognized as an oversimplification that can be useful for teaching object modeling to beginners. The truth is, though, that initial models usually are naive and superficial, based on shallow knowledge.

For example, I once worked on a shipping application for which my initial idea of an object model involved ships and containers. Ships moved from place to place. Containers were associated and disassociated through load and unload operations. That is an accurate description of some physical shipping activities. It does not turn out to be a very useful model for shipping business software.

Eventually, after months working with shipping experts through many iterations, we evolved a quite different model. It was less obvious to a layperson, but much more relevant to the experts. It was refocused on the business of delivering cargo.

The ships were still there, but abstracted in the form of a "vessel voyage," a particular trip scheduled for a ship, train, or other carrier. The ship itself was secondary, and could be substituted at the last minute for maintenance or a slipping schedule, while the vessel voyage went on as planned. The shipping container all but disappeared from the model. It did emerge in a cargo-handling application in a different, very complex form, but in the context of the original application, the container was an operational detail. The physical movement of the cargo took a back seat to the transfers of legal responsibility for that cargo. Less obvious objects, such as the "bill of lading," came to the fore.

Whenever new object modelers showed up on the project, what was their first suggestion? The missing classes: ship and container. They were smart people. They just hadn't gone through the processes of discovery.

A deep model provides a lucid expression of the primary concerns of the domain experts and their most relevant knowledge while it sloughs off the superficial aspects of the domain. This definition doesn't mention abstraction. A deep model usually has abstract elements, but it may well have concrete elements where those cut to the heart of the problem.

Versatility, simplicity, and explanatory power come from a model that is truly in tune with the domain. One feature such models almost always have is a simple, though possibly abstract, language that the business experts like to use.

Deep Model/Supple Design

In a process of constant refactoring, the design itself needs to support change. Chapter 10 looks at ways to make a design easy to work with, both for those changing it and for those integrating it with other parts of the system.

Certain characteristics of a design make it easier to change and use. They are not complicated, but they are challenging. "Supple design" and ways to approach it are the subjects of Chapter 10.

One bit of luck is that the very act of transforming the model and code again and again—if each change reflects new understanding— can bring about flexibility at just the points where change is most needed, along with easy ways of doing the common things. A well-worn glove becomes supple at the points where the fingers bend, while other parts are stiff and protective. So although there is a lot of trial and error involved in this approach to modeling and design, the changes can actually become easier to make, and the repeated changes actually move us toward a supple design.

In addition to facilitating change, a supple design contributes to the refinement of the model itself. A MODEL-DRIVEN DESIGN stands on two legs. A deep model makes possible an expressive design. At the same time, a design can actually feed insight into the model discovery process when it has the flexibility to let a developer experiment and the clarity to show a developer what is happening. This half of the feedback loop is essential, because the model we are looking for is not just a nice set of ideas: it is the foundation of the system.

The Discovery Process

To create a design really fitted to the problem at hand, you must first have a model that captures the central relevant concepts of the domain. Actively searching for these concepts and bringing them into the design is the subject of Chapter 9, "Making Implicit Concepts Explicit."

Because of the close relationship between model and design, the modeling process comes to a halt when the code is hard to refactor. Chapter 10, "Supple Design," discusses how to write software for software developers, not least yourself, so that it is productive to extend

---

and change. This effort goes hand in hand with further refinements to the model. It often entails more advanced design techniques and more rigor in model definitions.

You will usually depend on creativity and trial and error to find good ways to model the concepts you discover, but sometimes someone has laid down a pattern you can follow. Chapters 11 and 12 discuss the application of "analysis patterns" and "design patterns." Such patterns are not ready-made solutions, but they feed your knowledge crunching process and narrow your search.

But I'll start Part III with the most exciting event in domain-driven design. Sometimes, when the stage is set with a MODEL-DRIVEN DESIGN and explicit concepts, you have a breakthrough. An opportunity opens up to transform your software into something more expressive and versatile than you expected. This can mean new features or it can just mean the replacement of a big chunk of rigid code with a simple, flexible expression of a deeper model. Although such breakthroughs don't come along every day, they are so valuable that when they do happen, the opportunity needs to be recognized and grasped.

Chapter 8 tells the true story of a project on which a process of refactoring toward deeper insight led to a breakthrough. This experience is not something you can plan for. Nonetheless, it provides a good context for thinking about domain refactoring.

EIGHT

Breakthrough

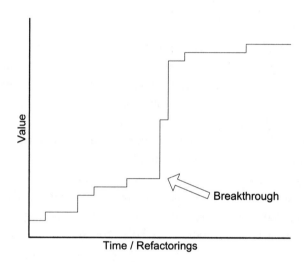

The returns from refactoring are not linear. Usually there is a marginal return for a small effort, and the small improvements add up. They fight entropy, and they are the frontline protection against a fossilized legacy. But some of the most important insights come abruptly and send a shock through the project.

Slowly but surely, the team assimilates knowledge and crunches it into a model. Deep models can emerge gradually through a sequence of small refactorings, an object at a time: a tweaked association here, a shifted responsibility there.

Often, though, continuous refactoring prepares the way for something less orderly. Each refinement of code and model gives developers a clearer view. This clarity creates the potential for a breakthrough of insights. A rush of change leads to a model that corresponds on a deeper level to the realities and priorities of the users. Versatility and explanatory power suddenly increase even as complexity evaporates.

This sort of breakthrough is not a technique; it is an event. The challenge lies in recognizing what is happening and deciding how to deal with it. To convey what this experience feels like, I'll tell a true story of a project I worked on some years ago, and how we arrived at a very valuable deep model.

Story of a Breakthrough

After a long New York winter of refactoring, we had arrived at a model that captured some of the key knowledge of the domain and a design that did some real work for the application. We were developing a core part of a large application for managing syndicated loans in an investment bank.

When Intel wants to build a billion-dollar factory, they need a loan that is too big for any single lending company to take on, so the lenders form a *syndicate* that pools its resources to support a *facility* (see sidebar). An investment bank usually acts as syndicate leader, coordinating transactions and other services. Our project was to build software to track and support this whole process.

A Decent Model, and Yet . . .

We were feeling pretty good. Four months before, we had been in deep trouble with a completely unworkable, inherited code base, which we had since wrestled into a coherent MODEL-DRIVEN DESIGN.

The model reflected in Figure 8.1 makes the common case very simple. The **Loan Investment** is a derived object that represents a particular investor's contribution to the **Loan,** proportional to its share in the **Facility.**

But there were some disconcerting signs. We kept stumbling over unexpected requirements that complicated the design. A major example was the creeping understanding that the shares in a **Facility** were only a *guideline* to participation in any particular loan drawdown. When the borrower requests its money, the leader of the syndicate calls all members for their shares.

What Is a "Facility"?
A "facility" in this context is not a building. As on most projects, specialized terminology from the domain experts entered our vocabulary and became part of the UBIQUITOUS LANGUAGE. In the domain of commercial banking, *a facility is a commitment by a company to lend.* Your credit card is a facility that entitles you to borrow on demand up to a prearranged limit at a predetermined interest rate. When you use the card, you create an outstanding loan, and each additional charge is a *drawdown* against your facility that increases the loan. Finally you pay back the loan principal. You may also pay an annual fee. This is a fee for the privilege of having the card (the facility) and is independent of your loan.

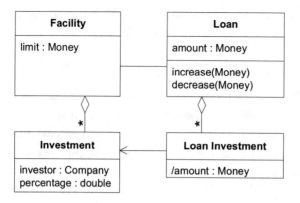

Figure 8.1
A model that assumes lender shares are fixed

When called, the investors usually cough up their share, but often they negotiate with other members of the syndicate and invest less (or more). We had accommodated this by adding **Loan Adjustments** to the model.

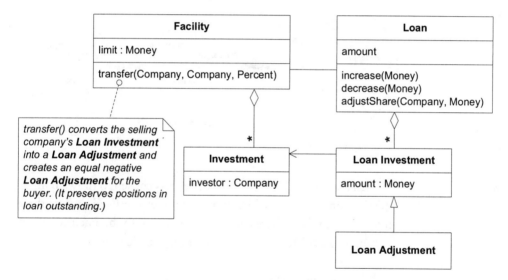

Figure 8.2
A model incrementally changed to solve problems. **Loan Adjustments** track departures from the share a lender originally agreed to in the **Facility**.

Refinements of this kind allowed us to keep up as the rules of various transactions became clearer. But complexity was increasing, and we did not seem to be converging quickly onto really solid functionality.

Even more troubling were subtle rounding inconsistencies that we had not been able to squash with increasingly complex algorithms. True, in a $100 million (MM) deal, no one cares about where the extra pennies go, but bankers don't trust software that cannot meticulously account for those pennies. We began to suspect that our difficulties were symptomatic of a basic design problem.

The Breakthrough

Suddenly one week it dawned on us what was wrong. Our model tied together the **Facility** and **Loan** shares in a way that was *not appropriate to the business*. This revelation had wide repercussions. With the business experts nodding, enthusiastically helping—and, I dare say, wondering what took us so long—we hashed out a new model on a whiteboard. Although the details hadn't jelled yet, we knew the crucial feature of the new model: shares of the **Loan** and those of the **Facility** could change independently of each other. With that insight, we walked through numerous scenarios using a visualization of the new model that looked something like this:

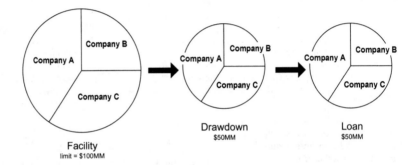

Figure 8.3
A drawdown distributed based on **Facility** shares

This diagram says that the borrower has chosen to draw an initial $50MM from the $100MM committed under the **Facility**. The three lenders chip in their shares in exact proportion to the **Facility** shares, resulting in a $50MM **Loan** divided among the lenders.

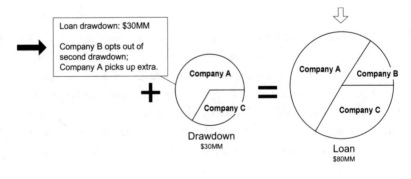

Figure 8.4
Lender B opts out of a second drawdown.

Then, in Figure 8.4, the borrower draws an additional $30MM, bringing his outstanding **Loan** to $80MM, still under the $100MM limit of the **Facility**. This time, Company B chooses not to participate, letting Company A take an extra share. The shares of the drawdown reflect these investment choices. When the drawdown amounts are added to the **Loan**, the shares of the **Loan** are no longer proportional to the shares of the **Facility**. This is common.

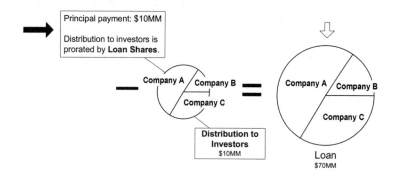

Figure 8.5
Principal payments are always distributed proportional to shares in the outstanding **Loan**.

When the borrower pays down the **Loan**, the money is divided among the lenders according to the shares of the **Loan**, not the **Facility**. Likewise, interest payments will be divided according to the **Loan** shares.

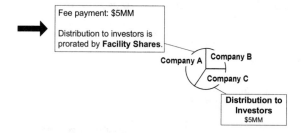

Figure 8.6
Fee payments are always distributed proportionally to shares in the **Facility**.

On the other hand, when the borrower pays a fee for the privilege of having the **Facility** available, this money is divided according to the **Facility** shares, regardless of who actually has lent money. The **Loan** is unchanged by fee payments. There are even scenarios in which lenders trade shares of fees separately from their shares of interest, and so on.

A Deeper Model

We had two deep insights. First was the realization that our "Investments" and "Loan Investments" were just two special cases of a general and fundamental concept: shares. Shares of a facility, shares of a loan, shares of a *payment distribution*. Shares, shares everywhere. Shares of any divisible value.

A few tumultuous days later I had sketched a model of shares, drawing on the language used in the discussions with experts and the scenarios we had explored together.

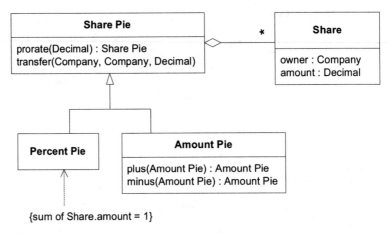

Figure 8.7
An abstract model of shares

I also sketched a new loan model to go with it.

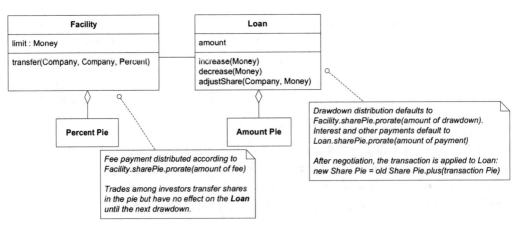

Figure 8.8
The **Loan** model using **Share Pie**

There were no longer specialized objects for the shares of a **Facility** or a **Loan**. They both were broken down into the more intuitive "**Share Pie.**" This generalization allowed the introduction of "shares math," vastly simplifying the calculation of shares in any transaction, and making those calculations more expressive, concise, and easily combined.

But most of all, problems went away because the new model removed an inappropriate constraint. It freed the **Loan's Shares** to depart from the proportions of the **Facility's Shares**, while keeping in place the valid constraints on totals, fee distributions, and so on. The **Share Pie** of the **Loan** could be adjusted directly, so the **Loan Adjustment** was no longer needed, and a large amount of special-case logic was eliminated.

The **Loan Investment** had disappeared, and at this point we realized that "loan investment" was not a banking term. In fact, the business experts had told us a number of times that they didn't understand it. They had deferred to our software knowledge and assumed it was useful to the technical design. Actually, we had created it based on our incomplete understanding of the domain.

Suddenly, on the basis of this new way of looking at the domain, we could run through every scenario we had ever encountered relatively effortlessly, much more simply than ever before. *And our model diagrams made perfect sense to the business experts, who had often indicated that the diagrams were "too technical" for them.* Even just sketching on a whiteboard, we could see that our most persistent rounding problems would be pulled out by the roots, allowing us to scrap some of the complicated rounding code.

Our new model worked well. Really, really well.

And we all felt sick!

A Sobering Decision

You might reasonably assume that we would have been elated at this point. We were not. We were under a severe deadline; the project was already dangerously behind schedule. Our dominant emotion was fear.

The gospel of refactoring is that you always go in small steps, always keeping everything working. But to refactor our code to this new model would require changing a lot of supporting code, and there would be few, if any, stable stopping points in between. We could see some small improvements we could make, but none that would take us closer to the new concept. We could see a sequence of small steps to get there, but parts of the application would be disabled along the way. And this was before the age when automated tests were widely used on such projects. We had none, so there was bound to be unforeseen breakage.

And it was going to take effort. We were already exhausted from months of pushing.

At this point, we had a meeting with our project manager that I will never forget. Our manager was an intelligent and bold man. He asked a series of questions:

Q: How long would it take to get back to current functionality with the new design?

A: About three weeks.

Q: Could we solve the problems without it?

A: Probably. But no way to be sure.

Q: Would we be able to move forward in the next release if we didn't do it now?

A: Forward movement would be slow without the change. And the change would be much harder once we had an installed base.

Q: Did *we* think it was the right thing to do?

A: We knew the political situation was unstable, so we'd cope if we had to. And we were tired. But, yes, it was a simpler solution that fit the business much better. In the long run it was lower risk.

He gave us the go-ahead and told us he would handle the heat. I've always had tremendous admiration for the courage and trust it took for him to make that decision.

We busted our butts and got it done in three weeks. It was a big job, but it went surprisingly smoothly.

The Payoff

The mystifyingly unexpected requirement changes stopped. The rounding logic, though never exactly simple, stabilized and made sense. We delivered version one and the way was clear to version two. My nervous breakdown was narrowly averted.

As version two evolved, this **Share Pie** became the unifying theme of the whole application. Technical people and business experts used it to discuss the system. *Marketing people used it to explain the features to prospective customers.* Those prospects and customers immediately grasped it and used it to discuss features. It truly became part of the UBIQUITOUS LANGUAGE because it got to the heart of what loan syndication is about.

Opportunities

When the prospect of a breakthrough to a deeper model presents itself, it is often scary. Such a change has higher opportunity *and* higher risk than most refactorings. And timing may be inopportune.

Much as we might like it to be otherwise, progress isn't a smooth ride. The transition to a really deep model is a profound shift in your thinking and demands a major change to the design. On many projects the most important progress in model and design come in these breakthroughs.

Focus on Basics

Don't become paralyzed trying to bring about a breakthrough. The possibility usually comes after many modest refactorings. Most of the time is spent making piecemeal improvements, with model insights emerging gradually during each successive refinement.

To set the stage for a breakthrough, concentrate on knowledge crunching and cultivating a robust UBIQUITOUS LANGUAGE. Probe for important domain concepts and make them explicit in the model (as discussed in Chapter 9). Refine the design to be suppler (see Chapter 10). Distill the model (see Chapter 15). Push on these more predictable levers, which increase clarity—usually a precursor of breakthroughs.

Don't hold back from modest improvements, which gradually deepen the model, even if confined within the same general conceptual framework. Don't be paralyzed by looking too far forward. Just be watchful for the opportunity.

Epilogue: A Cascade of New Insights

That breakthrough got us out of the woods, but it was not the end of the story. The deeper model opened unexpected opportunities to make the application richer and the design clearer.

Just weeks after the release of the **Share Pie** version of the software, we noticed another awkward aspect of the model that was complicating the design. An important ENTITY was missing, its absence leaving extra responsibilities to be taken up by other objects. Specifically, there were significant rules governing loan drawdowns, fee payments, and so on, and all this logic was crammed into various methods on the **Facility** and **Loan**. These design problems, which had been barely noticeable before the **Share Pie** breakthrough, became obvious with our clearer field of vision. Now we noticed terms popping up in our discussions that were nowhere to be found in the model—terms such as "transaction" (meaning a financial transaction)—that we started to realize were being implied by all those complicated methods.

Following a process similar to the one described earlier (although, thankfully, under much less time pressure) led to yet another round of insights and a still deeper model. This new model made those implicit concepts explicit, as kinds of **Transactions**, and at the same time simplified the **Positions** (an abstraction including the **Facility** and **Loan**). It became easy to define the diverse transactions we

Figure 8.9
Another model break-through that followed several weeks later. Constraints on **Transactions** could be expressed with easy precision.

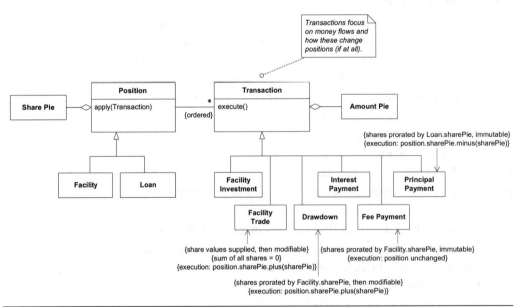

CHAPTER 8: BREAKTHROUGH

had, along with their rules, negotiating procedures, and approval processes, and all in relatively self-explanatory code.

As is often the case after a real breakthrough to a deep model, the clarity and simplicity of the new design, combined with the enhanced communication based on the new UBIQUITOUS LANGUAGE, had led to yet another modeling breakthrough.

Our pace of development was accelerating at a stage where most projects are beginning to bog down in the mass and complexity of what has already been built.

NINE

Making Implicit
Concepts Explicit

Deep modeling sounds great, but how do you actually do it? A deep model has power because it contains the central concepts and abstractions that can succinctly and flexibly express essential knowledge of the users' activities, their problems, and their solutions. The first step is to somehow represent the essential concepts of the domain in the model. Refinement comes later, after successive iterations of knowledge crunching and refactoring. But this process really gets into gear when an important concept is recognized and made explicit in the model and design.

Many transformations of domain models and the corresponding code happen when developers recognize a concept that has been hinted at in discussion or present implicitly in the design, and they then represent it explicitly in the model with one or more objects or relationships.

Occasionally, this transformation of a formerly implicit concept into an explicit one is a breakthrough that leads to a deep model. More often, though, the breakthrough comes later, after a number of important concepts are explicit in the model; after successive refactorings have tweaked their responsibilities repeatedly, changed their relationships with other objects, and even changed their names a few times. Everything finally snaps into focus. But the process starts with recognizing the implied concepts in some form, however crude.

Digging Out Concepts

Developers have to sensitize themselves to the hints that reveal lurking implicit concepts, and sometimes they have to proactively search them out. Most such discoveries come from listening to the language of the team, scrutinizing awkwardness in the design and seeming contradictions in the statements of experts, mining the literature of the domain, and doing lots and lots of experimentation.

Listen to Language

You may remember an experience like this: The users have always talked about some item on a report. The item is compiled from attributes of various objects and maybe even a direct database query. The same data set is assembled in another part of the application in order to present or report or derive something. But you have never seen the need for an object. Probably, you have never really understood what the users meant by a particular term and had not realized it was important.

Then suddenly a light comes on in your head. The name of the item on that report designates an important domain concept. You talk excitedly with your experts about your new insight. Maybe they show relief that you finally got it. Maybe they yawn because they've taken it for granted all along. Either way, you start to draw model diagrams on the board that fill in for some hand waving that you've always done before. The users correct you on the details of how the new model connects, but you can tell that there is a change in the quality of the discussion. You and the users understand each other more precisely, and demonstrations of model interactions to solve specific scenarios have become more natural. The language of the domain model has become more powerful. You refactor the code to reflect the new model and find you have a cleaner design.

Listen to the language the domain experts use. Are there terms that succinctly state something complicated? Are they correcting your word choice (perhaps diplomatically)? Do the puzzled looks on their faces go away when you use a particular phrase? These are hints of a concept that might benefit the model.

This is *not* the old "nouns are objects" notion. Hearing a new word produces a lead, which you follow up with conversation and knowledge crunching, with the goal of carving out a clean, useful concept. When the users or domain experts use vocabulary that is nowhere in the design, that is a warning sign. It is a doubly strong warning when both the developers and the domain experts are using terms that are not in the design.

Or perhaps it is better to look at it as an opportunity. The UBIQUITOUS LANGUAGE is made up of the vocabulary that pervades speech, documents, model diagrams, and even code. If a term is absent from the design, it is an opportunity to improve the model and design by including it.

Example

Hearing a Missing Concept in the Shipping Model

The team had already developed a working application that could book a cargo. They were starting to build an "operations support" application that would help juggle the work orders for loading and unloading cargos at the origin and destination and at transfers between ships.

The booking application used a routing engine to plan the trip for a cargo. Each leg of the journey was stored in a row of a database table, indicating the ID of the vessel voyage (a particular voyage by a particular ship) slated to carry the cargo, the location where it would be loaded, and the location where it would be unloaded.

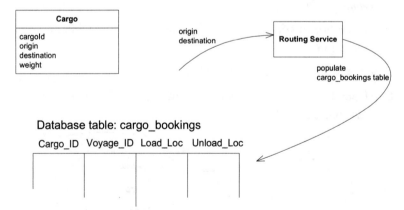

Figure 9.1

Let's eavesdrop on a conversation (heavily abbreviated) between the developer and a shipping expert.

Developer: I want to make sure the "cargo bookings" table has all the data that the operations application will need.

Expert: They're going to need the whole itinerary for the **Cargo**. What information does it have now?

Developer: The cargo ID, the vessel voyage, the loading port, and the unloading port for each leg.

Expert: What about the date? Operations will need to contract handling work based on the expected times.

Developer: Well, that can be derived from the schedule of the vessel voyage. The table data is normalized.

Expert: Yes, it is normal to need the date. Operations people use these kinds of itineraries to plan for upcoming handling work.

Developer: Yeah . . . OK, they'll definitely have access to the dates. The operations management application will be able to provide the whole loading and unloading sequence, with the date of each handling operation. The "itinerary," I guess you would say.

Expert: Good. The itinerary is the main thing they'll need. Actually, you know, the booking application has a menu item that will print an itinerary or e-mail it to the customer. Can you use that somehow?

Developer: That's just a report, I think. We won't be able to base the operations application on that.

[*Developer looks thoughtful, then excited.*]

Developer: So, this itinerary is really the link between booking and operations.

Expert: Yes, and some customer relations, too.

Developer: [*Sketching a diagram on the whiteboard.*] So would you say it is something like this?

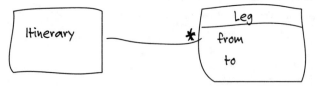

Figure 9.2

Expert: Yes, that looks basically right. For each leg you'd like to see the vessel voyage, the load and unload location, and time.

Developer: So once we create the **Leg** object, it can derive the times from the vessel voyage schedule. We can make the **Itinerary** object our main point of contact with the operations application. And we can rewrite that itinerary report to use this, so we'll get the domain logic back into the domain layer.

Expert: I didn't follow all of that, but you are right that the two main uses for the **Itinerary** are in the report in booking and in the operations application.

Developer: Hey! We can make the **Routing Service** interface return an itinerary object instead of putting the data in the database table. That way the routing engine doesn't need to know about our tables.

Expert: Huh?

Developer: I mean, I'll make the routing engine just return an **Itinerary**. Then it can be saved in the database by the booking application when the rest of the booking is saved.

Expert: You mean it isn't that way now?!

The developer then went off to talk with the other developers involved in the routing process. They hashed out the changes to the model and the implications for the design, calling on the shipping experts when needed. They came up with the diagram in Figure 9.3.

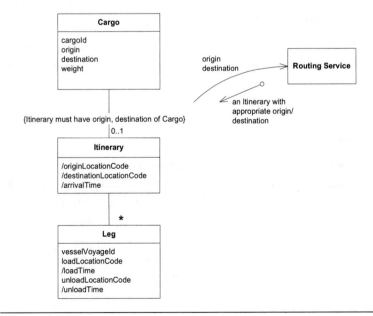

Figure 9.3

Next, the developers refactored the code to reflect the new model. They did it in a series of two or three refactorings, but in quick succession, within a week, except for simplifying the itinerary report in the booking application, which they took care of early the following week.

The developer had been listening closely enough to the shipping expert to notice how important the concept of an "itinerary" was to him. True, all the data was already being collected, and the behavior was implicit in the itinerary report, but the explicit **Itinerary** as part of the model opened up opportunities.

Benefits of refactoring to the explicit **Itinerary** object:

1. Defining the interface of the **Routing Service** more expressively

2. Decoupling the **Routing Service** from the booking database tables

3. Clarifying the relationship between the booking application and the operations support application (the sharing of the **Itinerary** object)

4. Reducing duplication, because the **Itinerary** derives loading/unloading times for both the booking report and the operations support application

5. Removing domain logic from the booking report and placing it in the isolated domain layer

6. Expanding the UBIQUITOUS LANGUAGE, allowing a more precise discussion of the model and design between developers and domain experts and among the developers themselves

Scrutinize Awkwardness

The concept you need is not always floating on the surface, emerging in conversation or documents. You may have to dig and invent. The place to dig is the most awkward part of your design. The place where procedures are doing complicated things that are hard to explain. The place where every new requirement seems to add complexity.

Sometimes it can be hard to recognize that there even is a missing concept. You may have objects doing all the work but find some of the responsibilities awkward. Or, if you do realize something is missing, a model solution may elude you.

Now you have to actively engage the domain experts in the search. If you are lucky, they may enjoy playing with ideas and experimenting with the model. If you are not that lucky, you and your fellow developers will have to come up with the ideas, using the domain expert as a validator, watching for discomfort or recognition on his or her face.

Example

Earning Interest the Hard Way

The next story is set in a hypothetical financial company that invests in commercial loans and other interest-bearing assets. An application that tracks those investments and the earnings from them has been evolving incrementally, feature by feature. Each night, one component was to run as a batch script, calculating all interest and fees for the day and then recording them appropriately in the company's accounting software.

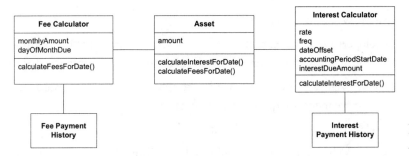

Figure 9.4
An awkward model

The nightly batch script iterated through each **Asset**, telling each to calculateInterestForDate() on that day's date. The script took the return value (the amount earned) and passed this amount, along with the name of a specific ledger, to a SERVICE that provided the public interface of the accounting program. That software posted the amount to the named ledger. The script went through a similar process to get the day's fees from each **Asset**, posting them to a different ledger.

A developer had been struggling with the increasing complexity of calculating interest. She started to suspect an opportunity for a model better suited to the task. This developer asked her favorite domain expert to help her dig into the problem area.

Developer: Our **Interest Calculator** is getting out of hand.

Expert: That is a complicated part. We still have more cases we've been holding back.

Developer: I know. We can add new interest types by substituting a different **Interest Calculator.** But what we're having the most trouble with right now is all these special cases when they don't pay the interest on schedule.

Expert: Those really aren't special cases. There's a lot of flexibility in when people pay.

Developer: Back when we factored out the **Interest Calculator** from the **Asset**, it helped a lot. We may need to break it up more.

Expert: OK.

Developer: I was thinking you might have a way of talking about this interest calculation.

Expert: What do you mean?

Developer: Well, for example, we're tracking the interest due but unpaid within an accounting period. Do you have a name for that?

Expert: Well, we don't really do it like that. The interest earned and the payment are quite separate postings.

Developer: So you don't need that number?

Expert: Well, sometimes we might look at it, but it isn't the way we do business.

Developer: OK, so if the payment and interest are separate, maybe we should model them that way. How does this look? [*Sketching on whiteboard*]

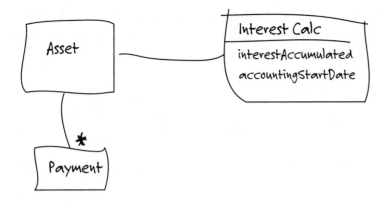

Figure 9.5

Expert: It makes sense, I guess. But you just moved it from one place to another.

Developer: Except now the **Interest Calculator** only keeps track of interest earned, and the **Payment** keeps that number separately. It hasn't simplified it a lot, but does it better reflect your business practice?

Expert: Ah. I see. Could we have interest history, too? Like the **Payment History**.

Developer: Yes, that has been requested as a new feature. But that could have been added onto the original design.

Expert: Oh. Well, when I saw interest and **Payment History** separated like that, I thought you were breaking up the interest to organize it more like the **Payment History**. Do you know anything about accrual basis accounting?

Developer: Please explain.

Expert: Each day, or whenever the schedule calls for, we have an interest accrual that gets posted to a ledger. The payments are posted a different way. This aggregate you have here is a little awkward.

Developer: You're saying that if we keep a list of "accruals," they could be aggregated or . . . "posted" as needed.

Expert: Probably posted on the accrual date, but yes, aggregated anytime. Fees work the same way, posted to a different ledger, of course.

Developer: Actually, the interest calculation would be simpler if it was done just for one day, or period. And then we could just hang on to them all. How about this?

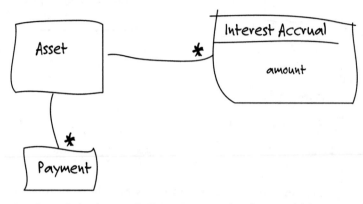

Figure 9.6

Expert: Sure. It looks good. I'm not sure why this would be easier for you. But basically, what makes any asset valuable is what it can accrue in interest, fees, and so on.

Developer: You said fees work the same way? They . . . what was it . . . post to different ledgers?

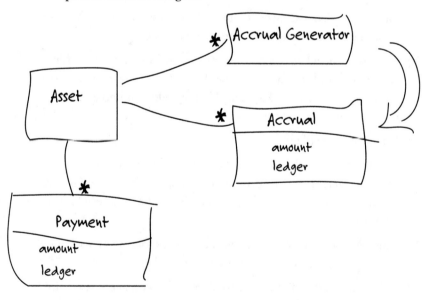

Figure 9.7

Developer: With this model, we get the interest calculation, or rather, the accrual calculation logic that was in the **Interest Calculator** separated from tracking. And I hadn't noticed until now how much duplication there is in the **Fee Calculator**. Also, now the different kinds of fees can easily be added.

Expert: Yes, the calculation was correct before, but I can see everything now.

Because the **Calculator** classes hadn't been directly coupled with other parts of the design, this was a fairly easy refactoring. The developer was able to rewrite the unit tests to use the new language in a few hours and had the new design working late the next day. She ended up with this.

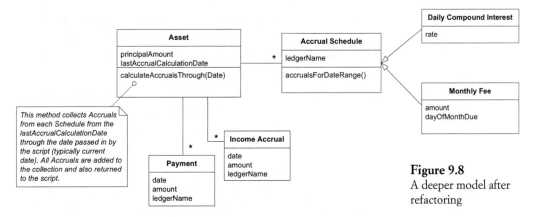

Figure 9.8
A deeper model after refactoring

In the refactored application, the nightly batch script tells each **Asset** to `calculateAccrualsThroughDate()`. The return value is a collection of **Accruals**, each of whose amounts it posts to the indicated ledger.

The new model has several advantages. The change

1. Enriches the UBIQUITOUS LANGUAGE with the term "accrual"

2. Decouples accrual from payment

3. Moves domain knowledge (such as which ledger to post to) from the script and into the domain layer

4. Brings fees and interest together in a way that fits the business and eliminates duplication in the code

5. Provides a straightforward path for adding new variations of fees and interest as **Accrual Schedules**

This time, the developer had to dig for the new concepts she needed. She could see the awkwardness of the interest calculations and made a committed effort to look for a deeper answer.

She was lucky to have an intelligent and motivated partner in the banking expert. With a more passive source of expertise, she would have made more false starts and depended more on other developers as brainstorming partners. Progress would have been slower, but still possible.

Contemplate Contradictions

Different domain experts see things different ways based on their experience and needs. Even the same person provides information that is logically inconsistent after careful analysis. Such pesky contradictions, which we encounter all the time when digging into program requirements, can be great clues to deeper models. Some are just variations in terminology or are based on misunderstanding. But there is a residue where two factual statements by experts seem to contradict.

The astronomer Galileo once posed a paradox. The evidence of the senses clearly indicates that the Earth is stationary: people are not being blown off and falling behind. Yet Copernicus had made a compelling argument that the Earth was moving around the sun quite rapidly. Reconciling this might reveal something profound about how nature works.

Galileo devised a thought experiment. If a rider dropped a ball from a running horse, where would it fall? Of course, the ball would move along with the horse until it hit the ground by the horse's feet, just as if the horse were standing still. From this he deduced an early form of the idea of inertial frames of reference, solving the paradox and leading to a much more useful model of the physics of motion.

OK. Our contradictions are usually not so interesting, nor the implications so profound. Even so, this same pattern of thought often helps pierce the superficial layers of a problem domain into a deeper insight.

It is not practical to reconcile all contradictions, and it may not even be desirable. (Chapter 14 delves into how to decide and how to manage the result.) However, even when a contradiction is left in place, contemplation of how two statements could both apply to the same external reality can be revealing.

Read the Book

Don't overlook the obvious when seeking model concepts. In many fields, you can find books that explain the fundamental concepts and conventional wisdom. You still have to work with your own domain experts to distill the part relevant to your problem and to crunch it into something suited to object-oriented software. But you may be able to start with a coherent, deeply considered view.

Example

Earning Interest by the Book

Let's imagine a different scenario for the investment-tracking application discussed in the previous example. Just as before, the story starts with the developer realizing that the design is getting unwieldy, particularly the **Interest Calculator**. But in this scenario, the domain expert's primary responsibilities lie elsewhere, and he doesn't have much interest in helping the software development project. In this scenario, the developer couldn't turn to the expert for a brainstorming session to probe for the missing concepts she suspected to be lurking under the surface.

Instead, she went to the bookstore. After a little browsing, she found an introductory accounting book she liked, and she skimmed it. She discovered a whole system of well-defined concepts. An excerpt that particularly fired her thinking:

> **Accrual Basis Accounting.** This method recognizes income when it is earned, even if it is not paid. *All* expenses also show when they are incurred whether they have been paid for or billed to be paid at a later date. Any obligation due, including taxes, will be shown as expense.
> —*Finance and Accounting: How to Keep Your Books and Manage Your Finances Without an MBA, a CPA or a Ph.D.,* by Suzanne Caplan (Adams Media, 2000)

The developer no longer needed to reinvent accounting. After some brainstorming with another developer, she came up with a model.

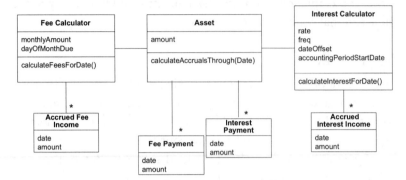

Figure 9.9
A somewhat deeper model based on book learning

She did not have the insight that **Assets** are income generators, and so the **Calculators** are still there. The knowledge of ledgers is still in the application, rather than the domain layer where it probably belongs. But she did separate the issue of payment from the accrual of income, which was the most problematic area, and she introduced the word "accrual" into the model and into the UBIQUITOUS LANGUAGE. Further refinement could come with later iterations.

When she did finally have the chance to talk with the domain expert, he was quite surprised. It was the first time a programmer had shown a glimmer of interest in what he did. Due to the way his responsibilities were assigned, the expert never engaged with her, sitting down to go over the model, as happened in the previous scenario. However, because this developer's knowledge allowed her to ask better questions, from then on the expert did listen to her carefully, and he made a special effort to answer her questions promptly.

Of course, this is not an either-or proposition. Even with ample support from domain experts, it pays to look at the literature to get a grasp of the theory of the field. Most businesses do not have models refined to the level of accounting or finance, but in many there have been thinkers in the field who have organized and abstracted the common practices of the business.

Yet another option the developer had was to read something written by another software professional with development experience in this domain. For example, Chapter 6 of the book *Analysis Patterns: Reusable Object Models* (Fowler 1997) would have sent her in quite a different direction, not necessarily better or worse. Such reading would not have provided an off-the-shelf solution. It would have given several new starting points for her own experiments, along with the distilled experience of people who have traveled the territory. She would have been spared reinventing the wheel. Chapter 11, "Applying Analysis Patterns," will delve further into this option.

Try, Try Again

The examples I've given don't convey the amount of trial and error involved. I might follow half a dozen leads in conversation before finding one that seems clear and useful enough to try out in the model. I'll end up replacing that one at least once later, as additional experience and knowledge crunching serve up better ideas. A modeler/designer cannot afford to get attached to his own ideas.

All these changes of direction are not just thrashing. Each change embeds deeper insight into the model. Each refactoring leaves the design more supple, easier to change the next time, ready to bend in the places that turn out to need to bend.

There really is no choice, anyway. Experimentation is the way to learn what works and doesn't. Trying to avoid missteps in design will result in a lower quality result because it will be based on less experience. And it can easily take longer than a series of quick experiments.

How to Model Less Obvious Kinds of Concepts

The object-oriented paradigm leads us to look for and invent certain kinds of concepts. Things, even very abstract ones such as "accruals," are the meat of most object models, along with the actions those things take. These are the "nouns and verbs" that introductory object-oriented design books talk about. But other important categories of concepts can be made explicit in a model as well.

I'll discuss three such categories that were not obvious to me when I started with objects. My designs became sharper with each one of these I learned.

Explicit Constraints

Constraints make up a particularly important category of model concepts. They often emerge implicitly, and expressing them explicitly can greatly improve a design.

Sometimes constraints find a natural home in an object or method. A "Bucket" object must guarantee the invariant that it does not hold more than its capacity.

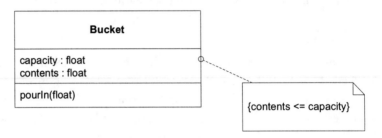

Figure 9.10

A simple invariant like this can be enforced using case logic in each operation capable of changing contents.

```
class Bucket  {
   private float capacity;
   private float contents;

   public void pourIn(float addedVolume) {
      if (contents + addedVolume > capacity) {
         contents = capacity;
      } else {
         contents = contents + addedVolume;
      }
   }
}
```

This logic is so simple that the rule is obvious. But you can easily imagine this constraint getting lost in a more complicated class. Let's factor it into a separate method, with a name that clearly and explicitly expresses the significance of the constraint.

```
class Bucket  {
   private float capacity;
   private float contents;
```

```
public void pourIn(float addedVolume) {
    float volumePresent = contents + addedVolume;
    contents = constrainedToCapacity(volumePresent);
}

private float constrainedToCapacity(float volumePlacedIn) {
    if (volumePlacedIn > capacity) return capacity;
    return volumePlacedIn;
}
}
```

Both versions of this code enforce the constraint, but the second has a more obvious relationship to the model (the basic requirement of MODEL-DRIVEN DESIGN). This very simple rule was understandable in its original form, but when the rules being enforced are more complex, they start to overwhelm the object or operation they apply to, as any implicit concept does. Factoring the constraint into its own method allows us to give it an intention-revealing name that makes the constraint explicit in our design. It is now a named thing we can discuss. This approach also gives the constraint room. A more complex rule than this might easily produce a method longer than its caller (the pourIn() method, in this case). This way, the caller stays simple and focused on its task while the constraint can grow in complexity if need be.

This separate method gives the constraint some room to grow, but there are lots of cases when a constraint just can't fit comfortably in a single method. Or even if the method stays simple, it may call on information that the object doesn't need for its primary responsibility. The rule may just have no good home in an existing object.

Here are some warning signs that a constraint is distorting the design of its host object.

1. Evaluating a constraint requires data that does not otherwise fit the object's definition.

2. Related rules appear in multiple objects, forcing duplication or inheritance between objects that are not otherwise a family.

3. A lot of design and requirements conversation revolves around the constraints, but in the implementation, they are hidden away in procedural code.

When the constraints are obscuring the object's basic responsibility, or when the constraint is prominent in the domain yet not prominent in the model, you can factor it out into an explicit object or even model it as a set of objects and relationships. (One in-depth, semiformal treatment of this subject can be found in *The Object Constraint Language: Precise Modeling with UML* [Warmer and Kleppe 1999].)

Example

Review: Overbooking Policy

In Chapter 1, we worked with a common shipping business practice: booking 10 percent more cargo than the transports could handle. (Experience has taught shipping firms that this overbooking compensates for last-minute cancellations, so their ships will sail nearly full.)

This constraint on the association between **Voyage** and **Cargo** was made explicit, both in the diagrams and in the code, by adding a new class that represented the constraint.

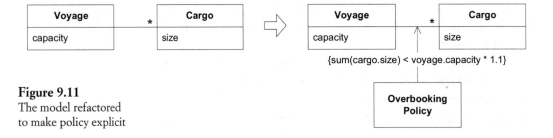

Figure 9.11
The model refactored
to make policy explicit

To review the code and reasoning in the full example, see page 17.

Processes as Domain Objects

Right up front, let's agree that we do *not* want to make procedures a prominent aspect of our model. Objects are meant to encapsulate the procedures and let us think about their goals or intentions instead.

What I am talking about here are processes that exist in the domain, which we have to represent in the model. When these emerge, they tend to make for awkward object designs.

The first example in this chapter described a shipping system that routed cargo. This routing process was something with business meaning. A SERVICE is one way of expressing such a process explicitly, while still encapsulating the extremely complex algorithms.

When there is more than one way to carry out a process, another approach is to make the algorithm itself, or some key part of it, an object in its own right. The choice between processes becomes a choice between these objects, each of which represents a different STRATEGY. (Chapter 12 will look in more detail at the use of STRATEGIES in the domain.)

The key to distinguishing a process that ought to be made explicit from one that should be hidden is simple: Is this something the domain experts talk about, or is it just part of the mechanism of the computer program?

Constraints and processes are two broad categories of model concepts that don't come leaping to mind when programming in an object-oriented language, yet they can really sharpen up a design once we start thinking about them as model elements.

Some useful categories of concepts are much narrower. I'll round out this chapter with one much more specific, yet quite common. SPECIFICATION provides a concise way of expressing certain kinds of rules, extricating them from conditional logic and making them explicit in the model.

I developed SPECIFICATION in collaboration with Martin Fowler (Evans and Fowler 1997). The simplicity of the concept belies the subtlety in application and implementation, so there is a lot of detail in this section. There will be even more discussion in Chapter 10, where the pattern is extended. After reading the initial explanation of the pattern that follows, you may want to skim the "Applying and Implementing SPECIFICATIONS" section, until you are actually attempting to apply the pattern.

SPECIFICATION

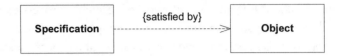

In all kinds of applications, Boolean test methods appear that are really parts of little rules. As long as they are simple, we handle them with testing methods, such as `anIterator.hasNext()` or `anInvoice.isOverdue()`. In an **Invoice** class, the code in `isOverdue()` is an algorithm that evaluates a rule. For example,

```
public boolean isOverdue() {
    Date currentDate = new Date();
    return currentDate.after(dueDate);
}
```

But not all rules are so simple. On the same **Invoice** class, another rule, `anInvoice.isDelinquent()` would presumably start with testing if the **Invoice** is overdue, but that would just be the beginning. A policy on grace periods could depend on the status of the customer's account. Some delinquent invoices will be ready for a second notice, while others will be ready to be sent to a collection agency. The payment history of the customer, company policy on different product lines . . . the clarity of **Invoice** as a request for payment will soon be lost in the sheer mass of rule evaluation code. The **Invoice** will also develop all sorts of dependencies on domain classes and subsystems that do not support that basic meaning.

At this point, in an attempt to save the **Invoice** class, a developer will often refactor the rule evaluation code into the application layer (in this case, a bill collection application). Now the rules have been separated from the domain layer altogether, leaving behind a dead data object that does not express the rules inherent in the business model. These rules need to stay in the domain layer, but they don't fit into the object being evaluated (the **Invoice** in this case). Not only that, but evaluating methods swell with conditional code, which make the rule hard to read.

Developers working in the logic-programming paradigm would handle this situation differently. Such rules would be expressed as *predicates*. Predicates are functions that evaluate to "true" or "false" and can be combined using operators such as "AND" and "OR" to express more complex rules. With predicates, we could declare rules explicitly and use them with the **Invoice**. If only we were in the logic paradigm.

Seeing this, people have made attempts at implementing logical rules in terms of objects. Some such attempts were very sophisticated, others naive. Some were ambitious, others modest. Some turned out valuable, some were tossed aside as failed experiments. A few attempts were allowed to derail their projects. One thing is clear: As appealing as the idea is, full implementation of logic in objects is a major undertaking. (After all, logic programming is a whole modeling and design paradigm in its own right.)

Business rules often do not fit the responsibility of any of the obvious ENTITIES **or** VALUE OBJECTS, **and their variety and combinations can overwhelm the basic meaning of the domain object. But moving the rules out of the domain layer is even worse, since the domain code no longer expresses the model.**

Logic programming provides the concept of separate, combinable, rule objects called "predicates," but full implementation of this concept with objects is cumbersome. It is also so general that it doesn't communicate intent as much as more specialized designs.

Fortunately, we don't really need to fully implement logic programming to get a large benefit. Most of our rules fall into a few special cases. We can borrow the concept of predicates and create specialized objects that evaluate to a Boolean. Those testing methods that get out of hand will neatly expand into objects of their own. They are little truth tests that can be factored out into a separate VALUE OBJECT. This new object can evaluate another object to see if the predicate is true for that object.

Figure 9.12

To put it another way, the new object is a *specification*. A SPECIFICATION states a constraint on the state of another object, which may or may not be present. It has multiple uses, but one that conveys the most basic concept is that a SPECIFICATION can test any object to see if it satisfies the specified criteria.

Therefore:

Create explicit predicate-like VALUE OBJECTS for specialized purposes. A SPECIFICATION is a predicate that determines if an object does or does not satisfy some criteria.

Many SPECIFICATIONS are simple, special-purpose tests, as in the delinquent invoice example. In cases where the rules are complex, the concept can be extended to allow simple specifications to be combined, just as predicates are combined with logical operators. (This technique will be discussed in the next chapter.) The fundamental pattern stays the same and provides a path from the simpler to more complex models.

The case of the delinquent invoice can be modeled using a SPECIFICATION that states what it means to be delinquent and that can evaluate any **Invoice** and make the determination.

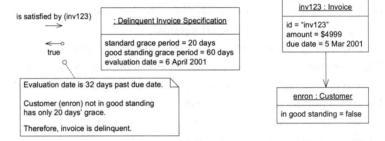

Figure 9.13
A more elaborate delinquency rule factored out as a SPECIFICATION

The SPECIFICATION keeps the rule in the domain layer. Because the rule is a full-fledged object, the design can be a more explicit reflection of the model. A FACTORY can configure a SPECIFICATION using information from other sources, such as the customer's account or the corporate policy database. Providing direct access to these sources from the **Invoice** would couple the objects in a way that does not relate to the request for payment (the basic responsibility of **Invoice**). In this case, the **Delinquent Invoice Specification** was to be created, used to evaluate some **Invoices**, and then discarded, so a specific evaluation date was built right in—a nice simplification. A SPECIFICATION can be given the information it will need to do its job in a simple, straightforward way.

✳ ✳ ✳

The basic concept of SPECIFICATION is very simple and helps us think about a domain modeling problem. But a MODEL-DRIVEN DESIGN requires an effective implementation that also expresses the concept. To pull that off requires digging a little deeper into how the pattern will be applied. A domain pattern is not just a neat idea for a UML diagram; it is a solution to a programming problem that retains a MODEL-DRIVEN DESIGN.

When you apply a pattern appropriately, you can tap into a whole body of thought about how to approach a class of domain modeling problem, and you can benefit from years of experience in finding effective implementations. There is a lot of detail in the discussion of SPECIFICATION that follows: many options for features and approaches to implementation. A pattern is not a cookbook. It lets you start from a base of experience to develop your solution, and it gives you some language to talk about what you are doing.

You may want to skim the key concepts when first reading. Later, when you run into the situation, you can come back and draw on the experience captured in the detailed discussion. Then you can go and figure out a solution to your problem.

Applying and Implementing SPECIFICATION

Much of the value of SPECIFICATION is that it unifies application functionality that may seem quite different. We might need to specify the state of an object for one or more of these three purposes.

1. To validate an object to see if it fulfills some need or is ready for some purpose

2. To select an object from a collection (as in the case of querying for overdue invoices)

3. To specify the creation of a new object to fit some need

These three uses—validation, selection, and building to order— are the same on a conceptual level. Without a pattern such as SPECIFICATION, the same rule may show up in different guises, and possibly contradictory forms. The conceptual unity can be lost. Applying the SPECIFICATION pattern allows a consistent model to be used, even when the implementation may have to diverge.

Validation

The simplest use of a SPECIFICATION is validation, and it is the use that demonstrates the concept most straightforwardly.

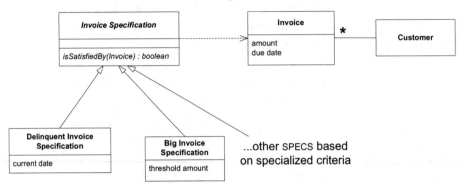

Figure 9.14
A model applying a
SPECIFICATION for
validation

```
class DelinquentInvoiceSpecification extends
        InvoiceSpecification {
    private Date currentDate;
    // An instance is used and discarded on a single date

    public DelinquentInvoiceSpecification(Date currentDate) {
        this.currentDate = currentDate;
    }

    public boolean isSatisfiedBy(Invoice candidate) {
        int gracePeriod =
            candidate.customer().getPaymentGracePeriod();
        Date firmDeadline =
            DateUtility.addDaysToDate(candidate.dueDate(),
                gracePeriod);
        return currentDate.after(firmDeadline);
    }

}
```

Now, suppose we need to display a red flag whenever a salesperson brings up a customer with delinquent bills. We just have to write a method in a client class, something like this.

```
public boolean accountIsDelinquent(Customer customer) {
    Date today = new Date();
    Specification delinquentSpec =
        new DelinquentInvoiceSpecification(today);
    Iterator it = customer.getInvoices().iterator();
```

```
    while (it.hasNext()) {
        Invoice candidate = (Invoice) it.next();
        if (delinquentSpec.isSatisfiedBy(candidate)) return true;
    }
    return false;
}
```

Selection (or Querying)

Validation tests an individual object to see if it meets some criteria, presumably so that the client can act on the conclusion. Another common need is to select a subset of a collection of objects based on some criteria. The same concept of SPECIFICATION can be applied here, but implementation issues are different.

Suppose there was an application requirement to list all customers with delinquent **Invoices.** In theory, the **Delinquent Invoice Specification** that we defined before will still serve, but in practice its implementation would probably have to change. To demonstrate that the *concept* is the same, let's assume first that the number of **Invoices** is small, maybe already in memory. In this case, the straightforward implementation developed for validation still serves. The **Invoice Repository** could have a generalized method to select **Invoices** based on a SPECIFICATION:

```
public Set selectSatisfying(InvoiceSpecification spec) {

    Set results = new HashSet();
    Iterator it = invoices.iterator();
    while (it.hasNext()) {
        Invoice candidate = (Invoice) it.next();
        if (spec.isSatisfiedBy(candidate)) results.add(candidate);
    }

    return results;
}
```

So a client could obtain a collection of all delinquent **Invoices** with a single code statement:

```
Set delinquentInvoices = invoiceRepository.selectSatisfying(
    new DelinquentInvoiceSpecification(currentDate));
```

That line of code establishes the concept behind the operation. Of course, the **Invoice** objects probably aren't in memory. There may be thousands of them. In a typical business system, the data is probably in a relational database. And, as pointed out in earlier chapters, the model focus tends to get lost at these intersections with other technologies.

Relational databases have powerful search capabilities. How can we take advantage of that power to solve this problem efficiently while retaining the model of a SPECIFICATION? MODEL-DRIVEN DESIGN demands that the model stay in lockstep with the implementation, but it allows freedom to choose any implementation that faithfully captures the meaning of the model. Lucky for us, SQL is a very natural way to write SPECIFICATIONS.

Here is a simple example, in which the query is encapsulated in the same class as the validation rule. A single method is added to the **Invoice Specification** and is implemented in the **Delinquent Invoice Specification** subclass:

```
public String asSQL() {
    return
        "SELECT * FROM INVOICE, CUSTOMER" +
        "  WHERE INVOICE.CUST_ID = CUSTOMER.ID" +
        "  AND INVOICE.DUE_DATE + CUSTOMER.GRACE_PERIOD" +
        "    < " + SQLUtility.dateAsSQL(currentDate);
}
```

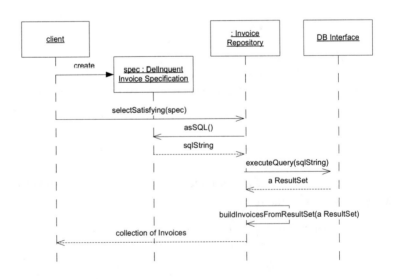

Figure 9.15
The interaction between REPOSITORY and SPECIFICATION

CHAPTER 9: MAKING IMPLICIT CONCEPTS EXPLICIT

SPECIFICATIONS mesh smoothly with REPOSITORIES, which are the building-block mechanisms for providing query access to domain objects and encapsulating the interface to the database (see Figure 9.15).

Now this design has some problems. Most important, the details of the table structure have leaked into the DOMAIN LAYER; they should be isolated in a mapping layer that relates the domain objects to the relational tables. Implicitly duplicating that information here could hurt the modifiability and maintainability of the **Invoice** and **Customer** objects, because any change to their mappings now have to be tracked in more than one place. But this example is a simple illustration of how to keep the rule in just one place. Some object-relational mapping frameworks provide the means to express such a query in terms of the model objects and attributes, generating the actual SQL in the infrastructure layer. This would let us have our cake and eat it too.

When the infrastructure doesn't come to the rescue, we can refactor the SQL out of the expressive domain objects by adding a specialized query method to the **Invoice Repository**. To avoid embedding the rule into the REPOSITORY, we have to express the query in a more generic way, one that doesn't capture the rule but can be combined or placed in context to work the rule out (in this example, by using a double dispatch).

```
public class InvoiceRepository {

    public Set selectWhereGracePeriodPast(Date aDate){
        //This is not a rule, just a specialized query
        String sql = whereGracePeriodPast_SQL(aDate);
        ResultSet queryResultSet =
            SQLDatabaseInterface.instance().executeQuery(sql);
        return buildInvoicesFromResultSet(queryResultSet);
    }

    public String whereGracePeriodPast_SQL(Date aDate) {
        return
            "SELECT * FROM INVOICE, CUSTOMER" +
            "  WHERE INVOICE.CUST_ID = CUSTOMER.ID" +
            "  AND INVOICE.DUE_DATE + CUSTOMER.GRACE_PERIOD" +
            "     < " + SQLUtility.dateAsSQL(aDate);
    }
```

```
    public Set selectSatisfying(InvoiceSpecification spec) {
        return spec.satisfyingElementsFrom(this);
    }
}
```

The asSql() method on **Invoice Specification** is replaced with
satisfyingElementsFrom(InvoiceRepository), which **Delinquent
Invoice Specification** implements as:

```
public class DelinquentInvoiceSpecification {
    // Basic DelinquentInvoiceSpecification code here

    public Set satisfyingElementsFrom(
                    InvoiceRepository repository) {
        //Delinquency rule is defined as:
        //   "grace period past as of current date"
        return repository.selectWhereGracePeriodPast(currentDate);
    }
}
```

This puts the SQL in the REPOSITORY, while the SPECIFICATION
controls what query should be used. The rules aren't as neatly collected into the SPECIFICATION, but the essential declaration is there
of what constitutes delinquency (that is, past grace period).

The REPOSITORY now has a very specialized query that most
likely will be used only in this case. That is acceptable, but depending
on the relative numbers of **Invoices** that are overdue compared to
those that are delinquent, an intermediate solution that leaves the
REPOSITORY methods more generic may still give good performance,
while keeping the SPECIFICATION more self-explanatory.

```
public class InvoiceRepository {

    public Set selectWhereDueDateIsBefore(Date aDate) {
        String sql = whereDueDateIsBefore_SQL(aDate);
        ResultSet queryResultSet =
            SQLDatabaseInterface.instance().executeQuery(sql);
        return buildInvoicesFromResultSet(queryResultSet);
    }
```

```
    public String whereDueDateIsBefore_SQL(Date aDate) {
        return
            "SELECT * FROM INVOICE" +
            "  WHERE INVOICE.DUE_DATE" +
            "     < " + SQLUtility.dateAsSQL(aDate);
    }

    public Set selectSatisfying(InvoiceSpecification spec) {
        return spec.satisfyingElementsFrom(this);
    }
}


public class DelinquentInvoiceSpecification {
    //Basic DelinquentInvoiceSpecification code here

    public Set satisfyingElementsFrom(
                        InvoiceRepository repository) {
        Collection pastDueInvoices =
            repository.selectWhereDueDateIsBefore(currentDate);

        Set delinquentInvoices = new HashSet();
        Iterator it = pastDueInvoices.iterator();
        while (it.hasNext()) {
            Invoice anInvoice = (Invoice) it.next();
            if (this.isSatisfiedBy(anInvoice))
                delinquentInvoices.add(anInvoice);
        }
        return delinquentInvoices;
    }
}
```

We'll take a performance hit with this code, because we pull out
more **Invoices** and then have to select from them in memory.
Whether this is an acceptable cost for the better factoring of responsibility depends entirely on circumstances. There are many ways to
implement the interactions between SPECIFICATIONS and REPOSITO-
RIES, to take advantage of the development platform, while keeping
the basic responsibilities in place.

Sometimes, to improve performance, or more likely to tighten security, queries may be implemented on the server as stored procedures. In that case, the SPECIFICATION could carry only the
parameters allowed by the stored procedure. For all that, there is no
difference in the model between these various implementations. The

choice of implementation is free except where specifically constrained by the model. The price comes in a more cumbersome way of writing and maintaining queries.

This discussion barely scratches the surface of the challenges of combining SPECIFICATIONS with databases, and I'll make no attempt to cover all the considerations that may arise. I just want to give a taste of the kind of choices that have to be made. Mee and Hieatt discuss a few of the technical issues involved in designing REPOSITORIES with SPECIFICATIONS in Fowler 2003.

Building to Order (Generating)

When the Pentagon wants a new fighter jet, officials write a specification. This specification may require that the jet reach Mach 2, that it have a range of 1800 miles, that it cost no more than $50 million, and so on. But however detailed it is, the specification is not a design for a plane, much less a plane. An aerospace engineering company will take the specification and create one or more designs based on it. Competing companies may produce different designs, all of which presumably satisfy the original spec.

Many computer programs generate things, and those things have to be specified. When you place a picture into a word-processing document, the text flows around it. You have specified the location of the picture, and perhaps the style of text flow. The exact placement of the words on the page is then worked out by the word processor in such a way that it meets your specification.

Although it may not be apparent at first, this is the same concept of a SPECIFICATION that was applied to validation and selection. We are specifying criteria for objects that are not yet present. The implementation will be quite different, however. This SPECIFICATION is not a filter for preexisting objects, as with querying. It is not a test for an existing object, as with validation. This time, a whole new object or set of objects will be made or reconfigured to satisfy the SPECIFICATION.

Without using SPECIFICATION, a generator can be written that has procedures or a set of instructions that create the needed objects. This code implicitly defines the behavior of the generator.

Instead, an interface of the generator that is defined in terms of a descriptive SPECIFICATION explicitly constrains the generator's products. This approach has several advantages.

- The generator's implementation is decoupled from its interface. The SPECIFICATION declares the requirements for the output but does not define how that result is reached.

- The interface communicates its rules explicitly, so developers can know what to expect from the generator without understanding all details of its operation. The only way to predict the behavior of a procedurally defined generator is to run cases or to understand every line of code.

- The interface is more flexible, or can be enhanced with more flexibility, because the statement of the request is in the hands of the client, while the generator is only obligated to fulfill the letter of the SPECIFICATION.

- Last, but not least, this kind of interface is easier to test, because the model contains an explicit way to define input into the generator *that is also a validation of the output*. That is, the same SPECIFICATION that is passed into the generator's interface to constrain the creation process can also be used, in its validation role (if the implementation supports it) to confirm that the created object is correct. (This is an example of an ASSERTION, discussed in Chapter 10.)

Building to order can mean creation of an object from scratch, but it can also be a configuration of preexisting objects to satisfy the SPEC.

Example

Chemical Warehouse Packer

There is a warehouse in which various chemicals are stored in stacks of large containers, similar to boxcars. Some chemicals are inert and can be stored just about anywhere. Some are volatile and have to be stored in specially ventilated containers. Some are explosive and have to be stored in specially armored containers. There are also rules about the combinations allowed in a container.

The goal is to write software that will find an efficient and safe way to put the chemicals in the containers.

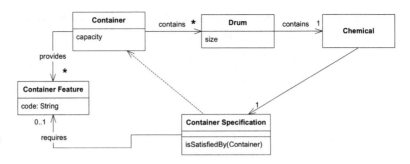

Figure 9.16
A model for warehouse storage

We could start by writing a procedure to take a chemical and place it in a container, but instead, let's start with the validation problem. This will force us to make the rules explicit, and it will give us a way to test the final implementation.

Each chemical will have a container SPECIFICATION:

Chemical	Container Specification
TNT	Armored container
Sand	
Biological Samples	Must not share container with explosives
Ammonia	Ventilated container

Now, if we write these as **Container Specifications**, we should be able to take a configuration of packed containers and test to see if it meets these constraints.

Container Features	Contents	Specification Satisfied?
Armored	20 lbs. TNT 500 lbs. sand	✓
	50 lbs. biological samples	✓
	Ammonia	✗

A method on **Container Specification**, `isSatisfied()`, would have to be implemented to check for needed **ContainerFeatures**. For example, the SPEC attached to an explosive chemical would look for the "armored" feature:

```
public class ContainerSpecification {
    private ContainerFeature requiredFeature;
```

```
public ContainerSpecification(ContainerFeature required) {
    requiredFeature = required;
}

boolean isSatisfiedBy(Container aContainer){
    return aContainer.getFeatures().contains(requiredFeature);
}
}
```

Here is sample client code to set up an explosive chemical:

```
tnt.setContainerSpecification(
        new ContainerSpecification(ARMORED));
```

A method on a **Container** object, isSafelyPacked(), will confirm that **Container** has all the features specified by the **Chemicals** it contains:

```
boolean isSafelyPacked(){
    Iterator it = contents.iterator();
    while (it.hasNext()) {
        Drum drum = (Drum) it.next();
        if (!drum.containerSpecification().isSatisfiedBy(this))
            return false;
    }
    return true;
}
```

At this point, we could write a monitoring application that would take the inventory database and report any unsafe situations.

```
Iterator it = containers.iterator();
while (it.hasNext()) {
    Container container = (Container) it.next();
    if (!container.isSafelyPacked())
        unsafeContainers.add(container);
}
```

This is not the software we've been asked to write. It would be good to let the business people know about the opportunity, but we have been charged with designing a packer. What we have is a test for a packer. This understanding of the domain and our SPECIFICATION-based model put us in a position to define a clear and simple interface for a SERVICE that will take collections of **Drums** and **Containers** and pack them in compliance with the rules.

```
public interface WarehousePacker {
    public void pack(Collection containersToFill,
        Collection drumsToPack) throws NoAnswerFoundException;

        /* ASSERTION: At end of pack(), the ContainerSpecification
        of each Drum shall be satisfied by its Container.
        If no complete solution can be found, an exception shall
        be thrown. */

}
```

Now the task of designing an optimized constraint solver to fulfill the responsibilities of the **Packer** service has been decoupled from the rest of the application, and those mechanisms will not clutter the part of the design that expresses the model. (See "Declarative Style of Design," Chapter 10, and COHESIVE MECHANISM, Chapter 15.) Yet the rules *governing* packing have not been pulled out of the domain objects.

Example

A Working Prototype of the Warehouse Packer

Writing the optimization logic to make the warehouse packing software work is a big job. A small team of developers and business experts have split off and have set to work on it, but they haven't even begun to code. Meanwhile, another small team is developing the application that will allow users to pull inventory from the database, feed it to the **Packer**, and interpret the results. They are trying to design for the anticipated **Packer**. But all they can do is mock up a UI and work on some database integration code. They can't show the users an interface with meaningful behavior to get good feedback. For the same reason, the **Packer** team is working in a vacuum too.

With the domain objects and SERVICE interface made in the warehouse packer example, the application team realizes they could build a very simple implementation of a **Packer** that could help the development process move along, allowing work to go forward in parallel and closing the feedback loop, which only reaches full effect with a working end-to-end system.

```
public class Container {
   private double capacity;
   private Set contents; //Drums

   public boolean hasSpaceFor(Drum aDrum) {
      return remainingSpace() >= aDrum.getSize();
   }

   public double remainingSpace() {
      double totalContentSize = 0.0;
      Iterator it = contents.iterator();
      while (it.hasNext()) {
         Drum aDrum = (Drum) it.next();
         totalContentSize = totalContentSize + aDrum.getSize();
      }
      return capacity - totalContentSize;
   }

   public boolean canAccommodate(Drum aDrum) {
      return hasSpaceFor(aDrum) &&
         aDrum.getContainerSpecification().isSatisfiedBy(this);
   }

}


public class PrototypePacker implements WarehousePacker {

   public void pack(Collection containers, Collection drums)
                              throws NoAnswerFoundException {

      /* This method fulfills the ASSERTION as written. However,
         when an exception is thrown, Containers' contents may
         have changed. Rollback must be handled at a higher
         level. */

      Iterator it = drums.iterator();
      while (it.hasNext()) {
         Drum drum = (Drum) it.next();
         Container container =
            findContainerFor(containers, drum);
         container.add(drum);
      }
   }
```

```
public Container findContainerFor(
            Collection containers, Drum drum)
        throws NoAnswerFoundException {
    Iterator it = containers.iterator();
    while (it.hasNext()) {
        Container container = (Container) it.next();
        if (container.canAccommodate(drum))
            return container;
    }
    throw new NoAnswerFoundException();
}


}
```

Clearing Development Logjams with Working Prototypes

One team has to wait for working code from another in order to move forward. Both teams have to wait for full integration to exercise their components or get feedback from users. This kind of congestion can often be eased by a MODEL-DRIVEN prototype of a key component, even if it does not satisfy all requirements. When implementation is decoupled from interface, then having any working implementation at all allows flexibility for project work to go in parallel. When the time is right, the prototype can be replaced by a more effective implementation. In the meantime, all other parts of the system have something to interact with during development.

Granted that this code leaves a lot to be desired. It might pack sand into specialty containers and then run out of room before it packs the hazardous chemicals. It certainly doesn't optimize revenues. But a lot of optimization problems are never solved perfectly anyway. This implementation does follow the rules that have been stated so far.

Having this prototype lets the application developers move at full speed, including all integrations with external systems. The **Packer** development team also gets feedback as domain experts interact with the prototype and firm up their ideas, helping clarify requirements and priorities. The **Packer** team decides to take over the prototype and tweak it to test ideas.

They also keep the interface up-to-date with their latest design, forcing refactoring of the application, and some domain objects, thereby tackling the integration problems early.

As soon as the sophisticated **Packer** is ready, integration is a breeze because it has been written to a well-characterized interface—the same interface and ASSERTIONS that the application was written for when interacting with the prototype.

It took specialists in optimization algorithms months to get it right. They benefited from the feedback they could get from users interacting with the prototype. In the meantime, all other parts of the system have something to interact with during development.

Here we have an example of a "simplest thing that could possibly work" that actually becomes possible because of a more sophisticated model. We can have a functioning prototype of a very complex

component in a couple dozen lines of easily understood code. A less
MODEL-DRIVEN approach would be harder to understand, would be
harder to upgrade (because the **Packer** would be more coupled to
the rest of the design), and in this case, would likely take longer to
prototype.

TEN

Supple Design

The ultimate purpose of software is to serve users. But first, that same software has to serve developers. This is especially true in a process that emphasizes refactoring. As a program evolves, developers will rearrange and rewrite every part. They will integrate the domain objects into the application and with new domain objects. Even years later, maintenance programmers will be changing and extending the code. People have to work with this stuff. But will they want to?

When software with complex behavior lacks a good design, it becomes hard to refactor or combine elements. Duplication starts to appear as soon as a developer isn't confident of predicting the full implications of a computation. Duplication is forced when design elements are monolithic, so that the parts cannot be recombined. Classes and methods can be broken down for better reuse, but it gets hard to keep track of what all the little parts do. When software doesn't have a clean design, developers dread even looking at the existing mess, much less making a change that could aggravate the tangle or break something through an unforeseen dependency. In any but the smallest systems, this fragility places a ceiling on the richness of behavior it is feasible to build. It stops refactoring and iterative refinement.

To have a project accelerate as development proceeds—rather than get weighed down by its own legacy—demands a design that is a pleasure to work with, inviting to change. A supple design.

Supple design is the complement to deep modeling. Once you've dug out implicit concepts and made them explicit, you have the raw material. Through the iterative cycle, you hammer that material into a useful shape, cultivating a model that simply and clearly captures the key concerns, and shaping a design that allows a client developer to really put that model to work. Development of the design and code leads to insight that refines model concepts. Round and round—we're back to the iterative cycle and refactoring toward deeper insight. But what kind of design are you trying to arrive at? What kind of experiments should you try along the way? That is what this chapter is about.

A lot of overengineering has been justified in the name of flexibility. But more often than not, excessive layers of abstraction and indirection get in the way. Look at the design of software that really empowers the people who handle it; you will usually see something simple. Simple is not easy. To create elements that can be assembled into elaborate systems and still be understandable, a dedication to MODEL-DRIVEN DESIGN has to be joined with a moderately rigorous design style. It may well require relatively sophisticated design skill to create *or to use*.

Developers play two roles, each of which must be served by the design. The same person might well play both roles—even switch back and forth in minutes—but the relationship to the code is different nonetheless. One role is the developer of a client, who weaves the domain objects into the application code or other domain layer code, utilizing capabilities of the design. A supple design reveals a deep underlying model that makes its potential clear. The client developer can flexibly use a minimal set of loosely coupled concepts to express a range of scenarios in the domain. Design elements fit together in a natural way with a result that is predictable, clearly characterized, and robust.

Equally important, the design must serve the developer working to change it. To be open to change, a design must be easy to understand, revealing that *same* underlying model that the client developer is drawing on. It must follow the contours of a deep model of the domain, so most changes bend the design at flexible points. The effects of its code must be transparently obvious, so the consequences of a change will be easy to anticipate.

Early versions of a design are usually stiff. Many never acquire any suppleness in the time frame or budget of the project. I've never seen a large program that had this quality throughout. But when complexity is holding back progress, honing the most crucial, intricate parts to a supple design makes the difference between getting sucked down into legacy maintenance and punching through the complexity ceiling.

There is no formula for designing software like this, but I have culled a set of patterns that, in my experience, tend to lend suppleness to a design when they fit. These patterns and examples should give a feel for what a supple design is like and the kind of thinking that goes into it.

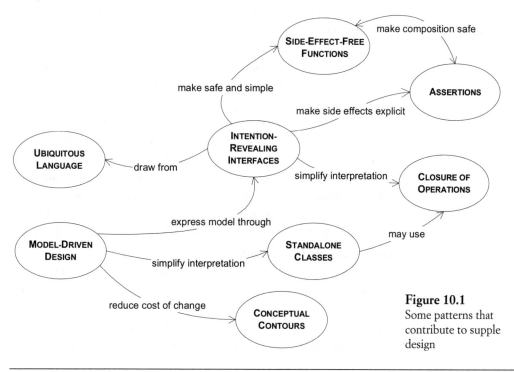

Figure 10.1
Some patterns that contribute to supple design

INTENTION-REVEALING INTERFACES

In domain-driven design, we want to think about meaningful domain logic. Code that produces the effect of a rule without explicitly stating the rule forces us to think of step-by-step software procedures. The same applies to a calculation that just results from running some code, but isn't explicit. Without a clear connection to the model, it is difficult to understand the effect of the code or anticipate the effect of a change. The previous chapter delved into modeling rules and calculations explicitly. Implementing such objects requires a lot of understanding of the gritty details of the calculation or the fine print of the rule. The beauty of objects is their ability to encapsulate all that, so that client code is simple and can be interpreted in terms of higher-level concepts.

But if the interface doesn't tell the client developer what he needs to know in order to use the object effectively, he will have to dig into the internals to understand the details anyway. A reader of the client code will have to do the same. Then most of the value of the encapsulation is lost. We are always fighting cognitive overload: If the client developer's mind is flooded with detail about how a component does its job, his mind isn't clear to work out the intricacies of the client design. This is true even when the same person is playing both roles, developing and using his own code, because even if he doesn't have to learn those details, there is a limit to how many factors he can consider at once.

If a developer must consider the implementation of a component in order to use it, the value of encapsulation is lost. If someone other than the original developer must infer the purpose of an object or operation based on its implementation, that new developer may infer a purpose that the operation or class fulfills only by chance. If that was not the intent, the code may work for the moment, but the conceptual basis of the design will have been corrupted, and the two developers will be working at cross-purposes.

To obtain the value of explicitly modeling a concept in the form of a class or method, we must give these program elements names that reflect those concepts. The names of classes and methods are great opportunities for improving communication between developers, and for improving the abstraction of the system.

Kent Beck wrote of making method names communicate their purpose with an INTENTION-REVEALING SELECTOR (Beck 1997). All public elements of a design together make up its interface, and the name of each of those elements presents an opportunity to reveal the intention of the design. Type names, method names, and argument names all combine to form an INTENTION-REVEALING INTERFACE.

Therefore:

Name classes and operations to describe their effect and purpose, without reference to the means by which they do what they promise. This relieves the client developer of the need to understand the internals. These names should conform to the UBIQUITOUS LANGUAGE so that team members can quickly infer their meaning. Write a test for a behavior before creating it, to force your thinking into client developer mode.

All the tricky mechanism should be encapsulated behind abstract interfaces that speak in terms of intentions, rather than means.

In the public interfaces of the domain, state relationships and rules, but not how they are enforced; describe events and actions, but not how they are carried out; formulate the equation but not the numerical method to solve it. Pose the question, but don't present the means by which the answer shall be found.

Example
Refactoring: A Paint-Mixing Application

A program for paint stores can show a customer the result of mixing standard paints. Here is the initial design, which has a single domain class.

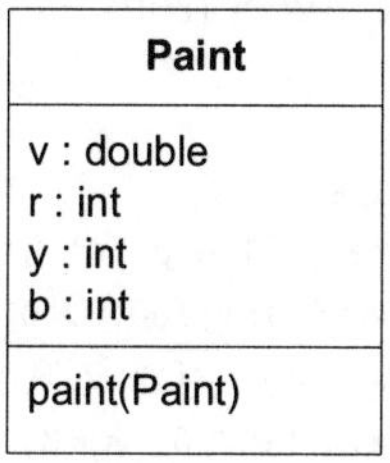

Figure 10.2

The only way to even guess what the `paint(Paint)` method does is to read the code.

```
public void paint(Paint paint) {
    v = v + paint.getV(); //After mixing, volume is summed
    // Omitted many lines of complicated color mixing logic
    // ending with the assignment of new r, b, and y values.
}
```

OK, so it looks like this method combines two **Paints** together, the result having a larger volume and a mixed color.

To shift our perspective, let's write a test for this method. (This code is based on the JUnit test framework.)

```
public void testPaint() {
    // Create a pure yellow paint with volume=100
    Paint yellow = new Paint(100.0, 0, 50, 0);
    // Create a pure blue paint with volume=100
    Paint blue = new Paint(100.0, 0, 0, 50);

    // Mix the blue into the yellow
    yellow.paint(blue);

    // Result should be volume of 200.0 of green paint
    assertEquals(200.0, yellow.getV(), 0.01);
    assertEquals(25, yellow.getB());
    assertEquals(25, yellow.getY());
    assertEquals(0, yellow.getR());
}
```

The passing test is the starting point. It is unsatisfying at this point because the code in the test doesn't tell us what it is doing. Let's rewrite the test to reflect the way we would *like* to use the **Paint** objects if we were writing a client application. Initially, this test will fail. In fact, it won't even compile. We are writing it to explore the interface design of the **Paint** object from the client developer's point of view.

```
public void testPaint() {
    // Start with a pure yellow paint with volume=100
    Paint ourPaint = new Paint(100.0, 0, 50, 0);
    // Take a pure blue paint with volume=100
    Paint blue = new Paint(100.0, 0, 0, 50);

    // Mix the blue into the yellow
    ourPaint.mixIn(blue);
```

```
    // Result should be volume of 200.0 of green paint
    assertEquals(200.0, ourPaint.getVolume(), 0.01);
    assertEquals(25, ourPaint.getBlue());
    assertEquals(25, ourPaint.getYellow());
    assertEquals(0, ourPaint.getRed());
}
```

We should take our time to write a test that reflects the way we would like to talk to these objects. After that, we refactor the **Paint** class to make the test pass.

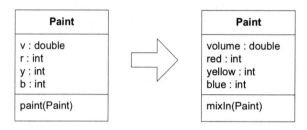

Figure 10.3

The new method name may not tell the reader everything about the effect of "mixing in" another **Paint** (for that we'll need ASSERTIONS, coming up in a few pages). But it will clue the reader in enough to get started using the class, especially with the example the test provides. And it will allow the reader of the client code to interpret the client's intent. In the next few examples in this chapter, we'll refactor this class again to make it even clearer.

＊　＊　＊

Entire subdomains can be carved off into separate modules and encapsulated behind INTENTION-REVEALING INTERFACES. Using such whittling to focus a project and manage the complexity of a large system will be discussed more in Chapter 15, "Distillation," with COHESIVE MECHANISMS and GENERIC SUBDOMAINS.

But in the next two patterns, we'll set out to make the consequences of using a method very predictable. Complex logic can be done safely in SIDE-EFFECT-FREE FUNCTIONS. Methods that change system state can be characterized with ASSERTIONS.

SIDE-EFFECT-FREE FUNCTIONS

Operations can be broadly divided into two categories, commands and queries. Queries obtain information from the system, possibly by simply accessing data in a variable, possibly performing a calculation based on that data. Commands (also known as modifiers) are operations that affect some change to the systems (for a simple example, by setting a variable). In standard English, the term *side effect* implies an unintended consequence, but in computer science, it means any effect on the state of the system. For our purposes, let's narrow that meaning to any change in the state of the system that will affect future operations.

Why was the term *side effect* adopted and applied to quite intentional changes affected by operations? I assume this was based on experience with complex systems. Most operations call on other operations, and those called invoke still other operations. As soon as this arbitrarily deep nesting is involved, it becomes very hard to anticipate all the consequences of invoking an operation. The developer of the client may not have intended the effects of the second-tier and third-tier operations—they've become side effects in every sense of the phrase. Elements of a complex design interact in other ways that are likely to produce the same unpredictability. The use of the term *side effect* underlines the inevitability of that interaction.

Interactions of multiple rules or compositions of calculations become extremely difficult to predict. The developer calling an operation must understand its implementation and the implementation of all its delegations in order to anticipate the result. The usefulness of any abstraction of interfaces is limited if the developers are forced to pierce the veil. Without safely predictable abstractions, the developers must limit the combinatory explosion, placing a low ceiling on the richness of behavior that is feasible to build.

Operations that return results without producing side effects are called *functions*. A function can be called multiple times and return the same value each time. A function can call on other functions without worrying about the depth of nesting. Functions are much easier to test than operations that have side effects. For these reasons, functions lower risk.

Obviously, you can't avoid commands in most software systems, but the problem can be mitigated in two ways. First, you can keep the commands and queries strictly segregated in different operations. Ensure that the methods that cause changes do not return domain data and are kept as simple as possible. Perform all queries and calculations in methods that cause no observable side effects (Meyer 1988).

Second, there are often alternative models and designs that do not call for an existing object to be modified at all. Instead, a new VALUE OBJECT, representing the result of the computation, is created and returned. This is a common technique, which will be illustrated in the example that follows. A VALUE OBJECT can be created in answer to a query, handed off, and forgotten—unlike an ENTITY, whose life cycle is carefully regulated.

VALUE OBJECTS are immutable, which implies that, apart from initializers called only during creation, *all* their operations are functions. VALUE OBJECTS, like functions, are safer to use and easier to test. An operation that mixes logic or calculations with state change should be refactored into two separate operations (Fowler 1999, p. 279). But by definition, this segregation of side effects into simple command methods only applies to ENTITIES. *After* completing the refactoring to separate modification from querying, consider a second refactoring to move the responsibility for the complex calculations into a VALUE OBJECT. The side effect often can be completely eliminated by deriving a VALUE OBJECT instead of changing existing state, or by moving the entire responsibility into a VALUE OBJECT.

Therefore:

Place as much of the logic of the program as possible into functions, operations that return results with no observable side effects. Strictly segregate commands (methods that result in modifications to observable state) into very simple operations that do not return domain information. Further control side effects by moving complex logic into VALUE OBJECTS when a concept fitting the responsibility presents itself.

SIDE-EFFECT-FREE FUNCTIONS, especially in immutable VALUE OBJECTS, allow safe combination of operations. When a FUNCTION is presented through an INTENTION-REVEALING INTERFACE, a developer can use it without understanding the detail of its implementation.

Example

Refactoring the Paint-Mixing Application Again

A program for paint stores can show a customer the result of mixing standard paints. Picking up where we left off in the last example, here is the single domain class.

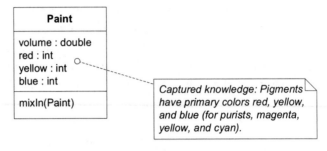

Figure 10.4

```
public void mixIn(Paint other) {
    volume = volume.plus(other.getVolume());
    // Many lines of complicated color-mixing logic
    // ending with the assignment of new red, blue,
    // and yellow values.
}
```

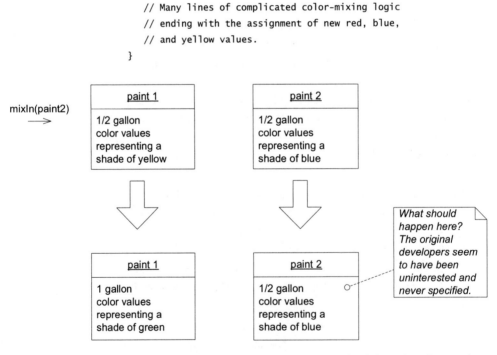

Figure 10.5
The side effects of the
mixIn() method

A lot is happening in the mixIn() method, but this design does follow the rule of separating modification from querying. One concern, which we'll take up later, is that the volume of the paint 2 object, the argument of the `mixIn()` method, has been left in limbo. Paint 2's volume is unchanged by the operation, which doesn't seem quite logical in the context of this conceptual model. This was not a problem for the original developers because, as near as we can tell, they had no interest in the paint 2 object after the operation, but it is hard to anticipate the consequences of side effects or their absence. We'll return to this question soon in the discussion of ASSERTIONS. For now, let's look at color.

Color is an important concept in this domain. Let's try the experiment of making it an explicit object. What should it be called? "Color" comes to mind first, but earlier knowledge crunching had already yielded the important insight that color mixing is different for paint than it is for the more familiar RGB light display. The name needs to reflect this.

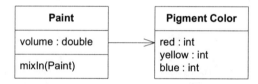

Figure 10.6

Factoring out **Pigment Color** does communicate more than the earlier version, but the computation is the same, still in the `mixIn()` method. When we moved out the color data, we should have taken related behavior with it. Before we do, note that **Pigment Color** is a VALUE OBJECT. Therefore, it should be treated as immutable. When we mixed paint, the **Paint** object itself was changed. It was an ENTITY with an ongoing life story. In contrast, a **Pigment Color** representing a particular shade of yellow is always exactly that. Instead, mixing will result in a new **Pigment Color** object representing the new color.

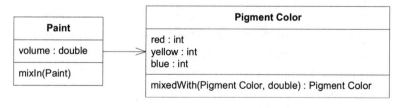

Figure 10.7

```
public class PigmentColor {

    public PigmentColor mixedWith(PigmentColor other,
                                             double ratio) {
        // Many lines of complicated color-mixing logic
        // ending with the creation of a new PigmentColor object
        // with appropriate new red, blue, and yellow values.
    }
}

public class Paint {

    public void mixIn(Paint other) {
        volume = volume + other.getVolume();
        double ratio = other.getVolume() / volume;
        pigmentColor =
            pigmentColor.mixedWith(other.pigmentColor(), ratio);
    }
}
```

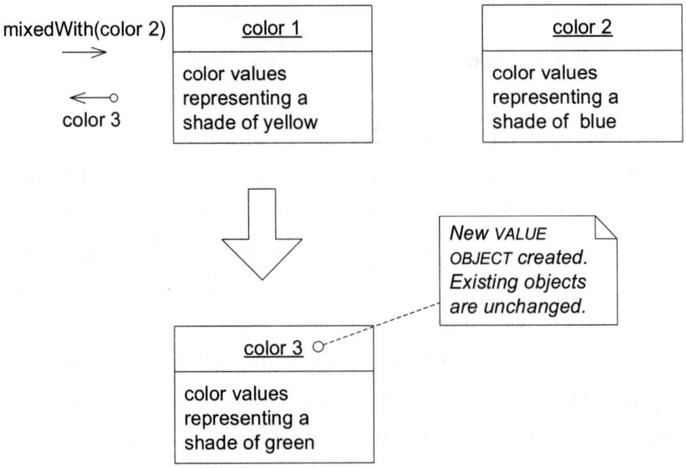

Figure 10.8

Now the modification code in **Paint** is as simple as possible. The new **Pigment Color** class captures knowledge and communicates it explicitly, and it provides a SIDE-EFFECT-FREE FUNCTION whose result is easy to understand, *easy to test*, and safe to use or combine with other operations. Because it is so safe, the complex logic of color mixing is truly encapsulated. Developers using this class don't have to understand the implementation.

❋ ❋ ❋

Assertions

Separating complex computations into SIDE-EFFECT-FREE FUNC-TIONS cuts the problem down to size, but there is still a residue of commands on the ENTITIES that produce side effects, and anyone using them must understand their consequences. ASSERTIONS make side effects explicit and easier to deal with.

✳   ✳   ✳

True, a command containing no complex computations may be fairly easy to interpret by inspection. But in a design where larger parts are built of smaller ones, a command may invoke other commands. The developer using the high-level command must understand the consequences of each underlying command. So much for encapsulation. And because object interfaces do not restrict side effects, two subclasses that implement the same interface can have different side effects. The developer using them will want to know which is which to anticipate the consequences. So much for abstraction and polymorphism.

When the side effects of operations are only defined implicitly by their implementation, designs with a lot of delegation become a tangle of cause and effect. The only way to understand a program is to trace execution through branching paths. The value of encapsulation is lost. The necessity of tracing concrete execution defeats abstraction.

We need a way of understanding the meaning of a design element and the consequences of executing an operation without delving into its internals. INTENTION-REVEALING INTERFACES carry us part of the way there, but informal suggestions of intentions are not always enough. The "design by contract" school goes the next step, making "assertions" about classes and methods that the developer guarantees will be true. This style is discussed in detail in Meyer 1988. Briefly, "post-conditions" describe the side effects of an operation, the guaranteed outcome of calling a method. "Preconditions" are like the fine print on the contract, the conditions that must be satisfied in order for the post-condition guarantee to hold. Class invariants make assertions about the state of an object at the end of any operation. Invariants can also be declared for entire AGGREGATES, rigorously defining integrity rules.

All these assertions describe state, not procedures, so they are easier to analyze. Class invariants help characterize the meaning of a class, and simplify the client developer's job by making the objects more predictable. If you trust the guarantee of a post-condition, you don't have to worry about how a method works. The effects of delegations should already be incorporated into the assertions.

Therefore:

State post-conditions of operations and invariants of classes and AGGREGATES. If ASSERTIONS cannot be coded directly in your programming language, write automated unit tests for them. Write them into documentation or diagrams where it fits the style of the project's development process.

Seek models with coherent sets of concepts, which lead a developer to infer the intended ASSERTIONS, accelerating the learning curve and reducing the risk of contradictory code.

Even though many object-oriented languages don't currently support ASSERTIONS directly, ASSERTIONS are still a powerful way of thinking about a design. Automated unit tests can partially compensate for the lack of language support. Because ASSERTIONS are all in terms of states, rather than procedures, they make tests easy to write. The test setup puts the preconditions in place; then, after execution, the test checks to see if the post-conditions hold.

Clearly stated invariants and pre- and post-conditions allow a developer to understand the consequences of using an operation or object. Theoretically, any noncontradictory set of assertions would work. But humans don't just compile predicates in their heads. They will be extrapolating and interpolating the concepts of the model, so it is important to find models that make sense to people as well as satisfying the needs of the application.

Example

Back to Paint Mixing

Recall that in the previous example I was concerned about the ambiguity of what happens to the argument of the `mixIn(Paint)` operation on the **Paint** class.

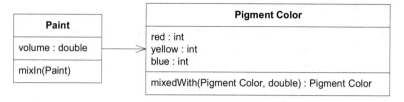

Figure 10.9

The receiver's volume is increased by the amount of the argument's volume. Drawing on our general understanding of physical paint, this mixing process should deplete the other paint by the same amount, draining it to zero volume, or eliminating it completely. The current implementation does not modify the argument, and modifying arguments is a particularly risky kind of side effect anyway.

To start on a solid footing, let's state the post-condition of the mixIn() method *as it is*:

After `p1.mixIn(p2)`:
    `p1.volume` is increased by amount of `p2.volume`.
    `p2.volume` is unchanged.

The trouble is, developers are going to make mistakes, because these properties don't fit the concepts we have invited them to think about. The straightforward fix would be change the volume of the other paint to zero. Changing an argument is a bad practice, but it would be easy and intuitive. We could state an invariant:

Total volume of paint is unchanged by mixing.

But wait! While developers were pondering this option, they made a discovery. It turns out that there was a compelling reason the original designers made it this way. At the end, the program *reports the list of unmixed paints that were added*. After all, the ultimate purpose of this application is to help a user figure out which paints to *put into* a mixture.

So, to make the volume model logically consistent would make it unsuitable for its application requirements. There seems to be a dilemma. Are we stuck with documenting the weird post-condition and trying to compensate with good communication? Not everything in this world is intuitive, and sometimes that is the best answer. But in this case, the awkwardness seems to point to missing concepts. Let's look for a new model.

We Can See Clearly Now

As we search for a better model, we have significant advantages over the original designers, because of the knowledge crunching and refactoring to deeper insight that has happened in the interim. For example, we compute color using a SIDE-EFFECT-FREE FUNCTION on a VALUE OBJECT. This means we can repeat the calculation any time we need to. We should take advantage of that.

We seem to be giving **Paint** two different basic responsibilities. Let's try splitting them.

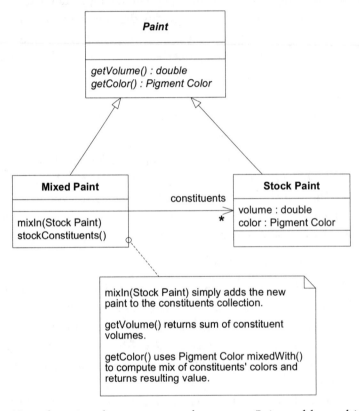

Figure 10.10

Now there is only one command, mixIn(). It just adds an object to a collection, an effect apparent from an intuitive understanding of the model. All other operations are SIDE-EFFECT-FREE FUNCTIONS.

A test method confirming one of the ASSERTIONS listed in Figure 10.10 could look something like this (using the JUnit test framework):

```
public void testMixingVolume {
    PigmentColor yellow = new PigmentColor(0, 50, 0);
    PigmentColor blue = new PigmentColor(0, 0, 50);

    StockPaint paint1 = new StockPaint(1.0, yellow);
    StockPaint paint2 = new StockPaint(1.5, blue);
    MixedPaint mix = new MixedPaint();

    mix.mixIn(paint1);
    mix.mixIn(paint2);
    assertEquals(2.5, mix.getVolume(), 0.01);
}
```

This model captures and communicates more of the domain. The invariants and post-conditions make common sense, which will make them easier to maintain and use.

✳ ✳ ✳

The communicativeness of the INTENTION-REVEALING INTERFACES, combined with the predictability given by SIDE-EFFECT-FREE FUNCTIONS and ASSERTIONS, should make encapsulation and abstraction safe.

The next ingredient in recombinable elements is effective decomposition. . . .

CONCEPTUAL CONTOURS

Sometimes people chop functionality fine to allow flexible combination. Sometimes they lump it large to encapsulate complexity. Sometimes they seek a consistent granularity, making all classes and operations to a similar scale. These are oversimplifications that don't work well as general rules. But they are motivated by a basic set of problems.

When elements of a model or design are embedded in a monolithic construct, their functionality gets duplicated. The external interface doesn't say everything a client might care about. Their meaning is hard to understand, because different concepts are mixed together.

On the other hand, breaking down classes and methods can pointlessly complicate the client, forcing client objects to understand how tiny pieces fit together. Worse, a concept can be lost completely. Half of a uranium atom is not uranium. And of course, it isn't just grain size that counts, but just where the grain runs.

Cookbook rules don't work. But there is a logical consistency deep in most domains, or else they would not be viable in their own sphere. This is not to say that domains are perfectly consistent, and certainly the ways people talk about them are not consistent. But there is rhyme and reason somewhere, or else modeling would be pointless. Because of this underlying consistency, when we find a model that resonates with some part of the domain, it is more likely to be consistent with other parts that we discover later. Sometimes the new discovery isn't easy for the model to adapt to, in which case we refactor to deeper insight, and hope to conform to the *next* discovery.

This is one reason why repeated refactoring eventually leads to suppleness. The CONCEPTUAL CONTOURS emerge as the code is adapted to newly understood concepts or requirements.

The twin fundamentals of high cohesion and low coupling play a role in design at all scales, from individual methods up through classes and MODULES to large-scale structures (see Chapter 16). These two principles apply to concepts as much as to code. To avoid slipping into a mechanistic view of them, temper your technical thinking by frequently touching base with your intuition for the domain. With each decision, ask yourself, "Is this an expedient based on a particular set of relationships in the current model and code, or does it echo some contour of the underlying domain?"

Find the conceptually meaningful unit of functionality, and the resulting design will be both flexible and understandable. For example, if an "addition" of two objects has a coherent meaning in the domain, then implement methods at that level. Don't break the add( ) into two steps. Don't proceed to the next step within the same operation. On a slightly larger scale, each object should be a single complete concept, a "WHOLE VALUE."[1]

By the same token, there are areas in any domain where detail isn't interesting to the kind of people the software serves. The users of our hypothetical paint mixing application don't add red pigment or blue pigment; they combine complete paints, which contain all three pigments. Clumping things that don't need to be dissected or rearranged avoids clutter and makes it easier to see the elements that really are meant to recombine. If our users' physical equipment allowed individual pigments to be added, the domain would be altered, and the individual pigments might be manipulated. A paint chemist would need still finer control, which would involve a whole other analysis, probably producing a much more detailed model of the makeup of paint than our abstracted pigment color that serves paint mixing. But it is simply irrelevant to anyone involved in the paint mixing application project.

Therefore:

Decompose design elements (operations, interfaces, classes, and AGGREGATES) into cohesive units, taking into consideration your intuition of the important divisions in the domain. Observe the axes of change and stability through successive refactorings and look for the underlying CONCEPTUAL CONTOURS that explain these shearing patterns. Align the model with the consistent aspects of the domain that make it a viable area of knowledge in the first place.

The goal is a simple set of interfaces that combine logically to make sensible statements in the UBIQUITOUS LANGUAGE, and without the distraction and maintenance burden of irrelevant options. This is typically an outcome of refactoring: it's hard to produce up

---

1. The WHOLE VALUE pattern, by Ward Cunningham.

front. But it may never emerge from technically oriented refactoring; it emerges from refactoring toward deeper insight.

Even when the design follows CONCEPTUAL CONTOURS, there will need to be modifications and refactoring. When successive refactoring tends to be localized, not shaking multiple broad concepts of the model, it is an indicator of model fit. Encountering a requirement that forces extensive changes in the breakdown of the objects and methods is a message: Our understanding of the domain needs refinement. It presents an opportunity to deepen the model and make the design more supple.

Example

The CONTOURS of Accruals

In Chapter 9, a loan tracking system was refactored based on deeper insight into accounting concepts:

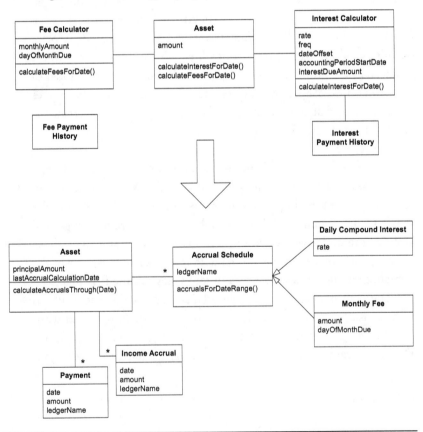

Figure 10.11

The new model contained only one more object than the old one, yet the partitioning of responsibility had been greatly changed.

Schedules, which had been worked out through case logic in the **Calculator** classes, were exploded into discrete classes for different types of fees and interest. On the other hand, payments of fees and interest, previously kept separate, were lumped together.

Because of the resonance of the newly explicit concepts and the cohesiveness of the **Accrual Schedule** hierarchy, the developer believed that this model better follows some of the domain's CONCEPTUAL CONTOURS.

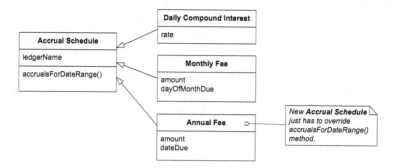

Figure 10.12
This model accommodates adding new kinds of **Accrual Schedules**.

The one change the developer could confidently predict was the addition of new **Accrual Schedules**. Those requirements were already waiting in the wings. So in addition to making existing functionality clearer and simpler, she chose a model that would make it easy to introduce new schedules. But had she found a CONCEPTUAL CONTOUR that will help the domain design change and grow as the application and the business evolve? There can be no guarantees about how a design will handle unanticipated change, but she thought it had improved the odds.

An Unanticipated Change

As the project proceeded, a requirement emerged for detailed rules for handling early and late payments. As she studied the problem, the developer was pleased to see that virtually the same rules applied to payments on interest and to payments on fees. This meant that the new model elements would connect naturally to the single **Payment** class.

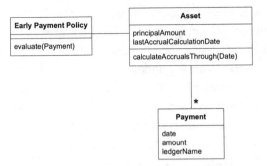

Figure 10.13

The old design would have forced duplication between the two **Payment History** classes. (This difficulty might have triggered an insight that the **Payment** class should be shared, leading by another path to a similar model.) This ease of extension did not come because she anticipated the change. Nor did it come because she made a design so versatile it could accommodate any conceivable change. It happened because in the previous refactoring, the design was aligned with underlying concepts of the domain.

❋ ❋ ❋

INTENTION-REVEALING INTERFACES allow clients to present objects as units of meaning rather than just mechanisms. SIDE-EFFECT-FREE FUNCTIONS and ASSERTIONS make it safe to use those units and make complex combinations. The emergence of CONCEPTUAL CONTOURS stabilizes parts of the model and also makes the units more intuitive to use and combine.

We can still run into conceptual overload when interdependencies force us to think about too many of these things at a time. . . .

Standalone Classes

Interdependencies make models and designs hard to understand. They also make them hard to test and maintain. And interdependencies pile up easily.

Every association is, of course, a dependency, and understanding a class requires understanding what it is attached to. Those attached things will be attached to still more things, and they have to be understood too. The type of every argument of every method is also a dependency. So is every return value.

With one dependency, you have to think about two classes at the same time, and the nature of their relationship. With two dependencies, you have to think about each of the three classes, the nature of the class's relationship to each of them, and any relationship they might have to each other. If they in turn have dependencies, you have to be wary of those also. With three dependencies . . . it snowballs.

Both MODULES and AGGREGATES are aimed at limiting the web of interdependencies. When a highly cohesive subdomain is carved out into a MODULE, a set of objects are decoupled from the rest of the system, so there are a finite number of interrelated concepts. But even a MODULE can be a lot to think about without an almost fanatical commitment to controlling dependencies within it.

Even within a MODULE, the difficulty of interpreting a design increases wildly as dependencies are added. This adds to mental overload, limiting the design complexity a developer can handle. Implicit concepts contribute to this load even more than explicit references.

Refined models are distilled until every remaining connection between concepts represents something fundamental to the meaning of those concepts. In an important subset, the number of dependencies can be reduced to zero, resulting in a class that can be fully understood all by itself, along with a few primitives and basic library concepts.

In every programming environment, a few basics are so pervasive that they are always in mind. For example, in Java development, primitives and a few standard libraries provide basics like numbers, strings, and collections. Practically speaking, "integers" don't add to the intellectual load. Beyond that, every additional concept that has to be held in mind in order to understand an object contributes to mental overload.

Implicit concepts, recognized or unrecognized, count just as much as explicit references. Although we can generally ignore dependencies on primitive values such as integers and strings, we can't ignore *what they represent*. For example, in the first paint mixing examples, the **Paint** object held three public integers representing red, yellow, and blue color values. The creation of the **Pigment Color** object did not increase the number of concepts involved or the dependencies. It did make the ones that were already there more explicit and easier to understand. On the other hand, the **Collection** `size()` operation returns an `int` that is simply a count, the basic meaning of an integer, so no new concept is implied.

Every dependency is suspect until proven basic to the concept behind the object. This scrutiny starts with the factoring of the model concepts themselves. Then it requires attention to each individual association and operation. Model and design choices can chip away at dependencies—often to zero.

Low coupling is fundamental to object design. When you can, go all the way. Eliminate *all* other concepts from the picture. Then the class will be completely self-contained and can be studied and understood alone. Every such self-contained class significantly eases the burden of understanding a MODULE.

Dependencies on other classes within the same module are less harmful than those outside. Likewise, when two objects are naturally tightly coupled, multiple operations involving the same pair can actually clarify the nature of the relationship. The goal is not to eliminate all dependencies, but to eliminate all nonessential ones. If every dependency can't be eliminated, each one that is removed frees the developer to concentrate on the remaining conceptual dependencies.

Try to factor the most intricate computations into STANDALONE CLASSES, perhaps by modeling VALUE OBJECTS held by the more connected classes.

The concept of paint is fundamentally related to the concept of color. But color, even of pigment, can be considered without paint. By making these two concepts explicit and distilling the relationship, the remaining one-way association says something important, and the

Pigment Color class, where most of the computational complexity lies, can be studied *and tested* alone.

✳ ✳ ✳

Low coupling is a basic way to reduce conceptual overload. A STANDALONE CLASS is an extreme of low coupling.

Eliminating dependencies should not mean dumbing down the model by arbitrarily reducing everything to primitives. The final pattern of this chapter, CLOSURE OF OPERATIONS, is an example of a technique for reducing dependency while keeping a rich interface. . . .

CLOSURE OF OPERATIONS

> If we take two real numbers and multiply them together, we get an-
> other real number. [The real numbers are all the rational numbers
> and all the irrational numbers.] Because this is always true, we say
> that the real numbers are "closed under the operation of multiplica-
> tion": there is no way to escape the set. When you combine any two
> elements of the set, the result is also included in the set.
>
> —*The Math Forum, Drexel University*

Of course, there will be dependencies, and that isn't a bad thing
when the dependency is fundamental to the concept. Stripping interfaces down to deal with nothing but primitives can impoverish them.
But a lot of unnecessary dependencies, and even entire concepts, get
introduced at interfaces.

**Most interesting objects end up doing things that can't be char-
acterized by primitives alone.**

Another common practice in refined designs is what I call "CLO-
SURE OF OPERATIONS." The name comes from that most refined of
conceptual systems, mathematics. $1 + 1 = 2$. The addition operation
is closed under the set of real numbers. Mathematicians are fanatical
about not introducing extraneous concepts, and the property of closure provides them a way of defining an operation without involving
any other concepts. We are so accustomed to the refinement of mathematics that it can be hard to grasp how powerful its little tricks are.
But this one is used extensively in software designs as well. The basic
use of XSLT is to transform one XML document into another XML
document. This sort of XSLT operation is closed under the set of
XML documents. The property of closure tremendously simplifies
the interpretation of an operation, and it is easy to think about chain-
ing together or combining closed operations.

Therefore:

**Where it fits, define an operation whose return type is the same
as the type of its argument(s). If the implementer has state that is
used in the computation, then the implementer is effectively an argument of the operation, so the argument(s) and return value
should be of the same type as the implementer. Such an operation is
closed under the set of instances of that type. A closed operation
provides a high-level interface without introducing any dependency
on other concepts.**

This pattern is most often applied to the operations of a VALUE OBJECT. Because the life cycle of an ENTITY has significance in the domain, you can't just conjure up a new one to answer a question. There are operations that are closed under an ENTITY type. You could ask an **Employee** object for its supervisor and get back another **Employee**. But in general, ENTITIES are not the sort of concepts that are likely to be the result of a computation. So, for the most part, this is an opportunity to look for in the VALUE OBJECTS.

An operation can be closed under an abstract type, in which case specific arguments can be of different concrete classes. After all, addition is closed under real numbers, which can be either rational or irrational.

As you're experimenting, looking for ways to reduce interdependence and increase cohesion, you sometimes get halfway to this pattern. The argument matches the implementer, but the return type is different, or the return type matches the receiver and the argument is different. These operations are not closed, but they do give some of the advantages of CLOSURE. When the extra type is a primitive or basic library class, it frees the mind almost as much as CLOSURE.

In the earlier example, the **Pigment Color** `mixedWith()` operation was closed under **Pigment Colors**, and there are several other examples scattered through the book. Here's an example that shows how useful this idea can be, even when true CLOSURE isn't reached.

Example

Selecting from Collections

In Java, if you want to select a subset of elements from a **Collection**, you request an **Iterator**. Then you iterate through the elements, testing each one, probably accumulating the matches into a new **Collection**.

```
Set employees = (some Set of Employee objects);
Set lowPaidEmployees = new HashSet();
Iterator it = employees.iterator();
while (it.hasNext()) {
    Employee anEmployee = it.next();
    if (anEmployee.salary() < 40000)
lowPaidEmployees.add(anEmployee);
}
```

Conceptually, I've selected a subset of a set. What do I need with this extra concept, **Iterator,** and all its mechanical complexity? In Smalltalk, I would call the "select" operation on the **Collection**, passing in the test as an argument. The return would be a new **Collection** containing just the elements that passed the test.

```
employees := (some Set of Employee objects).
lowPaidEmployees := employees select:
        [:anEmployee | anEmployee salary < 40000].
```

The Smalltalk **Collections** provide other such FUNCTIONS that return derived **Collections**, which can be of several concrete classes. The operations are not closed, because they take a "block" as an argument. But blocks are a basic library type in Smalltalk, so they don't add to the developer's mental load. Because the return value matches the implementer, they can be strung together, like a series of filters. They are easy to write and easy to read. They do not introduce extraneous concepts that are irrelevant to the problem of selecting subsets.

✳ ✳ ✳

The patterns presented in this chapter illustrate a general style of design and a way of thinking about design. Making software obvious, predictable, and communicative makes abstraction and encapsulation effective. Models can be factored so that objects are simple to use and understand yet still have rich, high-level interfaces.

These techniques require fairly advanced design skills to apply and sometimes even to write a client. The usefulness of a MODEL-DRIVEN DESIGN is sensitive to the quality of the detailed design and implementation decisions, and it only takes a few confused developers to derail a project from the goal.

That said, for the team willing to cultivate its modeling and design skills, these patterns and the way of thinking they reflect yield software that developers can work and rework to create complex software.

Declarative Design

ASSERTIONS can lead to much better designs, even with our relatively informal way of testing them. But there can be no real guarantees in handwritten software. To name just one way of evading ASSERTIONS, code could have additional side effects that were not specifically excluded. No matter how MODEL-DRIVEN our design is, we still end up writing procedures to produce the effect of the conceptual interactions. And we spend so much of our time writing boilerplate code that doesn't really add any meaning *or* behavior. This is tedious and fraught with error, and the bulk of it obscures the meaning of our model. (Some languages are better than others, but all require us to do a lot of grunt work.) INTENTION-REVEALING INTERFACES and the other patterns in this chapter help, but they can never give conventional object-oriented programs formal rigor.

These are some of the motivations behind *declarative design*. This term means many things to many people, but usually it indicates a way to write a program, or some part of a program, as a kind of executable specification. A very precise description of properties actually controls the software. In its various forms, this could be done through a reflection mechanism or at compile time through code generation (producing conventional code automatically, based on the declaration). This approach allows another developer to take the declaration at face value. It is an absolute guarantee.

Generating a running program from a declaration of model properties is a kind of Holy Grail of MODEL-DRIVEN DESIGN, but it does have its pitfalls in practice. For example, here are just two particular problems I've encountered more than once.

- A declaration language not expressive enough to do everything needed, but a framework that makes it very difficult to extend the software beyond the automated portion

- Code-generation techniques that cripple the iterative cycle by merging generated code into handwritten code in a way that makes regeneration very destructive

The unintended consequence of many attempts at declarative design is the dumbing-down of the model and application, as developers, trapped by the limitations of the framework, enact design triage in order to get *something* delivered.

Rule-based programming with an inference engine and a rule base is another promising approach to declarative design. Unfortunately, subtle issues can undermine this intention.

Although a rules-based program is declarative in principle, most systems have "control predicates" that were added to allow performance tuning. This control code introduces side effects, so that the behavior is no longer dictated completely by the declared rules. Adding, removing, or reordering the rules can cause unexpected, incorrect results. Therefore, a logic programmer has to be careful to keep the effect of code obvious, just as an object programmer does.

Many declarative approaches can be corrupted if the developers bypass them intentionally or unintentionally. This is likely when the system is difficult to use or overly restrictive. Everyone has to follow the rules of the framework in order to get the benefits of a declarative program.

The greatest value I've seen delivered has been when a narrowly scoped framework automates a particularly tedious and error-prone aspect of the design, such as persistence and object-relational mapping. The best of these unburden developers of drudge work while leaving them complete freedom to design.

Domain-Specific Languages

An interesting approach that is sometimes declarative is the *domain-specific language.* In this style, client code is written in a programming language tailored to a particular model of a particular domain. For example, a language for shipping systems might include terms such as *cargo* and *route*, along with syntax for associating them. The program is then compiled, often into a conventional object-oriented language, where a library of classes provides implementations for the terms in the language.

In such a language, programs can be extremely expressive, and make the strongest connection with the UBIQUITOUS LANGUAGE. This is an exciting concept, but domain-specific languages also have their drawbacks in the approaches I've seen based on object-oriented technology.

To refine the model, a developer needs to be able to modify the language. This may involve modifying grammar declarations and other language-interpreting features, as well as modifying underlying class libraries. I'm all in favor of learning advanced technology and design concepts, but we have to soberly assess the skills of a particular team, as well as the likely skills of future maintenance teams. Also, there is value in the seamlessness of an application and a model implemented in the same language. Another drawback is that it can be difficult to refactor client code to conform to a revised model and its associated domain-specific language. Of course, someone may come up with a technical fix for the refactoring problems.

This technique might be most useful for very mature models, perhaps where client code is being written by a different team. Generally, such setups lead to the poisonous distinction between highly technical framework builders and technically unskilled application builders, but it doesn't have to be that way.

In the scheme programming language, something very similar is part of standard programming style, so that the expressiveness of a domain-specific language can be created without bifurcating the system.

From the Ground Up
A different paradigm might handle domain-specific languages better than objects. In the Scheme programming language, a representative of the "functional programming" family, something very similar is part of standard programming style, so that the expressiveness of a domain-specific language can be created without bifurcating the system.

A Declarative Style of Design

Once your design has INTENTION-REVEALING INTERFACES, SIDE-EFFECT-FREE FUNCTIONS, and ASSERTIONS, you are edging into declarative territory. Many of the benefits of declarative design are obtained once you have combinable elements that communicate their meaning, and have characterized or obvious effects, or no observable effects at all.

A supple design can make it possible for the client code to use a declarative *style* of design. To illustrate, the next section will bring together some of the patterns in this chapter to make the SPECIFICATION more supple and declarative.

Extending SPECIFICATIONS in a Declarative Style

Chapter 9 covered the basic concept of SPECIFICATION, the roles it can play in a program, and some sense of what is involved in implementation. Now let's take a look at a few bells and whistles that can be very useful in some situations with complicated rules.

SPECIFICATION is an adaptation of an established formalism, the predicate. Predicates have other useful properties that we can draw on, selectively.

Combining SPECIFICATIONS Using Logical Operators

When using SPECIFICATIONS, you quickly come across situations in which you would like to combine them. As just mentioned, a SPECIFICATION is an example of a predicate, and predicates can be combined and modified with the operations "AND," "OR," and "NOT." These logical operations are closed under predicates, so SPECIFICATION combinations will exhibit CLOSURE OF OPERATIONS.

As significant generalized capability is built into SPECIFICATIONS, it becomes very useful to create an abstract class or interface that can be used for SPECIFICATIONS of all sorts. This means typing arguments as some high-level abstract class.

```
public interface Specification {
    boolean isSatisfiedBy(Object candidate);
}
```

This abstraction calls for a guard clause at the beginning of the method, but otherwise it does not affect functionality. For example, the **Container Specification** (from the example in Chapter 9, on page 236) would be modified this way:

```
public class ContainerSpecification implements Specification {
    private ContainerFeature requiredFeature;

    public ContainerSpecification(ContainerFeature required) {
        requiredFeature = required;
    }

    boolean isSatisfiedBy(Object candidate){
        if (!candidate instanceof Container) return false;

        return
(Container)candidate.getFeatures().contains(requiredFeature);
    }
}
```

Now, let's extend the **Specification** interface by adding the three new operations:

```
public interface Specification {
    boolean isSatisfiedBy(Object candidate);

    Specification and(Specification other);
    Specification or(Specification other);
    Specification not();
}
```

Recall that some **Container Specifications** were configured to require ventilated **Containers** and others to require armored **Containers**. A chemical that is both volatile *and* explosive would, presumably, need *both* of these SPECIFICATIONS. Easily done, using the new methods.

```
Specification ventilated = new ContainerSpecification(VENTILATED);
Specification armored = new ContainerSpecification(ARMORED);

Specification both = ventilated.and(armored);
```

The declaration defines a new **Specification** object with the expected properties. This combination would have required a more complicated **Container Specification**, and would still have been special purpose.

Suppose we had more than one kind of ventilated **Container**. It might not matter for some items which kind they were packed into. They could be placed in either type.

```
Specification ventilatedType1 =
        new ContainerSpecification(VENTILATED_TYPE_1);
Specification ventilatedType2 =
        new ContainerSpecification(VENTILATED_TYPE_2);

Specification either = ventilatedType1.or(ventilatedType2);
```

If it was considered wasteful to store sand in specialized containers, we could prohibit it by SPECIFYING a "cheap" container with no special features.

```
Specification cheap = (ventilated.not()).and(armored.not());
```

This constraint would have prevented some of the suboptimal behavior of the prototype warehouse packer discussed in Chapter 9.

The ability to build complex specifications out of simple elements increases the expressiveness of the code. The combinations are written in a declarative style.

Depending on how SPECIFICATIONS are implemented, these operators may be easy or difficult to provide. What follows is a very simple implementation, which would be inefficient in some situations and quite practical in others. It is meant as an *explanatory example*. Like any pattern, there are many ways to implement it.

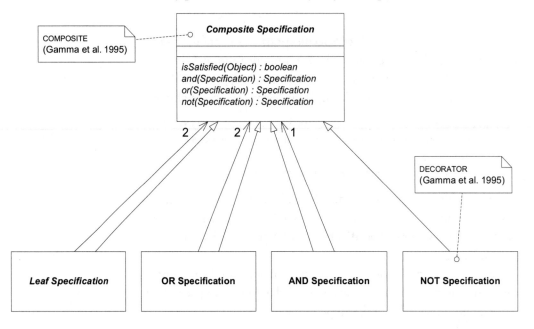

Figure 10.14
COMPOSITE design of
SPECIFICATION

```
public abstract class AbstractSpecification implements
        Specification {
    public Specification and(Specification other) {
        return new AndSpecification(this, other);
    }
    public Specification or(Specification other) {
        return new OrSpecification(this, other);
    }
    public Specification not() {
        return new NotSpecification(this);
    }
}

public class AndSpecification extends AbstractSpecification {
    Specification one;
    Specification other;
```

```
    public AndSpecification(Specification x, Specification y) {
       one = x;
       other = y;
    }
    public boolean isSatisfiedBy(Object candidate) {
       return one.isSatisfiedBy(candidate) &&
          other.isSatisfiedBy(candidate);
    }
}


public class OrSpecification extends AbstractSpecification {
    Specification one;
    Specification other;
    public OrSpecification(Specification x, Specification y) {
       one = x;
       other = y;
    }
    public boolean isSatisfiedBy(Object candidate) {
       return one.isSatisfiedBy(candidate) ||
          other.isSatisfiedBy(candidate);
    }
}


public class NotSpecification extends AbstractSpecification {
    Specification wrapped;

    public NotSpecification(Specification x) {
       wrapped = x;
    }
    public boolean isSatisfiedBy(Object candidate) {
       return !wrapped.isSatisfiedBy(candidate);
    }
}
```

This code was written to be as easy as possible to read in a book. As I said, there may be situations in which this is inefficient. However, other implementation options are possible that would minimize object count or boost speed, or perhaps be compatible with idiosyncratic technologies present in some project. The important thing is a model that captures the key concepts of the domain, along with an implementation that is faithful to that model. That leaves a lot of room to solve performance problems.

Also, this full generality is not needed in many cases. In particular, AND tends to be used a lot more than the others, and it also tends to create less implementation complexity. Don't be afraid to implement only AND, if that is all you need.

Way back in Chapter 2, in the example dialog on page 30, the developers had apparently not implemented the "satisfied by" behavior of their SPECIFICATION. Up to that point, the SPECIFICATION had been used only for building to order. Even so, the abstraction was intact, and adding functionality was relatively easy. Using a pattern doesn't mean building features you don't need. They can be added later, as long as the concepts don't get muddled.

Example

One Alternative Implementation of
COMPOSITE SPECIFICATION

Some implementation environments don't accommodate very fine grained objects very well. I once worked on a project with an object database that insisted on giving an object ID to every object and then tracking it. Each object had lots of overhead in memory space and performance, and total address space was a limiting factor. I employed SPECIFICATIONS at some important points in the domain design, which I think was a good decision. But I used a slightly more elaborate version of the implementation described in this chapter, which was definitely a mistake. It resulted in millions of very fine grained objects that contributed to bogging the system down.

Here is an example of an alternative implementation that encodes the composite SPECIFICATION as a string or array encoding the logical expression, to be interpreted at runtime.

(Don't worry if you do not see how you would implement this. The important thing is to realize that there are many ways of implementing a SPECIFICATION with logical operators, and so if the simple one is not practical in your situation, you have options.)

SPECIFICATION Stack Content for "Cheap Container"

Top	AndSpecificationOperator (FLY WEIGHT)
	NotSpecificationOperator (FLY WEIGHT)
	Armored
	NotSpecificationOperator
	Ventilated

When you want to test a candidate, you have to interpret this structure, which can be done by popping off each element, then evaluating it or popping off the next as required by an operator. You would end up with this:

```
and(not(armored), not(ventilated))
```

This design has pros (+) and cons (−):

+ Low object count

+ Efficient use of memory

− Requires more sophisticated developers

You have to find an implementation with trade-offs that work for your circumstances. The same pattern and model can underlie very different implementations.

Subsumption

This final feature is not usually needed and can be difficult to implement, but every now and then it solves a really hard problem. It also elucidates the meaning of a SPECIFICATION.

Consider again the chemical warehouse packer from the example on page 235. Recall that each **Chemical** had a **Container Specification,** and the **Packer** SERVICE guaranteed that all these would be satisfied when **Drums** are assigned to **Containers**. All is well . . . until someone changes the regulations.

Every few months a new set of rules is issued, and our users would like to be able to produce a list of the chemical types that now have more stringent requirements.

Of course, we could give a partial answer (and one the users probably also want) by running a validation of each **Drum** in the inventory, with the new SPECIFICATIONS in place, and finding all those that no longer meet the SPEC. This would tell the users which **Drums** in the existing inventory they need to move.

But what they *asked for* was a list of chemicals whose handling has become more stringent. Perhaps there are none in-house right now, or perhaps they just happened to be packed into a more stringent container. In either case, the report just described would not list them.

Let's introduce a new operation for directly comparing two SPECIFICATIONS.

```
boolean subsumes(Specification other);
```

A more stringent SPEC subsumes a less stringent one. It could take its place without any previous requirement being neglected.

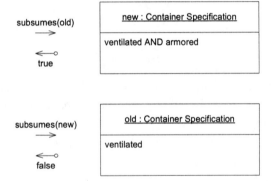

Figure 10.15
The SPECIFICATION for a gasoline container has been tightened.

In the language of SPECIFICATION, we would say that the new SPECIFICATION *subsumes* the old SPECIFICATION, because any candidate that would satisfy the new SPEC would also satisfy the old.

If each of these SPECIFICATIONS is viewed as a predicate, subsumption is equivalent to logical implication. Using conventional notation, $A \rightarrow B$ means that statement A implies statement B, so that if A is true, B is also true.

Let's apply this logic to our container-matching needs. When a SPECIFICATION is being changed, we would like to know if the proposed new SPEC meets all the conditions of the old one.

$$\text{New Spec} \rightarrow \text{Old Spec}$$

That is, if the new spec is true, then the old spec is also true. Proving a logical implication in a general way is very difficult, but special cases can be easy. For example, particular parameterized SPECS can define their own subsumption rule.

```
public class MinimumAgeSpecification {
    int threshold;

    public boolean isSatisfiedBy(Person candidate) {
        return candidate.getAge() >= threshold;
    }

    public boolean subsumes(MinimumAgeSpecification other) {
        return threshold >= other.getThreshold();
    }
}
```

A JUnit test might contain this:

```
drivingAge = new MinimumAgeSpecification(16);
votingAge = new MinimumAgeSpecification(18);
assertTrue(votingAge.subsumes(drivingAge));
```

Another practical special case, one suited to address the **Container Specification** problem, is a SPECIFICATION interface combining subsumption with the single logical operator AND.

```
public interface Specification {
    boolean isSatisfiedBy(Object candidate);
    Specification and(Specification other);
    boolean subsumes(Specification other);
}
```

Proving implication with only the AND operator is simple:

$$A \text{ AND } B \rightarrow A$$

or, in a more complicated case:

$$A \text{ AND } B \text{ AND } C \rightarrow A \text{ AND } B$$

So if the **Composite Specification** is able to collect all the leaf SPECIFICATIONS that are "ANDed" together, then all we have to do is check that the subsuming SPECIFICATION has all the leaves that the subsumed one has, and maybe some extra ones as well—its leaves are a superset of the other SPEC's set of leaves.

```
public boolean subsumes(Specification other) {
    if (other instanceof CompositeSpecification) {
        Collection otherLeaves =
            (CompositeSpecification) other.leafSpecifications();
        Iterator it = otherLeaves.iterator();
        while (it.hasNext()) {
            if (!leafSpecifications().contains(it.next()))
                return false;
        }
    } else {
        if (!leafSpecifications().contains(other))
            return false;
    }
    return true;
}
```

This interaction could be enhanced to compare carefully chosen parameterized leaf SPECIFICATIONS and some other complications. Unfortunately, when OR and NOT are included, these proofs become much more involved. In most situations it is best to avoid such complexity by making a choice, either forgoing some of the operators or forgoing subsumption. If both are needed, consider carefully if the benefit is great enough to justify the difficulty.

Aristotle on SPECIFICATIONS

All men are mortal.	`Specification manSpec = new ManSpecification();`
	`Specification mortalSpec = new MortalSpecification();`
	`assert manSpec.subsumes(mortalSpec);`

Aristotle is a man.	`Man aristotle = new Man();` `assert manSpec.isSatisfiedBy(aristotle);`
Therefore, Aristotle is mortal.	`assert mortalSpec.isSatisfiedBy(aristotle);`

Angles of Attack

This chapter has presented a raft of techniques to clarify the intent of code, to make the consequences of using it transparent, and to decouple model elements. Even so, this kind of design is difficult. You can't just look at an enormous system and say, "Let's make this supple." You have to choose targets. Here are a couple of broad approaches, followed by an extended example showing how the patterns are fit together and used to take on a bigger design.

Carve Off Subdomains

You just can't tackle the whole design at once. Pick away at it. Some aspects of the system will suggest approaches to you, and they can be factored out and worked over. You may see a part of the model that can be viewed as specialized math; separate that. Your application enforces complex rules restricting state changes; pull this out into a separate model or simple framework that lets you declare the rules. With each such step, not only is the new module clean, but also the part left behind is smaller and clearer. Part of what's left is written in a declarative style, a declaration in terms of the special math or validation framework, or whatever form the subdomain takes.

It is more useful to make a big impact on one area, making a part of the design really supple, than to spread your efforts thin. Chapter 15 discusses in more depth how to choose and manage subdomains.

Draw on Established Formalisms, When You Can

Creating a tight conceptual framework from scratch is something you can't do every day. Sometimes you discover and refine *one* of these over the course of the life of a project. But you can often use and adapt conceptual systems that are long established in your domain or others, some of which have been refined and distilled over centuries. Many business applications involve accounting, for example. Accounting defines a well-developed set of ENTITIES and rules that make for an easy adaptation to a deep model and a supple design.

There are many such formalized conceptual frameworks, but my personal favorite is math. It is surprising how useful it can be to pull out some twist on basic arithmetic. Many domains include math somewhere. Look for it. Dig it out. Specialized math is clean, combinable by clear rules, and people find it easy to understand. One example from my past is "Shares Math," which will end this chapter.

Integrating the Patterns: Shares Math

Chapter 8 told the story of a model breakthrough on a project to build a syndicated loan system. Now this example will go into detail, focusing on just one feature of a design comparable to the one on that project.

One requirement of that application was that when the borrower makes a principal payment, the money is, by default, prorated according to the lenders' shares in the loan.

Initial Design for Payment Distribution

As we refactor it, this code will get easier to understand, so don't get stuck on this version.

Figure 10.16

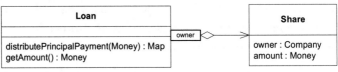

```
public class Loan {
    private Map shares;

    //Accessors, constructors, and very simple methods are excluded

    public Map distributePrincipalPayment(double paymentAmount) {
        Map paymentShares = new HashMap();
        Map loanShares = getShares();
        double total = getAmount();
        Iterator it = loanShares.keySet().iterator();
        while(it.hasNext()) {
            Object owner = it.next();
            double initialLoanShareAmount = getShareAmount(owner);
            double paymentShareAmount =
                initialLoanShareAmount / total * paymentAmount;
            Share paymentShare =
                new Share(owner, paymentShareAmount);
            paymentShares.put(owner, paymentShare);

            double newLoanShareAmount =
                initialLoanShareAmount - paymentShareAmount;
```

```
        Share newLoanShare =
            new Share(owner, newLoanShareAmount);
        loanShares.put(owner, newLoanShare);
    }
    return paymentShares;
}


public double getAmount() {
    Map loanShares = getShares();
    double total = 0.0;
    Iterator it = loanShares.keySet().iterator();
    while(it.hasNext()) {
        Share loanShare = (Share) loanShares.get(it.next());
        total = total + loanShare.getAmount();
    }
    return total;
}
}
```

Separating Commands and SIDE-EFFECT-FREE FUNCTIONS

This design already has INTENTION-REVEALING INTERFACES. But the distributePaymentPrincipal() method does a dangerous thing: It calculates the shares for distribution and also modifies the **Loan**. Let's refactor to separate the query from the modifier.

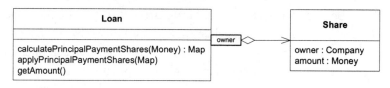

Figure 10.17

```
public void applyPrincipalPaymentShares(Map paymentShares) {
    Map loanShares = getShares();
    Iterator it = paymentShares.keySet().iterator();
    while(it.hasNext()) {
        Object lender = it.next();
        Share paymentShare = (Share) paymentShares.get(lender);
        Share loanShare = (Share) loanShares.get(lender);
        double newLoanShareAmount = loanShare.getAmount() -
            paymentShare.getAmount();
```

```
            Share newLoanShare = new Share(lender, newLoanShareAmount);
            loanShares.put(lender, newLoanShare);
        }
    }

    public Map calculatePrincipalPaymentShares(double paymentAmount) {
        Map paymentShares = new HashMap();
        Map loanShares = getShares();
        double total = getAmount();
        Iterator it = loanShares.keySet().iterator();
        while(it.hasNext()) {
            Object lender = it.next();
            Share loanShare = (Share) loanShares.get(lender);
            double paymentShareAmount =
                loanShare.getAmount() / total * paymentAmount;
            Share paymentShare = new Share(lender, paymentShareAmount);
            paymentShares.put(lender, paymentShare);
        }
        return paymentShares;
    }
```

Client code now looks like this:

```
Map distribution =
    aLoan.calculatePrincipalPaymentShares(paymentAmount);
aLoan.applyPrincipalPaymentShares(distribution);
```

Not too bad. The FUNCTIONS have encapsulated a lot of complexity behind INTENTION-REVEALING INTERFACES. But the code does begin to multiply some when we add applyDrawdown(), calculateFeePaymentShares(), and so on. Each extension complicates the code and weighs it down. This might be a point where the granularity is too coarse. The conventional approach would be to break the calculation methods down into subroutines. That could well be a good step along the way, but we ultimately want to see the underlying conceptual boundaries and deepen the model. The elements of a design with such a CONCEPT-CONTOURING grain could be combined to produce the needed variations.

Making an Implicit Concept Explicit

There are enough pointers now to start probing for that new model. The **Share** objects are passive in this implementation, and they are being manipulated in complex, low-level ways. This is because most of the rules and calculations about shares don't apply to single shares, but to groups of them. There is a missing concept: shares are related to each other as parts making up a whole. Making this concept explicit will let us express those rules and calculations more succinctly.

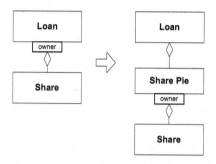

Figure 10.18

The **Share Pie** represents the total distribution of a specific **Loan**. It is an ENTITY whose identity is local within the AGGREGATE of the **Loan**. The actual distribution calculations can be delegated to the **Share Pie**.

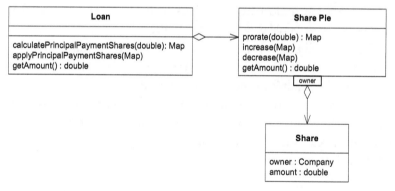

Figure 10.19

```java
public class Loan {
   private SharePie shares;

   //Accessors, constructors, and straightforward methods
   //are omitted

   public Map calculatePrincipalPaymentDistribution(
                                   double paymentAmount) {
     return getShares().prorated(paymentAmount);
   }
```

```
    public void applyPrincipalPayment(Map paymentShares) {
        shares.decrease(paymentShares);
    }
}
```

The **Loan** is simplified, and the **Share** calculations are centralized in a VALUE OBJECT focused on that responsibility. Still, the calculations haven't really become more versatile or easier to use.

Share Pie Becomes a VALUE OBJECT: Cascade of Insights

Often, the hands-on experience of implementing a new design will trigger a new insight into the model itself. In this case, the tight coupling of the **Loan** and **Share Pie** seems to be obscuring the relationship of the **Share Pie** and the **Shares**. What would happen if we made **Share Pie** a VALUE OBJECT?

This would mean that increase(Map) and decrease(Map) would not be allowed, because the **Share Pie** would have to be immutable. To change the **Share Pie**'s value, the whole **Pie** would have to be replaced. So you could have operations such as addShares(Map) that would return a whole new, larger **Share Pie**.

Let's go all the way to CLOSURE OF OPERATIONS. Instead of "increasing" a **Share Pie** or adding **Shares** to it, just add two **Share Pies** together: the result is the new, larger **Share Pie**.

We can partially close the prorate() operation over **Share Pie** just by changing the return type. Renaming it to prorated() emphasizes its lack of side effects. "Shares Math" starts to take shape, initially with four operations.

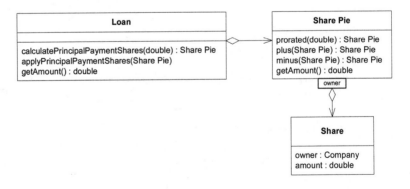

Figure 10.20

We can make some well-defined ASSERTIONS about our new
VALUE OBJECTS, the **Share Pies**. Each method means something.

```java
public class SharePie {
    private Map shares = new HashMap();

    //Accessors and other straightforward methods are omitted


    public double getAmount() {
        double total = 0.0;
        Iterator it = shares.keySet().iterator();
        while(it.hasNext()) {
            Share loanShare = getShare(it.next());
            total = total + loanShare.getAmount();
        }
        return total;
    }


    public SharePie minus(SharePie otherShares) {
        SharePie result = new SharePie();
        Set owners = new HashSet();
        owners.addAll(getOwners());
        owners.addAll(otherShares.getOwners());
        Iterator it = owners.iterator();
        while(it.hasNext()) {
            Object owner = it.next();
            double resultShareAmount = getShareAmount(owner) -
                otherShares.getShareAmount(owner);
            result.add(owner, resultShareAmount);
        }
        return result;
    }


    public SharePie plus(SharePie otherShares) {
        //Similar to implementation of minus()
    }

    public SharePie prorated(double amountToProrate) {
        SharePie proration = new SharePie();
        double basis = getAmount();
        Iterator it = shares.keySet().iterator();
        while(it.hasNext()) {
            Object owner = it.next();
            Share share = getShare(owner);
```

The whole is equal to the sum of its parts.

*The difference between two **Pies** is the difference between each owner's share.*

*The combination of two **Pies** is the combination of each owner's share.*

An amount can be divided proportionately among all shareholders.

```
      double proratedShareAmount =
          share.getAmount() / basis * amountToProrate;
      proration.add(owner, proratedShareAmount);
    }
    return proration;
  }

}
```

The Suppleness of the New Design

At this point, the methods in the all-important **Loan** class could be as simple as this:

```
public class Loan {
  private SharePie shares;

  //Accessors, constructors, and straightforward methods
  //are omitted

  public SharePie calculatePrincipalPaymentDistribution(
                                        double paymentAmount) {
    return shares.prorated(paymentAmount);
  }

  public void applyPrincipalPayment(SharePie paymentShares) {
    setShares(shares.minus(paymentShares));
  }
```

Each of these short methods states its *meaning*. Applying a principal payment means that you subtract the payment from the loan, share by share. Distributing a principal payment is done by dividing the amount *pro rata* among the shareholders. The design of the **Share Pie** has allowed us to use a declarative style in the **Loan** code, producing code that begins to read like a conceptual definition of the business transaction, rather than a calculation.

Other transaction types (too complicated to list before) can be declared easily now. For example, loan drawdowns are divided among lenders based on their shares of the **Facility**. The new drawdown is added to the outstanding **Loan**. In our new domain language:

```
public class Facility {
  private SharePie shares;
    . . .
```

```
public SharePie calculateDrawdownDefaultDistribution(
                                double drawdownAmount) {
    return shares.prorated(drawdownAmount);
  }
}

public class Loan {
  . . .
  public void applyDrawdown(SharePie drawdownShares) {
    setShares(shares.plus(drawdownShares));
  }
}
```

To see the deviation of each lender from its agreed contribution, take the theoretical distribution of the outstanding **Loan** amount and subtract it from the **Loan's** actual shares:

```
SharePie originalAgreement =
    aFacility.getShares().prorated(aLoan.getAmount());
SharePie actual = aLoan.getShares();
SharePie deviation = actual.minus(originalAgreement);
```

Certain characteristics of the **Share Pie** design make for this easy recombination and communication in the code.

- *Complex logic is encapsulated in specialized* VALUE OBJECTS *with* SIDE-EFFECT-FREE FUNCTIONS. Most complex logic has been encapsulated in these immutable objects. Because **Share Pies** are VALUE OBJECTS, the math operations can create new instances, which we can use freely to replace outdated instances.

  None of the **Share Pie** methods causes any change to any existing object. This allows us to use plus(), minus(), and prorated() freely in intermediate calculations, combining them, expecting them to do what their names suggest, and nothing more. It also allows us to build analytical features based on the same methods. (Before, they could be called only when an actual distribution was made, because the data would change after each call.)

- *State-modifying operations are simple and characterized with* AS-SERTIONS. The high-level abstractions of Shares Math allow invariants of transactions to be written concisely in a declarative

---

style. For example, the deviation is the actual pie minus the **Loan** amount prorated based on the **Facility's Share Pie**.

- *Model concepts are decoupled; operations entangle a minimum of other types.* Some methods on **Share Pie** exhibit CLOSURE OF OPERATIONS (the methods to add or subtract are closed under **Share Pies**). Others take simple amounts as arguments or return values; they are not closed, but they add little to the conceptual load. The **Share Pie** interacts closely with only one other class, **Share**. As a result, the **Share Pie** is self-contained, easily understood, easily tested, and easily combined to form declarative transactions. These properties were inherited from the math formalism.

- *Familiar formalism makes the protocol easy to grasp.* A wholly original protocol for manipulating shares could have been devised based on financial terminology. In principle, it could have been made supple. But it would have had two disadvantages. First, it would have to be invented, a difficult and uncertain task. Second, it would have to be learned by each person who dealt with it. People who see Shares Math recognize a system they already know, and because the design has been kept carefully consistent with the rules of arithmetic, those people are not misled.

Pulling out the part of the problem that corresponded to the formalism of math, we arrived at a supple design for **Shares** that further distills the core **Loan** and **Facility** methods. (See Chapter 15 for discussion of the CORE DOMAIN.)

Supple design has a profound effect on the ability of software to cope with change and complexity. As the examples in this chapter have shown, it often hinges on quite detailed modeling and design decisions. The impact can go beyond a specific modeling and design problem. Chapter 15 will discuss the strategic value of supple design as one of several tools for distilling a domain model to make large and complex projects more tractable.

ELEVEN

Applying
Analysis Patterns

Deep models and supple designs don't come easily. Progress comes from lots of learning about the domain, lots of talking, and lots of trial and error. Sometimes, though, we can get a leg up.

When an experienced developer looking at a domain problem sees a familiar sort of responsibility or a familiar web of relationships, he or she can draw on the memory of how the problem was solved before. What models were tried and which worked? What difficulties arose in implementation and how were they resolved? The trial and error of that earlier experience is suddenly relevant to the new situation. Some of these patterns have been documented and shared, allowing the rest of us to draw on the accumulated experience.

In contrast to the fundamental building block patterns presented in Part II, and the supple design principles of Chapter 10, these patterns are higher level and more specialized, involving the use of a few objects to represent some concept. They let us cut through expensive trial and error to start with a model that is already expressive and implementable and addresses subtleties that might be costly to learn. From that starting point, we refactor and experiment. These are not out-of-the-box solutions.

In *Analysis Patterns: Reusable Object Models,* Martin Fowler defined his patterns this way:

> Analysis patterns are groups of concepts that represent a common construction in business modeling. It may be relevant to only one domain or it may span many domains. [Fowler 1997, p. 8]

The analysis patterns Fowler presents arose from experience in the field, and so they are practical, in the right situation. Such patterns provide someone facing a challenging domain with very valuable starting points for their iterative development process. The name emphasizes their conceptual nature. Analysis patterns are not technological solutions; they are guides to help you work out a model in a particular domain.

What the name unfortunately does *not* convey is that there is significant discussion of implementation in these patterns, including some code. Fowler understands the pitfalls of analysis without thought for practical design. Here is an interesting example where he is looking even beyond deployment, to the implications of specific model choices on the long-term maintenance of the system in the field:

> When we build a new [accounting] practice, we create a network of new instances of the posting rule. We can do this without any recompilation or rebuilding of the system, while it is still up and running. There will be unavoidable occasions when we need a new subtype of posting rule, but these will be rare. [p. 151]

On a mature project, model choices are often informed by experience with the application. Multiple implementations of various components will have been tried. Some of these will have been carried into production and even will have faced the maintenance phase. Many problems can be avoided when such experience is available. Analysis patterns at their best can carry that kind of experience from other projects, combining model insights with extensive discussions of design directions and implementation consequences. To discuss model ideas out of that context makes them harder to apply and risks opening the deadly divide between analysis and design, which is antithetical to MODEL-DRIVEN DESIGN.

The principle and application of analysis patterns can be explained better by example than through abstract description. In this chapter, I will give two examples of developers making use of a small, representative sample of models from the chapter "Inventory and Accounting" in Fowler 1997. The analysis patterns will be summarized just enough to support the examples. This is obviously not an attempt to catalog patterns of this kind or even to fully explain the sample patterns. The point is to illustrate their integration into the domain-driven design process.

Example

Earning Interest with Accounts

Chapter 10 showed various possible ways that a developer might search for a deeper model for a particular specialty accounting application. Here is yet another scenario. This time, the developers will mine Fowler's *Analysis Patterns* book for useful ideas.

To review, an application for tracking loans and other interest-bearing assets calculates the interest and fees generated and tracks payments from the borrower. A nightly batch process takes those figures and passes them to the legacy accounting system, indicating the specific ledger each amount should be posted to. The design works, but it is awkward to use, tricky to change, and does not communicate well.

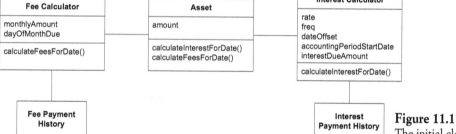

Figure 11.1
The initial class diagram

The developer decides to read Chapter 6 in *Analysis Patterns,* "Inventory and Accounting." Here is a summary of the part she found most relevant.

Accounting Models in *Analysis Patterns*

Business applications of all sorts track *accounts,* which hold things of value, typically money. In a lot of applications, it isn't enough to keep track of the amount in an account. It is essential to account for and control each change to that amount. That is the motivation for the most basic of the accounting models.

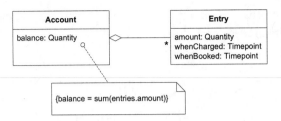

Figure 11.2
A basic accounting
model

Value can be added by inserting an *Entry.* Value can be removed by inserting a negative **Entry**. **Entries** are never removed, so the whole history is retained. The balance is the combined effect of all **Entries**. This balance could be computed on demand or cached, an implementation decision that is encapsulated by the **Account** interface.

A basic principle of accounting is *conservation*. Money doesn't appear out of nowhere, nor does it disappear without a trace. It is only moved from one **Account** to another.

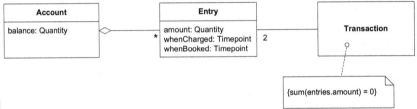

Figure 11.3
A transaction model

This is the well-established concept of *double-entry bookkeeping*: Every credit has a matching debit. Of course, like other conservation principles, it applies only to a closed system, one that includes all sources and sinks. Many simple applications do not require this rigor.

In his book, Fowler includes more elaborate forms of these models and considerable discussion of the trade-offs.

This reading gives the developer (**Developer 1**) several new ideas. She shows the chapter to a colleague (**Developer 2**) who has been working on some of the interest calculation logic with her and who wrote the nightly batch program. Together, they rough out a change to their model, incorporating some of the model elements they've read about.

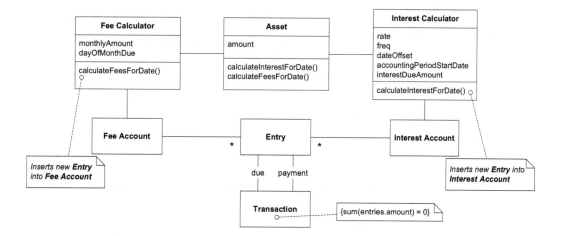

Then they pull in their domain expert (**Expert**) for a discussion of their new model ideas.

Figure 11.4
The new model proposal

Developer 1: With this new model, we make an **Entry** into the **Interest Account** for the interest earned, rather than just adjusting the interestDueAmount. Then, another **Entry** for the payment balances it out.

Expert: So now we'd be able to see a history of all the interest accruals as well as the payment history? That's something we've been wanting.

Developer 2: I'm not sure we've used "**Transaction**" quite right. The definition talks about moving money from one **Account** to another, not two entries that balance each other in the same **Account**.

Developer 1: That's a good point. I was also worried that the book seems to make quite a point about the transaction being created all at once. The interest payments can be several days late.

Expert: Those payments aren't necessarily late. There is a lot of flexibility in when they pay.

Developer 1: So this may be a blind alley. I was thinking we might have identified some implicit concepts. Having the **Interest Calculator** create **Entry** objects does seem to communicate better. And **Transaction** seemed to neatly tie together the calculated interest with the payment.

Expert: Why do we need to tie together the accrual to the payment? They are separate postings in the accounting system. The balance on the **Account** is the main thing. Along with the individual **Entries,** we really have what we need.

Developer 2: You mean you don't track whether they've made the interest payment?

Expert: Well, of course we do. But it isn't as simple as this one-accrual/one-payment scheme of yours.

Developer 2: It could actually simplify a lot of things to stop worrying about that connection.

Developer 1: OK, how about this? [*Takes copy of old class diagram and starts sketching modifications*] By the way, you used the word *accruals* a few times. Could you clarify what it means?

Expert: Sure. An accrual is just when you account for an expense or income at the time it is incurred, never mind when money actually changes hands. So, we accrue interest every day, but at the end of the month (for example) we receive a payment against it.

Developer 1: Yes, we really needed a word like that. OK, how does this look?

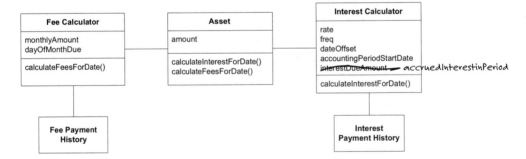

Figure 11.5
Original class diagram, accruals separated from payment

Developer 1: Now we can get rid of all the complications that were in the calculator from relating payments, and we've introduced the term *accruals*, which reveals the intent better.

Expert: So we're not going to have the **Account** object? I was looking forward to being able to see everything together there, with the accruals and the payments and a balance.

CHAPTER 11: APPLYING ANALYSIS PATTERNS

Developer 1: Really?! Well in that case, maybe *this* would work. [*Takes other diagram and sketches*]

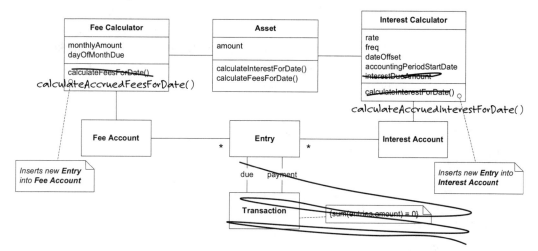

Expert: That actually looks pretty good!

Developer 2: The batch script will be easy to change to use these new objects.

Figure 11.6
The account-based diagram, without **Transaction**

Developer 1: It will take a few days to get the new **Interest Calculator** working. There are quite a few tests to change. But the test will read clearer afterward.

The two developers went off and started refactoring based on the new model. As they got their hands on the code, tightening up the design, they had insights that refined the model.

Entries were subclassed into **Payment** and **Accrual** because closer inspection revealed slightly different responsibilities in the application for these, and because they were both important domain concepts. On the other hand, there was no conceptual or behavioral distinction between **Entries** based on whether they resulted from fees or interest. They simply appeared in the appropriate **Account**.

Yet, unfortunately, the developers found they had to give up this last abstraction for the implementation. Data was stored in relational tables, and the project standard was to make those tables interpretable without running the program. This meant keeping fee entries and interest entries in separate tables. The only way for developers to do this, using their particular object-relational mapping framework, was to make concrete subclasses (**Fee Payments**, **Interest Payments**, and so on). With different infrastructure, they might have avoided this clumsy expansion.

I threw this twist into this largely fictitious story to represent the rub of reality that we encounter all the time. We have to make calculated compromises and then move on without letting it throw us off our MODEL-DRIVEN DESIGN.

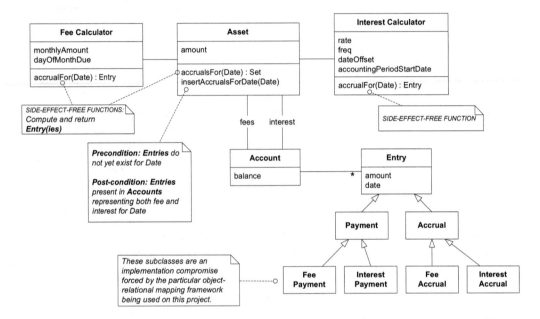

Figure 11.7
The class diagram after the implementation

The new design was much easier to analyze and test because the most complex functionality is in SIDE-EFFECT-FREE FUNCTIONS. The remaining command has simple code (because it calls various FUNCTIONS) and is characterized by ASSERTIONS.

Sometimes there are parts of our programs that we don't even suspect have the potential to benefit from a domain model. They may have started very simply and evolved mechanistically. They seem like complicated application code, rather than domain logic. Analysis patterns can be particularly helpful in showing us these blind spots.

In the following example, a developer has a new insight into the black box of the nightly batch, which had not been considered domain oriented.

Insight into the Nightly Batch

After a few weeks, the improved **Account**-based model had started to settle in. As often happens, the clarity of the new design made other problems more visible. The developer (**Developer 2**) who was adapting the nightly batch to interact with the new design began to see connections between the behavior of the batch and some of the concepts in *Analysis Patterns*. Here is a summary of some of the concepts he found most relevant.

Posting Rules

Accounting systems often provide multiple views of the same basic financial information. One account might track income while another might track an estimated tax on that income. If the system is expected to automatically update the estimated tax account, the implementation of those two accounts becomes very intertwined. There are systems in which the majority of account entries result from such rules; in such a system, the dependency logic gets to be a mess. Even in more modest systems, such cross-posting can be tricky. The first step toward taming the tangle of dependencies is to make these rules explicit by introducing a new object.

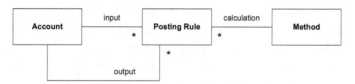

Figure 11.8
The class diagram of the basic posting rule

A posting rule is triggered by a new **Entry** in its "input" account. It then derives a new **Entry** (based on its own calculation **Method**) and inserts the new **Entry** into its "output" **Account**. In a payroll system, an **Entry** in a salary **Account** might trigger a **Posting Rule** that would calculate a 30 percent estimated income tax and insert it as an **Entry** in the tax withholding **Account**.

Executing Posting Rules

The **Posting Rule** has established the conceptual dependency between **Accounts**, but if the pattern stopped there, it could be difficult to follow. One of the trickiest parts of dependency designs is the timing and control of updates. Fowler discusses three options.

1. "Eager firing" is the most obvious, but typically the least practical. Whenever an **Entry** is inserted into an **Account**, it immediately triggers the **Posting Rules** and all updates are made immediately.

2. "**Account**-based firing" allows processing to be deferred. At some point, a message is sent to an **Account** and it triggers its **Posting Rules** to process all **Entries** inserted since its last firing.

3. Finally, "**Posting-Rule**-based firing" is initiated by an external agent, which tells the **Posting Rule** to fire. The **Posting Rule** is responsible for looking up all **Entries** made to its input **Accounts** since the last time it fired.

Although firing modes can be mixed in a system, each particular set of rules needs to have one clearly defined point of initiation and responsibility for identifying input **Account Entries**. The addition of the three firing modes to the UBIQUITOUS LANGUAGE is as important to the success of the pattern as the model object definitions themselves. It eliminates ambiguity and guides decision making directly to a clearly defined set of choices. These modes identify an easily overlooked challenge and provide vocabulary to support clear discussion.

Developer 2 needed a sounding board to discuss his new ideas. He met up his colleague (**Developer 1**), the developer who had been primarily responsible for modeling the accruals.

Developer 2: At some point, the nightly batch started being a place where we swept stuff under the rug. There is domain logic implicit in what the script does, and it's been getting more and more complicated. For a long time I've wanted to do a model-driven design for the batch, separate out a domain layer, and make the script itself a simple layer on top of the domain. But I could never figure out what that domain model would be like. It seemed like maybe it was just some procedures that didn't really make sense as objects. As I've been reading the section in *Analysis Patterns* on **Posting Rules**, I've been getting some ideas. Here's what I had in mind. [*Hands over a sketch*]

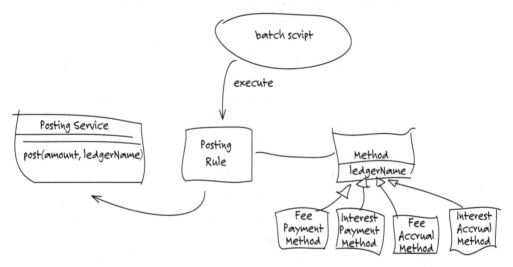

Developer 1: What is this "**Posting Service**"?

Developer 2: That is a FACADE that exposes the accounting application's API and presents it as a SERVICE. I actually made that a while back to simplify the batch code, and it also gave me an INTENTION-REVEALING INTERFACE for posting to the legacy system.

Developer 1: Interesting. So, which firing style do you plan to use for these **Posting Rules**?

Developer 2: I hadn't really gotten that far.

Developer 1: Eager Firing would work for **Accruals**, since the batch actually tells the **Asset** to insert them, but it wouldn't work for **Payments**, which get entered during the day.

Developer 2: I don't think we would want to couple the calculation method that tightly to the batch anyway. If we ever decided to trigger interest calculations at a different time, it would mess things up. And it just doesn't seem right, conceptually.

Figure 11.9
A shot at using **Posting Rules** in the batch

Developer 1: It sounds like **Posting-Rule**-based firing. The batch tells each **Posting Rule** to execute, and the rule goes and looks for appropriate new **Entries** and then does its thing. That's pretty much the way you've drawn it.

Developer 2: So then we avoid creating a lot of dependencies on the batch design, and the batch keeps control. That sounds right.

Developer 1: I'm still a little vague on the interaction of these objects with the **Accounts** and **Entries**.

Developer 2: You and me both. The examples in the book create a direct link between the **Accounts** and the **Posting Rules**. That is kind of logical, but I don't think it will work very well for us. We have to instantiate these objects from data each time, so we would have to figure out which rule applies in order to associate it. Meanwhile, the **Asset** object is the one that knows the content of each **Account**, and therefore which rule to apply. Anyway, what about the rest of this?

Developer 1: I hate to nitpick, but I don't think that we're using "**Method**" right. I think the concept is that the **Method** computes the amount to be posted—like, say, a 20 percent tax withholding on income. But in our case, that's simple: it's always the full amount being posted. I think the **Posting Rule** itself is supposed to know which **Account** to post to, which corresponds to our "ledger name."

Developer 2: Oh. So if the **Posting Rule** is responsible for knowing the correct ledger name, we probably don't need **Method** at all.

Actually, this whole business of choosing the right ledger name is getting more and more complicated. It is already a combination of the type of income (fee or interest) with the "asset class" (a category the business applies to each **Asset**). That is one place I'm hoping this new model will help.

Developer 1: OK, let's focus there. The **Posting Rule** is responsible for choosing the ledger based on attributes of the **Account**. For now, we can make it a straightforward way to handle asset class and the distinction between interest and fees. In the future, you'll have an OBJECT MODEL you can enhance to handle more complex cases.

Developer 2: I need to think about this some more. Let me mull it over, and reread the patterns, and then I'll take another stab at it. Could I talk with you about this again tomorrow afternoon?

Over the next few days, the two developers worked out a model and refactored the code so that the batch simply iterated through the **Assets**, sending a few self-explanatory messages to each and then committing the database transactions. The complexity was shifted into the domain layer, where an object model made it both more explicit and more abstract.

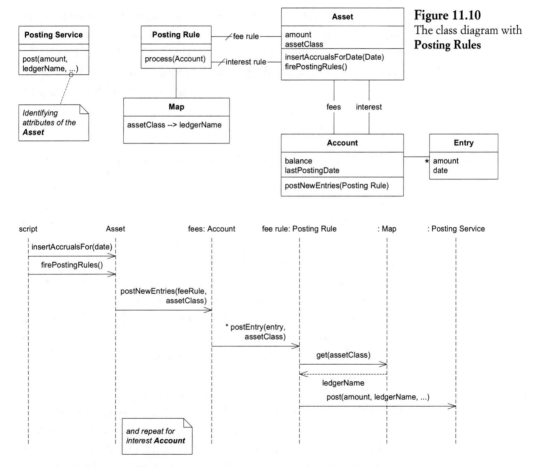

Figure 11.10
The class diagram with **Posting Rules**

Figure 11.11
Sequence diagram showing rule firing

The developers departed considerably from the details of the models presented in *Analysis Patterns,* yet they felt they had preserved the essence of the concepts. They were a little uncomfortable about involving the **Asset** in the selection of the **Posting Rule**. They went that way because the **Asset** had the knowledge of the nature of each **Account** (fee or interest) and was also the natural access point for the script. To have associated the rule object directly with the **Account** would have required a collaboration with the **Asset** object on each instantiation of the objects (each time the batch was run). Instead, they let the **Asset** object look up the two relevant rules through their SINGLETON access and pass them the appropriate **Account**. It seemed to make the code much more direct and so they made a pragmatic decision.

They both felt that conceptually it would have been better to associate **Posting Rules** only with **Accounts**, while keeping the **Asset** focused on its job of generating **Accruals**. They hoped that subsequent refactorings and deeper insight would bring them back to this and show them a way to make this clean division without losing the obviousness of the code.

Analysis Patterns Are Knowledge to Draw On

When you are lucky enough to have an analysis pattern, it hardly ever is the answer to your particular needs. Yet it offers valuable leads in your investigation, and it provides cleanly abstracted vocabulary. It should also give you guidance about implementation consequences that will save you pain down the road.

All this feeds into the dynamo of knowledge crunching and refactoring toward deeper insight and stimulates development. The result often resembles the form documented in the analysis pattern, but adapted to circumstances. Sometimes the result doesn't even obviously relate to the analysis pattern itself, yet was stimulated by the insights from the pattern.

There is one kind of change you should avoid. When you use a term from a well-known analysis pattern, take care to keep the basic concept it designates intact, however much the superficial form might change. There are two reasons for this. First, the pattern may embed understanding that will help you avoid problems. Second, and more important, your UBIQUITOUS LANGUAGE is enhanced when it includes terms that are widely understood or at least well explained. If your model definitions change through the natural evolution of the model, take the trouble to change the names too.

Quite a lot of object models have been written about, some specialized for one kind of application in one industry and some quite general. Most of them provide the seed of an idea, but only a few have captured the reasoning behind the choices and the consequences that follow, which are the most useful parts of an analysis pattern. More of these refined analysis patterns would be valuable, to help save us from reinventing the wheel again and again. I'd be surprised ever to see a comprehensive catalog, but industry-specific catalogs might arise. And patterns for some domains that cross many applications could be widely shared.

This kind of reapplication of organized knowledge is completely different from attempts to reuse code through frameworks or components, except that either could provide the seed of an idea that is not obvious. A model, even a generalized framework, is a complete working whole, while an analysis is a kit of model fragments. Analysis patterns focus on the most critical and difficult decisions and illuminate alternatives and choices. They anticipate downstream consequences that are expensive if you have to discover them for yourself.

TWELVE

Relating Design Patterns to the Model

The patterns explored in this book so far are intended specifically for solving problems in a domain model in the context of a MODEL-DRIVEN DESIGN. Actually, though, most of the patterns published to date are more technical in focus. What is the difference between a design pattern and a domain pattern? For starters, the authors of the seminal book, *Design Patterns,* had this to say:

> Point of view affects one's interpretation of what is and isn't a pattern. One person's pattern can be another person's primitive building block. For this book we have concentrated on patterns at a certain level of abstraction. Design patterns are not about designs such as linked lists and hash tables that can be encoded in classes and reused as is. Nor are they complex, domain-specific designs for an entire application or subsystem. The design patterns in this book are descriptions of communicating objects and classes that are customized to solve a general design problem in a particular context. [Gamma et al. 1995, p. 3]

Some, not all, of the patterns in *Design Patterns* can be used as domain patterns. Doing so requires a shift in emphasis. *Design Patterns* presents a catalog of design elements that have solved problems commonly encountered in a variety of contexts. The motivations of these patterns and the patterns themselves are presented in purely technical terms. But a subset of these elements can be applied in the broader context of domain modeling and design, because they correspond to general concepts that emerge in many domains.

In addition to those in *Design Patterns,* there have been many other technical design patterns presented over the years. Some of them correspond to deep concepts that emerge in domains. It would be nice to draw on this work. To make use of such patterns in domain-driven design, we have to look at the patterns on two levels simultaneously. On one level, they are technical design patterns in the code. On the other level, they are conceptual patterns in the model.

A sample of specific patterns from *Design Patterns* will show how a pattern conceived as a design pattern can be applied in the domain model, and it will clarify the distinction between a technical design pattern and a domain pattern. COMPOSITE and STRATEGY demonstrate how some of the classic design patterns can be applied to domain problems by thinking about them in a different way. . . .

STRATEGY (A.K.A. POLICY)

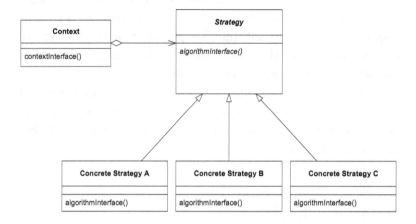

Define a family of algorithms, encapsulate each one, and make them interchangeable. STRATEGY lets the algorithm vary independently from clients that use it. [Gamma et al. 1995]

Domain models contain processes that are not technically motivated but actually meaningful in the problem domain. When alternative processes must be provided, the complexity of choosing the appropriate process combines with the complexity of the multiple processes themselves, and things get out of hand.

When we model processes, we often realize that there is more than one legitimate way of doing them. As we start to describe these options, our definition of the process becomes clumsy and complicated. The actual behavioral alternatives we are choosing between are obscured as they are mixed in with the rest of the behavior.

We would like to separate this variation from the main concept of the process. Then we would be able to see both the main process and the options more clearly. The STRATEGY pattern, already well established in the software design community, addresses this very issue, though the focus is technical. Here it is being applied as a concept in a model and reflected in the code implementation of that model. There is the same need to decouple the highly variable part of the process from the more stable part.

Therefore:

Factor the varying part of a process into a separate "strategy" object in the model. Factor apart a rule and the behavior it governs. Implement the rule or substitutable process following the STRATEGY design pattern. Multiple versions of the strategy object represent different ways the process can be done.

Whereas the conventional view of STRATEGY as a design pattern focuses on the ability to substitute different algorithms, its use as a domain pattern focuses on its ability to express a concept, usually a process or a policy rule.

Example

Route-Finding Policies

A **Route Specification** is being passed to a **Routing Service**, whose job is to construct a detailed **Itinerary** that satisfies the SPECIFICATION. This SERVICE is an optimization engine that can be tuned to find either the fastest route or the cheapest one.

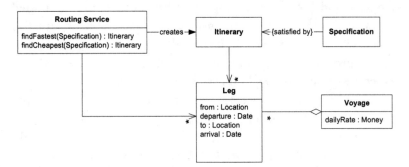

Figure 12.1
A SERVICE interface with options will need conditional logic.

This setup looks OK, but a detailed look at the routing code would reveal conditionals in every computation, making the decision between fastest or cheapest appear all over the place. More trouble will come when new criteria are added to make more subtle choices between routes.

One approach is to separate those tuning parameters into STRATEGIES. Then they can be represented explicitly, passed into the **Routing Service** as a parameter.

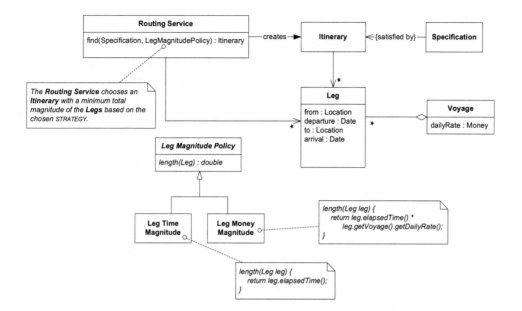

The **Routing Service** now handles all requests in the same, unconditional way, looking for a sequence of **Legs** with a low magnitude, as computed by the **Leg Magnitude Policy**.

This design has the advantages that motivate the STRATEGY pattern in *Design Patterns*. On the level of application versatility and flexibility, the behavior of the **Routing Service** can now be controlled and extended by installing an appropriate **Leg Magnitude Policy**. The STRATEGIES illustrated in Figure 12.2 (fastest or cheapest) are only the most obvious ones. Combinations that balance speed and cost are likely. There may be other factors altogether, such as a bias toward booking cargo on the company's own transports rather than subcontracting to carry them on the transports of other shipping companies. These modifications could have been made without resorting to STRATEGIES, but the logic would have wound through the internals of the **Routing Service** and bloated its interface. The decoupling does make it clear and easily testable.

A fundamentally important rule in the domain, the basis of choosing one **Leg** over another when building an **Itinerary**, is now explicit and distinct. It conveys the knowledge that a specific attribute (potentially derived) of an individual leg, boiled down to a single number, is the basis for routing. This makes possible a simple statement in the language of the domain that defines the **Routing Service's**

Figure 12.2
Options determined by choice of STRATEGY (POLICY) passed as argument

behavior: The **Routing Service** chooses an **Itinerary** with a minimum total magnitude of the **Legs** based on the chosen STRATEGY.

Note: This discussion implies that the **Routing Service** is actually evaluating **Legs** as it searches for an **Itinerary**. This approach is conceptually straightforward, and it could make a reasonable prototype implementation, but it is probably unacceptably inefficient. This application will be taken up again in Chapter 14, "Maintaining Model Integrity," where the same interface will be used with a completely different implementation of the **Routing Service**.

* * *

When we use the technical design pattern in the domain layer, we have to add an additional motivation, another layer of meaning. When the STRATEGY corresponds to an actual business strategy or policy, the pattern becomes more than just a useful implementation technique (though that too is valuable as far as it goes).

The *consequences* of the design pattern fully apply. For example, in *Design Patterns,* Gamma et al. point out that clients must be aware of different STRATEGIES, which is also a modeling concern. A concern purely of implementation is that STRATEGIES can increase the number of objects in the application. If that is a problem, the overhead can be reduced by implementing STRATEGIES as stateless objects that contexts can share. The extensive discussion of implementation approaches in *Design Patterns* all applies here. This is because we are still using a STRATEGY. Our motivations are partially different, which will affect some choices, but the experience embedded in the design pattern is at our disposal.

Composite

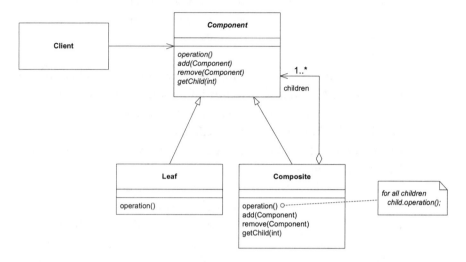

Compose objects into tree structures to represent part-whole hierarchies. COMPOSITE lets clients treat individual objects and compositions of objects uniformly. [Gamma et al. 1995]

We often encounter, while modeling complex domains, an important object that is composed of parts, which are themselves made up of parts, which are made up of parts—occasionally even nesting to arbitrary depth. In some domains, each of these levels is conceptually distinct, but in other cases, there is a sense in which the parts are the same kind of thing as the whole, only smaller.

When the relatedness of nested containers is not reflected in the model, common behavior has to be duplicated at each level of the hierarchy, and nesting is rigid (for example, containers can't usually contain other containers at their own level, and the number of levels is fixed). Clients must deal with different levels of the hierarchy through different interfaces, even though there may be no conceptual difference they care about. Recursion through the hierarchy to produce aggregated information is very complicated.

When applying any design pattern in the domain, the first concern should be whether the pattern idea really is a good fit for the domain concept. It might be convenient to move recursively through some associated objects, but is there a true whole-part hierarchy? Have you found an abstraction under which all the parts truly are the same conceptual type? If you have, COMPOSITE will make those aspects of the model clearer, while allowing you to tap into the carefully thought-out design and implementation considerations of the design pattern.

Therefore:

Define an abstract type that encompasses all members of the COMPOSITE. Methods that return information are implemented on containers to return aggregated information about their contents. "Leaf" nodes implement those methods based on their own values. Clients deal with the abstract type and have no need to distinguish leaves from containers.

This is a relatively obvious pattern on the structural level, but designers often do not push themselves to flesh out the operational level of the pattern. The COMPOSITE offers the same behavior at every structural level, and meaningful questions can be asked of small or large parts that transparently reflect their makeup. That rigorous symmetry is the key to the power of the pattern.

Example
Shipment Routes Made of Routes

A complete cargo shipment route is complicated. First the container must be trucked to a railhead, then carried to a port, then transported on a ship to another port, possibly transferred to other ships, and finally transported by ground on the other end.

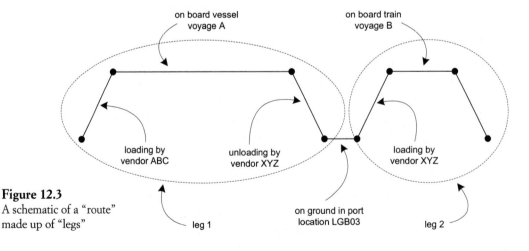

Figure 12.3
A schematic of a "route" made up of "legs"

An application development team has created an object model to express these arbitrarily long strings of legs that assemble into a route.

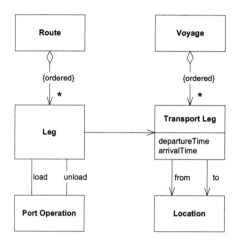

Figure 12.4
A class diagram of a
Route made up of **Legs**

Using this model, the developers are able to create **Route** objects based on booking requests. They are able to process the **Legs** into the operational plan for the step-by-step handling of the cargo. Then they discover something.

The developers had always thought of a route as an arbitrary, un-differentiated string of legs.

Figure 12.5
The developers'
conception of a route

It turns out the domain experts see the route as a sequence of five logical segments.

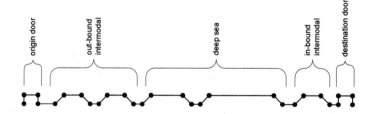

Figure 12.6
The business experts'
conception of a route

Among other things, these subroutes may be planned at different times by different people, so they have to be viewed as distinct. And on closer inspection, the "door legs" are quite different from the other legs, involving locally hired trucks or even customer haulage, in contrast to the elaborately scheduled rail and ship transports.

An object model reflecting all these distinctions starts to get complicated.

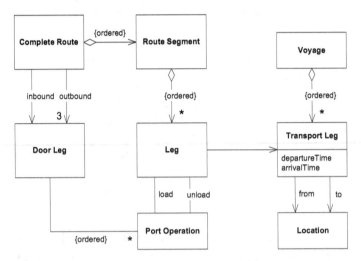

Figure 12.7
The elaborated class diagram of Route

Structurally the model isn't so bad, but the uniformity of processing the operational plan is lost, so the code, or even a description of behavior, becomes much more complicated. Other complications begin to surface, too. Any traversal of a route involves multiple collections of different types of objects.

Enter COMPOSITE. It would be nice, for certain clients, to treat the different levels in this construct uniformly, as routes made up of routes. Conceptually this view is sound. Every level of **Route** is a movement of a container from one point to another, all the way down to an individual leg. (See Figure 12.8.)

Now, the static class diagram does not tell us as much about how door legs and other segments fit together as the previous one did. But the model is more than a static class diagram. We'll convey assembly information through other diagrams (see Figure 12.9) and through the (now much simpler) code. This model captures the deep relatedness of all these different kinds of "**Route**." Generating the operational plan is simple again, as are other route-traversing operations.

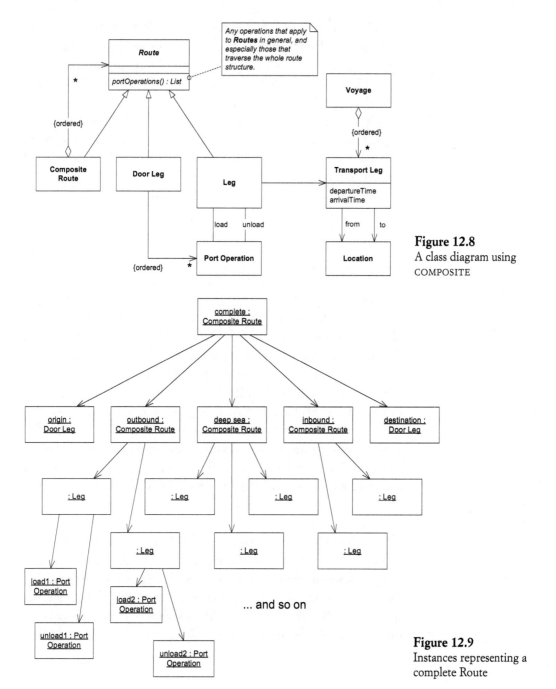

Figure 12.8
A class diagram using
COMPOSITE

Note (attached to Route): Any operations that apply to **Routes** in general, and especially those that traverse the whole route structure.

Figure 12.9
Instances representing a complete Route

... and so on

With a route made of other routes, pieced together end to end to get from one place to another, you can have route implementations of varying detail. You can chop off the end of a route and splice on a new ending, you can have arbitrary nesting of detail, and you can exploit all sorts of possibly useful options.

Of course, we don't yet need such options. And before we needed those route segments and distinct door legs, we were doing just fine without COMPOSITE. A design pattern should be applied only when it is needed.

✳ ✳ ✳

Why Not FLYWEIGHT?

Because I referred to the FLYWEIGHT pattern earlier (in Chapter 5), you might have assumed that it is an example of a pattern to be applied to domain models. In fact, FLYWEIGHT is a good example of a design pattern that has *no correspondence* to the domain model.

When a limited set of VALUE OBJECTS is used many times (as in the example of electrical outlets in a house plan), it may make sense to implement them as FLYWEIGHTS. This is an *implementation* option available for VALUE OBJECTS and not for ENTITIES. Contrast this with COMPOSITE, in which conceptual objects are composed of other conceptual objects. In that case, the pattern applies to both model and implementation, which is an essential trait of a domain pattern.

I'm not going to try to compile a list of the design patterns that can be used as domain patterns. Although I can't think of an example of using an interpreter as a domain pattern, I'm not prepared to say that there is no conception of any domain that would fit. The only requirement is that the pattern should say something about the conceptual domain, not just be a technical solution to a technical problem.

THIRTEEN

Refactoring Toward Deeper Insight

Refactoring toward deeper insight is a multifaceted process. It will be helpful to stop for a moment to pull together the major points. There are three things you have to focus on.

1. Live in the domain.

2. Keep looking at things a different way.

3. Maintain an unbroken dialog with domain experts.

Seeking insight into the domain creates a broader context for the process of refactoring.

The classic refactoring scenario involves a developer or two sitting at the keyboard, recognizing that some code can be improved, and then changing it on the fly (with unit tests to verify their results, of course). This practice should happen all the time, but it isn't the whole story.

The previous five chapters present an expanded view of refactoring, superimposed on the conventional micro-refactoring approach.

Initiation

Refactoring toward deeper insight can begin in many ways. It may be a response to a problem in the code—some complexity or awkwardness. Rather than apply a standard transformation of the code, the developers sense that the root of the problem is in the domain model. Perhaps a concept is missing. Maybe some relationship is wrong.

In a departure from the conventional view of refactoring, this same realization could come when the code looks tidy, if the language of the model seems disconnected from the domain experts, or if new requirements are not fitting in naturally. Refactoring might result from learning, as a developer who has gained deeper understanding sees an opportunity for a more lucid or useful model.

Seeing the trouble spot is often the hardest and most uncertain part. After that, developers can systematically seek out the elements of a new model. They can brainstorm with colleagues and domain experts. They can draw on systematized knowledge written as analysis patterns or design patterns.

Exploration Teams

Whatever the source of dissatisfaction, the next step is to seek a refinement that will make the model communicate clearly and naturally. This might require only some modest change that is immediately evident and can be accomplished in a few hours. In that case, the change resembles traditional refactoring. But the search for a new model may well call for more time and the involvement of more people.

The initiators of the change pick a couple of other developers who are good at thinking through that kind of problem, who know that area of the domain, or who have strong modeling skills. If there are subtleties, they make sure a domain expert is involved. This group of four or five people goes to a conference room or a coffee shop and brainstorms for half an hour to an hour and a half. They sketch UML diagrams; they try walking through scenarios using the objects. They make sure the subject matter expert understands the model and finds it useful. When they find something they are happy with, they go back and code it. Or they decide to mull it over for a few days, and they go back and work on something else. A couple of days later, the group reconvenes and goes through the exercise again. This time they are more confident, having slept on their earlier thoughts, and they reach some conclusions. They go back to their computers and code the new design.

There are a few keys to keeping this process productive.

- *Self-determination.* A small team can be assembled on the fly to explore a design problem. The team can operate for a few days and then disband. There is no need for long-term, elaborate organizational structures.

- *Scope and sleep.* Two or three short meetings spaced out over a few days should produce a design worth trying. Dragging it out doesn't help. If you get stuck, you may be taking on too much at once. Pick a smaller aspect of the design and focus on that.

- *Exercising the* UBIQUITOUS LANGUAGE. Involving the other team members—particularly the subject matter expert—in the brainstorming session creates an opportunity to exercise and refine the UBIQUITOUS LANGUAGE. The end result of the effort is a refinement of that LANGUAGE which the original developer(s) will take back and formalize in code.

Earlier chapters in this book have presented several dialogs in which developers and domain experts probe for better models. A full-blown brainstorming session is dynamic, unstructured, and incredibly productive.

Prior Art

It isn't always necessary to reinvent the wheel. The process of brainstorming for missing concepts and better models has a great capacity to absorb ideas from any source, combine them with local knowledge, and continue crunching to find answers to the current situation.

You can get ideas from books and other sources of knowledge about the domain itself. Although the people in the field may not have created a model suitable for running software, they may well have organized the concepts and found some useful abstractions. Feeding the knowledge-crunching process this way leads to richer, quicker results that also will probably seem more familiar to domain experts.

Sometimes you can draw on the experience of others in the form of analysis patterns. This kind of input has some of the effect of reading about the domain, but in this case it is geared specifically toward software development, and it should be based directly on experience implementing software in your domain. Analysis patterns can give you subtle model concepts and help you avoid lots of mistakes. But they don't give you a cookbook recipe. They feed the knowledge-crunching process.

As the pieces are fit together, model concerns and design concerns must be dealt with in parallel. Again, it doesn't always mean inventing everything from scratch. Design patterns can often be employed in the domain layer when they fit both an implementation need and the model concept.

Likewise, when a common formalism, such as arithmetic or predicate logic, fits some part of a domain, you can factor that part out and adapt the rules of the formal system. This provides very tight and readily understood models.

A Design for Developers

Software isn't just for users. It's also for developers. Developers have to integrate code with other parts of the system. In an iterative process, developers change the code again and again. Refactoring toward deeper insight both leads to and benefits from a supple design.

A supple design communicates its intent. The design makes it easy to anticipate the effect of running code—and therefore it easy to anticipate the consequences of changing it. A supple design helps limit mental overload, primarily by reducing dependencies and side effects. It is based on a deep model of the domain that is fine-grained only where most critical to the users. This makes for flexibility where change is most common, and simplicity elsewhere.

Timing

If you wait until you can make a complete justification for a change, you've waited too long. Your project is already incurring heavy costs, and the postponed changes will be harder to make because the target code will have been more elaborated and more embedded in other code.

Continuous refactoring has come to be considered a "best practice," but most project teams are still too cautious about it. They see the risk of changing code and the cost of developer time to make a change; but what's harder to see is the risk of keeping an awkward design and the cost of working around that design. Developers who want to refactor are often asked to justify the decision. Although this seems reasonable, it makes an already difficult thing impossibly difficult, and tends to squelch refactoring (or drive it underground). Software development is not such a predictable process that the benefits of a change or the costs of not making a change can be accurately calculated.

Refactoring toward deeper insight needs to become part of the ongoing exploration of the subject matter of the domain, the education of the developers, and the meeting of the minds of developers and domain experts. Therefore, refactor when

- The design does not express the team's current understanding of the domain;

- Important concepts are implicit in the design (and you see a way to make them explicit); or

- You see an opportunity to make some important part of the design suppler.

This aggressive attitude does not justify any change at any time. Don't refactor the day before a release. Don't introduce "supple designs" that are just demonstrations of technical virtuosity but fail to cut to the core of the domain. Don't introduce a "deeper model" that you couldn't convince a domain expert to use, no matter how elegant it seems. Don't be absolute about things, but push beyond the comfort zone in the direction of favoring refactoring.

Crisis as Opportunity

For over a century after Charles Darwin introduced it, the standard model of evolution was that species changed gradually, somewhat steadily, over time. Suddenly, in the 1970s, this model was displaced by the "punctuated equilibrium" model. In this expanded view of evolution, long periods of gradual change or stability are interrupted by relatively short bursts of rapid change. Then things settle down into a new equilibrium. Software development has an intentional direction behind it that evolution lacks (although it may not be evident on some projects), but nonetheless it follows this kind of rhythm.

Classical descriptions of refactoring sound very steady. Refactoring toward deeper insight usually isn't. A period of steady refinement of a model can suddenly bring you to an insight that shakes up everything. These breakthroughs don't happen every day, yet a large proportion of the changes that lead to a deep model and supple design emerge from them.

Such a situation often does not look like an opportunity; it seems more like a crisis. Suddenly there is some obvious inadequacy in the model. There is a gaping hole in what it can express, or some critical area where it is opaque. Maybe it makes statements that are just wrong.

This means the team has reached a new level of understanding. From their now-elevated viewpoint, the old model looks poor. From that viewpoint, they can conceive a far better one.

Refactoring toward deeper insight is a continuing process. Implicit concepts are recognized and made explicit. Parts of the design are made suppler, perhaps taking on a declarative style. Development suddenly comes to the brink of a breakthrough and plunges through to a deep model—and then steady refinement starts again.

IV
Strategic
Design

As systems grow too complex to know completely at the level of individual objects, we need techniques for manipulating and comprehending large models. This part of the book presents principles that enable the modeling process to scale up to very complicated domains. Most such decisions must be made at team level or even negotiated between teams. These are the decisions where design and politics often intersect.

The goal of the most ambitious enterprise system is a tightly integrated system spanning the entire business. Yet the entire business model for almost any such organization is too large and complex to manage or even understand as a single unit. The system must be broken into smaller parts, in both concept and implementation. The challenge is to accomplish this modularity *without losing the benefits of integration,* allowing different parts of the system to interoperate to support the coordination of various business operations. A monolithic, all-encompassing domain model will be unwieldy and loaded with subtle duplications and contradictions. A set of small, distinct subsystems glued together with ad hoc interfaces will lack the power to solve enterprise-wide problems and allows consistency problems to arise at every integration point. The pitfalls of both extremes can be avoided with a systematic, evolving design strategy.

Even at this scale, domain-driven design does not produce models unconnected to the implementation. Every decision must have a direct impact on system development, or else it is irrelevant. Strategic design principles must guide design decisions to reduce the interdependence of parts and improve clarity without losing critical interoperability and synergy. They must focus the model to capture the conceptual core of the system, the "vision" of the system. *And they must do all this without bogging the project down.* To help accomplish these goals, Part IV explores three broad themes: context, distillation, and large-scale structure.

Context, the least obvious of the principles, is actually the most fundamental. A successful model, large or small, has to be logically consistent throughout, without contradictory or overlapping definitions. Enterprise systems sometimes integrate subsystems with varying origins or have applications so distinct that very little in the domain is viewed in the same light. It may be asking too much to unify the models implicit in these disparate parts. By explicitly defining a BOUNDED CONTEXT within which a model applies and then, when necessary, defining its relationship with other contexts, the modeler can avoid bastardizing the model.

Distillation reduces the clutter and focuses attention appropriately. Often a great deal of effort is spent on peripheral issues in the domain. The overall domain model needs to make prominent the most value-adding and special aspects of your system and be structured to give that part as much power as possible. While some supporting components are critical, they must be put into their proper perspective. This focus not only helps to direct efforts toward vital parts of the system, but it keeps the vision of the system from being lost. Strategic distillation can bring clarity to a large model. And with a clearer view, the design of the CORE DOMAIN can be made more useful.

Large-scale structure completes the picture. In a very complex model, you may not see the forest for the trees. Distillation helps, by focusing the attention on the core and presenting the other elements in their supporting roles, but the relationships can still be too confusing without an overarching theme, applying some system-wide design elements and patterns. I'll give an overview of a few approaches to large-scale structure and then go into depth on one such pattern, RESPONSIBILITY LAYERS, to explore the implications of using such a structure. The specific structures discussed are only examples; they are not a comprehensive catalog. New ones should be invented as needed, or these should be modified, through a process of EVOLVING ORDER. Some such structure can bring a uniformity to the design that accelerates development and improves integration.

These three principles, useful separately but particularly powerful taken together, help to produce good designs—even in a sprawling system that no one completely understands. Large-scale structure brings consistency to disparate parts to help those parts mesh. Structure and distillation make the complex relationships between parts comprehensible while keeping the big picture in view. BOUNDED CONTEXTS allow work to proceed in different parts without corrupting the model or unintentionally fragmenting it. Adding these concepts to the team's UBIQUITOUS LANGUAGE helps developers work out their own solutions.

FOURTEEN

Maintaining Model Integrity

I once worked on a project where several teams were working in parallel on a major new system. One day, the team working on the customer-invoicing module was ready to implement an object they called **Charge**, when they discovered that another team had already built one. Diligently, they set out to reuse the existing object. They discovered it didn't have an "expense code," so they added one. It already had the "posted amount" attribute they needed. They had been planning to call it "amount due," but—what's in a name?—they changed it. Adding a few more methods and associations, they got something that looked like what they wanted, without disturbing what was there. They had to ignore many associations they didn't need, but their application module ran.

A few days later, mysterious problems surfaced in the bill-payment application module for which the **Charge** had originally been written. Strange **Charges** appeared that no one remembered entering and that didn't make any sense. The program began to crash when some functions were used, particularly the month-to-date tax report. Investigation revealed that the crash resulted when a function was used that summed up the amount deductible for all the current month's payments. The mystery records had no value in the "percent deductible" field, although the validation of the data-entry application required it and even put in a default value.

The problem was that these two groups had *different models*, but they did not realize it, and there were no processes in place to detect it. Each made assumptions about the nature of a charge that were useful in their context (billing customers versus paying vendors). When their code was combined without resolving these contradictions, the result was unreliable software.

If only they had been more aware of this reality, they could have consciously decided how to deal with it. That might have meant working together to hammer out a common model and then writing an automated test suite to prevent future surprises. Or it might simply have meant an agreement to develop separate models and keep hands off each other's code. Either way, it starts with an explicit agreement on the boundaries within which each model applies.

What did they do once they knew about the problem? They created separate **Customer Charge** and **Supplier Charge** classes and defined each according to the needs of the corresponding team. The immediate problem having been solved, they went back to doing things just as before. Oh well.

Although we seldom think about it explicitly, the most fundamental requirement of a model is that it be internally consistent; that its terms always have the same meaning, and that it contain no contradictory rules. The internal consistency of a model, such that each term is unambiguous and no rules contradict, is called *unification*. A model is meaningless unless it is logically consistent. In an ideal world, we would have a single model spanning the whole domain of the enterprise. This model would be unified, without any contradictory or overlapping definitions of terms. Every logical statement about the domain would be consistent.

But the world of large systems development is not the ideal world. To maintain that level of unification in an entire enterprise system is more trouble than it is worth. It is necessary to allow multiple models to develop in different parts of the system, but we need to make careful choices about which parts of the system will be allowed to diverge and what their relationship to each other will be. We need ways of keeping crucial parts of the model tightly unified. None of this happens by itself or through good intentions. It happens only through conscious design decisions and institution of specific processes. **Total unification of the domain model for a large system will not be feasible or cost-effective.**

Sometimes people fight this fact. Most people see the price that multiple models exact by limiting integration and making communication cumbersome. On top of that, having more than one model somehow seems inelegant. This resistance to multiple models sometimes leads to very ambitious attempts to unify all the software in a large project under a single model. I know I've been guilty of this kind of overreaching. But consider the risks.

1. Too many legacy replacements may be attempted at once.

2. Large projects may bog down because the coordination overhead exceeds their abilities.

3. Applications with specialized requirements may have to use models that don't fully satisfy their needs, forcing them to put behavior elsewhere.

4. Conversely, attempting to satisfy everyone with a single model may lead to complex options that make the model difficult to use.

What's more, model divergences are as likely to come from political fragmentation and differing management priorities as from technical concerns. And the emergence of different models can be a result of team organization and development process. So even when no technical factor prevents full integration, the project may still face multiple models.

Given that it isn't feasible to maintain a unified model for an entire enterprise, we don't have to leave ourselves at the mercy of events. Through a combination of proactive decisions about what should be unified and pragmatic recognition of what is not unified, we can create a clear, shared picture of the situation. With that in hand, we can set about making sure that the parts we want to unify stay that way, and the parts that are not unified don't cause confusion or corruption.

We need a way to mark the boundaries and relationships between different models. We need to choose our strategy consciously and then follow our strategy consistently.

This chapter lays out techniques for recognizing, communicating, and choosing the limits of a model and its relationships to others. It all starts with mapping the current terrain of the project. A BOUNDED CONTEXT defines the range of applicability of each model, while a CONTEXT MAP gives a global overview of the project's contexts and the relationships between them. This reduction of ambiguity will, in and of itself, change the way things happen on the project, but it isn't necessarily enough. Once we have a CONTEXT BOUNDED, a process of CONTINUOUS INTEGRATION will keep the model unified.

Then, starting from this stable situation, we can start to migrate toward more effective strategies for BOUNDING CONTEXTS and relating them, ranging from closely allied contexts with SHARED KERNELS to loosely coupled models that go their SEPARATE WAYS.

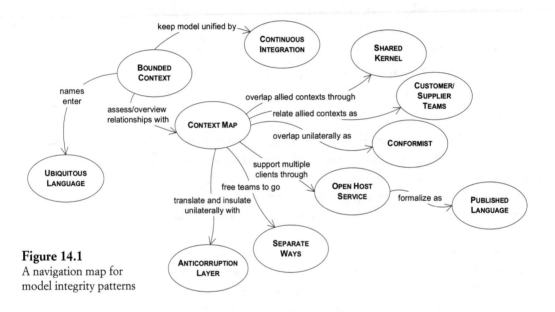

Figure 14.1
A navigation map for
model integrity patterns

Bounded Context

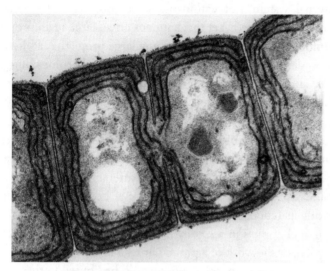

Cells can exist because their membranes define what is in and out and determine what can pass.

Multiple models coexist on big projects, and this works fine in many cases. Different models apply in different contexts. For example, you may have to integrate your new software with an external system over which your team has no control. A situation like this is probably clear to everyone as a distinct context where the model under development doesn't apply, but other situations can be more vague and confusing. In the story that opened this chapter, two teams were working on different functionality for the same new system. Were they working on the same model? Their intention was to share at least part of what they did, but there was no demarcation to tell them what they did or did not share. And they had no process in place to hold a shared model together or quickly detect divergences. They realized they had diverged only after their system's behavior suddenly became unpredictable.

Even a single team can end up with multiple models. Communication can lapse, leading to subtly conflicting interpretations of the model. Older code often reflects an earlier conception of the model that is subtly different from the current model.

Everyone is aware that the data format of another system is different and calls for a data conversion, but this is only the mechanical dimension of the problem. More fundamental is the difference in the models implicit in the two systems. When the discrepancy is not with an external system, but within the same code base, it is even less likely to be recognized. Yet this happens on *all* large team projects.

Multiple models are in play on any large project. Yet when code based on distinct models is combined, software becomes buggy, unreliable, and difficult to understand. Communication among team members becomes confused. It is often unclear in what context a model should *not* be applied.

Failure to keep things straight is ultimately revealed when the running code doesn't work right, but the problem starts in the way teams are organized and the way people interact. Therefore, to clarify the context of a model, we have to look at both the project and its end products (code, database schemas, and so on).

A model applies in a *context.* The context may be a certain part of the code, or the work of a particular team. For a model invented in a brainstorming session, the context could be limited to that particular conversation. The context of a model used in an example in this book is that particular example section and any later discussion of it. The model context is whatever set of conditions must apply in order to be able to say that the terms in a model have a specific meaning.

To begin to solve the problems of multiple models, we need to define explicitly the scope of a particular model as a bounded part of a software system within which a single model will apply and will be kept as unified as possible. This definition has to be reconciled with the team organization.

Therefore:

Explicitly define the context within which a model applies. Explicitly set boundaries in terms of team organization, usage within specific parts of the application, and physical manifestations such as code bases and database schemas. Keep the model strictly consistent within these bounds, but don't be distracted or confused by issues outside.

A BOUNDED CONTEXT delimits the applicability of a particular model so that team members have a clear and shared understanding of what has to be consistent and how it relates to other CONTEXTS. Within that CONTEXT, work to keep the model logically unified, but do not worry about applicability outside those bounds. In other CONTEXTS, other models apply, with differences in terminology, in concepts and rules, and in dialects of the UBIQUITOUS LANGUAGE.

BOUNDED CONTEXTS Are Not MODULES
The issues are confused sometimes, but these are different patterns with different motivations. True, when two sets of objects are recognized as making up different models, they are almost always placed in separate MODULES. Doing so does provide different name spaces (essential for different CONTEXTS) and some demarcation.

But MODULES also organize the elements within one model; they don't necessarily communicate an intention to separate CONTEXTS. The separate name spaces that MODULES create *within* a BOUNDED CONTEXT actually make it harder to spot accidental model fragmentation.

By drawing an explicit boundary, you can keep the model pure, and therefore potent, where it is applicable. At the same time, you avoid confusion when shifting your attention to other CONTEXTS. Integration across the boundaries necessarily will involve some translation, which you can analyze explicitly.

Example

Booking Context

A shipping company has an internal project to develop a new application for booking cargo. This application is to be driven by an object model. What is the BOUNDED CONTEXT within which this model applies? To answer this question, we have to look at what is happening on the project. Keep in mind, this is a look at the project *as it is*, not as it ideally should be.

One project team is working on the booking application itself. They are not expected to modify the model objects, but the application they are building has to display and manipulate those objects. This team is a consumer of the model. The model is valid within the application (its primary consumer), and therefore the booking application is in bounds.

The completed bookings have to be passed to the legacy cargo-tracking system. A decision was made up front that the new model would depart from that of the legacy, so the legacy cargo-tracking system is outside the boundary. Necessary translation between the new model and the legacy is to be the responsibility of the legacy maintenance team. The translation mechanism is not driven by the model. It is not in the BOUNDED CONTEXT. (It is part of the boundary itself, which will be discussed in CONTEXT MAP.) It is good that translation is out of CONTEXT (not based on the model). It would be unrealistic to ask the legacy team to make any real use of the model because their primary work is out of CONTEXT.

The team responsible for the model deals with the whole life cycle of each object, including persistence. Because this team has control of the database schema, they've been deliberately keeping the object-relational mapping straightforward. In other words, the schema is being driven by the model and therefore is in bounds.

Yet another team is working on a model and application for scheduling the voyages of the cargo ships. The scheduling and booking teams were initiated together, and both teams had intended to produce a single, unified system. The two teams have casually coordinated with each other, and they occasionally share objects, but they are not systematic about it. They are *not* working in the same BOUNDED CONTEXT. This is a risk, because they do not think of themselves as working on separate models. To the extent they integrate, there will be problems unless they put in place processes to manage the situation. (The SHARED KERNEL, discussed later in this chapter, might be a good choice.) The first step, though, is to recognize the situation *as it is*. They are not in the same CONTEXT and should stop trying to share code until some changes are made.

This BOUNDED CONTEXT is made up of all those aspects of the system that are driven by this particular model: the model objects, the database schema that persists the model objects, and the booking application. Two teams work primarily in this CONTEXT: the modeling team and the application team. Information has to be exchanged with the legacy tracking system, and the legacy team has primary responsibility for the translation at this boundary, with cooperation from the modeling team. There is no clearly defined relationship between the booking model and the voyage schedule model, and defining that relationship should be one of those teams' first actions. In the meantime, they should be very careful about sharing code or data.

So, what has been gained by defining this BOUNDED CONTEXT? For the teams working in CONTEXT: clarity. Those two teams know they must stay consistent with one model. They make design decisions in that knowledge and watch for fractures. For the teams outside: freedom. They don't have to walk in the gray zone, not using the same model, yet somehow feeling they should. But the most concrete gain in this particular case is probably realizing the risk of the informal sharing between the booking model team and the voyage schedule team. To avoid problems, they really need to decide on the cost/benefit trade-offs of sharing and put in processes to make it work. This won't happen unless everyone understands where the bounds of the model contexts are.

* * *

Of course, boundaries are special places. The relationships between a BOUNDED CONTEXT and its neighbors require care and attention. The CONTEXT MAP charts the territory, giving the big picture of the CONTEXTS and their connections, while several patterns define the nature of the various relationships between CONTEXTS. And a process of CONTINUOUS INTEGRATION preserves unity of the model within a BOUNDED CONTEXT.

But before proceeding to all that, what does it look like when unification of a model is breaking down? How do you recognize conceptual splinters?

Recognizing Splinters Within a BOUNDED CONTEXT

Many symptoms may indicate unrecognized model differences. Some of the most obvious are when coded interfaces don't match up. More subtly, unexpected behavior is a likely sign. The CONTINUOUS INTEGRATION process with automated tests can help catch these kinds of problems. But the early warning is usually a confusion of language.

Combining elements of distinct models causes two categories of problems: *duplicate concepts* and *false cognates*. Duplication of concepts means that there are two model elements (and attendant implementations) that actually represent the same concept. Every time this information changes, it has to be updated in two places with conversions. Every time new knowledge leads to a change in one of the objects, the other has to be reanalyzed and changed too. Except the reanalysis doesn't happen in reality, so the result is two versions of the same concept that follow different rules and even have different data. On top of that, the team members must learn not one but two ways of doing the same thing, along with all the ways they are being synchronized.

False cognates may be slightly less common, but more insidiously harmful. This is the case when two people who are using the same term (or implemented object) think they are talking about the same thing, but really are not. The example in the beginning of this chapter (two different business activities both called **Charge**) is typical, but conflicts can be even subtler when the two definitions are actually related to the same aspect in the domain, but have been conceptualized in slightly different ways. False cognates lead to development teams that step on each other's code, databases that have weird contradictions, and confusion in communication within the team. The term *false cognate* is ordinarily applied to natural languages. For example, English speakers learning Spanish often misuse the word *embarazada*. This word does not mean "embarrassed"; it means "pregnant." Oops.

When you detect these problems, your team will have to make a decision. You may want to pull the model back together and refine the processes to prevent fragmentation. Or the fragmentation may be a result of groups who want to pull the model in different directions for good reasons, and you may decide to let them develop independently. Dealing with these issues is the subject of the remaining patterns in this chapter.

Continuous Integration

Having defined a BOUNDED CONTEXT, we must keep it sound.

* * *

When a number of people are working in the same BOUNDED CONTEXT, there is a strong tendency for the model to fragment. The bigger the team, the bigger the problem, but as few as three or four people can encounter serious problems. Yet breaking down the system into ever-smaller CONTEXTS eventually loses a valuable level of integration and coherency.

Sometimes developers do not fully understand the intent of some object or interaction modeled by someone else, and they change it in a way that makes it unusable for its original purpose. Sometimes they don't realize that the concepts they are working on are already embodied in another part of the model and they duplicate (inexactly) those concepts and behavior. Sometimes they are aware of those other expressions but are afraid to tamper with them, for fear of corrupting the existing functionality, and so they proceed to duplicate concepts and functionality.

It is very hard to maintain the level of communication needed to develop a unified system of any size. We need ways of increasing communication and reducing complexity. We also need safety nets that prevent overcautious behavior, such as developers duplicating functionality because they are afraid they will break existing code.

It is in this environment that Extreme Programming (XP) really comes into its own. Many XP practices are aimed at this specific problem of maintaining a coherent design that is being constantly changed by many people. XP in its purest form is a nice fit for maintaining model integrity within a single BOUNDED CONTEXT. However, whether or not XP is being used, it is essential to have some process of CONTINUOUS INTEGRATION.

CONTINUOUS INTEGRATION means that all work within the context is being merged and made consistent frequently enough that when splinters happen they are caught and corrected quickly. CONTINUOUS INTEGRATION, like everything else in domain-driven design, operates at two levels: (1) the integration of model concepts and (2) the integration of the implementation.

Concepts are integrated by constant communication among team members. The team must cultivate a shared understanding of the ever-changing model. Many practices help, but the most fundamental is constantly hammering out the UBIQUITOUS LANGUAGE. Meanwhile, the implementation artifacts are being integrated by a systematic merge/build/test process that exposes model splinters early. Many processes for integration are used, but most of the effective ones share these characteristics:

- A step-by-step, reproducible merge/build technique;

- Automated test suites; and

- Rules that set some reasonably small upper limit on the lifetime of unintegrated changes.

The other side of the coin in effective processes, although it is seldom formally included, is *conceptual* integration.

- Constant exercise of the UBIQUITOUS LANGUAGE in discussions of the model and application

Most Agile projects have at least daily merges of each developer's code changes. The frequency can be adjusted to the pace of change, as long as any unintegrated change would be merged before a significant amount of incompatible work could be done by other team members.

In a MODEL-DRIVEN DESIGN, the integration of concepts smooths the way for the integration of the implementation, while the integration of the implementation proves the validity and consistency of the model and exposes splinters.

Therefore:

Institute a process of merging all code and other implementation artifacts frequently, with automated tests to flag fragmentation quickly. Relentlessly exercise the UBIQUITOUS LANGUAGE to hammer out a shared view of the model as the concepts evolve in different people's heads.

Finally, do not make the job any bigger than it has to be. CONTINUOUS INTEGRATION is essential only within a BOUNDED CONTEXT. Design issues involving neighboring CONTEXTS, including translation, don't have to be dealt with at the same pace.

✳ ✳ ✳

CONTINUOUS INTEGRATION would be applied within any individual BOUNDED CONTEXT that is larger than a two-person task. It maintains the integrity of that single model. When multiple BOUNDED CONTEXTS coexist, you have to decide on their relationships and design any necessary interfaces. . . .

CONTEXT MAP

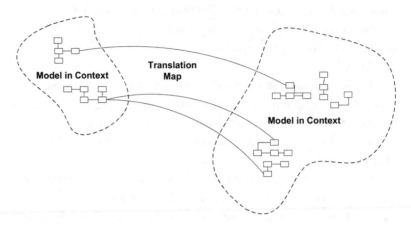

An individual BOUNDED CONTEXT still does not provide a global view. The context of other models may still be vague and in flux.

❋ ❋ ❋

People on other teams won't be very aware of the CONTEXT bounds and will unknowingly make changes that blur the edges or complicate the interconnections. When connections must be made between different contexts, they tend to bleed into each other.

Code reuse between BOUNDED CONTEXTS is a hazard to be avoided. Integration of functionality and data must go through a translation. You can reduce confusion by defining the relationship between the different contexts and creating a global view of all the model contexts on the project.

A CONTEXT MAP is in the overlap between project management and software design. The natural course of events is for the boundaries to follow the contours of team organization. People who work closely will naturally share a model context. People on different teams, or those that don't talk, even if they are on the same team, will split off into different contexts. Physical office space can have an impact too, as team members on opposite ends of a building—not to mention different cities—will probably diverge without extra integration effort. Most project managers intuitively recognize these factors and broadly organize teams around subsystems. But the interrelationship between team organization and software model and design is still not prominent enough. Both managers and team members need a clear view into the ongoing conceptual subdivision of the software model and design.

Therefore:

Identify each model in play on the project and define its BOUNDED CONTEXT. This includes the implicit models of non-object-oriented subsystems. Name each BOUNDED CONTEXT, and make the names part of the UBIQUITOUS LANGUAGE.

Describe the points of contact between the models, outlining explicit translation for any communication and highlighting any sharing.

Map the *existing* terrain. Take up transformations later.

Within each BOUNDED CONTEXT, you will have a coherent dialect of the UBIQUITOUS LANGUAGE. The names of the BOUNDED CONTEXTS will themselves enter that LANGUAGE so that you can speak unambiguously about the model of any part of the design by making your CONTEXT clear.

The MAP does not have to be documented in any particular form. I find diagrams like the ones in this chapter to be helpful in visualizing and communicating the map. Others may prefer a more textual description or a different graphical representation. In some situations, discussion among teammates may be sufficient. The level of detail can vary according to need. Whatever form the MAP takes, it must be shared and understood by everyone on the project. It must provide a clear name for each BOUNDED CONTEXT, and it must make the points of contact and their natures clear.

The relationships between BOUNDED CONTEXTS take many forms depending on both design issues and project organizational issues. Later, this chapter will lay out various patterns of relationships between CONTEXTS that are effective in different situations, and that can provide terms to describe the relationships you find in your own MAP. Keeping in mind that the CONTEXT MAP always represents *the situation as it stands*, the relationships you find may not fit these patterns initially. If they fall close, you may wish to use the pattern name, but don't force it. Just describe the relationships you find. Later you can begin to migrate toward more standardized relationships.

So, what do you do if you've discovered a splinter—a model that is completely entangled but contains inconsistencies? Put a dragon on the map and finish describing everything. Then, with an accurate global view, address the points of confusion. A minor splinter can be repaired, and processes can be put in place to shore it up. If a relationship is vague, you can choose the nearest pattern and move toward it. Your first order of business is to arrive at a clear CONTEXT MAP, and this may mean fixing real problems you have found. But don't let this necessary repair lead to wholesale reorganization. Until you have an unambiguous CONTEXT MAP that places all your work into some BOUNDED CONTEXT, with explicit relationships between all connected models, change only the outright contradictions.

Once you have a coherent CONTEXT MAP, you'll see things you want to change. You can make considered changes to the organization of teams or to the design. Remember, don't change the map until the change in reality is *done*.

Example

Two CONTEXTS in a Shipping Application

We return again to the shipping system. One of the application's major features was to be the automatic routing of cargos at booking time. The model was something like this:

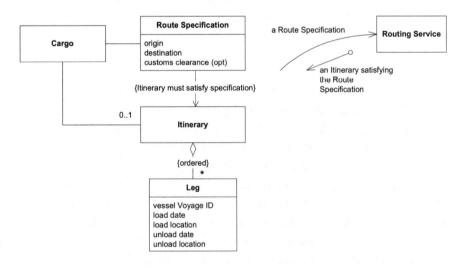

Figure 14.2

The **Routing Service** is a SERVICE that encapsulates a mechanism behind an INTENTION-REVEALING INTERFACE made up of SIDE-EFFECT-FREE FUNCTIONS. The results of those functions are characterized with ASSERTIONS.

1. The interface declares that when a **Route Specification** is passed in, an **Itinerary** will be returned.

2. The ASSERTION states that the returned **Itinerary** will satisfy the **Route Specification** that was passed in.

Nothing is stated about *how* this very difficult task is performed. Now let's go behind the curtain to see the mechanism.

Initially on the project on which this example is based, I was too dogmatic about the internals of the **Routing Service**. I wanted the actual routing operation to be done with an extended domain model that would represent vessel voyages and directly relate them to the **Legs** in the **Itinerary**. But the team working on the routing problem pointed out that, to make it perform well and to draw on well-established algorithms, the solution needed to be implemented as an optimized network, with each leg of a voyage represented as an element in a matrix. They insisted on a distinct model of shipping operations for this purpose.

They were clearly right about the computational demands of the routing process as then designed, and so, lacking any better idea, I yielded. In effect, we created two separate BOUNDED CONTEXTS, each of which had its own conceptual organization of shipping operations. (See Figure 14.3.)

Our requirement was to take a **Routing Service** request, translate it into terms the **Network Traversal Service** could understand, then take the result and translate it into the form a **Routing Service** is expected to give.

This means it was not necessary to map everything in these two models, but only to be able to make two specific translations:

> **Route Specification** → **List** of location codes

> List of **Node** IDs → **Itinerary**

To do this, we have to look at the meaning of an element of one model and figure out how to express it in terms of the other.

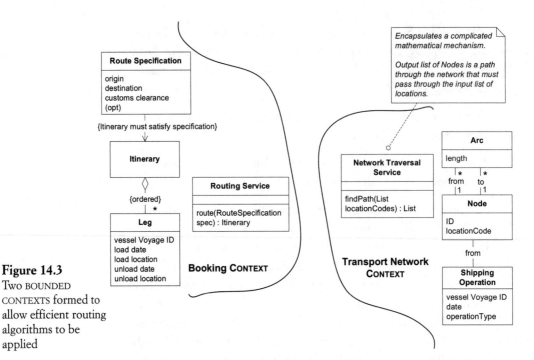

Figure 14.3
Two BOUNDED
CONTEXTS formed to
allow efficient routing
algorithms to be
applied

Starting with the first translation (**Route Specification** → **List** of location codes), we have to think about the meaning of the sequence of locations in the list. The first in the list will be the beginning of the path, which will then be forced to pass through each location in turn until it reaches the last location in the list. So the origin and destination are the first and last in the list, with the customs clearance location (if there is one) in the middle.

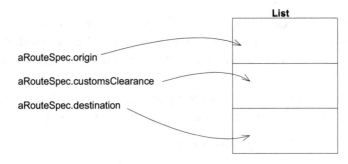

Figure 14.4
Translation of a query
to the **Network
Traversal Service**

(Mercifully, the two teams used the same location codes, so we don't have to deal with that level of translation.)

Notice that the reverse translation would be ambiguous, because the network traversal input allows any number of intermediate points, not just one specifically designated as customs clearance point. Fortunately, this is no problem because we don't need to translate in that direction, but it gives a glimpse of why some translations are impossible.

Now, let's translate the result (**List** of **Node** IDs → **Itinerary**). We'll assume that we can use a REPOSITORY to look up the **Node** and **Shipping Operation** objects based on the **Node** IDs we receive. So, how do those **Nodes** map to **Legs**? Based on the `operationType-Code`, we can break the list of **Nodes** into departure/arrival pairs. Each pair then relates to one **Leg**.

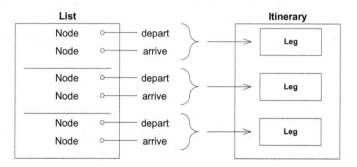

Figure 14.5
Translation of a route found by the **Network Traversal Service**

The attributes for each **Node** pair would be mapped as follows:

```
departureNode.shippingOperation.vesselVoyageId →
                                    leg.vesselVoyageId
departureNode.shippingOperation.date → leg.loadDate
departureNode.locationCode → leg.loadLocationCode
arrivalNode.shippingOperation.date → leg.unloadDate
arrivalNode.locationCode → leg.unloadLocationCode
```

This is the conceptual translation map between these two models. Now we have to implement something that can do the translation for us. In a simple case like this, I typically create an object for the purpose, and then find or create another object to provide the service to the rest of our subsystem.

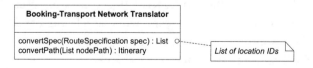

Figure 14.6
A two-way translator

This is the one object that both teams have to work together to maintain. The design should make it very easy to unit-test, and it would be a particularly good idea for the teams to collaborate on a test suite for it. Other than that, they can go their separate ways.

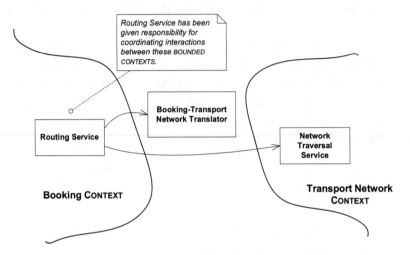

Figure 14.7

The **Routing Service** implementation now becomes a matter of delegating to the Translator and the Network Traversal Service. Its single operation would look something like this:

```
public Itinerary route(RouteSpecification spec) {
    Booking_TransportNetwork_Translator translator =
        new Booking_TransportNetwork_Translator();

    List constraintLocations =
        translator.convertConstraints(spec);

    // Get access to the NetworkTraversalService
    List pathNodes =
        traversalService.findPath(constraintLocations);

    Itinerary result = translator.convert(pathNodes);
    return result;
}
```

Not bad. The BOUNDED CONTEXTS served to keep each of the models relatively clean, let the teams work largely independently, and if initial assumptions had been correct, would probably have served well. (We'll return to that later in this chapter.)

The interface between the two contexts is fairly small. The interface of the **Routing Service** insulates the rest of the Booking CONTEXT's design from events in the route-finding world. The interface is easy to test because it is made up of SIDE-EFFECT-FREE FUNCTIONS. One of the secrets to comfortable coexistence with other CONTEXTS is to have effective sets of tests for the interfaces. "Trust, but verify," said President Reagan when negotiating arms reductions.[1]

It should be easy to devise a set of automated tests that would feed **Route Specifications** into the **Routing Service** and check the returned **Itinerary**.

Model contexts always exist, but without conscious attention they may overlap and fluctuate. By explicitly defining BOUNDED CONTEXTS and a CONTEXT MAP, your team can begin to direct the process of unifying models and connecting distinct ones.

Testing at the CONTEXT Boundaries

Contact points with other BOUNDED CONTEXTS are particularly important to test. Tests help compensate for the subtleties of translation and the lower level of communication that typically exist at boundaries. They can act as a valuable early warning system, especially reassuring in cases where you depend on the details of a model you don't control.

Organizing and Documenting CONTEXT MAPS

There are only two important points here:

1. The BOUNDED CONTEXTS should have names so that you can talk about them. Those names should enter the UBIQUITOUS LANGUAGE of the team.

2. Everyone has to know where the boundaries lie, and be able to recognize the CONTEXT of any piece of code or any situation.

---

1. Reagan translated an old Russian saying that summed up the heart of the matter for both sides—another metaphor for bridging contexts.

The second requirement could be met in many ways depending on the culture of the team. Once the BOUNDED CONTEXTS have been defined, it comes naturally to segregate the code of different CONTEXTS into different MODULES, which leaves the question of how to keep track of which MODULE belongs in which CONTEXT. A naming convention might be used to indicate this, or any other mechanism that is easy and avoids confusion.

Equally important is communicating the conceptual boundaries in such a way that everyone on the team understands them the same way. For this communication purpose, I like informal diagrams like the ones in the example. More rigorous diagrams or textual lists could be made, showing all packages in each CONTEXT, along with the points of contact and the mechanisms responsible for connecting and translating. Some teams will be more comfortable with this approach, while others will get by fine based on spoken agreement and lots of discussion.

In any case, working the CONTEXT MAP into discussions is essential if the names are to enter the UBIQUITOUS LANGUAGE. Don't say, "George's team's stuff is changing, so we're going to have to change our stuff that talks to it." Say instead, "The *Transport Network* model is changing, so we're going to have to change the *translator* for the *Booking context*."

Relationships Between BOUNDED CONTEXTS

The following patterns cover a range of strategies for relating two models that can be composed to encompass an entire enterprise. These patterns serve the dual purpose of providing targets for successfully organizing development work, and supplying vocabulary for describing the existing organization.

An existing relationship may, by chance or by design, fall near one of these patterns, in which case you can describe it using that term, variations duly noted. Then, with each small design change, the relationship can be drawn closer to the chosen pattern.

On the other hand, you may find that an existing relationship is muddled or overcomplicated. Some reorganization might be necessary just to make an unambiguous CONTEXT MAP possible. In this situation, or any situation in which you are considering reorganization, these patterns present a range of choices that are favored in different circumstances. Prominent variables include the level of control you have over the other model, the level and type of cooperation between teams, and the degree of integration of features and data.

The following set of patterns covers some of the most common and important cases, which should give you a good idea of how to approach other cases. A crack team working closely on a tightly integrated product can deploy a large unified model. The need to serve different user communities or a limitation on the coordination abilities of the team might lead to a SHARED KERNEL or CUSTOMER/SUPPLIER relationships. Sometimes a good hard look at the requirements reveals that integration is not essential and it is best for systems to go their SEPARATE WAYS. And, of course, most projects have to integrate to some degree with legacy and external systems, which can lead to OPEN HOST SERVICES or ANTICORRUPTION LAYERS.

SHARED KERNEL

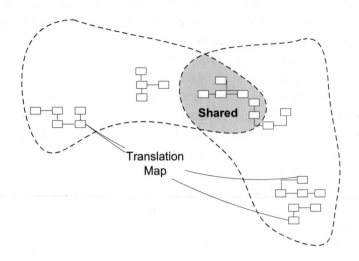

When functional integration is limited, the overhead of CONTINUOUS INTEGRATION may be deemed too high. This may especially be true when the teams do not have the skill or the political organization to maintain continuous integration, or when a single team is simply too big and unwieldy. So separate BOUNDED CONTEXTS might be defined and multiple teams formed.

✳ ✳ ✳

Uncoordinated teams working on closely related applications can go racing forward for a while, but what they produce may not fit together. They can end up spending more on translation layers and retrofitting than they would have on CONTINUOUS INTEGRATION in the first place, meanwhile duplicating effort and losing the benefits of a common UBIQUITOUS LANGUAGE.

On many projects I've seen the infrastructure layer shared among teams that worked largely independently. An analogy to this can work well within the domain as well. It may be too much overhead to fully synchronize the entire model and code base, but a carefully selected subset can provide much of the benefit for less cost.

Therefore:

Designate some subset of the domain model that the two teams agree to share. Of course this includes, along with this subset of the

model, the subset of code or of the database design associated with that part of the model. This explicitly shared stuff has special status, and shouldn't be changed without consultation with the other team.

Integrate a functional system frequently, but somewhat less often than the pace of CONTINUOUS INTEGRATION within the teams. At these integrations, run the tests of both teams.

It is a careful balance. The SHARED KERNEL cannot be changed as freely as other parts of the design. Decisions involve consultation with another team. Automated test suites must be integrated because all tests of both teams must pass when changes are made. Usually, teams make changes on separate copies of the KERNEL, integrating with the other team at intervals. (For example, on a team that CONTINUOUSLY INTEGRATES daily or better, the KERNEL merger might be weekly.) Regardless of when code integration is scheduled, the sooner both teams talk about the changes, the better.

The SHARED KERNEL is often the CORE DOMAIN, some set of GENERIC SUBDOMAINS, or both (see Chapter 15), but it can be any part of the model that is needed by both teams. The goal is to reduce duplication (but not to eliminate it, as would be the case if there were just one BOUNDED CONTEXT) and make integration between the two subsystems relatively easy.

CUSTOMER/SUPPLIER
DEVELOPMENT TEAMS

Often one subsystem essentially feeds another; the "downstream" component performs analysis or other functions that feed back very little into the "upstream" component, and all dependencies go one way. The two subsystems commonly serve very different user communities, who do different jobs, where different models may be useful. The tool set may also be different, so that program code cannot be shared.

✳ ✳ ✳

Upstream and downstream subsystems separate naturally into two BOUNDED CONTEXTS. This is especially true when the two components require different skills or employ a different tool set for implementation. Translation is easier for having to operate in one direction only. But problems can emerge, depending on the political relationship of the two teams.

The freewheeling development of the upstream team can be cramped if the downstream team has veto power over changes, or if procedures for requesting changes are too cumbersome. The upstream team may even be inhibited, worried about breaking the downstream system. Meanwhile, the downstream team can be helpless, at the mercy of upstream priorities.

Downstream needs things from upstream, but upstream is not responsible for downstream deliverables. It takes a lot of extra effort to anticipate what will affect the other team, and human nature being what it is, and time pressures being what they are, well . . . . It makes everyone's life easier to formalize the relationship between the teams. The process can be organized to balance the needs of the two user communities and schedule work on features needed downstream.

On an Extreme Programming project, there already is a mechanism in place for doing just that: the iteration planning process. All we have to do is define the relationship between the two teams in terms of the planning process. Representatives of the downstream team can function much like the user representatives, joining them in planning sessions, discussing directly with their fellow "customers" the trade-offs for the tasks they want. The result is an iteration plan for the supplier team that includes tasks the downstream team needs most or defers tasks by agreement, so there is no expectation of delivery.

If a process other than XP is used, whatever analogous method serves to balance the concerns of different users can be expanded to include the downstream application's needs.

Therefore:

Establish a clear customer/supplier relationship between the two teams. In planning sessions, make the downstream team play the customer role to the upstream team. Negotiate and budget tasks for downstream requirements so that everyone understands the commitment and schedule.

Jointly develop automated acceptance tests that will validate the interface expected. Add these tests to the upstream team's test suite, to be run as part of its continuous integration. This testing will free the upstream team to make changes without fear of side effects downstream.

During the iteration, the downstream team members need to be available to the upstream developers just as conventional customers are, to answer questions and help resolve problems.

Automating the acceptance tests is a vital part of this customer relationship. Even on the most cooperative project, although the customer can identify and communicate its dependencies, and the supplier can diligently try to communicate changes, without tests, surprises will happen. They will disrupt the downstream team's work and force the upstream team to take on unscheduled, emergency fixes. Instead, have the customer team, in collaboration with the supplier team, develop automated acceptance tests that will validate the interface it expects. The upstream team will run these tests as part of its standard test suite. Any change to these tests calls for communication with the other team, because changing the tests implies changing the interface.

Customer/supplier relationships also emerge between projects in separate companies, in situations where a single customer is very important to the business of the supplier. The tail can wag the dog: an influential customer can make demands that are important to the upstream project's success, but those demands can also be disruptive to the upstream project's development. Both parties benefit from the formalization of the process of responding to requirements, because the cost/benefit trade-offs are even harder to see in external relationships than they are in the internal IT situation.

There are two crucial elements to this pattern.

1. The relationship must be that of customer and supplier, with the implication that the customer's needs are paramount. Because the downstream team is not the only customer, the different customers' demands have to be balanced in negotiation—but they remain priorities. This situation is in contrast to the poor-cousin relationship that often emerges, in which the downstream team has to come begging to the upstream team for its needs.

2. There must be an automated test suite that allows the upstream team to change its code without fear of breaking the downstream, and lets the downstream team concentrate on its own work without constantly monitoring the upstream team.

In a relay race, the forward runner can't be looking backward all the time, checking. He or she has to be able to trust the baton carrier to make the handoff precisely, or else the team will be hopelessly slowed down.

Example
Yield Analysis Versus Booking

Back to our trusty shipping example. A highly specialized team has been set up to analyze all the bookings that flow through the firm, to see how to maximize income. Team members might find that ships have empty space and might recommend more overbooking. They might find that the ships are filling up with bulk freight early, forcing the company to turn away more lucrative specialty cargoes. In that case they might recommend reserving space for these types of cargo or raising prices on the bulk freight.

To do this analysis, they use their own complex models. For implementation, they use a data warehouse with tools for building analytical models. And they need lots of information from the Booking application.

From the start, it is clear that these are two BOUNDED CONTEXTS, because they use different implementation tools and, most important, different domain models. What should the relationship between them be?

A SHARED KERNEL might seem logical, because yield analysis is interested in a subset of the Booking's model, and their own model has some overlapping concepts of cargos, prices, and so on. But SHARED KERNEL is difficult in a case where different implementation technologies are being used. Besides, the modeling needs of the yield analysis team are quite specialized, and they continuously play with their models and try alternative ones. They may well be better off translating what they need from the Booking CONTEXT into their own. (On the other hand, if they can use a SHARED KERNEL, their translation burden will be much lighter. They will still have to reimplement the model and translate the data to the new implementation, but if the model is the same, the transfer should be simple.)

The Booking application has no dependency on the yield analysis, because there is no intention of automatically adjusting policies. Human specialists will make the decisions and convey them to the needed people and systems. So we have an upstream/downstream relationship. What downstream needs is this:

1. Some data not needed by any booking operation

2. Some stability in database schema (or at least reliable notification of change) or an export utility

Fortunately, the project manager of the Booking application development team is motivated to help the yield analysis team. This could have been a problem, because the operations department that actually does day-to-day booking reports to a different vice president than the people who actually do yield analysis. But the upper management cares deeply about yield management and, having seen past cooperation problems between the two departments, structured the software development project so that the project managers of both teams report to the same person.

Therefore, all the requirements are in place to apply CUSTOMER/ SUPPLIER DEVELOPMENT TEAMS.

I've seen this scenario evolve in multiple places, where analysis software developers and operations software developers had a customer/supplier relationship. When the upstream team members thought of their role as serving a customer, things worked out pretty well. It was almost always organized informally, and in each case it worked out about as well as the personal relationship of the two project managers.

On one XP project, I saw this relationship formalized in the sense that, for each iteration, representatives of the downstream team played the "planning game" in the role of customers, huddling with the more conventional customer representatives (of application functionality) to negotiate which tasks made it into the iteration plan. This project was at a small company, and so the nearest shared boss was not far up the chain. It worked very well.

CUSTOMER/SUPPLIER TEAMS are more likely to succeed if the two teams work under the same management, so that ultimately they do share goals, or where they are in different companies that actually have those roles. When there is nothing to motivate the upstream team, the situation is very different. . . .

Conformist

When two teams with an upstream/downstream relationship are not effectively being directed from the same source, a cooperative pattern such as CUSTOMER/SUPPLIER TEAMS is not going to work. Naively trying to apply it will get the downstream team into trouble. This can be the case in a large company in which the two teams are far apart in the management hierarchy or where the shared supervisor is indifferent to the relationship of the two teams. It also arises between teams in different companies when the customer's business is not individually important to the supplier. Perhaps the supplier has many small customers, or perhaps the supplier is changing market direction and no longer values the old customers. The supplier may just be poorly run. It may have gone out of business. Whatever the reason, the reality is that the downstream is on its own.

When two development teams have an upstream/downstream relationship in which the upstream has no motivation to provide for the downstream team's needs, the downstream team is helpless. Altruism may motivate upstream developers to make promises, but they are unlikely to be fulfilled. Belief in those good intentions leads

---

When using an off-the-shelf component that has a large interface, you should typically CONFORM to the model implicit in that component. Because the component and the application are clearly different BOUNDED CONTEXTS, based on team organization and control, adapters may be needed for minor format changes, but the model should be equivalent. Otherwise, you should question the value of having the component. If it is good enough to give you value, there is probably knowledge crunched into its design. Within its narrow sphere, it may well be much more advanced than your own understanding. Your model presumably extends beyond the scope of this component, and your own concepts will evolve for those other parts. But where they connect, your model is a CONFORMIST, following the lead of the component's model. In effect, you could be dragged into a better design.

When your interface with a component is small, sharing a unified model is less essential, and translation is a viable option. But when the interface is large and integration is more significant, it usually makes sense to follow the leader.

the downstream team to make plans based on features that will never be available. The downstream project will be delayed until the team ultimately learns to live with what it is given. An interface tailored to the needs of the downstream team is not in the cards.

In this situation, there are three possible paths. One is to abandon use of the upstream altogether. This option should be evaluated realistically, making no assumptions that the upstream will accommodate downstream needs. Sometimes we overestimate the value or underestimate the cost of such a dependency. If the downstream team decides to cut the strings, they are going their SEPARATE WAYS (see the pattern description later in this chapter).

Sometimes the value of using the upstream software is so great that the dependency has to be maintained (or a political decision has been made that the team cannot change). In this case, two paths remain open; the choice depends on the quality and style of the upstream design. If the design is very difficult to work with, perhaps for lack of encapsulation, awkward abstractions, or modeling in a paradigm the team cannot use, then the downstream team will still need to develop its own model. They will have to take full responsibility for a translation layer that is likely to be complex. (See ANTICORRUPTION LAYER, later in this chapter.).

On the other hand, if the quality is not so bad, and the style is reasonably compatible, then it may be best to give up on an independent model altogether. This is the circumstance that calls for a CONFORMIST.

Therefore:

Eliminate the complexity of translation between BOUNDED CONTEXTS by slavishly adhering to the model of the upstream team. Although this cramps the style of the downstream designers and probably does not yield the ideal model for the application, choosing CONFORMITY enormously simplifies integration. Also, you will share a UBIQUITOUS LANGUAGE with your supplier team. The supplier is in the driver's seat, so it is good to make communication easy for them. Altruism may be sufficient to get them to share information with you.

This decision deepens your dependency on the upstream and limits your application to the capabilities of the upstream model—plus purely additive enhancements. It is very unappealing emotionally, which is why we choose it less often than we probably should.

If these trade-offs are not acceptable, but the upstream dependency is indispensable, the second option still remains: Insulate yourself as much as possible by creating an ANTICORRUPTION LAYER, an aggressive approach to implementing a translation map that will be discussed later.

❋ ❋ ❋

CONFORMIST resembles SHARED KERNEL in that both have an overlapping area where the model is the same, areas where your model has been extended by addition, and areas where the other model does not affect you. The difference between the patterns is in the decision-making and development processes. Where the SHARED KERNEL is a collaboration between two teams that coordinate tightly, CONFORMIST deals with integration with a team that is not interested in collaboration.

We've been proceeding down a spectrum of cooperation in the integration between BOUNDED CONTEXTS, from highly cooperative SHARED KERNELS or CUSTOMER/SUPPLIER DEVELOPER TEAMS to the one-sidedness of the CONFORMIST. Now we'll take the final step to an even more pessimistic view of the relationship, assuming neither cooperation nor a usable design on the other side. . . .

ANTICORRUPTION LAYER

New systems almost always have to be integrated with legacy or other systems, which have their own models. Translation layers can be simple, even elegant, when bridging well-designed BOUNDED CONTEXTS with cooperative teams. But when the other side of the boundary starts to leak through, the translation layer may take on a more defensive tone.

When a new system is being built that must have a large interface with another, the difficulty of relating the two models can eventually overwhelm the intent of the new model altogether, causing it to be modified to resemble the other system's model, in an ad hoc fashion. The models of legacy systems are usually weak, and even the exception that is well developed may not fit the needs of the current project. Yet there may be a lot of value in the integration, and sometimes it is an absolute requirement.

The answer is not to avoid all integration with other systems. I've been on projects where people enthusiastically set out to replace all the legacy, but this is just too much to take on at once. Besides, integrating with existing systems is a valuable form of reuse. On a large project, one subsystem will often have to interface with several other, independently developed subsystems. These will reflect the problem domain differently. When systems based on different models are combined, the need for the new system to adapt to the semantics of the other system can lead to a corruption of the new system's own model. Even when the other system is well designed, it is not based on the *same* model as the client. And often the other system is not well designed.

There are many hurdles in interfacing with an external system. For example, the infrastructure layer must provide the means to communicate with another system that might be on a different platform or use different protocols. The data types of the other system must be translated into those of your system. But often overlooked is the certainty that the other system does not use the same conceptual domain model.

It seems clear enough that errors will result if you take some data from one system and misinterpret it in another. You may even corrupt the database. But even so, this problem tends to sneak up on us because we think that what we are transporting between systems is primitive data, whose meaning is unambiguous and must be the same on both sides. This assumption is usually wrong. Subtle yet important differences in meaning arise from the way the data are associated in each system. And even if primitive data elements do have exactly the same meaning, it is usually a mistake to make the interface to the other system operate at such a low level. A low-level interface takes away the power of the other system's model to explain the data and constrain its values and relationships, while saddling the new system with the burden of interpreting primitive data that is not in terms of its own model.

We need to provide a translation between the parts that adhere to different models, so that the models are not corrupted with undigested elements of foreign models.

Therefore:

Create an isolating layer to provide clients with functionality in terms of their own domain model. The layer talks to the other system through its existing interface, requiring little or no modification to the other system. Internally, the layer translates in both directions as necessary between the two models.

✳ ✳ ✳

This discussion of a mechanism to link two systems might bring to mind issues of transporting the data from one program to another or from one server to another. I'll discuss the incorporation of the technical communications mechanism shortly. But such details shouldn't

be confused with an ANTICORRUPTION LAYER, which is not a mechanism for sending messages to another system. Rather, it is a mechanism that translates conceptual objects and actions from one model
and protocol to another.

An ANTICORRUPTION LAYER can become a complex piece of
software in its own right. Next I'll outline some of the design considerations for creating one.

Designing the Interface of the ANTICORRUPTION LAYER

The public interface of the ANTICORRUPTION LAYER usually appears as
a set of SERVICES, although occasionally it can take the form of an EN-
TITY. Building a whole new layer responsible for the translation between the semantics of the two systems gives us an opportunity to
reabstract the other system's behavior and offer its services and information to our system consistently with our model. It may not even make
sense, in our model, to represent the external system as a single component. It may be best to use multiple SERVICES (or occasionally ENTI-
TIES), each of which has a coherent responsibility in terms of our model.

Implementing the ANTICORRUPTION LAYER

One way of organizing the design of the ANTICORRUPTION LAYER is
as a combination of FACADES, ADAPTERS (both from Gamma et al.
1995), and translators, along with the communication and transport
mechanisms usually needed to talk between systems.

We often have to integrate with systems that have large, complicated, messy interfaces. This is an implementation issue, not an issue
of conceptual model differences that motivated the use of ANTI-
CORRUPTION LAYERS, but it is a problem you'll encounter trying to
create them. Translating from one model to another (especially if one
model is fuzzy) is a hard enough job without simultaneously dealing
with a subsystem interface that is hard to talk to. Fortunately, that is
what FACADES are for.

A FACADE is an alternative interface for a subsystem that simplifies access for the client and makes the subsystem easier to use. Because we know exactly what functionality of the other system we
want to use, we can create a FACADE that facilitates and streamlines
access to those features and hides the rest. The FACADE does *not*

change the model of the underlying system. It should be written strictly in accordance with the other system's model. Otherwise, you will at best diffuse responsibility for translation into multiple objects and overload the FACADE and at worst end up creating yet another model, one that doesn't belong to the other system *or* your own BOUNDED CONTEXT. The FACADE belongs in the BOUNDED CONTEXT of the other system. It just presents a friendlier face specialized for your needs.

An ADAPTER is a wrapper that allows a client to use a different protocol than that understood by the implementer of the behavior. When a client sends a message to an ADAPTER, it is converted to a semantically equivalent message and sent on to the "adaptee." The response is converted and passed back. I'm using the term *adapter* a little loosely, because the emphasis in Gamma et al. 1995 is on making a wrapped object conform to a standard interface that clients expect, whereas we get to choose the adapted interface, and the adaptee is probably not even an object. Our emphasis is on translation between two models, but I think this is consistent with the intent of ADAPTER.

For each SERVICE we define, we need an ADAPTER that supports the SERVICE's interface and knows how to make equivalent requests of the other system or its FACADE.

The remaining element is the translator. The ADAPTER's job is to know how to make a request. The actual conversion of conceptual objects or data is a distinct, complex task that can be placed in its own object, making them both much easier to understand. A translator can be a lightweight object that is instantiated when needed. It needs no state and does not need to be distributed, because it belongs with the ADAPTER(s) it serves.

Figure 14.8
The structure of an
ANTICORRUPTION LAYER

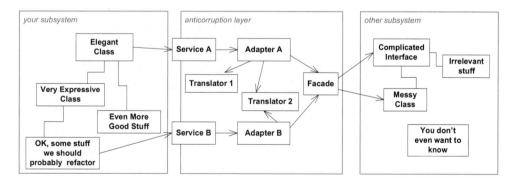

Those are the basic elements I use to create an ANTICORRUPTION LAYER. There are a few other considerations.

- Typically, the system under design (your subsystem) will be initiating action, as implied by Figure 14.8. There are cases, however, when the other subsystem may need to request something of your subsystem or notify it of some event. An ANTICORRUPTION LAYER can be bidirectional, defining SERVICES on both interfaces with their own ADAPTERS, potentially using the same translators with symmetrical translations. Although implementing the ANTICORRUPTION LAYER doesn't usually require any change to the other subsystem, it might be necessary in order to make the other system call on SERVICES of the ANTICORRUPTION LAYER.

- You'll usually need some communications mechanism to connect the two subsystems, and they could well be on separate servers. In this case, you have to decide where to place these communication links. If you have no access to the other subsystem, you may have to put the links between the FACADE and the other subsystem. However, if the FACADE can be integrated directly with the other subsystem, then a good option is to put the communication link between the ADAPTER and FACADE, because the protocol of the FACADE is presumably simpler than what it covers. There also will be cases where the entire ANTICORRUPTION LAYER can live with the other subsystem, placing communication links or distribution mechanisms between your subsystem and the SERVICES that make up the ANTICORRUPTION LAYER's interface. These are implementation and deployment decisions to be made pragmatically. They have no bearing on the conceptual role of the ANTICORRUPTION LAYER.

- If you do have access to the other subsystem, you may find that a little refactoring over there can make your job easier. In particular, try to write more explicit interfaces for the functionality you'll be using, starting with automated tests, if possible.

- Where integration requirements are extensive, the cost of translation goes way up. It may be necessary to make choices in the model of the system under design that keep it closer to the external system, in order to make translation easier. Do this very carefully, without compromising the integrity of the model. It is only something to do selectively when translation difficulty gets out of hand. If this approach seems the most natural solution for much of the important part of the problem, consider making your subsystem a CONFORMIST pattern, eliminating translation.

- If the other subsystem is simple or has a clean interface, you may not need the FACADE.

- Functionality can be added to the ANTICORRUPTION LAYER if it is *specific to the relationship of the two subsystems*. An audit trail for use of the external system or trace logic for debugging the calls to the other interface are two useful features that come to mind.

Remember, an ANTICORRUPTION LAYER is a means of linking two BOUNDED CONTEXTS. Ordinarily, we are thinking of a system created by someone else; we have incomplete understanding of the system and little control over it. But that is not the only situation where you need a little padding between subsystems. There are even situations in which it makes sense to connect two subsystems of your own design with an ANTICORRUPTION LAYER, if they are based on different models. Presumably, in such a case, you will have full control over both sides and typically can use a simple translation layer. However, if two BOUNDED CONTEXTS have gone SEPARATE WAYS yet still have some need of functional integration, an ANTICORRUPTION LAYER can reduce the friction between them.

Example
The Legacy Booking Application

In order to have a small, quick first release, we will write a minimal application that can set up a shipment and then pass that to the legacy system through a translation layer for booking and support operations. Because we built the translation layer specifically to protect our developing model from the influence of the legacy design, this translation is an ANTICORRUPTION LAYER.

Initially, the ANTICORRUPTION LAYER will accept the objects representing a shipment, convert them, pass them to the legacy system and request a booking, and then capture the confirmation and translate it back into the confirmation object of the new design. This isolation will allow us to develop our new application mostly independently of the old one, though we'll have to invest quite a bit in translation.

With each successive release, the new system can either take over more functions of the legacy or simply add new value without replacing existing capabilities, depending on later decisions. This flexibility, and the ability to continually operate the combined system while making a gradual transition, probably makes it worth the expense to build the ANTICORRUPTION LAYER.

A Cautionary Tale

To protect their frontiers from raids by neighboring nomadic warrior tribes, the early Chinese built the Great Wall. It was not an impenetrable barrier, but it allowed a regulated commerce with neighbors while providing an impediment to invasion and other unwanted influence. For two thousand years it defined a boundary that helped the Chinese agricultural civilization to define itself with less disruption from the chaos outside.

Although China might not have become so distinct a culture without the Great Wall, the Wall's construction was immensely expensive and bankrupted at least one dynasty, probably contributing to its fall. The benefits of isolation strategies must be balanced against their costs. There is a time to be pragmatic and make measured revisions to the model, so that it can fit more smoothly with foreign ones.

There is overhead involved in any integration, from full-on CONTINUOUS INTEGRATION inside a single BOUNDED CONTEXT, through the lesser commitments of SHARED KERNELS or CUSTOMER/SUPPLIER DEVELOPER TEAMS, to the one-sidedness of the CONFORMIST and the defensive posture of the ANTICORRUPTION LAYER. Integration can be very valuable, but it is always expensive. We should be sure it is really needed. . . .

Separate Ways

We must ruthlessly scope requirements. Two sets of functionality with no indispensable relationship can be cut loose from each other.

❋ ❋ ❋

Integration is always expensive. Sometimes the benefit is small.

In addition to the usual expense of coordinating teams, integration forces compromises. The simple specialized model that can satisfy a particular need must give way to the more abstract model that can handle all situations. Perhaps some completely different technology could provide certain features very easily, but it is difficult to integrate. Maybe some team is just so hard to get along with that nothing works very well when other teams try to collaborate with them.

In many circumstances, integration provides no significant benefit. If two functional parts do not call upon each other's functionality, or require interactions between objects that are touched by both, or share data during their operations, then integration, even through a translation layer, may not be necessary. Just because features are related in a use case does not mean they must be integrated.

Therefore:

Declare a BOUNDED CONTEXT to have no connection to the others at all, allowing developers to find simple, specialized solutions within this small scope.

The features can still be organized in middleware or the UI layer, but there will be no sharing of logic, and an absolute minimum of data transfer through translation layers—preferably none.

Example

An Insurance Project Slims Down

One project team had set out to develop new software for insurance claims that would integrate into one system everything a customer service agent or a claims adjuster needed. After a year of effort, team members were stuck. A combination of analysis paralysis and a major up-front investment in infrastructure had found them with nothing to show an increasingly impatient management. More seriously, the scope of what they were trying to do was overwhelming them.

A new project manager forced everyone into a room for a week to form a new plan. First they made lists of requirements and tried to estimate their difficulty and assign importance. They ruthlessly chopped the difficult and unimportant ones. Then they started to bring order to the remaining list. Many smart decisions were made in that room that week, but in the end, only one turned out to be important. At some point it was recognized that *there were some features for which integration provided little added value.* For example, adjusters needed access to some existing databases, and their current access was very inconvenient. *But, although the users needed to have this data, none of the other features of the proposed software system would use it.*

Team members proposed various ways of providing easy access. In one case, a key report could be exported as HTML and placed on the intranet. In another case, adjusters could be provided with a specialized query written using a standard software package. All these functions could be integrated by organizing links on an intranet page or by placing buttons on the user's desktop.

The team launched a set of small projects that attempted no more integration than launching from the same menu. Several valuable capabilities were delivered almost overnight. Dropping the baggage of these extraneous features left a distilled set of requirements that seemed for a while to give hope for delivery of the main application.

It could have gone that way, but unfortunately the team slipped back into old habits. They paralyzed themselves again. In the end, their only legacy turned out to be those small applications that had gone their SEPARATE WAYS.

***

Taking SEPARATE WAYS forecloses some options. Although continuous refactoring can eventually undo any decision, it is hard to merge models that have developed in complete isolation. If integration turns out to be needed after all, translation layers will be necessary and may be complex. Of course, this is something you will face anyway.

Now, turning back to more cooperative relationships, let's look at ways to scale up integration. . . .

OPEN HOST SERVICE

Typically for each BOUNDED CONTEXT, you will define a translation layer for each component outside the CONTEXT with which you have to integrate. Where integration is one-off, this approach of inserting a translation layer for each external system avoids corruption of the models with a minimum of cost. But when you find your subsystem in high demand, you may need a more flexible approach.

✳ ✳ ✳

When a subsystem has to be integrated with many others, customizing a translator for each can bog down the team. There is more and more to maintain, and more and more to worry about when changes are made.

The team may be doing the same thing again and again. If there is any coherence to the subsystem, it is probably possible to describe it as a set of SERVICES that cover the common needs of other subsystems.

It is a lot harder to design a protocol clean enough to be understood and used by multiple teams, so it pays off only when the subsystem's resources can be described as a cohesive set of SERVICES and when there are a significant number of integrations. Under those circumstances, it can make the difference between maintenance mode and continuing development.

Therefore:

Define a protocol that gives access to your subsystem as a set of SERVICES. Open the protocol so that all who need to integrate with you can use it. Enhance and expand the protocol to handle new integration requirements, except when a single team has idiosyncratic needs. Then, use a one-off translator to augment the protocol for that special case so that the shared protocol can stay simple and coherent.

✳ ✳ ✳

This formalization of communication implies some shared model vocabulary—the basis of the SERVICE interfaces. As a result, the other subsystems become coupled to the model of the OPEN HOST, and other teams are forced to learn the particular dialect used by the HOST team. In some situations, using a well-known PUBLISHED LANGUAGE as the interchange model can reduce coupling and ease understanding. . . .

Published Language

The translation between the models of two BOUNDED CONTEXTS requires a common language.

❋　❋　❋

When two domain models must coexist and information must pass between them, the translation process itself can become complex and hard to document and understand. If we are building a new system, we will typically believe that our new model is the best available, and so we will think in terms of translating directly into it. But sometimes we are enhancing a set of older systems and trying to integrate them. Choosing one messy model over the other may be choosing the lesser of two evils.

Another situation: When businesses want to exchange information with one another, how do they do it? Not only is it unrealistic to expect one to adopt the domain model of the other, it may be undesirable for both parties. A domain model is developed to solve problems for its users; such a model may contain features that needlessly complicate communication with another system. Also, if the model underlying one of the applications is used as the communications medium, it cannot be changed freely to meet new needs, but must be very stable to support the ongoing communication role.

Direct translation to and from the existing domain models may not be a good solution. Those models may be overly complex or poorly factored. They are probably undocumented. If one is used as a data interchange language, it essentially becomes frozen and cannot respond to new development needs.

The OPEN HOST SERVICE uses a standardized protocol for multiparty integration. It employs a model of the domain for interchange between systems, even though that model may not be used internally by those systems. Here we go a step further and publish that language, or find one that is already published. By *publish* I simply mean that the language is readily available to the community that might be interested in using it, and is sufficiently documented to allow independent interpretations to be compatible.

Recently, the world of e-commerce has become very excited about a new technology: Extensible Markup Language (XML) promises to make interchange of data much easier. A very valuable feature of XML is that, through the document type definition (DTD) or through XML schemas, XML allows the formal definition of a specialized domain language into which data can be translated. Industry groups have begun to form for the purpose of defining a single standard DTD for their industry so that, say, chemical formula information or genetic coding can be communicated between many parties. Essentially these groups are creating a shared domain model in the form of a language definition.

Therefore:

Use a well-documented shared language that can express the necessary domain information as a common medium of communication, translating as necessary into and out of that language.

The language doesn't have to be created from scratch. Many years ago, I was contracted by a company that had a software product written in Smalltalk that used DB2 to store its data. The company wanted the flexibility to distribute the software to users without a DB2 license and contracted me to build an interface to Btrieve, a lighter-weight database engine that had a free runtime distribution license. Btrieve is not fully relational, but my client was using only a small part of DB2's power and was within the lowest common denominator of the two databases. The company's developers had built on top of DB2 some abstractions that were in terms of the storage of objects. I decided to use this work as the interface for my Btrieve component.

This approach did work. The software smoothly integrated with my client's system. However, the lack of a formal specification or documentation of the abstractions of persistent objects in the client's design meant a lot of work for me to figure out the requirements of the new component. Also, there wasn't much opportunity to reuse the component to migrate some other application from DB2 to Btrieve. And the new software more deeply entrenched the company's model of persistence, so that refactoring that model of persistent objects would have been even more difficult.

A better way might have been to identify the subset of the DB2 interface that the company was using and then support that. The interface of DB2 is made up of SQL and a number of proprietary protocols. Although it is very complex, the interface is tightly specified and thoroughly documented. The complexity would have been mitigated because only a small subset of the interface was being used. If a component had been developed that emulated the necessary subset of the DB2 interface, it could have been very effectively documented for developers simply by identifying the subset. The application it was integrated into already knew how to talk to DB2, so little additional work would have been needed. Future redesign of the persistence layer would have been constrained only to the use of the DB2 subset, just as before the enhancement.

The DB2 interface is an example of a PUBLISHED LANGUAGE. In this case, the two models are not in the business domain, but all the principles apply just the same. Because one of the models in the collaboration is already a PUBLISHED LANGUAGE, there is no need to introduce a third language.

Example

A PUBLISHED LANGUAGE for Chemistry

Innumerable programs are used to catalog, analyze, and manipulate chemical formulas in industry and academia. Exchanging data has always been difficult, because almost every program uses a different domain model to represent chemical structures. And of course, most of them are written in languages, such as FORTRAN, that do not express the domain model very fully anyway. Whenever anyone wanted to share data, they had to unravel the details of the other system's database and work out some sort of translation scheme.

Enter the Chemical Markup Language (CML), a dialect of XML intended as a common interchange language for this domain, developed and managed by a group representing academics and industry (Murray-Rust et al. 1995).

Chemical information is very complex and diverse, and it changes all the time with new discoveries. So they developed a language that could describe the basics, such as the chemical formulas of organic and inorganic molecules, protein sequences, spectra, or physical quantities.

Now that the language has been published, tools can be developed that would never have been worth the trouble to write before, when they would have only been usable for one database. For example, a Java application, called the JUMBO Browser, was developed that creates graphical views of chemical structures stored in CML. So if you put your data in the CML format, you'll have access to such visualization tools.

In fact, CML gained a double advantage by using XML, a sort of "published meta-language." The learning curve of CML is flattened by people's familiarity with XML; the implementation is eased by various off-the-shelf tools, such as parsers; and documentation is helped by the many books written on all aspects of handling XML.

Here is a tiny sample of CML. It is only vaguely intelligible to nonspecialists like myself, but the principle is clear.

```
<CML.ARR ID="array3" EL.TYPE=FLOAT NAME="ATOMIC ORBITAL ELECTRON POPULATIONS"
    SIZE=30 GLO.ENT=CML.THE.AOEPOPS>
   1.17947    0.95091    0.97175    1.00000    1.17947    0.95090    0.97174    1.00000
   1.17946    0.98215    0.94049    1.00000    1.17946    0.95091    0.97174    1.00000
   1.17946    0.95091    0.97174    1.00000    1.17946    0.98215    0.94049    1.00000
   0.89789    0.89790    0.89789    0.89789    0.89790    0.89788
</CML.ARR>
```

✳ ✳ ✳

Unifying an Elephant

It was six men of Indostan
To learning much inclined,
Who went to see the Elephant
(Though all of them were blind),
That each by observation
Might satisfy his mind.

The *First* approached the Elephant,
And happening to fall
Against his broad and sturdy side,
At once began to bawl:
"God bless me! but the Elephant
Is very like a wall!"

. . .

The *Third* approached the animal,
And happening to take
The squirming trunk within his hands,
Thus boldly up and spake:
"I see," quoth he, "the Elephant
Is very like a snake."

The *Fourth* reached out his eager hand,
And felt about the knee.
"What most this wondrous beast is like
Is mighty plain," quoth he;
" 'Tis clear enough the Elephant
Is very like a tree!"

. . .

The *Sixth* no sooner had begun
About the beast to grope,
Than, seizing on the swinging tail
That fell within his scope,
"I see," quoth he, "the Elephant
Is very like a rope!"

And so these men of Indostan
Disputed loud and long,
Each in his own opinion
Exceeding stiff and strong,
Though each was partly in the right,
And all were in the wrong!

. . .

*—From "The Blind Men and the Elephant," by John Godfrey Saxe
(1816–1887), based on a story in the* Udana, *a Hindu text*

Depending on their goals in interacting with the elephant, the various blind men may still be able to make progress, even if they don't fully agree on the nature of the elephant. If no integration is required, then it doesn't matter that the models are not unified. If they require some integration, they may not actually have to agree on what an elephant is, but they will get a lot of value from merely recognizing that they don't agree. This way, at least they don't unknowingly talk at cross-purposes.

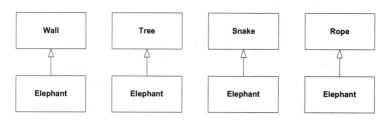

Figure 14.9
Four contexts: no integration

The diagrams in Figure 14.9 are UML representations of the models the blind men have formed of the elephant. Having established separate BOUNDED CONTEXTS, the situation is clear enough for them to work out a way to communicate with each other about the few aspects they care about in common: the location of the elephant, perhaps.

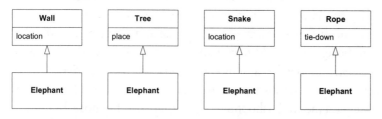

Translations: {Wall.location ↔ Tree.place ↔ Snake.location ↔ Rope.tie-down}

Figure 14.10
Four contexts: minimal integration

As the blind men want to share more information about the elephant, the value of sharing a single BOUNDED CONTEXT goes up. But unifying the disparate models is a challenge. None of them is likely to give up his model and adopt one of the others. After all, the man who touched the tail *knows* the elephant is not like a tree, and that model would be meaningless and useless to him. Unifying multiple models almost always means creating a new model.

With some imagination and continued discussion (probably heated), the blind men could eventually recognize that they have been describing and modeling different parts of a larger whole. For many purposes, a part-whole unification may not require much additional work. At least the first stage of integration only requires figuring out how the parts are related. It may be adequate for some needs to view an elephant as a wall, held up by tree trunks, with a rope at one end and a snake at the other.

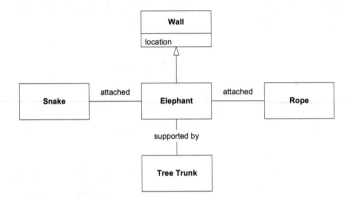

Figure 14.11
One context: crude integration

The unification of the various elephant models is easier than most such mergers. Unfortunately, it is the exception when two models purely describe different parts of the whole, although this is often one aspect of the difference. Matters are more difficult when two models are looking at the same part in a different way. If two men had touched the trunk and one described it as a snake and the other described it as a fire hose, they would have had more difficulty. Neither can accept the other's model, because it contradicts his own experience. In fact, they need a new abstraction that incorporates the "aliveness" of a snake with the water-shooting functionality of a fire hose, but one that leaves out the inapt implications of the first models, such as the expectation of possibly venomous fangs, or the ability to be detached from the body and rolled up into a compartment in a fire truck.

Even though we have combined the parts into a whole, the resulting model is crude. It is incoherent, lacking any sense of following contours of an underlying domain. New insights could lead to a deeper model in a process of continuous refinement. New application requirements can also force the move to a deeper model. If the elephant starts moving, the "tree" theory is out, and our blind modelers may break through to the concept of "legs."

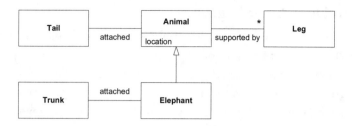

Figure 14.12
One context: deeper model

This second pass of model integration tends to slough off incidental or incorrect aspects of the individual models and creates new concepts—in this case, "animal" with parts "trunk," "leg," "body," and "tail"—each of which has its own properties and clear relationships to other parts. Successful model unification, to a large extent, hinges on minimalism. An elephant trunk is both more and less than a snake, but the "less" is probably more important than the "more." Better to lack the water-spewing ability than to have an incorrect poison-fang feature.

If the goal is simply to find the elephant, then translating between each model's expression of location will do. When more integration is needed, the unified model doesn't have to reach full maturity in the first version. It may be adequate for some needs to view an elephant as a wall, held up by tree trunks, with a rope at one end and a snake at the other. Later, driven by new requirements and by improved understanding and communication, the model can be deepened and refined.

Recognizing multiple, clashing domain models is really just facing reality. By explicitly defining a context within which each model applies, you can maintain the integrity of each and clearly see the implications of any particular interface you want to create between the two. There is no way for the blind men to see the whole elephant, but their problem would be manageable if only they recognized the incompleteness of their perception.

Choosing Your Model Context Strategy

It is important always to draw the CONTEXT MAP to reflect the current situation at any given time. Once that's done, though, you may very well want to change that reality. Now you can begin to consciously choose CONTEXT boundaries and relationships. Here are some guidelines.

Team Decision or Higher

First, teams have to make decisions about where to define BOUNDED CONTEXTS and what sort of relationships to have between them. *Teams* have to make these decisions, or at least the decisions have to be propagated to the entire team and understood by everyone. In fact, such decisions often involve agreements beyond your own team. On the merits, decisions about whether to expand or to partition BOUNDED CONTEXTS should be based on the cost-benefit trade-off between the value of independent team action and the value of direct and rich integration. In practice, political relationships between teams often determine how systems are integrated. A technically advantageous unification may be impossible because of reporting structure. Management may dictate an unwieldy merger. You won't always get what you want, but at least you may be able to assess and communicate something of the cost incurred, and take steps to mitigate it. Start with a realistic CONTEXT MAP and be pragmatic in choosing transformations.

Putting Ourselves in Context

When we are working on a software project, we are interested primarily in the parts of the system our team is changing (the "system under design") and secondarily in the systems it will communicate with. In a typical case, the system under design is going to get carved into one or two BOUNDED CONTEXTS that the main development teams will be working on, perhaps with another CONTEXT or two in a supporting role. In addition to that are the relationships between these CONTEXTS and the external systems. This is a simple, typical view, to give some rough expectation for what you are likely to encounter.

We really are *part of* that primary CONTEXT we are working in, and that is bound to be reflected in our CONTEXT MAP. This isn't a problem if we are aware of the bias and are mindful of when we step outside the limits of that MAP's applicability.

Transforming Boundaries

There are an unlimited variety of situations and an unlimited number of options for drawing the boundaries of BOUNDED CONTEXTS. But typically the struggle is to balance some subset of the following forces:

Favoring Larger BOUNDED CONTEXTS

- Flow between user tasks is smoother when more is handled with a unified model.

- It is easier to understand one coherent model than two distinct ones plus mappings.

- Translation between two models can be difficult (sometimes impossible).

- Shared language fosters clear team communication.

Favoring Smaller BOUNDED CONTEXTS

- Communication overhead between developers is reduced.

- CONTINUOUS INTEGRATION is easier with smaller teams and code bases.

- Larger contexts may call for more versatile abstract models, requiring skills that are in short supply.

- Different models can cater to special needs or encompass the jargon of specialized groups of users, along with specialized dialects of the UBIQUITOUS LANGUAGE.

Deep integration of functionality between different BOUNDED CONTEXTS is impractical. Integration is limited to those parts of one model that can be rigorously stated in terms of the other model, and even this level of integration may take considerable effort. This makes sense when there will be a small interface between two systems.

Accepting That Which We Cannot Change: Delineating the External Systems

It is best to start with the easiest decisions. Some subsystems will clearly not be in any BOUNDED CONTEXT of the system under development. Examples would be major legacy systems that you are not immediately replacing and external systems that provide services you'll need. You can identify these immediately and prepare to segregate them from your design.

Here we must be careful about our assumptions. It is convenient to think of each of these systems as constituting its own BOUNDED CONTEXT, but most external systems only weakly meet the definition. First, a BOUNDED CONTEXT is defined by an *intention* to unify the model within certain boundaries. You may have control of maintenance of the legacy system, in which case you can declare the intention, or the legacy team may be well coordinated and be carrying out an informal form of CONTINUOUS INTEGRATION, but don't take it for granted. Check into it, and if the development is not well integrated, be particularly cautious. It is not unusual to find semantic contradictions in different parts of such systems.

Relationships with the External Systems

There are three patterns that can apply here. First, to consider SEPARATE WAYS. Yes, you wouldn't have included them if you didn't need integration. But be really sure. Would it be sufficient to give the user easy access to both systems? Integration is expensive and distracting, so unburden your project as much as you can.

If the integration is really essential, you can choose between two extremes: CONFORMIST or ANTICORRUPTION LAYER. It is not fun to be a CONFORMIST. Your creativity and your options for new functionality will be limited. In building a major new system, it is unlikely to be practical to adhere to the model of a legacy or external system (after all, why are you building a new system?). However, sticking with the legacy model may be appropriate in the case of peripheral extensions to a large system that will continue to be the dominant system. Examples of this choice include the lightweight decision-support tools that are often written in Excel or other simple tools. If your application is really an extension to the existing system and your interface with that system is going to be large, the translation between CONTEXTS can easily be a bigger job than the application functionality itself. And there is still some room for good design work, even though you have placed yourself in the BOUNDED CONTEXT of the other system. If there is a discernable domain model behind the other system, you can improve your implementation by making that model more explicit than it was in the old system, just as long as you strictly conform to the old model. If you decide on a CONFORMIST design, you must do it wholeheartedly. You restrict yourself to extension only, with no modification of the existing model.

When the functionality of the system under design is going to be more involved than an extension to an existing system, where your interface to the other system is small, or where the other system is very badly designed, you'll really want your own BOUNDED CONTEXT, which means building a translation layer, or even an ANTI-CORRUPTION LAYER.

The System Under Design

The software your project team is actually building is the *system under design*. You can declare BOUNDED CONTEXTS within this zone and apply CONTINUOUS INTEGRATION within each to keep them unified. But how many should you have? What relationships should they have to each other? The answers are less cut and dried than with the external systems because we have more freedom and control.

It could be quite simple: a single BOUNDED CONTEXT for the entire system under design. For example, this would be a likely choice for a team of fewer than ten people working on highly interrelated functionality.

As the team grows larger, CONTINUOUS INTEGRATION may become difficult (although I have seen it maintained for somewhat larger teams). You may look for a SHARED KERNEL and break off relatively independent sets of functionality into separate BOUNDED CONTEXTS, each with fewer than ten people. If all of the dependencies between two of these go in one direction, you could set up CUSTOMER/SUPPLIER DEVELOPMENT TEAMS.

You may recognize that the mind-sets of two groups are so different that their modeling efforts constantly clash. It may be that they actually need quite different things from the model, it may be just a difference in background knowledge, or it may be a result of the management structure the project is embedded in. If the cause of the clash is something you can't change, or don't want to change, you may choose to allow the models to go SEPARATE WAYS. Where integration is needed, a translation layer can be developed and maintained jointly by the two teams as the single point of CONTINUOUS INTEGRATION. This is in contrast with integration with external systems, where the ANTICORRUPTION LAYER typically has to accommodate the other system as is and without much support from the other side.

Generally speaking, there is a correspondence of one team per BOUNDED CONTEXT. One team can maintain multiple BOUNDED CONTEXTS, but it is hard (though not impossible) for multiple teams to work on one together.

Catering to Special Needs with Distinct Models

Different groups within the same business have often developed their own specialized terminologies, which may have diverged from one another. These local jargons may be very precise and tailored to their needs. Changing them (for example, by imposing a standardized, enterprise-wide terminology) requires extensive training and analysis to resolve the differences. Even then, the new terminology may not serve as well as the finely tuned version they already had.

You may decide to cater to these special needs in separate BOUNDED CONTEXTS, allowing the models to go SEPARATE WAYS, except for CONTINUOUS INTEGRATION of translation layers. Different dialects of the UBIQUITOUS LANGUAGE will evolve around these models and the specialized jargon they are based on. If the two dialects have a lot of overlap, a SHARED KERNEL may provide the needed specialization while minimizing the translation cost.

Where integration is not needed, or is relatively limited, this allows continued use of customary terminology and avoids corruption of the models. It also has its costs and risks.

- The loss of shared language will reduce communication.

- There is extra overhead in integration.

- There will be some duplication of effort, as different models of the same business activities and entities evolve.

But perhaps the biggest risk is that it can become an argument against change and a justification for any quirky, parochial model. How much do you need to tailor this individual part of the system to meet specialized needs? Most important, *how valuable is the particular jargon of this user group?* You have to weigh the value of more independent action of teams against the risks of translation, keeping an eye out for rationalizing terminology variations that have no value.

Sometimes a deep model emerges that can unify these distinct languages and satisfy both groups. The catch is that deep models emerge later in the life cycle, after a lot of development and knowledge crunching, if at all. You can't plan on a deep model; you just have to accept the opportunity when it arises, change your strategy, and refactor.

Keep in mind that, where integration requirements are extensive, the cost of translation goes way up. Some coordination of the teams, from the pinpoint modifications of one object that has a complicated translation ranging up to a SHARED KERNEL, can make translation easier while still not requiring full unification.

Deployment

Coordinating the packaging and deployment of complex systems is one of those boring tasks that are almost always a lot harder than they look. The choice of BOUNDED CONTEXT strategy has an impact on the deployment. For example, when CUSTOMER/SUPPLIER TEAMS deploy new versions, they have to coordinate with each other to release versions that have been tested together. Both code and data migrations have to work in these combinations. In a distributed system, it may help to keep the translation layers between CONTEXTS together within a single process, so that you don't have multiple versions coexisting.

Even deployment of the components of a single BOUNDED CONTEXT can be challenging when data migration takes time or when distributed systems can't be updated instantaneously, resulting in two versions of the code and data coexisting.

Many technical considerations come into play depending on the deployment environment and technology. But the BOUNDED CONTEXT relationships can point you toward the hot spots. The translation interfaces have been marked out.

The feasibility of a deployment plan should feed back into the drawing of the CONTEXT boundaries. When two CONTEXTS are bridged by a translation layer, one CONTEXT can be updated just so a new translation layer provides the same interface to the other CONTEXT. A SHARED KERNEL imposes a much greater burden of coordination, not just in development but also in deployment. SEPARATE WAYS can make life much simpler.

The Trade-off

To sum up these guidelines, there is a range of strategies for unifying or integrating models. In general terms, you will trade off the benefits of seamless integration of functionality against the additional effort of coordination and communication. You trade more independent action against smoother communication. More ambitious unification requires control over the design of the subsystems involved.

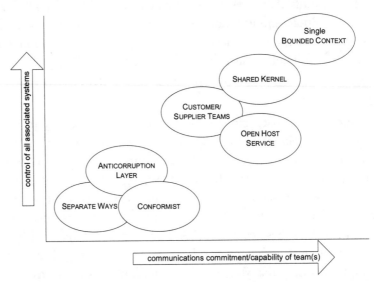

Figure 14.13
The relative demands of CONTEXT relationship patterns

When Your Project Is Already Under Way

Most likely, you are not starting a project but are looking to improve a project that is already under way. In this case, the first step is to define BOUNDED CONTEXTS *according to the way things are now*. This is crucial. To be effective, the CONTEXT MAP must reflect the true practice of the teams, *not* the ideal organization you might decide on by following the guidelines just described.

Once you have delineated your true current BOUNDED CONTEXTS and described the relationships they currently have, the next step is to tighten up the team's practices *around that current organization*. Improve your CONTINUOUS INTEGRATION within the CONTEXTS. Refactor any stray translation code into your ANTICORRUPTION LAYERS. Name the existing BOUNDED CONTEXTS and make sure they are in the UBIQUITOUS LANGUAGE of the project.

Now you are ready to consider changes to the boundaries and relationships themselves. These changes will naturally be driven by the same principles I've already described for a new project, but they will have to be bitten off in small pieces, chosen pragmatically to give the most value for the least effort and disruption.

The next section discusses how to go about actually making changes to your CONTEXT boundaries once you have decided to.

Transformations

Like any other aspect of modeling and design, decisions about BOUNDED CONTEXTS are not irrevocable. Inevitably, there will be many cases in which you have to change your initial decision about the boundaries and relationships between BOUNDED CONTEXTS. Generally speaking, breaking up CONTEXTS is pretty easy, but merging them or changing the relationships between them is challenging. I'll describe a few representative changes that are difficult yet important. These transformations are usually much too big to be taken in a single refactoring or possibly even in a single project iteration. For that reason, I've outlined game plans for making these transformations as a series of manageable steps. These are, of course, guidelines that you will have to adapt to your particular circumstances and events.

Merging CONTEXTS:
SEPARATE WAYS → SHARED KERNEL

Translation overhead is too high. Duplication is too obvious. There are many motivations for merging BOUNDED CONTEXTS. This is hard to do. It's not too late, but it takes some patience.

Even if your eventual goal is to merge completely to a single CONTEXT with CONTINUOUS INTEGRATION, start by moving to a SHARED KERNEL.

1. Evaluate the initial situation. Be sure that the two CONTEXTS are indeed internally unified before beginning to unify them with each other.

2. Set up the process. You'll need to decide how the code will be shared and what the module naming conventions will be. There

must be at least weekly integration of the SHARED KERNEL code. And it must have a test suite. Set this up before developing any shared code. (The test suite will be empty, so it should be easy to pass!)

3. Choose some small subdomain to start with—something duplicated in both CONTEXTS, but *not* part of the CORE DOMAIN. This first merger is going to establish the process, so it is best to use something simple and relatively generic or noncritical. Examine the integrations and translations that already exist. Choosing something that is being translated has the advantage of starting out with a proven translation, plus you'll be thinning your translation layer.

At this point, you have two models that address the same subdomain. There are basically three approaches to merging. You can choose one model and refactor the other CONTEXT to be compatible. This decision can be made wholesale, setting the intention of systematically replacing one CONTEXT's model and retaining the coherence of a model that was developed as a unit. Or you can choose one piece at a time, presumably ending up with the best of both (but taking care not to end up with a jumble).

The third option is to find a new model, presumably deeper than either of the originals, capable of assuming the responsibilities of both.

4. Form a group of two to four developers, drawn from both teams, to work out a shared model for the subdomain. Regardless of how the model is derived, it must be ironed out in detail. This includes the hard work of identifying synonyms and mapping any terms that are not already being translated. This joint team outlines a basic set of tests for the model.

5. Developers from either team take on the task of implementing the model (or adapting existing code to be shared), working out details and making it function. If these developers run into problems with the model, they reconvene the team from step 3 and participate in any necessary revisions of the concepts.

6. Developers of each team take on the task of integrating with the new SHARED KERNEL.

7. Remove translations that are no longer needed.

At this point, you will have a very small SHARED KERNEL, with a process in place to maintain it. In subsequent project iterations, repeat steps 3 through 7 to share more. As the processes firm up and the teams gain confidence, you can take on more complicated subdomains, multiple ones at the same time, or subdomains that are in the CORE DOMAIN.

A note: As you take on more domain-specific parts of the models, you may encounter cases where the two models have conformed to the specialized jargon of different user communities. It is wise to defer merging these into the SHARED KERNEL unless a breakthrough to a deep model has occurred, providing you with a language capable of superseding both specialized ones. An advantage of a SHARED KERNEL is that you can have some of the advantages of CONTINUOUS INTEGRATION while retaining some of the advantages of SEPARATE WAYS.

Those are some guidelines for merging into a SHARED KERNEL. Before going ahead, consider one alternative that satisfies some of the needs addressed by this transformation. If one of the two models is definitely preferred, consider shifting toward it without integrating. Instead of sharing common subdomains, just systematically transfer full responsibility for those subdomains from one BOUNDED CONTEXT to the other by refactoring the applications to call on the model of the more favored CONTEXT, and making any enhancements that model needs. Without any ongoing integration overhead, you have eliminated redundancy. Potentially (but not necessarily), the more favored BOUNDED CONTEXT could eventually take over completely, and you'll have created the same effect as a merger. In the transition (which can be quite long or indefinite), this will have the usual advantages and disadvantages of going SEPARATE WAYS, and you have to weigh them against the pros and cons of a SHARED KERNEL.

Merging CONTEXTS:
SHARED KERNEL → CONTINUOUS INTEGRATION

If your SHARED KERNEL is expanding, you may be lured by the advantages of full unification of the two BOUNDED CONTEXTS. This is not just a matter of resolving the model differences. You are going to be changing team structures and ultimately the language people speak.

Start by preparing the people and the teams.

1. Be sure that all the processes needed for CONTINUOUS INTEGRA-TION (shared code ownership, frequent integration, and so on) are in place on *each team*, separately. Harmonize integration procedures on the two teams so that everyone is doing things in the same way.

2. Start circulating team members between teams. This will create a pool of people who understand both models, and will begin to connect the people of the two teams.

3. Clarify the distillation of each model individually. (See Chapter 15.)

4. At this point, confidence should be high enough to begin merging the core domain into the SHARED KERNEL. This can take several iterations, and sometimes temporary translation layers are needed between the newly shared parts and the not-yet-shared parts. Once into merging the CORE DOMAIN, it is best to go pretty fast. It is a high-overhead phase, fraught with errors, and should be shortened as much as possible, taking priority over most new development. But don't take on more than you can handle.

To merge the CORE models, you have a few choices. You can stick with one model and modify the other to be compatible with it, or you can create a new model of the subdomain and adapt both contexts to use it. Watch out if the two models have been tailored to address distinct user needs. You may need the specialized power of both original models. This calls for developing a deeper model that can supersede both original models. Developing a deeper unifying model is very difficult, but if you are committed to the full merger of the two CONTEXTS, you no longer have the option of multiple dialects. There will be a reward in terms of the clarity of integration of the resulting model and code. Be careful that it doesn't come at the cost of your ability to address the specialized needs of your users.

5. As the SHARED KERNEL grows, increase the integration frequency to daily and finally to CONTINUOUS INTEGRATION.

6. As the SHARED KERNEL approaches the point of encompassing all of the two former BOUNDED CONTEXTS, you will find yourself with either one large team or two smaller teams that have a shared code base that they INTEGRATE CONTINUOUSLY, and that trade members back and forth frequently.

Phasing Out a Legacy System

All good things must come to an end, even legacy computer software. But it doesn't happen on its own. These old systems can be so woven into the business and other systems that extricating them can take many years. Fortunately, it doesn't have to be done all at once.

The possibilities are too various for me to do more than scratch the surface here. But I'll discuss a common case: An old system that is used daily in the business has been supplemented recently by a handful of more modern systems that communicate with the legacy system through an ANTICORRUPTION LAYER.

One of the first steps should be to decide on a testing strategy. Automated unit tests should be written for new functionality in the new systems, but phasing out legacy introduces special testing needs. Some organizations run new and old in parallel for some period of time.

In any given iteration:

1. Identify specific functionality of the legacy that could be added to one of the favored systems within a single iteration.

2. Identify additions that will be required in the ANTICORRUPTION LAYER.

3. Implement.

4. Deploy.

Sometimes it will be necessary to spend more than one iteration writing equivalent functionality to a unit that can be phased out of the legacy, but still plan the new functions in small, iteration-sized units, only waiting multiple iterations for deployment.

Deployment is another point at which too much variation exists to cover all the bases. It would be nice for development if these small, incremental changes could be rolled out to production, but usually it is necessary to organize bigger releases. The users must be trained to use the new software. A parallel period sometimes must be completed successfully. Many logistical problems will have to be worked out.

Once it is finally running in the field:

5. Identify any unnecessary parts of the ANTICORRUPTION LAYER and remove them.

6. Consider excising the now-unused modules of the legacy system, though this may not turn out to be practical. Ironically, the better designed the legacy system is, the easier it will be to phase it out. But badly designed software is hard to dismantle a little at a time. It may be possible to just ignore the unused parts until a later time when the remainder has been phased out and the whole thing can be switched off.

Repeat this over and over. The legacy system should become less involved in the business, and eventually it will be possible to see the light at the end of the tunnel and finally switch off the old system. Meanwhile, the ANTICORRUPTION LAYER will alternately shrink *and* swell as various combinations increase or decrease the interdependence between the systems. All else being equal, of course, you should migrate first those functions that lead to smaller ANTICORRUPTION LAYERS. But other factors are likely to dominate, and you may have to live with some hairy translations during some transitions.

OPEN HOST SERVICE → PUBLISHED LANGUAGE

You have been integrating with other systems with a series of ad hoc protocols, but the maintenance burden is mounting as more systems want access, or perhaps the interaction is becoming very difficult to understand. You need to formalize the relationship between the systems with a PUBLISHED LANGUAGE.

1. If an industry-standard language is available, evaluate it and use it if at all possible.

2. If no standard or prepublished language is available, then begin by sharpening up the CORE DOMAIN of the system that will serve as the host. (See Chapter 15.)

3. Use the CORE DOMAIN as the basis of an interchange language, using a standard interchange paradigm such as XML, if at all possible.

4. Publish the new language to all involved in the collaboration (at least).

5. If a new system architecture is involved, publish that too.

6. Build translation layers for each collaborating system.

7. Switch over.

At this point, additional collaborators should be able to enter with minimal disruption.

Remember, the PUBLISHED LANGUAGE must be stable, yet you'll still need the freedom to change the host's model as you continue your relentless refactoring. Therefore, *do not equate the interchange language and the model of the host.* Keeping them close together will reduce translation overhead, and you may choose to make your host a CONFORMIST. But reserve the right to beef up the translation layer and diverge if the cost-benefit trade-off favors that.

Project leaders should define BOUNDED CONTEXTS based on functional integration requirements and relationships of development teams. Once BOUNDED CONTEXTS and a CONTEXT MAP are explicitly defined and respected, then logical consistency should be protected. Related communication problems will at least be exposed so they can be dealt with.

However, sometimes model contexts, whether consciously bounded or naturally occurring, are misapplied to solve problems other than logical inconsistency within a system. The team may find that the model of a large CONTEXT seems too complex to comprehend as a whole, or to analyze completely. By choice or by chance, this often leads to breaking down the CONTEXTS into more manageable pieces. This fragmentation leads to lost opportunities. Now, it is worth scrutinizing a decision to establish a large model in a broad CONTEXT, and if it is not organizationally or politically possible to keep together, if it is in reality fragmenting, then redraw the map and define boundaries you can keep. But if a large BOUNDED CONTEXT addresses compelling integration needs, and if it seems feasible apart from the complexity of the model itself, then breaking up the CONTEXT may not be the best answer.

There are other means of making large models tractable that should be considered before making this sacrifice. The next two chapters focus on managing complexity within a big model by applying two more broad principles: distillation and large-scale structure.

FIFTEEN

Distillation

$$\nabla \cdot \mathbf{D} = \rho$$

$$\nabla \cdot \mathbf{B} = 0$$

$$\nabla \times \mathbf{E} = -\frac{\partial \mathbf{B}}{\partial t}$$

$$\nabla \times \mathbf{H} = \mathbf{J} + \frac{\partial \mathbf{D}}{\partial t}$$

—*James Clerk Maxwell,* A Treatise on Electricity and Magnetism, *1873*

*These four equations, along with the definitions of their terms
and the body of mathematics they rest on, express the entirety
of classical nineteenth-century electromagnetism.*

How do you focus on your central problem and keep from drowning in a sea of side issues? A LAYERED ARCHITECTURE separates domain concepts from the technical logic that makes a computer system run, but in a large system, even the isolated domain may be unmanageably complex.

Distillation is the process of separating the components of a mixture to extract the essence in a form that makes it more valuable and useful. A model is a distillation of knowledge. With every refactoring to deeper insight, we abstract some crucial aspect of domain knowledge and priorities. Now, stepping back for a strategic view, this chapter looks at ways to distinguish broad swaths of the model and distill the domain model as a whole.

As with many chemical distillations, the separated by-products are themselves made more valuable by the distillation process (as GENERIC SUBDOMAINS and COHERENT MECHANISMS), but the effort is motivated by the desire to extract that one particularly valuable part, the part that distinguishes our software and makes it worth building: the "CORE DOMAIN."

Strategic distillation of a domain model does all of the following:

1. Aids all team members in grasping the overall design of the system and how it fits together

2. Facilitates communication by identifying a core model of manageable size to enter the UBIQUITOUS LANGUAGE

3. Guides refactoring

4. Focuses work on areas of the model with the most value

5. Guides outsourcing, use of off-the-shelf components, and decisions about assignments

Figure 15.1
A navigation map for strategic distillation

This chapter lays out a systematic approach to strategic distillation of the CORE DOMAIN, and it explains how to effectively share a view of it within the team and provides the language to talk about what we are doing.

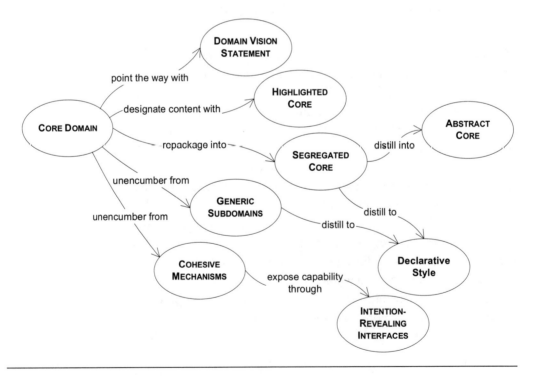

Like a gardener pruning a tree, clearing the way for the growth of the main branches, we are going to apply a suite of techniques to hew away distractions in the model and focus our attention on the part that matters most. . . .

CORE DOMAIN

In designing a large system, there are so many contributing components, all complicated and all absolutely necessary to success, that the essence of the domain model, the real business asset, can be obscured and neglected.

A system that is hard to understand is hard to change. The effect of a change is hard to foresee. A developer who wanders outside his or her own area of familiarity gets lost. (This is particularly true when bringing new people into a team, but even an established member of the team will struggle unless code is very expressive and organized.) This forces people to specialize. When developers confine their work to specific modules, it further reduces knowledge transfer. With the compartmentalization of work, smooth integration of the system suffers, and flexibility in assigning work is lost. Duplication crops up when a developer does not realize that a behavior already exists elsewhere, and so the system becomes even more complex.

Those are some of the consequences of any design that is hard to understand, but there is another, equally serious risk from losing the big picture of the domain:

The harsh reality is that not all parts of the design are going to be equally refined. Priorities must be set. To make the domain model an asset, the model's critical core has to be sleek and fully leveraged to create application functionality. But scarce, highly skilled developers tend to gravitate to technical infrastructure or neatly definable domain problems that can be understood without specialized domain knowledge.

Such parts of the system seem interesting to computer scientists, and are perceived to build transferable professional skills and provide better resume material. The specialized core, that part of the model that really differentiates the application and makes it a business asset, typically ends up being put together by less skilled developers who work with DBAs to create a data schema and then code feature-by-feature without drawing on any conceptual power in the model at all.

Poor design or implementation of this part of the software leads to an application that never does compelling things for the users, no matter how well the technical infrastructure works, no matter how nice the supporting features are. This insidious problem can take root when a project lacks a sharp picture of the overall design and the relative significance of the various parts.

One of the most successful projects I've joined initially suffered from this syndrome. The goal was to develop a very complex syndicated loan system. Most of the strong talent was happily working on database mapping layers and messaging interfaces while the business model was in the hands of developers new to object technology.

The single exception, an experienced object developer working on a domain problem, devised a way of attaching comments to any of the long-lived domain objects. These comments could be organized so that traders could see the rationale they or others recorded for some past decision. He also built an elegant user interface that gave intuitive access to the flexible features of the comment model.

These features were useful and well designed. They went into production.

Unfortunately, they were peripheral. This talented developer modeled his interesting, generic way of commenting, implemented it cleanly, and put it into users' hands. Meanwhile an incompetent developer was turning the mission-critical "loan" module into an incomprehensible tangle that the project very nearly did not recover from.

The planning process must drive resources to the most crucial points in the model and design. To do that, those points must be identified and understood by everyone during planning and development.

Those parts of the model distinctive and central to the purposes of the intended applications make up the CORE DOMAIN. The CORE DOMAIN is where the most value should be added in your system.

Therefore:

Boil the model down. Find the CORE DOMAIN and provide a means of easily distinguishing it from the mass of supporting model and code. Bring the most valuable and specialized concepts into sharp relief. Make the CORE small.

Apply top talent to the CORE DOMAIN, and recruit accordingly. Spend the effort in the CORE to find a deep model and develop a supple design—sufficient to fulfill the vision of the system. Justify investment in any other part by how it supports the distilled CORE.

Distilling the CORE DOMAIN is not easy, but it does lead to some easy decisions. You'll put a lot of effort into making your CORE distinctive, while keeping the rest of the design as generic as is practical. If you need to keep some aspect of your design secret as a competitive advantage, it is the CORE DOMAIN. There is no need to waste effort concealing the rest. And whenever a choice has to be made (due to time limitations) between two desirable refactorings, the one that most affects the CORE DOMAIN should be chosen first.

✳ ✳ ✳

The patterns in this chapter make the CORE DOMAIN easier to see and use and change.

Choosing the CORE

We are looking at those parts of the model particular to representing your business domain and solving your business problems.

The CORE DOMAIN you choose depends on your point of view. For example, many applications need a generic model of money that could represent various currencies and their exchange rates and conversions. On the other hand, an application to support currency trading might need a more elaborate model of money, which would be considered part of the CORE. Even in such a case, there may be a part of the money model that is very generic. As insight into the domain deepens with experience, the distillation process can continue by separating the generic money concepts and retaining only the specialized aspects of the model in the CORE DOMAIN.

In a shipping application, the CORE could be the model of how cargoes are consolidated for shipping, how liability is transferred when containers change hands, or how a particular container is routed on various transports to reach its destination. In investment banking, the CORE could include the models of syndication of assets among assignees and participants.

One application's CORE DOMAIN is another application's generic supporting component. Still, throughout one project, and usually throughout one company, a consistent CORE can be defined. Like every other part of the design, the identification of the CORE DOMAIN should evolve through iterations. The importance of a particular set of relationships might not be apparent at first. The objects that seem obviously central at first may turn out to have supporting roles.

The discussion in the following sections, particularly GENERIC SUBDOMAINS, will give more guidelines for these decisions.

Who Does the Work?

The most technically proficient members of project teams seldom have much knowledge of the domain. This limits their usefulness and reinforces the tendency to assign them to supporting components, sustaining a vicious circle in which lack of knowledge keeps them away from the work that would build domain knowledge.

It is essential to break this cycle by assembling a team matching up a set of strong developers who have a long-term commitment and an interest in becoming repositories of domain knowledge with one or more domain experts who know the business deeply. Domain design is interesting, technically challenging work when approached seriously, and developers can be found who see it this way.

It is usually not practical to hire short-term, outside design expertise for the nuts and bolts of creating the CORE DOMAIN, because the team needs to accumulate domain knowledge, and a temporary member is a leak in the bucket. On the other hand, an expert in a teaching/mentoring role can be very valuable by helping the team build its domain design skills and facilitating the use of sophisticated principles that team members probably have not mastered.

For similar reasons, it is unlikely that the CORE DOMAIN can be purchased. Efforts have been made to build industry-specific model frameworks, conspicuous examples being the semiconductor industry consortium SEMATECH's CIM framework for semiconductor manufacturing automation, and IBM's "San Francisco" frameworks for a wide range of businesses. Although this is a very enticing idea, so far the results have not been compelling, except perhaps as PUB-LISHED LANGUAGES facilitating data interchange (see Chapter 14). The book *Domain-Specific Application Frameworks* (Fayad and John-son 2000) gives an overview of the state of this art. As the field advances, more workable frameworks may be available.

Even so, there is a more fundamental reason for caution: The greatest value of custom software comes from the total control of the CORE DOMAIN. A well-designed framework may be able to provide high-level abstractions that you can specialize for your use. It may save you from developing the more generic parts and leave you free to concentrate on the CORE. But if it constrains you more than that, then there are three likely possibilities.

1. You are losing an essential software asset. Back off restrictive frameworks in your CORE DOMAIN.

2. The area treated by the framework is not as pivotal as you thought. Redraw the boundaries of the CORE DOMAIN to the truly distinctive part of the model.

3. You don't have special needs in your CORE DOMAIN. Consider a lower-risk solution, such as purchasing software to integrate with your applications.

One way or another, creating distinctive software comes back to a stable team accumulating specialized knowledge and crunching it into a rich model. No shortcuts. No magic bullets.

An Escalation of Distillations

The various distillation techniques that make up the rest of this chapter can be applied in almost any order, but there is a range in how radically they modify the design.

A simple DOMAIN VISION STATEMENT communicates the basic concepts and their value with a minimum investment. The HIGH-LIGHTED CORE can improve communication and help guide decision making—and still requires little or no modification to the design.

More aggressive refactoring and repackaging explicitly separate GENERIC SUBDOMAINS, which can then be dealt with individually. COHESIVE MECHANISMS can be encapsulated with versatile, communicative, and supple design. Removing these distractions disentangles the CORE.

Repackaging a SEGREGATED CORE makes the CORE directly visible, even in the code, and facilitates future work on the CORE model.

And most ambitious is the ABSTRACT CORE, which expresses the most fundamental concepts and relationships in a pure form (and requires extensive reorganizing and refactoring of the model).

Each of these techniques requires a successively greater commitment, but a knife gets sharper as its blade is ground finer. Successive distillation of a domain model produces an asset that gives the project speed, agility, and precision of execution.

To start, we can boil off the least distinctive aspects of the model. GENERIC SUBDOMAINS provide a contrast to the CORE DOMAIN that clarifies the meaning of each. . . .

Generic Subdomains

Some parts of the model add complexity without capturing or communicating specialized knowledge. Anything extraneous makes the CORE DOMAIN harder to discern and understand. The model clogs up with general principles everyone knows or details that belong to specialties which are not your primary focus but play a supporting role. Yet, however generic, these other elements are essential to the functioning of the system and the full expression of the model.

There is a part of your model that you would like to take for granted. It is undeniably part of the domain model, but it abstracts concepts that would probably be needed for a great many businesses. For example, a corporate organization chart is needed in some form by businesses as diverse as shipping, banking, or manufacturing. For another example, many applications track receivables, expense ledgers, and other financial matters that could all be handled using a generic accounting model.

Often a great deal of effort is spent on peripheral issues in the domain. I personally have witnessed two separate projects that have employed their best developers for weeks in redesigning dates and times with time zones. While such components must work, they are not the conceptual core of the system.

Even if such a generic model element is deemed critical, the overall domain model needs to make prominent the most value-adding and special aspects of your system, and needs to be structured to give that part as much power as possible. This is hard to do when the CORE is mixed with all the interrelated factors.

Therefore:

Identify cohesive subdomains that are not the motivation for your project. Factor out generic models of these subdomains and place them in separate MODULES. Leave no trace of your specialties in them.

Once they have been separated, give their continuing development lower priority than the CORE DOMAIN, and avoid assigning your core developers to the tasks (because they will gain little domain knowledge from them). Also consider off-the-shelf solutions or published models for these GENERIC SUBDOMAINS.

❋ ❋ ❋

You may have a few extra options when developing these packages.

Option 1: An Off-the-Shelf Solution

Sometimes you can buy an implementation or use open source code.

Advantages

- Less code to develop.

- Maintenance burden externalized.

- Code is probably more mature, used in multiple places, and therefore more bulletproof and complete than homegrown code.

Disadvantages

- You still have to spend the time to evaluate it and understand it before using it.

- Quality control being what it is in our industry, you can't count on it being correct and stable.

- It may be overengineered for your purposes; integration could be more work than a minimalist homegrown implementation.

- Foreign elements don't usually integrate smoothly. There may be a distinct BOUNDED CONTEXT. Even if not, it may be difficult to smoothly reference ENTITIES from your other packages.

- It may introduce platform dependencies, compiler version dependencies, and so on.

Off-the-shelf subdomain solutions are worth investigating, but they are usually not worth the trouble. I've seen success stories in applications with very elaborate workflow requirements that used commercially available external workflow systems with API hooks. I've also seen success with an error-logging package that was deeply integrated into the application. Sometimes GENERIC SUBDOMAIN solutions are packaged in the form of frameworks, which implement a very abstract model that can be integrated with and specialized for your application. The more generic the subcomponent, and the more distilled its own model, the better the chance that it will be useful.

Option 2: A Published Design or Model

Advantages

- More mature than a homegrown model and reflects many people's insights

- Instant, high-quality documentation

Disadvantage

- May not quite fit your needs or may be overengineered for your needs

Tom Lehrer (the comedic songwriter from the 1950s and 1960s) said the secret to success in mathematics was, "Plagiarize! Plagiarize. Let no one's work evade your eyes. . . . Only be sure always to call it please, *research*." Good advice in domain modeling, and especially when attacking a GENERIC SUBDOMAIN.

This works best when there is a widely distributed model, such as the ones in *Analysis Patterns* (Fowler 1996). (See Chapter 11.)

When the field already has a highly formalized and rigorous model, use it. Accounting and physics are two examples that come to mind. Not only are these very robust and streamlined, but they are widely understood by people everywhere, reducing your present and future training burden. (See Chapter 10, on using established formalisms.)

Don't feel compelled to implement all aspects of a published model, if you can identify a simplified subset that is self-consistent and satisfies your needs. But in cases where there is a well-traveled and well-documented—or better yet, formalized—model available, it makes no sense to reinvent the wheel.

Option 3: An Outsourced Implementation

Advantages

- Keeps core team free to work on the CORE DOMAIN, where most knowledge is needed and accumulated.

- Allows more development to be done without permanently enlarging the team, but without dissipating knowledge of the CORE DOMAIN.

- Forces an interface-oriented design, and helps keep the subdomain generic, because the specification is being passed outside.

Disadvantages

- Still requires time from the core team, because the interface, coding standards, and any other important aspects need to be communicated.

- Incurs significant overhead of transferring ownership back inside, because code has to be understood. (Still, overhead is less than for specialized subdomains, because a generic model presumably requires no special background to understand.)

- Code quality can vary. This could be good or bad, depending on the relative caliber of the two teams.

Automated tests can play an important role in outsourcing. The implementers should be required to provide unit tests for the code they deliver. A really powerful approach—one that helps ensure a degree of quality, clarifies the spec, and smooths reintegration—is to specify or even write automated acceptance tests for the outsourced components. Also, "outsourced implementation" can be an excellent combination with "published design or model."

Option 4: An In-House Implementation

Advantages

- Easy integration.

- You get just what you want and nothing extra.

- Temporary contractors can be assigned.

Disadvantages

- Ongoing maintenance and training burden.

- It is easy to underestimate the time and cost of developing such packages.

Of course, this too combines well with "published design or model."

GENERIC SUBDOMAINS are the place to try to apply outside design expertise, because they do not require deep understanding of your specialized CORE DOMAIN, and they do not present a major opportunity to learn that domain. Confidentiality is of less concern, because little proprietary information or business practice will be involved in such modules. A GENERIC SUBDOMAIN lessens the training burden for those not committed to deep knowledge of the domain.

Over time, I believe our ideas of what constitutes the CORE model will narrow, and more and more generic models will be available as implemented frameworks, or at least as published models or analysis patterns. For now, we still have to develop most of these ourselves, but there is great value in partitioning them from the CORE DOMAIN model.

Example

A Tale of Two Time Zones

Twice I've watched as the best developers on a project spent weeks of their time solving the problem of storing and converting times with time zones. While I'm always suspicious of such activities, sometimes it is necessary, and these two projects provide almost perfect contrast.

The first was an effort to design scheduling software for cargo shipping. To schedule international transports, it is critical to have accurate time calculations, and because all such schedules are tracked in local time, it is impossible to coordinate transports without conversions.

Having clearly established their need for this functionality, the team proceeded with development of the CORE DOMAIN and some early iterations of the application using the available time classes and some dummy data. As the application began to mature, it was clear that the existing time classes were not adequate, and that the problem was very intricate because of the variations between the many countries and the complexity of the International Date Line. With their requirements by now even clearer, they searched for an off-the-shelf solution, but found none. They had no option but to build it themselves.

The task would require research and precision engineering, so the team leaders assigned one of their best programmers. But the task did not require any special knowledge of shipping and would not cultivate that knowledge, so they chose a programmer who was on the project on a temporary contract.

This programmer did not start from scratch. He researched several existing implementations of time zones, most of which did not meet requirements, and decided to adapt the public-domain solution from BSD Unix, which had an elaborate database and an implementation in C. He reverse-engineered the logic and wrote an import routine for the database.

The problem turned out to be even harder than expected (involving, for example, the import of databases of special cases), but the code got written and integrated with the CORE and the product was delivered.

Things went very differently on the other project. An insurance company was developing a new claims-processing system, and planned to capture the times of various events (time of car crash, time of hail storm, and so on). This data would be recorded in local time, so time zone functionality was needed.

When I arrived, they had assigned a junior, but very smart, developer to the task, although the exact requirements of the app were still in play and not even an initial iteration had been attempted. He had dutifully set out to build a time zone model *a priori*.

Not knowing what would be needed, it was assumed that it should be flexible enough to handle anything. The programmer assigned to the task needed help with such a difficult problem, so a senior developer was assigned to it also. They wrote complex code, but no specific application was using it, so it was never clear that the code worked correctly.

The project ran aground for various reasons, and the time zone code was never used. But if it had been, simply storing local times tagged with the time zone might have been sufficient, even with no conversion, because this was primarily reference data and not the basis of computations. Even if conversion had turned out to be necessary, all the data was going to be gathered from North America, where time zone conversions are relatively simple.

The main cost of this attention to the time zones was the neglect of the CORE DOMAIN model. If the same energy had been placed there, they might have produced a functioning prototype of their own application and a first cut at a working domain model. Furthermore, the developers involved, who were committed long-term to the project, should have been steeped in the insurance domain, building up critical knowledge within the team.

One thing both projects did right was to cleanly segregate the GENERIC time zone model from the CORE DOMAIN. A shipping-specific or insurance-specific model of time zones would have coupled the model to this generic supporting model, making the CORE harder to understand (because it would contain irrelevant detail about time zones). It would have made the time zone MODULE harder to maintain (because the maintainer would have to understand the CORE and its interrelationship with time zones).

Shipping Project's Strategy	Insurance Project's Strategy
Advantages • GENERIC model decoupled from CORE. • CORE model mature, so resources could be diverted without stunting it. • Knew exactly what they needed. • Critical support functionality for international scheduling. • Programmer on short-term contract used for GENERIC task. *Disadvantage* • Diverted top programmer from core.	*Advantage* • GENERIC model decoupled from CORE. *Disadvantages* • CORE model undeveloped, so attention to other issues continued this neglect. • Unknown requirements led to attempt at full generality, where simpler North America-specific conversion might have sufficed. • Long-term programmers were assigned who could have been repositories of domain knowledge.

We technical people tend to enjoy definable problems like time zone conversion, and we can easily justify spending our time on them. But a disciplined look at priorities usually points to the CORE DOMAIN.

Generic Doesn't Mean Reusable

Note that while I have emphasized the generic quality of these subdomains, I have not mentioned the reusability of code. Off-the-shelf solutions may or may not make sense for a particular situation, but assuming that you are implementing the code yourself, in-house or outsourced, you should specifically not concern yourself with the reusability of that code. This would go against the basic motivation of distillation: that you should be applying as much of your effort to the CORE DOMAIN as possible and investing in supporting GENERIC SUB-DOMAINS only as necessary.

Reuse does happen, but not always code reuse. The model reuse is often a better level of reuse, as when you use a published design or model. And if you have to create your own model, it may well be valuable in a later related project. But while the concept of such a model may be applicable to many situations, you do not have to develop the model in its full generality. You can model and implement only the part you need for your business.

Though you should seldom design for reusability, you must be strict about keeping within the generic concept. Introducing industry-specific model elements will have two costs. First, it will impede future development. Although you need only a small part of the subdomain model now, your needs will grow. By introducing anything to the design that is not part of the concept, you make it much more difficult to expand the system cleanly without completely rebuilding the older part and redesigning the other modules that use it.

The second, and more important, reason is that those industry-specific concepts belong either in the CORE DOMAIN or in their own, more specialized, subdomains, and those specialized models are even more valuable than the generic ones.

Project Risk Management

Agile processes typically call for managing risk by tackling the riskiest tasks early. XP specifically calls for getting an end-to-end system up and running immediately. This initial system often proves a technical architecture, and it is tempting to build a peripheral system that handles some supporting GENERIC SUBDOMAIN because these are usually easier to analyze. But be careful; this can defeat the purpose of risk management.

Projects face risk from both sides, with some projects having greater technical risks and others greater domain modeling risks. The end-to-end system mitigates risk only to the extent that it is an embryonic version of the challenging parts of the actual system. It is easy to underestimate the domain modeling risk. It can take the form of

---

unforeseen complexity, inadequate access to business experts, or gaps in key skills of the developers.

Therefore, except when the team has proven skills and the domain is very familiar, the first-cut system should be based on some part of the CORE DOMAIN, however simple.

The same principle applies to any process that tries to push high-risk tasks forward: the CORE DOMAIN is high risk because it is often unexpectedly difficult and because without it, the project cannot succeed.

Most of the distillation patterns in this chapter show how to change the model and code to distill the CORE DOMAIN. However, the next two patterns, DOMAIN VISION STATEMENT and HIGHLIGHTED CORE, show how the use of supplemental documents can, with a very minor investment, improve communication and awareness of the CORE and focus development effort. . . .

Domain Vision Statement

At the beginning of a project, the model usually doesn't even exist, yet the need to focus its development is already there. In later stages of development, there is a need for an explanation of the value of the system that does not require an in-depth study of the model. Also, the critical aspects of the domain model may span multiple BOUNDED CONTEXTS, but by definition these distinct models can't be structured to show their common focus.

Many project teams write "vision statements" for management. The best of these documents lay out the specific value the application will bring to the organization. Some mention the creation of the domain model as a strategic asset. Usually the vision statement document is abandoned after the project gets funding, and it is never used in the actual development process or even read by the technical staff.

A DOMAIN VISION STATEMENT is modeled after such documents, but it focuses on the nature of the domain model and how it is valuable to the enterprise. It can be used directly by the management and technical staff during all phases of development to guide resource allocation, to guide modeling choices, and to educate team members. If the domain model serves many masters, this document can show how their interests are balanced.

Therefore:

Write a short description (about one page) of the CORE DOMAIN and the value it will bring, the "value proposition." Ignore those aspects that do not distinguish this domain model from others. Show how the domain model serves and balances diverse interests. Keep it narrow. Write this statement early and revise it as you gain new insight.

A DOMAIN VISION STATEMENT can be used as a guidepost that keeps the development team headed in a common direction in the ongoing process of distilling the model and code itself. It can be shared with nontechnical team members, management, and even customers (except where it contains proprietary information, of course).

This is part of a DOMAIN VISION STATEMENT

Airline Booking System
The model can represent passenger priorities and airline booking strategies and balance these based on flexible policies. The model of a passenger should reflect the "relationship" the airline is striving to develop with repeat customers. Therefore, it should represent the history of the passenger in useful condensed form, participation in special programs, affiliation with strategic corporate clients, and so on.

Different roles of different users (such as passenger, agent, manager) are represented to enrich the model of relationships and to feed necessary information to the security framework.

Model should support efficient route/seat search and integration with other established flight booking systems.

This, though important, is *not* part of a DOMAIN VISION STATEMENT

Airline Booking System
The UI should be streamlined for expert users but accessible to first-time users.

Access will be offered over the Web, by data transfer to other systems, and maybe through other UIs, so interface will be designed around XML with transformation layers to serve Web pages or translate to other systems.

A colorful animated version of the logo needs to be cached on the client machine so that it can come up quickly on future visits.

When customer submits a reservation, make visual confirmation within 5 seconds.

A security framework will authenticate a user's identity and then limit access to specific features based on privileges assigned to defined user roles.

This is part of a DOMAIN VISION STATEMENT

Semiconductor Factory Automation
The domain model will represent the status of materials and equipment within a wafer fab in such a way that necessary audit trails can be provided and automated product routing can be supported.

The model will not include the human resources required in the process, but must allow selective process automation through recipe download.

The representation of the state of the factory should be comprehensible to human managers, to give them deeper insight and support better decision making.

This, though important, is *not* part of a DOMAIN VISION STATEMENT

Semiconductor Factory Automation
The software should be Web enabled through a servlet, but structured to allow alternative interfaces.

Industry-standard technologies should be used whenever possible to avoid in-house development and maintenance costs and to maximize access to outside expertise. Open source solutions are preferred (such as Apache Web server).

The Web server will run on a dedicated server. The application will run on a single dedicated server.

A DOMAIN VISION STATEMENT gives the team a shared direction. Some bridge between the high-level STATEMENT and the full detail of the code or model will usually be needed. . . .

HIGHLIGHTED CORE

A DOMAIN VISION STATEMENT identifies the CORE DOMAIN in broad terms, but it leaves the identification of the specific CORE model elements up to the vagaries of individual interpretation. Unless there is an exceptionally high level of communication on the team, the VISION STATEMENT alone will have little impact.

✳ ✳ ✳

Even though team members may know broadly what constitutes the CORE DOMAIN, different people won't pick out quite the same elements, and even the same person won't be consistent from one day to the next. The mental labor of constantly filtering the model to identify the key parts absorbs concentration better spent on design thinking, and it requires comprehensive knowledge of the model. The CORE DOMAIN must be made easier to see.

Significant structural changes to the code are the ideal way of identifying the CORE DOMAIN, but they are not always practical in the short term. In fact, such major code changes are difficult to undertake without the very view the team is lacking.

Structural changes in the organization of the model, such as partitioning GENERIC SUBDOMAINS and a few others to come later in this chapter, can allow the MODULES to tell the story. But as the only means of communicating the CORE DOMAIN, this is too ambitious to shoot for straight away.

You will probably need a lighter solution to supplement these aggressive techniques. You may have constraints that prevent you from physically separating the CORE. Or you may be starting out with existing code that does not differentiate the CORE well, but you really need to see the CORE, and share that view, to effectively refactor toward better distillation. And even at an advanced stage, a few carefully selected diagrams or documents provide mental anchor points and entry points for the team.

These issues arise equally for projects that use elaborate UML models and those (such as XP projects) that keep few external documents and use the code as the primary repository of the model. An Extreme Programming team might be more minimalist, keeping these supplements more casual and more transient (for example, a hand-drawn diagram on the wall for all to see), but these techniques can fold nicely into the process.

Marking off a privileged part of a model, along with the implementation that embodies it, is a reflection on the model, not necessarily part of the model itself. Any technique that makes it easy for everyone to know the CORE DOMAIN will do. Two specific techniques can represent this class of solutions.

The Distillation Document

Often I create a separate document to describe and explain the CORE DOMAIN. It can be as simple as a list of the most essential conceptual objects. It can be a set of diagrams focused on those objects, showing their most critical relationships. It can walk through the fundamental interactions at an abstract level or by example. It can use UML class or sequence diagrams, nonstandard diagrams particular to the domain, carefully worded textual explanations, or combinations of these. *A distillation document is not a complete design document.* It is a minimalist entry point that delineates and explains the CORE and suggests reasons for closer scrutiny of particular pieces. The reader is given a broad view of how the pieces fit and guided to the appropriate part of the code for more details.

Therefore (as one form of HIGHLIGHTED CORE):

Write a very brief document (three to seven sparse pages) that describes the CORE DOMAIN and the primary interactions among CORE elements.

All the usual risks of separate documents apply.

1. The document may not be maintained.

2. The document may not be read.

3. By multiplying the information sources, the document may defeat its own purpose of cutting through complexity.

The best way to limit these risks is to be absolutely minimalist. Staying away from mundane detail and focusing on the central abstractions and their interactions allows the document to age more slowly, because this level of the model is usually more stable.

Write the document to be understood by the nontechnical members of the team. Use it as a shared view that delineates what everyone needs to know, and a guide by which all team members may start their exploration of the model and code.

The Flagged CORE

On my first day on a project at a major insurance company, I was given a copy of the "domain model," a two-hundred-page document, purchased at great expense from an industry consortium. I spent a few days wading through a jumble of class diagrams covering everything from the detailed composition of insurance policies to extremely abstract models of relationships between people. The quality of the factoring of these models ranged from high-school project to rather good (a few even described business rules, at least in the accompanying text). But where to start? Two hundred pages.

The project culture heavily favored abstract framework building, and my predecessors had focused on a very abstract model of the relationship of people with each other, with things, and with activities or agreements. It was actually a nice analysis of these relationships, and their experiments with the model had the quality of an academic research project. But it wasn't getting us anywhere near an insurance application.

My first instinct was to start slashing, finding a small CORE DOMAIN to fall back on, then refactoring that and reintroducing other complexities as we went. But the management was alarmed by this attitude. The document was invested with great authority. Its production had involved experts from across the industry, and in any event they had paid the consortium far more than they were paying me, so they were unlikely to weigh my recommendations for radical change too heavily. But I knew we had to get a shared picture of our CORE DOMAIN and get everyone's efforts focused on that.

Instead of refactoring, I went through the document and, with the help of a business analyst who knew a great deal about the insurance industry in general and the requirements of the application we were to build in particular, I identified the handful of sections that presented the essential, differentiating concepts we needed to work with. I provided a navigation of the model that clearly showed the CORE and its relationship to supporting features.

A new prototyping effort started from this perspective, and quickly yielded a simplified application that demonstrated some of the required functionality.

Two pounds of recyclable paper was turned into a business asset by a few page tabs and some yellow highlighter.

This technique is not specific to object diagrams on paper. A team that uses UML diagrams extensively could use a "stereotype" to identify core elements. A team that uses the code as the sole repository of the model might use comments, maybe structured as Java Doc, or might use some tool in its development environment. The particular technique doesn't matter, as long as a developer can effortlessly see what is in and what is out of the CORE DOMAIN.

Therefore (as another form of HIGHLIGHTED CORE):

Flag each element of the CORE DOMAIN within the primary repository of the model, without particularly trying to elucidate its role. Make it effortless for a developer to know what is in or out of the CORE.

The CORE DOMAIN is now clearly visible to those working with the model, with a fairly small effort and low maintenance, at least to the extent that the model is factored fine enough to distinguish the contributions of parts.

The Distillation Document as Process Tool

Theoretically on an XP project, any pair (two programmers working together) can change any code in the system. In practice, some changes have major implications, and call for more consultation and coordination. When working in the infrastructure layer, the impact of a change may be clear, but it may not be so obvious in the domain layer, as typically organized.

With the concept of the CORE DOMAIN, this impact can be made clear. Changes to the model of the CORE DOMAIN should have a big effect. Changes to widely used generic elements may require a lot of code updating, but they still shouldn't create the conceptual shift that CORE changes do.

Use the distillation document as a guide. When developers realize that the distillation document itself requires change to stay in sync with their code or model change, then consultation is called for. Either they are fundamentally changing the CORE DOMAIN elements or relationships, or they are changing the boundaries of the CORE, including or excluding something different. Dissemination of the model change to the whole team is necessary by whatever communication channels the team uses, including distribution of a new version of the distillation document.

If the distillation document outlines the essentials of the CORE DOMAIN, then it serves as a practical indicator of the significance of a model change. When a model or code change affects the distillation document, it requires consultation with other team members. When the change is made, it requires immediate notification of all team members, and the dissemination of a new version of the document. Changes outside the CORE or to details not included in the distillation document can be integrated without consultation or notification and will be encountered by other members in the course of their work. Then the developers have the full autonomy that XP suggests.

Although the VISION STATEMENT and HIGHLIGHTED CORE inform and guide, they do not actually modify the model or the code itself. Partitioning GENERIC SUBDOMAINS physically removes some distracting elements. The next patterns look at ways to structurally change the model and the design itself to make the CORE DOMAIN more visible and manageable. . . .

Cohesive Mechanisms

Encapsulating mechanisms is a standard principle of object-oriented design. Hiding complex algorithms in methods with intention-revealing names separates the "what" from the "how." This technique makes a design simpler to understand and use. Yet it runs into natural limits.

Computations sometimes reach a level of complexity that begins to bloat the design. The conceptual "what" is swamped by the mechanistic "how." A large number of methods that provide algorithms for resolving the problem obscure the methods that express the problem.

This proliferation of procedures is a symptom of a problem in the model. Refactoring toward deeper insight can yield a model and design whose elements are better suited to solving the problem. The first solution to seek is a model that makes the computation mechanism simple. But now and then the insight emerges that some part of the mechanism is itself conceptually coherent. This conceptual computation will probably not include all of the messy computations you need. We are not talking about some kind of catch-all "calculator." But extracting the coherent part should make the remaining mechanism easier to understand.

Therefore:

Partition a conceptually COHESIVE MECHANISM into a separate lightweight framework. Particularly watch for formalisms or well-documented categories of algorithms. Expose the capabilities of the framework with an INTENTION-REVEALING INTERFACE. Now the other elements of the domain can focus on expressing the problem ("what"), delegating the intricacies of the solution ("how") to the framework.

These separated mechanisms are then placed in their supporting roles, leaving a smaller, more expressive CORE DOMAIN that uses the mechanism through the interface in a more declarative style.

Recognizing a standard algorithm or formalism moves some of the complexity of the design into a studied set of concepts. With such a guide, we can implement a solution with confidence and little trial and error. We can count on other developers knowing about it or at least being able to look it up. This is similar to the benefits of a published GENERIC SUBDOMAIN model, but a documented algorithm or formal computation may be found more often because this level of computer science has been studied more. Still, more often than not you will have to create something new. Make it narrowly focused on the computation and avoid mixing in the expressive domain model. There is a separation of responsibilities: The model of the CORE DOMAIN or a GENERIC SUBDOMAIN formulates a fact, rule, or problem. A COHESIVE MECHANISM resolves the rule or completes the computation as specified by the model.

Example

A Mechanism in an Organization Chart

I went through this process on a project that needed a fairly elaborate model of an organization chart. This model represented the fact that one person worked for another, and in which branches of the organization, and it provided an interface by which relevant questions might be asked and answered. Because most of these questions were along the lines of "Who, in this chain of command, has authority to approve this?" or "Who, in this department, is capable of handling an issue like this?" the team realized that most of the complexity involved traversing specific branches of the organizational tree, searching for specific people or relationships. This is exactly the kind of problem solved by the well-developed formalism of a *graph*, a set of nodes connected by arcs (called *edges*) and the rules and algorithms needed to traverse the graph.

A subcontractor implemented a graph traversal framework as a COHESIVE MECHANISM. This framework used standard graph terminology and algorithms familiar to most computer scientists and abundantly documented in textbooks. By no means did he implement a fully general graph. It was a subset of that conceptual framework that covered the features needed for our organization model. And with an INTENTION-REVEALING INTERFACE, the means by which the answers are obtained are not a primary concern.

Now the organization model could simply state, using standard graph terminology, that each person is a node, and that each relationship between people is an edge (arc) connecting those nodes. After that, presumably, mechanisms within the graph framework could find the relationship between any two people.

If this mechanism had been incorporated into the domain model, it would have cost us in two ways. The model would have been coupled to a particular method of solving the problem, limiting future options. More important, the model of an organization would have been greatly complicated and muddied. Keeping mechanism and model separate allowed a declarative style of describing organizations that was much clearer. And the intricate code for graph manipulation was isolated in a purely mechanistic framework, based on proven algorithms, that could be maintained and unit-tested in isolation.

Another example of a COHESIVE MECHANISM would be a framework for constructing SPECIFICATION objects and supporting the basic comparison and combination operations expected of them. By employing such a framework, the CORE DOMAIN and GENERIC SUBDOMAINS can declare their SPECIFICATIONS in the clear, easily understood language described in that pattern (see Chapter 10). The intricate operations involved in carrying out the comparisons and combinations can be left to the framework.

※   ※   ※

GENERIC SUBDOMAIN Versus COHESIVE MECHANISM

Both GENERIC SUBDOMAINS and COHESIVE MECHANISMS are motivated by the same desire to unburden the CORE DOMAIN. The difference is the nature of the responsibility taken on. A GENERIC SUBDOMAIN is based on an expressive model that represents some aspect of how the team views the domain. In this it is no different than the CORE DOMAIN, just less central, less important, less specialized. A COHESIVE MECHANISM does not represent the domain; it solves some sticky computational problem posed by the expressive models.

A model proposes; a COHESIVE MECHANISM disposes.

In practice, unless you recognize a formalized, published computation, this distinction is usually not pure, at least not at first. In successive refactoring it could either be distilled into a purer mechanism or be transformed into a GENERIC SUBDOMAIN with some previously unrecognized model concepts that would make the mechanism simple.

When a MECHANISM Is Part of the CORE DOMAIN

You almost always want to remove MECHANISMS from the CORE DOMAIN. The one exception is when a MECHANISM is itself proprietary and a key part of the value of the software. This is sometimes the case with highly specialized algorithms. For example, if one of the distinguishing features of a shipping logistics application were a particularly effective algorithm for working out schedules, that MECHANISM could be considered part of the conceptual CORE. I once worked on a project at an investment bank in which highly proprietary algorithms for rating risk were definitely in the CORE DOMAIN. (In fact, they were held so closely that even most of the CORE developers were not allowed to see them.) Of course, these algorithms are probably a particular implementation of a set of rules that really predict risk. Deeper analysis might lead to a deeper model that would allow those rules to be explicit, with an encapsulated solving mechanism.

But that would be another incremental improvement in the design, for another day. The decision as to whether to go that next step would be based on a cost-benefit analysis: How difficult would it be to work out that new design? How difficult is the current design to understand and modify? How much easier would it be with a more advanced design, for the type of people who would be expected to do the work? And of course, does anyone have any idea what form the new model might take?

Example
Full Circle: Organization Chart Reabsorbs Its MECHANISM

Actually, a year after we completed the organization model in the previous example, other developers redesigned it to eliminate the separation of the graph framework. They felt the increased object count and the complication of separating the MECHANISM into a separate package were not warranted. Instead, they added node behavior to the parent class of the organizational ENTITIES. Still, they retained the declarative public interface of the organization model. They even kept the MECHANISM encapsulated, within the organizational ENTITIES.

These full circles are common, but they do not return to their starting point. The end result is usually a deeper model that more clearly differentiates facts, goals, and MECHANISMS. Pragmatic refactoring retains the important virtues of the intermediate stages while shedding the unneeded complications.

Distilling to a Declarative Style

Declarative design and "declarative style" is a topic of Chapter 10, but that design style deserves special mention in this chapter on strategic distillation. The value of distillation is being able to see what you are doing: cutting to the essence without being distracted by irrelevant detail. Important parts of the CORE DOMAIN may be able to follow a declarative style, when the supporting design provides an economical language for expressing the concepts and rules of the CORE while encapsulating the means of computing or enforcing them.

COHESIVE MECHANISMS are by far most useful when they provide access through an INTENTION-REVEALING INTERFACE, with conceptually coherent ASSERTIONS and SIDE-EFFECT-FREE FUNCTIONS. MECHANISMS and supple designs allow the CORE DOMAIN to make meaningful statements rather than calling obscure functions. But an exceptional payoff comes when part of the CORE DOMAIN itself breaks through to a deep model and starts to function as a language that can express the most important application scenarios flexibly and concisely.

A deep model often comes with a corresponding supple design. When a supple design reaches maturity, it provides an easily understood set of elements that can be combined unambiguously to accomplish complex tasks or express complex information, just as words are combined into sentences. At that point, client code takes on a declarative style and can be much more distilled.

Factoring out GENERIC SUBDOMAINS reduces clutter, and COHESIVE MECHANISMS serve to encapsulate complex operations. This leaves behind a more focused model, with fewer distractions that add no particular value to the way users conduct their activities. But you are unlikely ever to find good homes for *everything* in the domain model that is not CORE. The SEGREGATED CORE takes a direct approach to structurally marking off the CORE DOMAIN. . . .

Segregated Core

Elements in the model may partially serve the CORE DOMAIN and partially play supporting roles. CORE elements may be tightly coupled to generic ones. The conceptual cohesion of the CORE may not be strong or visible. All this clutter and entanglement chokes the CORE. Designers can't clearly see the most important relationships, leading to a weak design.

By factoring out GENERIC SUBDOMAINS, you clear away some of the obscuring detail from the domain, making the CORE more visible. But it is hard work identifying and clarifying all these subdomains, and some of them don't seem worth the trouble. Meanwhile, the all-important CORE DOMAIN is left entangled with the residue.

Therefore:

Refactor the model to separate the CORE concepts from supporting players (including ill-defined ones) and strengthen the cohesion of the CORE while reducing its coupling to other code. Factor all generic or supporting elements into other objects and place them into other packages, even if this means refactoring the model in ways that separate highly coupled elements.

This is basically taking the same principles we applied to GENERIC SUBDOMAINS but from the other direction. The cohesive subdomains that are central to our application can be identified and partitioned into coherent packages of their own. What is done with the undifferentiated mass left behind is important, but not as important. It can be left more or less where it was, or placed into packages based on prominent classes. Eventually, more and more of the residue can be factored into GENERIC SUBDOMAINS, but in the short term any easy solution will do, just so the focus on the SEGREGATED CORE is retained.

❈ ❈ ❈

The steps needed to refactor to SEGREGATED CORE are typically something like these:

1. Identify a CORE subdomain (possibly drawing from the distillation document).

2. Move related classes to a new MODULE, named for the concept that relates them.

3. Refactor code to sever data and functionality that are not directly expressions of the concept. Put the removed aspects into (possibly new) classes in other packages. Try to place them with conceptually related tasks, but don't waste too much time being perfect. Keep focused on scrubbing the CORE subdomain and making the references from it to other packages explicit and self-explanatory.

4. Refactor the newly SEGREGATED CORE MODULE to make its relationships and interactions simpler and more communicative, and to minimize and clarify its relationships with other MODULES. (This becomes an ongoing refactoring objective.)

5. Repeat with another CORE subdomain until the SEGREGATED CORE is complete.

The Costs of Creating a SEGREGATED CORE

Segregating the CORE will sometimes make relationships with tightly coupled non-CORE classes more obscure or even more complicated, but that cost is outweighed by the benefit of clarifying the CORE DOMAIN and making it much easier to work on.

The SEGREGATED CORE will let you enhance the cohesion of that CORE DOMAIN. There are many meaningful ways of breaking down a model, and sometimes in the creation of a SEGREGATED CORE a nicely cohesive MODULE may be broken, sacrificing that cohesion for the sake of bringing out the cohesiveness of the CORE DOMAIN. This is a net gain, because the greatest value-added of enterprise software comes from the enterprise-specific aspects of the model.

The other cost, of course, is that segregating the CORE is a lot of work. It must be acknowledged that a decision to go to a SEGREGATED CORE will potentially absorb developers in changes all over the system.

The time to chop out a SEGREGATED CORE is when you have a large BOUNDED CONTEXT that is critical to the system, but where the essential part of the model is being obscured by a great deal of supporting capability.

Evolving Team Decision

As with many strategic design decisions, an entire team must move to a SEGREGATED CORE together. This step requires a team decision process and a team disciplined and coordinated enough to carry out the decision. The challenge is to constrain everyone to use the same definition of the CORE while not freezing that decision. Because the CORE DOMAIN evolves just like every other aspect of a design, experience working with a SEGREGATED CORE will lead to new insights into what is essential and what is a supporting element. Those insights should feed back into a refined definition of the CORE DOMAIN and of the SEGREGATED CORE MODULES.

This means that new insights must be shared with the team on an ongoing basis, but an individual (or programming pair) cannot act on those insights unilaterally. Whatever the process is for joint decisions, whether consensus or team leader directive, it must be agile enough to make repeated course corrections. Communication must be effective enough to keep everyone together in one view of the CORE.

Example

Segregating the CORE of a Cargo Shipping Model

We start with the model shown in Figure 15.2 as the basis of software for cargo shipping coordination.

Note that this is highly simplified compared to what would likely be needed for a real application. A realistic model would be too cumbersome for an example. Therefore, although this example may not be complicated enough to drive us to a SEGREGATED CORE, take a leap of imagination to treat this model as being too complex to interpret easily and deal with as a whole.

Now, what is the essence of the shipping model? Usually a good place to start looking is the "bottom line." This might lead us to focus on pricing and invoices. But we really need to look at the DOMAIN VISION STATEMENT. Here is an excerpt from this one.

> . . . Increase visibility of operations and provide tools to fulfill customer requirements faster and more reliably . . .

This application is not being designed for the sales department. It is going to be used by the front-line operators of the company. So

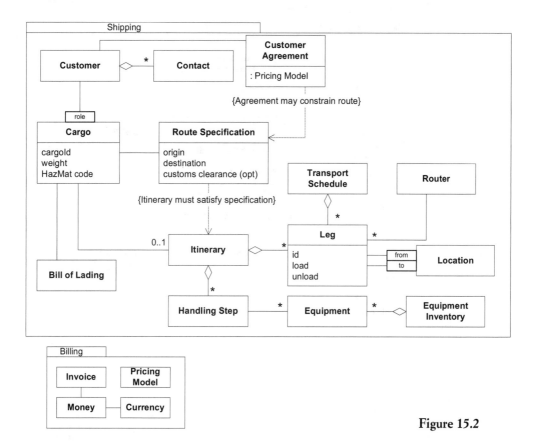

Figure 15.2

let's relegate all money-related issues to (admittedly important) supporting roles. Someone has already placed some of these items into a separate package (**Billing**). We can keep that, and further recognize that it plays a supporting role.

The focus needs to be on the cargo handling: delivery of the cargo according to customer requirements. Extracting the classes most directly involved in these activities produces a SEGREGATED CORE in a new package called **Delivery**, as shown in Figure 15.3.

For the most part, classes have just moved into the new package, but there have been a few changes to the model itself.

First, the **Customer Agreement** now constrains the **Handling Step**. This is typical of the insights that tend to arise as the team segregates the CORE. As attention is focused on effective, correct delivery, it becomes clear that the delivery constraints in the **Customer Agreement** are fundamental and should be *explicit* in the model.

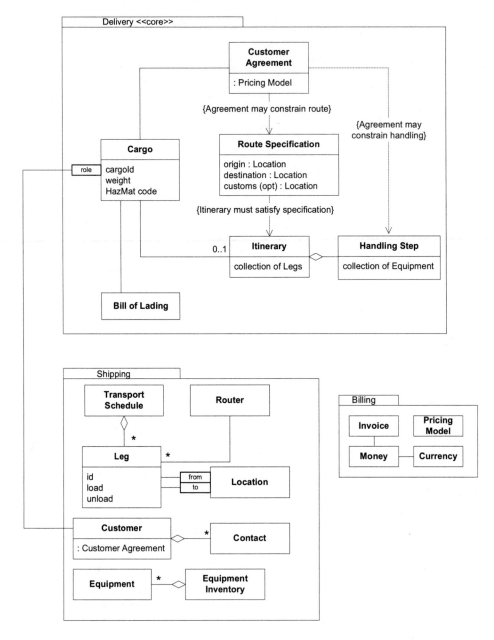

Figure 15.3
Reliable delivery in adherence with customer requirements is the core goal of this project.

The other change is more pragmatic. In the refactored model, the **Customer Agreement** is attached directly to the **Cargo**, rather than requiring a navigation through the **Customer**. (It will have to be attached when the **Cargo** is booked, just as the **Customer** is.) At actual delivery time, the **Customer** is not as relevant to operations as the agreement itself. In the other model, the correct **Customer** had to be found, according to the role it played in the shipment, and then queried for its **Customer Agreement**. This interaction would clog up every story you set out to tell about the model. The new association makes the most important scenarios as simple and direct as possible. Now it becomes easy to pull the **Customer** out of the CORE altogether.

And what about pulling **Customer** out, anyway? The focus is on fulfilling the **Customer's** requirements, so at first **Customer** seems to belong in the CORE. Yet the interactions during delivery do not usually need to involve the **Customer** class now that the **Customer Agreement** is available directly. And the basic model of a **Customer** is pretty generic.

A strong argument could be made for **Leg** to remain in the CORE. I tend to be minimalist in the CORE, and the **Leg** has tighter cohesion with **Transport Schedule**, **Routing Service**, and **Location**, none of which needed to be in the CORE. But if a lot of the stories I wanted to tell about this model involved **Legs**, I'd move it into the **Delivery** package and suffer the awkwardness of its separation from those other classes.

In this example, all the class definitions are the same as before, but often distillation requires refactoring the classes themselves to separate the generic and domain-specific responsibilities, which can then be segregated.

Now that we have a SEGREGATED CORE, the refactoring is complete. But the **Shipping** package we are left with is just "everything left over after we pulled out the CORE." We can follow up with other refactorings to get more communicative packaging, as shown in Figure 15.4.

It might take several refactorings to get to this point; it doesn't have to be done all at once. Here, we've ended up with one SEGREGATED CORE package, one GENERIC SUBDOMAIN, and two domain-specific packages in supporting roles. Deeper insight might eventually produce a GENERIC SUBDOMAIN for **Customer**, or it might end up more specialized for shipping.

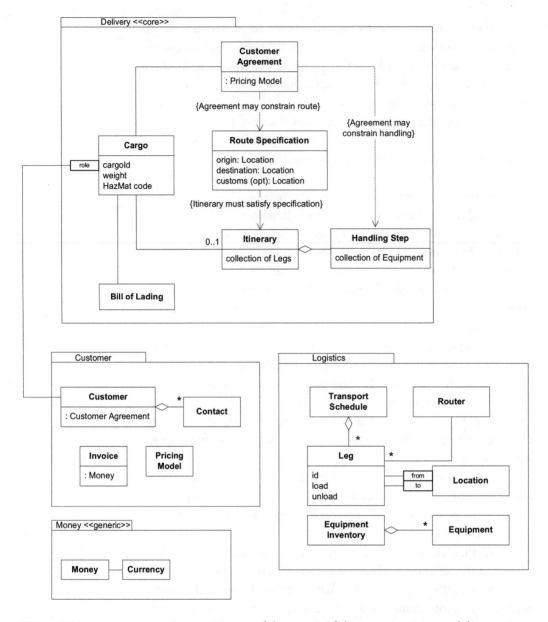

Figure 15.4
Meaningful MODULES
for non-CORE sub-
domains follow after the
SEGREGATED CORE is
complete.

Recognizing useful, meaningful MODULES is a modeling activity
(as discussed in Chapter 5). Developers and domain experts collaborate in strategic distillation as part of the knowledge crunching
process.

Abstract Core

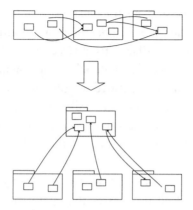

Even the CORE DOMAIN model usually has so much detail that communicating the big picture can be difficult.

✳ ✳ ✳

We usually deal with a large model by breaking it into narrower subdomains that are small enough to be grasped and placing them in separate MODULES. This reductive style of packaging often works to make a complicated model manageable. But sometimes creating separate MODULES can obscure or even complicate the interactions between the subdomains.

When there is a lot of interaction between subdomains in separate MODULES, either many references will have to be created between MODULES, which defeats much of the value of the partitioning, or the interaction will have to be made indirect, which makes the model obscure.

Consider slicing horizontally rather than vertically. Polymorphism gives us the power to ignore a lot of the detailed variation among instances of an abstract type. If most of the interactions across MODULES can be expressed at the level of polymorphic interfaces, it may make sense to refactor these types into a special CORE MODULE.

We are not looking for a technical trick here. This is a valuable technique only when the polymorphic interfaces correspond to fundamental concepts in the domain. In that case, separating these abstractions decouples the MODULES while distilling a smaller and more cohesive CORE DOMAIN.

Therefore:

Identify the most fundamental concepts in the model and factor them into distinct classes, abstract classes, or interfaces. Design this abstract model so that it expresses most of the interaction between significant components. Place this abstract overall model in its own MODULE, while the specialized, detailed implementation classes are left in their own MODULES defined by subdomain.

Most of the specialized classes will now reference the ABSTRACT CORE MODULE but not the other specialized MODULES. The ABSTRACT CORE gives a succinct view of the main concepts and their interactions.

The process of factoring out the ABSTRACT CORE is not mechanical. For example, if all the classes that were frequently referenced across MODULES were automatically moved into a separate MODULE, the likely result would be a meaningless mess. Modeling an ABSTRACT CORE requires a deep understanding of the key concepts and the roles they play in the major interactions of the system. In other words, it is an example of refactoring to deeper insight. And it usually requires considerable redesign.

The ABSTRACT CORE should end up looking a lot like the distillation document (if both were used on the same project, and the distillation document had evolved with the application as insight deepened). Of course, the ABSTRACT CORE will be written in code, and therefore more rigorous and more complete.

※　※　※

Deep Models Distill

Distillation does not operate only on the gross level of separating parts of the domain away from the CORE. It also means refining those subdomains, especially the CORE DOMAIN, through continuously refactoring toward deeper insight, driving toward a deep model and supple design. The goal is a design that makes the model obvious, a model that expresses the domain simply. A deep model distills the most essential aspects of a domain into simple elements that can be combined to solve the important problems of the application.

Although a breakthrough to a deep model provides value anywhere it happens, it is in the CORE DOMAIN that it can change the trajectory of an entire project.

Choosing Refactoring Targets

When you encounter a large system that is poorly factored, where do you start? In the XP community, the answer tends to be either one of these:

1. Just start anywhere, because it all has to be refactored.

2. Start wherever it is hurting. I'll refactor what I need to in order to get my specific task done.

I don't hold with either of these. The first is impractical except in a few projects staffed entirely with top programmers. The second tends to pick around the edges, treating symptoms and ignoring root causes, shying away from the worst tangles. Eventually the code becomes harder and harder to refactor.

So, if you can't do it all, and you can't be pain-driven, what do you do?

1. In a pain-driven refactoring, you look to see if the root involves the CORE DOMAIN or the relationship of the CORE to a supporting element. If it does, you bite the bullet and fix that first.

2. When you have the luxury of refactoring freely, you focus first on better factoring of the CORE DOMAIN, on improving the segregation of the CORE, and on purifying supporting subdomains to be GENERIC.

This is how to get the most bang for your refactoring buck.

SIXTEEN

Large-Scale Structure

Thousands of people worked independently
to create the AIDS Quilt.

A small Silicon Valley design firm had been contracted to create a simulator for a satellite communications system. Work was progressing well. A MODEL-DRIVEN DESIGN was developing that could express and simulate a wide range of network conditions and failures.

But the lead developers on the project were uneasy. The problem was inherently complex. Driven by the need to clarify the intricate relationships in the model, they had decomposed the design into coherent MODULES of manageable size. Now there were a *lot* of MODULES. Which package should a developer look in to find a particular aspect of functionality? Where should a new class be placed? What did some of these little packages really mean? How did they all fit together? And there was still more to build.

The developers communicated well with one another and could still figure out what to do from day to day, but the project leaders were not content to skirt the edge of comprehensibility. They wanted some way of organizing the design so that it could be understood and manipulated as it moved to the next level of complexity.

They brainstormed. There were a lot of possibilities. Alternative packaging schemes were proposed. Maybe some document could give an overview of the system, or some new views of the class diagram in the modeling tool could guide a developer to the right MODULE. But the project leaders weren't satisfied with these gimmicks.

They could tell a simple story of their simulation, of the way data would be marshaled through an infrastructure, its integrity and routing assured by layers of telecommunications technology. Every detail of that story was in the model, yet the broad arc of the story could not be seen.

Some essential concept from the domain was missing. But this time it was not a class or two missing from the object model, it was a missing structure for the model as a whole.

After the developers mulled over the problem for a week or two, the idea began to jell. They would impose a structure on the design. The entire simulator would be viewed as a series of layers related to aspects of the communications system. The bottom layer would represent the physical infrastructure, the basic ability to transmit bits from one node to another. Then there would be a packet-routing layer that brought together the concerns of how a particular data stream would be directed. Other layers would identify other conceptual levels of the problem. *These layers would outline their story of the system.*

They set out to refactor the code to conform to the new structure. MODULES had to be redefined so as not to span layers. In some cases, object responsibilities were refactored so that each object would clearly belong to one layer. Conversely, throughout this process the definitions of the conceptual layers themselves were refined based on the hands-on experience of applying them. The layers, MODULES, and objects coevolved until, in the end, the entire design followed the contours of this layered structure.

These layers were not MODULES or any other artifact in the code. They were an overarching set of rules that constrained the boundaries and relationships of any particular MODULE or object throughout the design, even at interfaces with other systems.

Imposing this order brought the design back to comfortable intelligibility. People knew roughly where to look for a particular function. Individuals working independently could make design decisions that were broadly consistent with each other. The complexity ceiling had been lifted.

Even with a MODULAR breakdown, a large model can be too complicated to grasp. The MODULES chunk the design into manageable bites, but there may be many of them. Also, modularity does not necessarily bring uniformity to the design. Object to object, package to package, a jumble of design decisions may be applied, each defensible but idiosyncratic.

The strict segregation imposed by BOUNDED CONTEXTS prevents corruption and confusion, but it does not, in itself, make it easier to see the system as a whole.

Distillation does help by focusing attention on the CORE DOMAIN and casting other subdomains in their supporting roles. But it is still necessary to understand the supporting elements and their relationships to the CORE DOMAIN—and to each other. And while the CORE DOMAIN would ideally be so clear and easily understood that no additional guidance would be needed, we are not always at that point.

On a project of any size, people must work somewhat independently on different parts of the system. Without any coordination or rules, a confusion of different styles and distinct solutions to the same problems arises, making it hard to understand how the parts fit together and impossible to see the big picture. Learning about one part of the design will not transfer to other parts, so the project will end up with specialists in different MODULES who cannot help each other outside their narrow range. CONTINUOUS INTEGRATION breaks down and the BOUNDED CONTEXT fragments.

In a large system without any overarching principle that allows elements to be interpreted in terms of their role in patterns that span the whole design, developers cannot see the forest for the trees. We need to be able to understand the role of an individual part in the whole without delving into the details of the whole.

A "large-scale structure" is a language that lets you discuss and understand the system in broad strokes. A set of high-level concepts or rules, or both, establishes a pattern of design for an entire system. This organizing principle can guide design as well as aid understanding. It helps coordinate independent work because there is a shared concept of the big picture: how the roles of various parts shape the whole.

Devise a pattern of rules or roles and relationships that will span the entire system and that allows some understanding of each part's place in the whole—even without detailed knowledge of the part's responsibility.

Structure may be confined to one BOUNDED CONTEXT but will usually span more than one, providing the conceptual organization to hold together all the teams and subsystems involved in the project. A good structure gives insight into the model and complements distillation.

You can't represent most large-scale structures in UML, and you don't need to. Most large-scale structures shape and explain the model and design but do not appear in it. They provide an extra level of communication about the design. In the examples of this chapter, you'll see many informal UML diagrams on which I've superimposed information about the large-scale structure.

When a team is reasonably small and the model is not too complicated, decomposition into well-named MODULES, a certain amount of distillation, and informal coordination among developers can be sufficient to keep the model organized.

Large-scale structure can save a project, but an ill-fitting structure can severely hinder development. This chapter explores patterns for successfully structuring a design at this level.

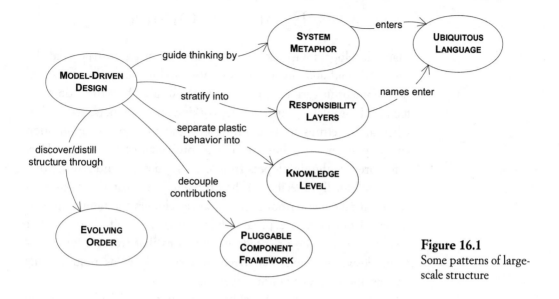

Figure 16.1
Some patterns of large-scale structure

Evolving Order

Many developers have experienced the cost of an unstructured design. To avoid anarchy, projects impose architectures that constrain development in various ways. Some technical architectures do solve technical problems, such as networking or data persistence, but when architectures start venturing into the arena of the application and domain model, they can create problems of their own. They often prevent the developers from creating designs and models that work well for the specifics of the problem. The most ambitious ones can even take away from application developers the familiarity and technical power of the programming language itself. And whether technical or domain oriented, architectures that freeze a lot of up-front design decisions can become a straitjacket as requirements change and as understanding deepens.

While some technical architectures (such as J2EE) have become prominent over the years, large-scale structure in the domain layer has not been explored much. Needs vary widely from one application to the next.

An up-front imposition of a large-scale structure is likely to be costly. As development proceeds, you will almost certainly find a more suitable structure, and you may even find that the prescribed structure is prohibiting you from taking a design route that would greatly clarify or simplify the application. You may be able to use some of the structure, but you're forgoing opportunities. Your work slows down as you try workarounds or try to negotiate with the architects. But your managers think the architecture is done. It was supposed to make this application easy, so why aren't you working on the application instead of dealing with all these architecture problems? The managers and architecture teams may even be open to input, but if each change is a heroic battle, it is too exhausting.

Design free-for-alls produce systems no one can make sense of as a whole, and they are very difficult to maintain. But architectures can straitjacket a project with up-front design assumptions and take too much power away from the developers/designers of particular parts of the application. Soon, developers will dumb down the application to fit the structure, or they will subvert it and have no structure at all, bringing back the problems of uncoordinated development.

The problem is not the existence of guiding rules, but rather the rigidity and source of those rules. If the rules governing the design really fit the circumstances, they will not get in the way but actually push development in a helpful direction, as well as provide consistency.

Therefore:

Let this conceptual large-scale structure evolve with the application, possibly changing to a completely different type of structure along the way. Don't overconstrain the detailed design and model decisions that must be made with detailed knowledge.

Individual parts have natural or useful ways of being organized and expressed that may not apply to the whole, so imposing global rules makes these parts less ideal. Choosing to use a large-scale structure favors manageability of the model as a whole over optimal structuring of the individual parts. Therefore, there will be some compromise between unifying structure and freedom to express individual components in the most natural way. This can be mitigated by selecting the structure based on actual experience and knowledge of the domain and by avoiding over-constrictive structures. A really nice fit of structure to domain and requirements actually makes detailed modeling and design easier, by helping to quickly eliminate a lot of options.

The structure can also give shortcuts to design decisions that could, in principle, be found by working on the individual object level, but would, in practice, take too long and have inconsistent results. Of course, continuous refactoring is still necessary, but this will make it a more manageable process and can help make different people come up with consistent solutions.

A large-scale structure generally needs to be applicable across BOUNDED CONTEXTS. Through iteration on a real project, a structure will lose features that tightly bind it to a particular model and evolve features that correspond to CONCEPTUAL CONTOURS of the domain. This doesn't mean that it will have *no* assumptions about the model, but it will not impose upon the entire project ideas tailored to a particular local situation. It has to leave freedom for development teams in distinct CONTEXTS to vary the model in ways that address their local needs.

Also, large-scale structures must accommodate practical constraints on development. For example, designers may have no control over the model of some parts of the system, especially in the case of external or legacy subsystems. This could be handled by changing the structure to better fit the specific external elements. It could be handled by specifying ways in which the application relates to externals. It might be handled by making the structure loose enough to flex around awkward realities.

Unlike the CONTEXT MAP, a large-scale structure is optional. One should be imposed when costs and benefits favor it, and when a fitting structure is found. In fact, it is not needed for systems that are simple enough to be understood when broken into MODULES. **Large-scale structure should be applied when a structure can be found that greatly clarifies the system without forcing unnatural constraints on model development. Because an ill-fitting structure is worse than none, it is best not to shoot for comprehensiveness, but rather to find a minimal set that solves the problems that have emerged. Less is more.**

A large-scale structure can be very helpful and still have a few exceptions, but those exceptions need to be flagged somehow, so that developers can assume the structure is being followed unless otherwise noted. And if those exceptions start to get numerous, the structure needs to be changed or discarded.

As mentioned, it is no mean feat to create a structure that gives the necessary freedom to developers while still averting chaos. Although a lot of work has been done on technical architecture for software systems, little has been published on the structuring of the domain layer. Some approaches weaken the object-oriented paradigm, such as those that break down the domain by application task or by use case. This whole area is still undeveloped. I've observed a few general patterns of large-scale structures that have emerged on various projects. I'll discuss four in this chapter. One of these may fit your needs or lead to ideas for a structure tailored to your project.

SYSTEM METAPHOR

Metaphorical thinking is pervasive in software development, especially with models. But the Extreme Programming practice of "metaphor" has come to mean a particular way of using a metaphor to bring order to the development of a whole system.

✳ ✳ ✳

Just as a firewall can save a building from a fire raging through neighboring buildings, a software "firewall" protects the local network from the dangers of the larger networks outside. This metaphor has influenced network architectures and shaped a whole product category. Multiple competing firewalls—developed independently, understood to be somewhat interchangeable—are available for consumers. Novices to networking readily grasp the concept. This shared understanding throughout the industry and among customers is due in no small part to the metaphor.

Yet it is an inexact analogy, and its power cuts both ways. The use of the firewall metaphor has led to development of software barriers that are sometimes insufficiently selective and impede desirable exchanges, while offering no protection against threats originating within the wall. Wireless LANs, for example, are vulnerable. The clarity of the firewall has been a boon, but all metaphors carry baggage.[1]

Software designs tend to be very abstract and hard to grasp. Developers and users alike need tangible ways to understand the system and share a view of the system as a whole.

On one level, metaphor runs so deeply in the way we think that it pervades every design. Systems have "layers" that "lay on top" of each other. They have "kernels" at their "centers." But sometimes a metaphor comes along that can convey the central theme of a whole design and provide a shared understanding among all team members.

When this happens, the system is actually shaped by the metaphor. A developer will make design decisions consistent with the system metaphor. This consistency will enable other developers to interpret the many parts of a complex system in terms of the same

---

1. SYSTEM METAPHOR finally made sense to me when I heard Ward Cunningham use this firewall example in a workshop lecture.

metaphor. The developers and experts have a reference point in discussions that may be more concrete than the model itself.

A SYSTEM METAPHOR is a loose, easily understood, large-scale structure that it is harmonious with the object paradigm. Because the SYSTEM METAPHOR is only an analogy to the domain anyway, different models can map to it in an approximate way, which allows it to be applied in multiple BOUNDED CONTEXTS, helping to coordinate work between them.

SYSTEM METAPHOR has become a popular approach because it is one of the core practices of Extreme Programming (Beck 2000). Unfortunately, few projects have found really useful METAPHORS, and people have tried to push the idea into domains where it is counterproductive. A persuasive metaphor introduces the risk that the design will take on aspects of the analogy that are not desirable for the problem at hand, or that the analogy, while seductive, may not be apt.

That said, SYSTEM METAPHOR is a well-known form of large-scale structure that is useful on some projects, and it nicely illustrates the general concept of a structure.

Therefore:

When a concrete analogy to the system emerges that captures the imagination of team members and seems to lead thinking in a useful direction, adopt it as a large-scale structure. Organize the design around this metaphor and absorb it into the UBIQUITOUS LANGUAGE. The SYSTEM METAPHOR should both facilitate communication about the system and guide development of it. This increases consistency in different parts of the system, potentially even across different BOUNDED CONTEXTS. But because all metaphors are inexact, continually reexamine the metaphor for overextension or inaptness, and be ready to drop it if it gets in the way.

✳ ✳ ✳

The "Naive Metaphor" and Why We Don't Need It

Because a useful metaphor doesn't present itself on most projects, some in the XP community have come to talk of the *naive metaphor*, by which they mean the domain model itself.

One trouble with this term is that a mature domain model is anything but naive. In fact, "payroll processing is like an assembly line" is likely a much more naive view than a model that is the product of many iterations of knowledge crunching with domain experts, and that has been proven by being tightly woven into the implementation of a working application.

The term *naive metaphor* should be retired.

SYSTEM METAPHORS are not useful on all projects. Large-scale structure in general is not essential. In the 12 practices of Extreme Programming, the role of a SYSTEM METAPHOR could be fulfilled by a UBIQUITOUS LANGUAGE. Projects should augment that LANGUAGE with SYSTEM METAPHORS or other large-scale structures when they find one that fits well.

RESPONSIBILITY LAYERS

Throughout this book, individual objects have been assigned narrow sets of related responsibilities. Responsibility-driven design also applies to larger scales.

✳ ✳ ✳

When each individual object has handcrafted responsibilities, there are no guidelines, no uniformity, and no ability to handle large swaths of the domain together. To give coherence to a large model, it is useful to impose some structure on the assignment of those responsibilities.

When you gain a deep understanding of a domain, broad patterns start to become visible. Some domains have a natural stratification. Certain concepts and activities take place against a background of other elements that change independently and at a different rate for different reasons. How can we take advantage of this natural structure, make it more visible and useful? This stratification suggests layering, one of the most successful architectural design patterns (Buschmann et al. 1996, among others).

Layers are partitions of a system in which the members of each partition are aware of and are able to use the services of the layers "below," but unaware of and independent of the layers "above." When the dependencies of MODULES are drawn, they are often laid out so that a MODULE with dependents appears below its dependents. In this way, layers sometimes sort themselves out so that none of the objects in the lower levels is conceptually dependent on those in higher layers.

But this ad hoc layering, while it can make tracing dependencies easier—and sometimes makes some intuitive sense—doesn't give much insight into the model or guide modeling decisions. We need something more intentional.

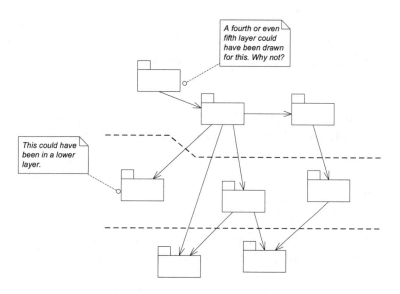

Figure 16.2
Ad hoc layering: What are these packages about?

In a model with a natural stratification, conceptual layers can be defined around major responsibilities, uniting the two powerful principles of layering and responsibility-driven design.

These responsibilities must be considerably broader than those typically assigned to individual objects, as examples will illustrate shortly. As individual MODULES and AGGREGATES are designed, they are factored to keep them within the bounds of one of these major responsibilities. This named grouping of responsibilities by itself could enhance the comprehensibility of a modularized system, since the responsibilities of MODULES could be more readily interpreted. But combining high-level responsibilities with layering gives us an organizing principle for a system.

The layering pattern that serves best for RESPONSIBILITY LAYERS is the variant called RELAXED LAYERED SYSTEM (Buschmann et al. 1996, p. 45), which allows components of a layer to access any lower layer, not just the one immediately below.

Therefore:

Look at the conceptual dependencies in your model and the varying rates and sources of change of different parts of your domain. If you identify natural strata in the domain, cast them as broad abstract responsibilities. These responsibilities should tell a story of the high-level purpose and design of your system. Refactor the model so that the responsibilities of each domain object, AGGREGATE, and MODULE fit neatly within the responsibility of one layer.

This is a pretty abstract description, but it will become clear with a few examples. The satellite communications simulator whose story opened this chapter layered its responsibility. I have seen RESPONSIBILITY LAYERS used to good effect in domains as various as manufacturing control and financial management.

✳ ✳ ✳

The following example explores RESPONSIBILITY LAYERS in detail to give a feel for the discovery of a large-scale structure of *any* sort, and the way it guides and constrains modeling and design.

Example

In Depth: Layering a Shipping System

Let's look at the implications of applying RESPONSIBILITY LAYERS to the cargo shipping application discussed in the examples of previous chapters.

As we rejoin the story, the team has made considerable progress creating a MODEL-DRIVEN DESIGN and distilling a CORE DOMAIN. But as the design fleshes out, they are having trouble coordinating how all the parts fit together. They are looking for a large-scale structure that can bring out the main themes of their system and keep everyone on the same page.

Here is a look at a representative part of the model.

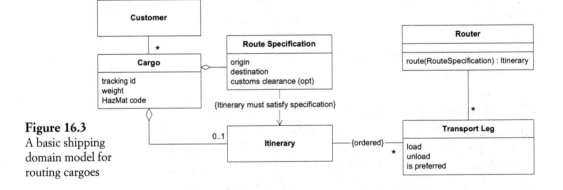

Figure 16.3
A basic shipping domain model for routing cargoes

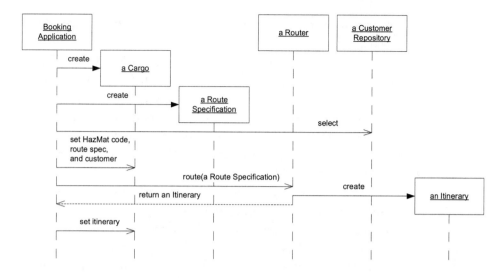

The team members have been steeped in the domain of shipping for months, and they have noticed some natural stratification of its concepts. It is quite reasonable to discuss transport schedules (the scheduled voyages of ships and trains) without referring to the cargoes aboard those transports. It is harder to talk about tracking a cargo without referring to the transport carrying it. The conceptual dependencies are pretty clear. The team can readily distinguish two layers: "Operations" and the substrate of those operations, which they dub "Capability."

Figure 16.4
Using the model to route a cargo during booking

"Operational" Responsibilities

Activities of the company, past, current, and planned, are collected into the Operations layer. The most obvious Operations object is **Cargo**, which is the focus of most of the day-to-day activity of the company. The **Route Specification** is an integral part of **Cargo**, indicating delivery requirements. The **Itinerary** is the operational delivery plan. Both of these objects are part of the **Cargo's** AGGREGATE, and their life cycles are tied to the time frame of an active delivery.

"Capability" Responsibilities

This layer reflects the resources the company draws upon in order to carry out operations. The **Transit Leg** is a classic example. The ships are scheduled to run and have a certain capacity to carry cargo, which may or may not be fully utilized.

True, if we were focused on operating a shipping fleet, **Transit Leg** would be in the Operations layer. But the users of this system aren't worried about that problem. (If the company were involved in both those activities and wanted the two coordinated, the development team might have to consider a different layering scheme, perhaps with two distinct layers, such as "Transport Operations" and "Cargo Operations.")

A trickier decision is where to place **Customer**. In some businesses, customers tend to be transient: they're interesting while a package is being delivered and then mostly forgotten until next time. This quality would make customers only an operational concern for a parcel delivery service aimed at individual consumers. But our hypothetical shipping company tends to cultivate long-term relationships with customers, and most work comes from repeat business. *Given these intentions of the business users*, the **Customer** belongs in the potential layer. As you can see, *this was not a technical decision*. It was an attempt to capture and communicate knowledge of the domain.

Because the association between **Cargo** and **Customer** can be traversed in only one direction, the **Cargo** REPOSITORY will need a query that finds all **Cargoes** for a particular **Customer**. There were good reasons to design it that way anyway, but with the imposition of the large-scale structure, it is now a requirement.

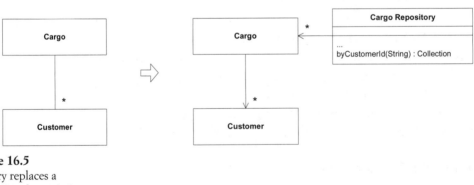

Figure 16.5
A query replaces a bidirectional association that violates the layering.

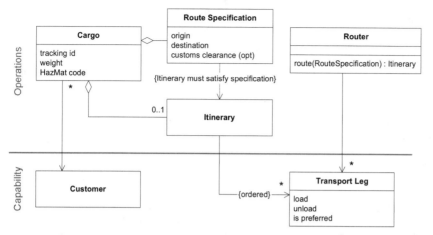

While the distinction between Operations and Capability clarifies the picture, order continues to evolve. After a few weeks of experimentation, the team zeroes in on another distinction. For the most part, both initial layers focus on situations or plans *as they are*. But the **Router** (and many other elements excluded from this example) isn't part of current operational realities or plans. It helps make decisions about changing those plans. The team defines a new layer responsible for "Decision Support."

"Decision Support" Responsibilities

This layer of the software provides the user with tools for planning and decision making, and it could potentially automate some decisions (such as automatically rerouting **Cargoes** when a transport schedule changes).

The **Router** is a SERVICE that helps a booking agent choose the best way to send a **Cargo**. This places the **Router** squarely in Decision Support.

The references within this model are all consistent with the three layers except for one discordant element: the "is preferred" attribute on **Transport Leg**. This attribute exists because the company prefers to use its own ships when it can, or the ships of certain other companies with which it has favorable contracts. The "is preferred" attribute is used to bias the **Router** toward these favored transports. This attribute has nothing to do with "Capability." It is a policy that directs decision making. To use the new RESPONSIBILITY LAYERS, the model will have to be refactored.

Figure 16.6
A first-pass layered model

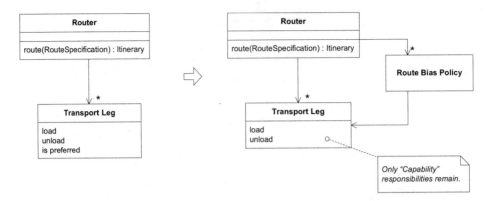

Figure 16.7
Refactoring the model to conform to the new layering structure

This factoring makes the **Route Bias Policy** more explicit while making **Transport Leg** more focused on the fundamental concept of transportation capability. A large-scale structure based on a deep understanding of the domain will often push the model in directions that clarify its meaning.

This new model now smoothly fits into the large-scale structure.

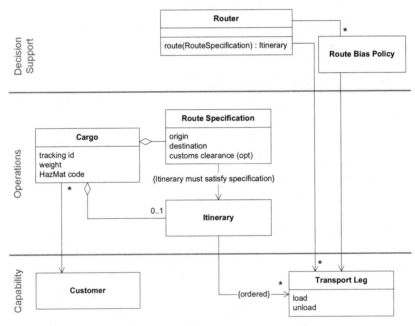

Figure 16.8
The restructured and refactored model

A developer accustomed to the chosen layers can more readily discern the roles and dependencies of the parts. The value of the large-scale structure increases as the complexity grows.

Note that although I'm illustrating this example with a modified UML diagram, the drawing is just a way of *communicating* the layering. UML doesn't include this notation, so this is additional information imposed for the sake of the reader. If code is the ultimate design document for your project, it would be helpful to have a tool for browsing classes by layer or at least for reporting them by layer.

How Does This Structure Affect Ongoing Design?

Once a large-scale structure has been adopted, subsequent modeling and design decisions must take it into account. To illustrate, suppose that we must add a new feature to this already layered design. The domain experts have just told us that routing restrictions apply for certain categories of hazardous materials. Certain materials may not be allowed on some transports or in some ports. We have to make the **Router** obey these regulations.

There are many possible approaches. In the absence of a large-scale structure, one appealing design would be to give the responsibility of incorporating these routing rules to the object that owns the **Route Specification** and the Hazardous Material (HazMat) code—namely the **Cargo**.

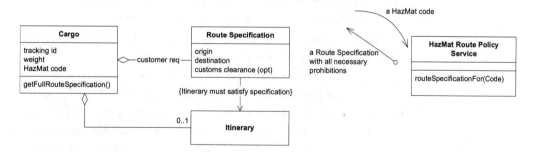

Figure 16.9
A possible design for routing hazardous cargo

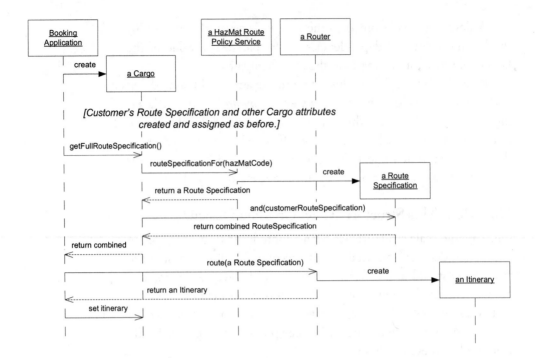

Figure 16.10
The trouble is, this design doesn't fit the large-scale structure. The **HazMat Route Policy Service** is not the problem; it fits neatly into the responsibility of the Decision Support layer. The problem is the dependency of **Cargo** (an Operational object) on **HazMat Route Policy Service** (a Decision Support object). As long as the project is committed to these layers, this model cannot be allowed. It would confuse developers who expected the structure to be followed.

There are always many design possibilities, and we'll just have to choose another one—one that follows the rules of the large-scale structure. The **HazMat Route Policy Service** is all right, but we need to move the responsibility for using the policy. Let's try giving the **Router** the responsibility for collecting appropriate policies before searching for a route. This means changing the **Router** interface to include objects that policies might depend on. Here is a possible design.

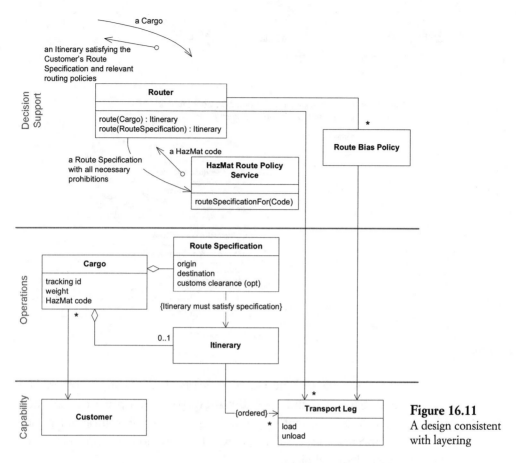

Figure 16.11
A design consistent with layering

A typical interaction is shown in Figure 16.12 on the next page.

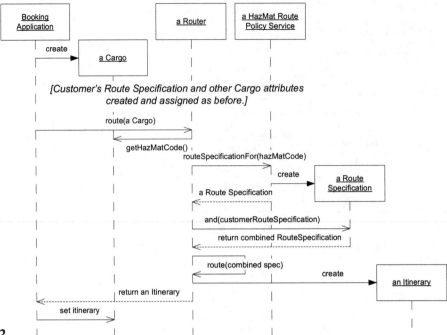

Figure 16.12

Now, this isn't necessarily a *better* design than the other. They both have pros and cons. But if everyone on a project makes decisions in a consistent way, the design as a whole will be much more comprehensible, and that is worth some modest trade-offs on detailed design choices.

If the structure is forcing many awkward design choices, then in keeping with EVOLVING ORDER, it should be evaluated and perhaps modified or even discarded.

Choosing Appropriate Layers

Finding good RESPONSIBILITY LAYERS, or any large-scale structure, is a matter of understanding the problem domain and experimenting. If you allow EVOLVING ORDER, the initial starting point is not critical, although a poor choice does add work. The structure may well evolve into something unrecognizable. So the guidelines suggested here should be applied when considering transformations of the structure as much as when choosing from scratch.

As layers get switched out, merged, split, and redefined, here are some useful characteristics to look for and preserve.

- *Storytelling*. The layers should communicate the basic realities or priorities of the domain. Choosing a large-scale structure is less a technical decision than a business modeling decision. The layers should bring out the priorities of the business.

- *Conceptual dependency*. The concepts in the "upper" layers should have meaning against the backdrop of the "lower" layers, while the lower-layer concepts should be meaningful standing alone.

- CONCEPTUAL CONTOURS. If the objects of different layers should have different rates of change or different sources of change, the layer accommodates the shearing between them.

It isn't always necessary to start from scratch in defining layers for each new model. Certain layers show up in whole families of related domains.

For example, in businesses based on exploiting large fixed capital assets, such as factories or cargo ships, logistical software can often be organized into a "Potential" layer (another name for the "Capability" layer in the example) and an "Operations" layer.

- *Potential*. What can be done? Never mind what we are planning to do. What *could* we do? The resources of the organization, including its people, and the way those resources are organized are the core of the Potential layer. Contracts with vendors also define potentials. This layer could be recognized in almost any business domain, but it is a prominent part of the story in those businesses, such as transportation and manufacturing, that have relatively large fixed capital investments that enable the business. Potential includes transient assets as well, but a business driven primarily by transient assets might choose layers that emphasize this, as discussed later. (This layer was called "Capability" in the example.)

- *Operation*. What is being done? What have we managed to make of those potentials? Like the Potential layer, this layer should reflect the reality of the situation, rather than what we want it to be. In this layer we are trying to see our own efforts and activities: What we are selling, rather than what enables us to sell. It is very typical of Operational objects to reference or even be composed of Potential objects, but a Potential object shouldn't reference the Operations layer.

In many, perhaps most, existing systems in domains of this kind, these two layers cover everything (although there could be some entirely different and more revealing breakdown). They track the current situation and active operational plans and issue reports or documents about it. But tracking is not always enough. When projects seek to guide or assist users, or to automate decision making, there is an additional set of responsibilities that can be organized into another layer, above Operations.

- *Decision Support.* What action should be taken or what policy should be set? This layer is for analysis and decision making. It bases its analysis on information from lower layers, such as Potential or Operations. Decision Support software may use historical information to actively seek opportunities for current and future operations.

Decision Support systems have conceptual dependencies on other layers such as Operations or Potential because decisions aren't made in a vacuum. A lot of projects implement Decision Support using data warehouse technology. The layer becomes a distinct BOUNDED CONTEXT, with a CUSTOMER/SUPPLIER relationship with the Operations software. In other projects, it is more deeply integrated, as in the preceding extended example. And one of the intrinsic advantages of layers is that the lower layers can exist without the higher ones. This can facilitate phased introductions or higher-level enhancements built on top of older operational systems.

Another case is software that enforces elaborate business rules or legal requirements, which can constitute a RESPONSIBILITY LAYER.

- *Policy.* What are the rules and goals? Rules and goals are mostly passive, but constrain the behavior in other layers. Designing these interactions can be subtle. Sometimes a Policy is passed in as an argument to a lower level method. Sometimes the STRATEGY pattern is applied. Policy works well in conjunction with a

Decision Support layer, which provides the means to seek the goals set by Policy, constrained by the rules set by Policy.

Policy layers can be written in the same language as the other layers, but they are sometimes implemented using rules engines. This doesn't necessarily place them in a separate BOUNDED CONTEXT. In fact, the difficulty of coordinating such different implementation technologies can be eased by fastidiously using the same model across both. When rules are written based on a different model than the objects they apply to, either the complexity goes way up or the objects get dumbed down to keep things manageable.

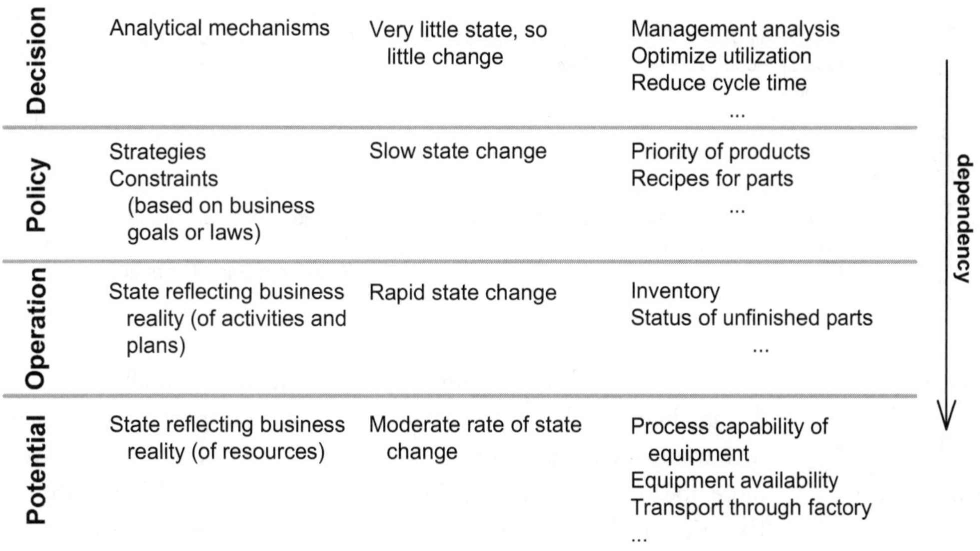

Decision	Analytical mechanisms	Very little state, so little change	Management analysis Optimize utilization Reduce cycle time ...
Policy	Strategies Constraints (based on business goals or laws)	Slow state change	Priority of products Recipes for parts ...
Operation	State reflecting business reality (of activities and plans)	Rapid state change	Inventory Status of unfinished parts ...
Potential	State reflecting business reality (of resources)	Moderate rate of state change	Process capability of equipment Equipment availability Transport through factory ...

dependency ↓

Figure 16.13
Conceptual dependencies and shearing points in a factory automation system

Many businesses do not base their capability on plant and equipment. In financial services or insurance, to name two, the potential is to a large extent determined by current operations. An insurance company's ability to take on a new risk by underwriting a new policy agreement is based on the diversification of its current business. The Potential layer would probably merge into Operations, and a different layering would evolve.

One area that often comes to the fore in these situations is commitments made to customers.

- *Commitment.* What have we promised? This layer has the nature of Policy, in that it states goals that direct future operations, but it has the nature of Operations in that commitments emerge and change as a part of ongoing business activity.

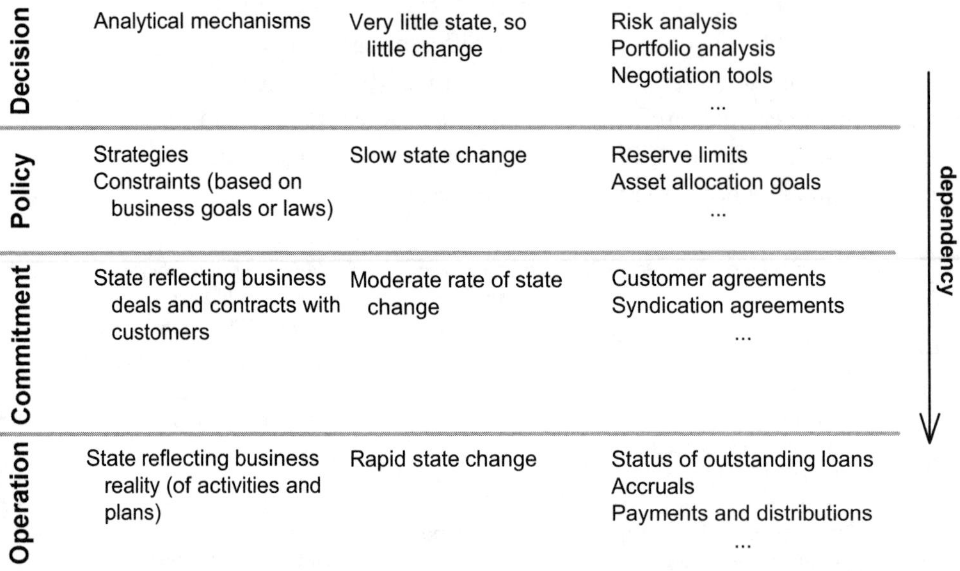

Decision	Analytical mechanisms	Very little state, so little change	Risk analysis Portfolio analysis Negotiation tools ...
Policy	Strategies Constraints (based on business goals or laws)	Slow state change	Reserve limits Asset allocation goals ...
Commitment	State reflecting business deals and contracts with customers	Moderate rate of state change	Customer agreements Syndication agreements ...
Operation	State reflecting business reality (of activities and plans)	Rapid state change	Status of outstanding loans Accruals Payments and distributions ...

dependency ↓

Figure 16.14
Conceptual dependencies and shearing points in an investment banking system

The Potential and Commitment layers are not mutually exclusive. A domain in which both are prominent, say a transportation company with a lot of custom shipping services, might use both. Other layers more specific to those domains might be useful too. Change things. Experiment. But it is best to keep the layering system simple; going beyond four or possibly five becomes unwieldy. Having too many layers isn't as effective at telling the story, and the problems of complexity the large-scale structure was meant to solve will come back in a new form. The large-scale structure must be ferociously distilled.

Although these five layers are applicable to a range of enterprise systems, they do not capture the salient responsibilities of all domains. In other cases, it would be counterproductive to try to force the design into this shape, but there may be a natural set of RESPONSIBILITY LAYERS that do work. For a domain completely unrelated to those we've discussed, these layers might have to be completely original. Ultimately, you have to use your intuition, start somewhere, and let the ORDER EVOLVE.

KNOWLEDGE LEVEL

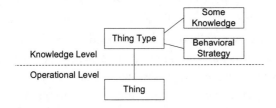

[A KNOWLEDGE LEVEL is] a group of objects that describes how another group of objects should behave. [Martin Fowler, "Accountability," www.martinfowler.com]

KNOWLEDGE LEVEL untangles things when we need to let some part of the model itself be plastic in the user's hands yet constrained by a broader set of rules. It addresses requirements for software with configurable behavior, in which the roles and relationships among ENTITIES must be changed at installation or even at runtime.

In *Analysis Patterns* (Fowler 1996, pp. 24–27), the pattern emerges from a discussion of modeling accountability within organizations, and it is later applied to posting rules in accounting. Although the pattern appears in several chapters, it doesn't have a chapter of its own because it is different from most patterns in the book. Rather than modeling a domain, as the other analysis patterns do, KNOWLEDGE LEVEL structures a model.

To see the problem concretely, consider models of "accountability." Organizations are made up of people and smaller organizations, and define the roles they play and the relationships between them. The rules governing those roles and relationships vary greatly for different organizations. At one company, a "department" might be headed by a "Director" who reports to a "Vice President." In another company, a "module" is headed by a "Manager" who reports to a "Senior Manager." Then there are "matrix" organizations, in which each person reports to different managers for different purposes.

A typical application would make some assumptions. When those didn't fit, users would start to use data-entry fields in a different way than they were intended. Any behavior the application had would misfire, as the semantics were changed by the users. Users would develop workarounds for the behavior, or would get the higher level features of the application shut off. They would be forced to learn complicated mappings between what they did in their jobs and the way the software works. They would never be served well.

When the system had to be changed or replaced, developers would discover (sooner or later) that the meanings of the features were not what they seemed. They might mean very different things in different user communities or in different situations. Changing anything without breaking these overlaid usages would be daunting. Data migration to a more tailored system would require understanding and coding for all those quirks.

Example

Employee Payroll and Pension, Part 1

The HR department of a medium-sized company has a simple program for calculating payroll and pension contributions.

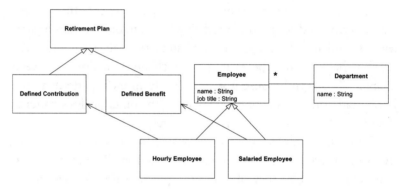

Figure 16.15
The old model, overconstrained for new requirements

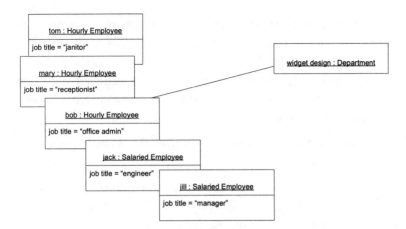

Figure 16.16
Some employees
represented using the
old model

But now, the management has decided that the office administrators should go into the "defined benefit" retirement plan. The trouble is that office administrators are paid hourly, and this model does not allow mixing. The model will have to change.

The next model proposal is quite simple: just remove the constraints.

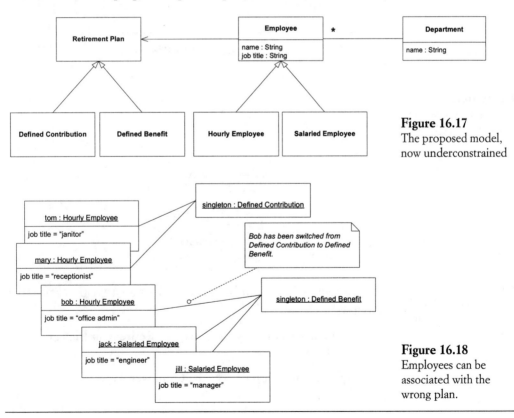

Figure 16.17
The proposed model,
now underconstrained

Figure 16.18
Employees can be
associated with the
wrong plan.

This model allows each employee to be associated with either kind of retirement plan, so each office administrator can be switched. This model is rejected by management because it does not reflect company policy. Some administrators could be switched and others not. Or the janitor could be switched. Management wants a model that enforces the policy:

> Office administrators are hourly employees with defined-benefit retirement plans.

This policy suggests that the "job title" field now represents an important domain concept. Developers could refactor to make that concept explicit as an "**Employee Type**."

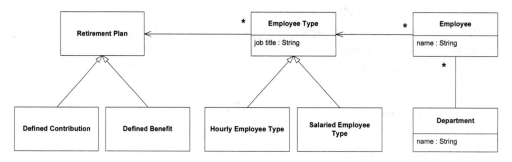

Figure 16.19
The **Type** object allows requirements to be met.

Figure 16.20
Each **Employee Type** is assigned a **Retirement Plan**.

The requirements can be stated in the UBIQUITOUS LANGUAGE as follows:

> An **Employee Type** is assigned to either **Retirement Plan** or either payroll.

> **Employees** are constrained by the **Employee Type**.

Access to edit the **Employee Type** object will be restricted to a "superuser," who will make changes only when company policy changes. An ordinary user in the personnel department can change **Employees** or point them at a different **Employee Type**.

This model satisfies the requirements. The developers sense an implicit concept or two, but it is just a nagging feeling at the moment. They don't have any solid ideas to pursue, so they call it a day.

A static model can cause problems. But problems can be just as bad with a fully flexible system that allows any possible relationship to be presented. Such a system would be inconvenient to use and wouldn't allow the organization's own rules to be enforced.

Fully customizing software for each organization is not practical because, even if each organization could pay for custom software, the organizational structure will likely change frequently.

So such software must provide options to allow the *user* to configure it to reflect the current structure of the organization. The trouble is that adding such options to the model objects makes them unwieldy. The more flexibility you add, the more complex it all becomes.

In an application in which the roles and relationships between ENTITIES vary in different situations, complexity can explode. Neither fully general models nor highly customized ones serve the users' needs. Objects end up with references to other types to cover a variety of cases, or with attributes that are used in different ways in different situations. Classes that have the same data and behavior may multiply just to accommodate different assembly rules.

Nestled *into* our model is another model that is *about* our model. A KNOWLEDGE LEVEL separates that self-defining aspect of the model and makes its constraints explicit.

KNOWLEDGE LEVEL is an application to the domain layer of the REFLECTION pattern, used in many software architectures and technical infrastructures and described well in Buschmann et al. 1996. REFLECTION accommodates changing needs by making the software "self-aware," and making selected aspects of its structure and behavior accessible for adaptation and change. This is done by splitting the software into a "base level," which carries the operational responsibility for the application, and a "meta level," which represents knowledge of the structure and behavior of the software.

Significantly, the pattern is not called a knowledge "layer." As much as it resembles layering, REFLECTION involves mutual dependencies running in both directions.

Java has some minimal built-in REFLECTION in the form of protocols for interrogating a class for its methods and so forth. Such mechanisms allow a program to ask questions about its own design. CORBA has somewhat more extensive but similar REFLECTION protocols. Some persistence technologies extend the richness of that self-description to support partially automated mapping between database tables and objects. There are other technical examples. This pattern can also be applied within the domain layer.

Fowler Terminology	**POSA Terminology**[2]
Knowledge Level	Meta Level
Operations Level	Base Level

Comparing the terminology of KNOWLEDGE LEVEL and REFLECTION

Just to be clear, the reflection tools of the programming language are *not* for use in implementing the KNOWLEDGE LEVEL of a domain model. Those meta-objects describe the structure and behavior of the language constructs themselves. Instead, the KNOWLEDGE LEVEL must be built of ordinary objects.

The KNOWLEDGE LEVEL provides two useful distinctions. First, it focuses on the application domain. in contrast to familiar uses of REFLECTION. Second, it does not strive for full generality. Just as a SPECIFICATION can be more useful than a general predicate, a very specialized set of constraints on a set of objects and their relationships can be more useful than a generalized framework. The KNOWLEDGE LEVEL is simpler and can communicate the specific intent of the designer.

---

2. POSA is short for *Pattern-Oriented Software Architecture,* by Buschmann et al. 1996.

Therefore:

Create a distinct set of objects that can be used to describe and constrain the structure and behavior of the basic model. Keep these concerns separate as two "levels," one very concrete, the other reflecting rules and knowledge that a user or superuser is able to customize.

Like all powerful ideas, REFLECTION and KNOWLEDGE LEVELS can be intoxicating. This pattern should be used sparingly. It can unravel complexity by freeing operations objects from the need to be jacks-of-all-trades, but the indirection it introduces does add some of that obscurity back in. If the KNOWLEDGE LEVEL becomes complex, the system's behavior becomes hard to understand for developers and users alike. The users (or superuser) who configure it will end up needing the skills of a programmer—and a meta-level programmer at that. If they make mistakes, the application will behave incorrectly.

Also, the basic problems of data migration don't completely disappear. When a structure in the KNOWLEDGE LEVEL is changed, existing operations-level objects have to be dealt with. It may be possible for old and new to coexist, but one way or another, careful analysis is needed.

All of these issues put a major burden on the designer of a KNOWLEDGE LEVEL. The design has to be robust enough to handle not only the scenarios presented in development, but also any scenario for which a user could configure the software in the future. Applied judiciously, to the points where customization is crucial and would otherwise distort the design, KNOWLEDGE LEVELS can solve problems that are very hard to handle any other way.

Example

Employee Payroll and Pension, Part 2: KNOWLEDGE LEVEL

Our team members are back, and, refreshed from a night's sleep, one of them has started to close in on one of the awkward points. Why were certain objects being secured while others were freely edited? The cluster of restricted objects reminded him of the KNOWLEDGE LEVEL pattern, and he decided to try it as a way of viewing the model. He found that the existing model could already be viewed this way.

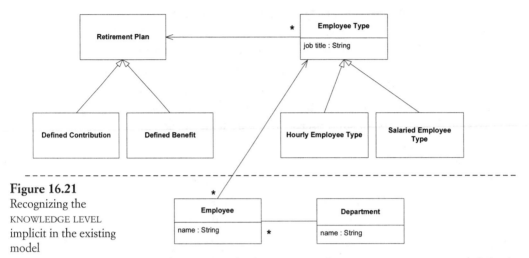

Figure 16.21
Recognizing the KNOWLEDGE LEVEL implicit in the existing model

The restricted edits were in the KNOWLEDGE LEVEL, while the day-to-day edits were in the operational level. A nice fit. All the objects above the line described types or longstanding policies. The **Employee Type** effectively imposed behavior on the **Employee**.

The developer was sharing his insight with his colleagues when one of the other developers had another insight. The clarity of seeing the model organized by KNOWLEDGE LEVEL had let her spot what had been bothering *her* the previous day. Two distinct concepts were being combined in the same object. She had heard it in the language used on the previous day but hadn't put her finger on it:

> An **Employee Type** is assigned to either **Retirement Plan** or either payroll.

But that was *not* really a statement in the UBIQUITOUS LANGUAGE. There was no "payroll" in the model. They had spoken in the language they *wanted*, rather than the one they had. The concept of payroll was implicit in the model, lumped together with **Employee Type**. It hadn't been so obvious before the KNOWLEDGE LEVEL was separated out, and the very elements in that key phrase all appeared in the same level together . . . except one.

Based on this insight, she refactored again to a model that does support that statement.

The need for user control of the rules for associating objects drove the team to a model that had an implicit KNOWLEDGE LEVEL.

Figure 16.22
Payroll is now explicit, distinct from **Employee Type**.

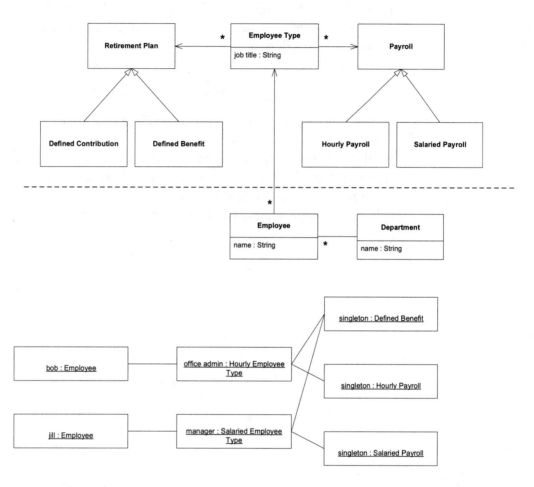

Figure 16.23
Each **Employee Type** now has a **Retirement Plan** and a **Payroll**.

KNOWLEDGE LEVEL was hinted at by the characteristic access restrictions and a "thing-thing" type relationship. Once it was in place, the clarity it afforded helped produce another insight that disentangled two important domain concepts by factoring out **Payroll**.

KNOWLEDGE LEVEL, like other large-scale structures, isn't strictly necessary. The objects will still work without it, and the insight that separated **Employee Type** from **Payroll** could still have been found and used. There may come a time when this structure doesn't seem to be pulling its weight and can be dropped. But for now, it seems to tell a useful story about the system and helps developers grapple with the model.

✳ ✳ ✳

At first glance, KNOWLEDGE LEVEL looks like a special case of RESPONSIBILITY LAYERS, especially the "policy" layer, but it is not. For one thing, dependencies run in both directions between the levels, but with LAYERS, lower layers are independent of upper layers.

In fact, KNOWLEDGE LEVEL can coexist with most other large-scale structures, providing an additional dimension of organization.

Pluggable Component Framework

Opportunities arise in a very mature model that is deep and distilled. A PLUGGABLE COMPONENT FRAMEWORK usually only comes into play after a few applications have already been implemented in the same domain.

* * *

When a variety of applications have to interoperate, all based on the same abstractions but designed independently, translations between multiple BOUNDED CONTEXTS limit integration. A SHARED KERNEL is not feasible for teams that do not work closely together. Duplication and fragmentation raise costs of development and installation, and interoperability becomes very difficult.

Some successful projects break down their design into components, each with responsibility for certain categories of functions. Usually all the components plug into a central hub, which supports any protocols they need and knows how to talk to the interfaces they provide. Other patterns of connecting components are also possible. The design of these interfaces and the hub that connects them must be coordinated, while more independence is possible designing the interiors.

Several widely used technical frameworks support this pattern, but that is a secondary issue. A technical framework is needed only if it solves some essential technical problem such as distribution, or sharing a component among different applications. The basic pattern is a conceptual organization of responsibilities. It can easily be applied within a single Java program.

Therefore:

Distill an ABSTRACT CORE of interfaces and interactions and create a framework that allows diverse implementations of those interfaces to be freely substituted. Likewise, allow any application to use those components, so long as it operates strictly through the interfaces of the ABSTRACT CORE.

High-level abstractions are identified and shared across the breadth of the system; specialization occurs in MODULES. The central hub of the application is an ABSTRACT CORE within a SHARED KERNEL. But multiple BOUNDED CONTEXTS can lie behind the encapsulated component

---

interfaces, so that this structure can be especially convenient when many components are coming from many different sources, or when components are encapsulating preexisting software for integration.

This is not to say that components must have divergent models. Multiple components can be developed within a single CONTEXT if the teams CONTINUOUSLY INTEGRATE, or they can define another SHARED KERNEL held in common by a closely related set of components. All these strategies can coexist easily within a large-scale structure of PLUGGABLE COMPONENTS. Another option, in some cases, is to use a PUBLISHED LANGUAGE for the plug-in interface of the hub.

There are a few downsides to a PLUGGABLE COMPONENT FRAMEWORK. One is that this is a very difficult pattern to apply. It requires precision in the design of the interfaces and a deep enough model to capture the necessary behavior in the ABSTRACT CORE. Another major downside is that applications have limited options. If an application needs a very different approach to the CORE DOMAIN, the structure will get in the way. Developers can specialize the model, but they can't change the ABSTRACT CORE without changing the protocol of all the diverse components. As a result, the process of continuous refinement of the CORE, refactoring toward deeper insight, is more or less frozen in its tracks.

Fayad and Johnson (2000) give a good look at ambitious attempts at PLUGGABLE COMPONENT FRAMEWORKS in several domains, including a discussion of SEMATECH CIM. The success of such frameworks is a mixed story. Probably the biggest obstacle is the maturity of understanding needed to design a useful framework. A PLUGGABLE COMPONENT FRAMEWORK should not be the first large-scale structure applied on a project, nor the second. The most successful examples have followed after the full development of multiple specialized applications.

Example

The SEMATECH CIM Framework

In a factory producing computer chips, groups (called *lots*) of silicon wafers are moved from one machine to another through hundreds of steps of processing until the microscopic circuitry being printed and etched into them is complete. The factory needs software that can track each individual lot, recording the exact processing that has been done to it, and then direct either factory workers or automated equipment to take it to the next appropriate machine and apply the next appropriate process. Such software is called a *manufacturing execution system* (MES).

Hundreds of different machines from dozens of vendors are used, with carefully tailored recipes at each step of the way. Developing MES software that could deal with such a complex mix was daunting and prohibitively expensive. In response, an industry consortium, SEMATECH, developed the CIM Framework.

The CIM Framework is big and complicated and has many aspects, but two are relevant here. First, the framework defines abstract interfaces for the basic concepts of the semiconductor MES domain—in other words, the CORE DOMAIN in the form of an ABSTRACT CORE. These interface definitions include both behavior and semantics.

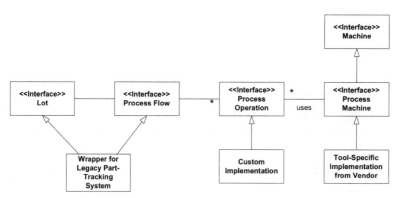

Figure 16.24
A highly simplified subset of the CIM interfaces, with sample implementations

If a vendor produces a new machine, they have to develop a specialized implementation of the **Process Machine** interface. If they adhere to that interface, their machine-control component should plug into any application based on the CIM Framework.

Having defined these interfaces, SEMATECH defined the rules by which they could interact in an application. Any application based on the CIM Framework would have to implement a protocol that hosted objects implementing some subset of those interfaces. If this protocol were implemented, and the application strictly observed the abstract interfaces, then the application could count on the promised services of those interfaces, regardless of implementation. The combination of those interfaces and the protocol for using them constitutes a tightly restrictive large-scale structure.

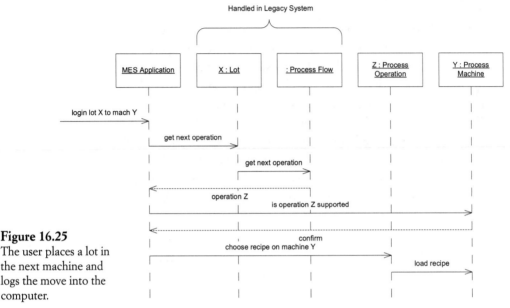

Figure 16.25
The user places a lot in the next machine and logs the move into the computer.

The framework has very specific infrastructure requirements. It is tightly coupled to CORBA to provide persistence, transactions, events, and other technical services. But the interesting thing about it is the definition of a PLUGGABLE COMPONENT FRAMEWORK, which allows people to develop software independently and smoothly integrate them into immense systems. No one knows all the details of such a system, but everyone understands an overview.

❋   ❋   ❋

How can thousands of people work independently to create a quilt of more than 40,000 panels?

A few simple rules provide a large-scale structure for the AIDS Memorial Quilt, leaving the details to individual contributors. Notice how the rules focus on the overall mission (memorializing people who have died of AIDS), the features of a component that make integration practical, and the ability to handle the quilt in larger sections (such as folding it).

Here's How to Create a Panel for the Quilt
[From the AIDS Memorial Quilt Project Web site, www.aidsquilt.org]

Design the panel
Include the name of the person you are remembering. Feel free to include additional information such as the dates of birth and death, and a hometown. . . . [P]lease limit each panel to one individual . . . .

Choose your materials
Remember that the Quilt is folded and unfolded many times, so durability is crucial. Since glue deteriorates with time, it is best to sew things to the panel. A medium-weight, non-stretch fabric such as a cotton duck or poplin works best.

Your design can be vertical or horizontal, but the finished, hemmed panel must be 3 feet by 6 feet (90 cm × 180 cm)—no more and no less! When you cut the fabric, leave an extra 2–3 inches on each side for a hem. If you can't hem it yourself, we'll do it for you. Batting for the panels is not necessary, but backing is recommended. Backing helps to keep panels clean when they are laid out on the ground. It also helps retain the shape of the fabric.

Create the panel
In constructing your panel you might want to use some of the following techniques:

- Appliqué: Sew fabric, letters and small mementos onto the background fabric. Do not rely on glue—it won't last.

- Paint: Brush on textile paint or color-fast dye, or use an indelible ink pen. Please don't use "puffy" paint; it's too sticky.

- Stencil: Trace your design onto the fabric with a pencil, lift the stencil, then use a brush to apply textile paint or indelible markers.

- Collage: Make sure that whatever materials you add to the panel won't tear the fabric (avoid glass and sequins for this reason), and be sure to avoid very bulky objects.

- Photos: The best way to include photos or letters is to photocopy them onto iron-on transfers, iron them onto 100% cotton fabric and sew that fabric to the panel. You may also put the photo in clear plastic vinyl and sew it to the panel (off-center so it avoids the fold).

How Restrictive Should a Structure Be?

The large-scale structure patterns discussed in this chapter range from the very loose SYSTEM METAPHOR to the restrictive PLUGGABLE COMPONENT FRAMEWORK. Other structures are possible, of course, and even within a general structural pattern, there is a lot of choice about how restrictive to make the rules.

For example, RESPONSIBILITY LAYERS dictate a kind of factoring of model concepts and their dependencies, but you could add rules that would specify communication patterns between the layers.

Consider a manufacturing plant where software directs each part to a machine where it is processed according to some recipe. The correct process is ordered from a Policy layer and executed in an Operations layer. But inevitably there will be mistakes made on the factory floor. The actual situation will not be consistent with the rules of the software. Now, an Operations layer *must reflect the world as it is*, which means that when a part is occasionally put in the wrong machine, that information must be accepted unconditionally. Somehow, this exceptional condition needs to be communicated to a higher layer. A decision-making layer can then use other policies to correct the situation, perhaps by rerouting the part to a repair process or by scrapping it. But Operations does not know anything about higher layers. The communication has to be done in a way that doesn't create two-way dependencies from the lower layers to the higher ones.

Typically, this signaling would be done through some kind of event mechanism. The Operations objects would generate events whenever their state changed. Policy layer objects would listen for events of interest from the lower layers. When an event occurred that violated a rule, the rule would execute an action (part of the rule's definition) that makes the appropriate response, or it might generate an event for the benefit of some still higher layer.

In the banking example, the values of assets change (Operations), shifting the values of segments of a portfolio. When these values exceed portfolio allocation limits (Policy), perhaps a trader is alerted, who can buy or sell assets to redress the balance.

We could figure this out on a case-by-case basis, or we could decide on a consistent pattern for everyone to follow in interactions of objects of particular layers. A more restrictive structure increases uniformity, making the design easier to interpret. If the structure fits, the rules are likely to push developers toward good designs. Disparate pieces are likely to fit together better.

On the other hand, the restrictions may take away flexibility that developers need. Very particular communication paths might be impractical to apply across BOUNDED CONTEXTS, especially in different implementation technologies, in a heterogeneous system.

So you have to fight the temptation to build frameworks and regiment the implementation of the large-scale structure. The most important contribution of the large-scale structure is conceptual coherence, and giving insight into the domain. *Each structural rule should make development easier.*

Refactoring Toward a Fitting Structure

In an era when the industry is shaking off excessive up-front design, some will see large-scale structure as a throwback to the bad old days of waterfall architecture. But in fact, the only way a useful structure can be found is from a very deep understanding of the domain and the problem, and the practical way to that understanding is an iterative development process.

A team committed to EVOLVING ORDER must fearlessly rethink the large-scale structure throughout the project life cycle. The team should not saddle itself with a structure conceived of early on, when no one understood the domain or the requirements very well.

Unfortunately, that evolution means that your final structure will not be available at the start, and that means that you will have to refactor to impose it as you go along. This can be expensive and difficult, but it is *necessary*. There are some general ways of controlling the cost and maximizing the gain.

Minimalism

One key to keeping the cost down is to keep the structure simple and lightweight. Don't attempt to be comprehensive. Just address the most serious concerns and leave the rest to be handled on a case-by-case basis.

Early on, it can be helpful to choose a loose structure, such as a SYSTEM METAPHOR or a couple of RESPONSIBILITY LAYERS. A minimal, loose structure can nonetheless provide lightweight guidelines that will help prevent chaos.

Communication and Self-Discipline

The entire team must follow the structure in new development and refactoring. To do this, the structure must be understood by the entire team. The terminology and relationships must enter the UBIQUITOUS LANGUAGE.

Large-scale structure can provide a vocabulary for the project to deal with the system broadly, and for different people independently to make harmonious decisions. But because most large-scale structures are loose conceptual guidelines, the teams must exercise self-discipline.

Without consistent adherence by the many people involved, structures have a tendency to decay. The relationship of the structure to detailed parts of the model or implementation is not usually explicit in the code, and functional tests do not rely on the structure. Plus, the structure tends to be abstract, so that consistency of application can be difficult to maintain across a large team (or multiple teams).

The kinds of conversations that take place on most teams are not enough to maintain a consistent large-scale structure in a system. It is critical to incorporate it into the UBIQUITOUS LANGUAGE of the project, and for everyone to exercise that language relentlessly.

Restructuring Yields Supple Design

Second, any change to the structure may lead to a lot of refactoring. The structure is evolving as system complexity increases and understanding deepens. Each time the structure changes, *the entire system has to be changed to adhere to the new order.* Obviously that is a lot of work.

This isn't quite as bad as it sounds. I've observed that a design with a large-scale structure is usually much easier to transform than one without. This seems to be true even when changing from one kind of structure to another, say from METAPHOR to LAYERS. I can't entirely explain this. Part of the answer is that it is easier to rearrange something when you can understand its current arrangement, and the preexisting structure makes that easier. Partly it is that the discipline that it took to maintain the earlier structure permeates all aspects of the system. But there is something more, I think, because it is *even easier* to change a system that has had *two* previous structures.

A new leather jacket is stiff and uncomfortable, but after the first day of wear the elbows have flexed a few times and are becoming easier to bend. After a few more wearings, the shoulders have loosened up, and the jacket is easier to put on. After months of wear, the leather becomes supple and is comfortable and easy to move in. So it seems to be with models that are transformed repeatedly with sound transformations. Ever-increasing knowledge is embedded into them and *the principal axes of change have been identified and made flexible,* while stable aspects have been simplified. The broader CONCEPTUAL CONTOURS of the underlying domain are emerging in the model structure.

Distillation Lightens the Load

Another crucial force that should be applied to the model is continuous distillation. This reduces the difficulty of changing the structure in various ways. First, by removing mechanisms, GENERIC SUBDOMAINS, and other support structure from the CORE DOMAIN, there may simply be less to restructure.

If possible, these supporting elements should be defined to fit into the large-scale structure in a simple way. For example, in a system of RESPONSIBILITY LAYERS, a GENERIC SUBDOMAIN could be defined in such a way that it would fit within a single layer. With PLUGGABLE COMPONENTS, a GENERIC SUBDOMAIN could be owned entirely by a single component, or it could be a SHARED KERNEL among a set of related components. These supporting elements may have to be refactored to find their place in the structure; but they move independently of the CORE DOMAIN, and tend to be more narrowly focused, which makes it easier. And ultimately they are less critical, so refinement matters less.

The principles of distillation and refactoring toward deeper insight apply even to the large-scale structure itself. For example, the layers may initially be chosen based on a superficial understanding of the domain; they are gradually replaced with deeper abstractions that express the fundamental responsibilities of the system. This sharp-edged clarity lets people see deep into the design, which is the goal. It is also part of the means, as it makes manipulation of the system on a large scale easier and safer.

Bringing the Strategy Together

The preceding three chapters presented many principles and techniques for domain-driven strategic design. In a large, complex system, you may need to bring several of them to bear on the same design. How does a large-scale structure coexist with a CONTEXT MAP? Where do the building blocks fit in? What do you do first? Second? Third? How do you go about devising your strategy?

Combining Large-Scale Structures and BOUNDED CONTEXTS

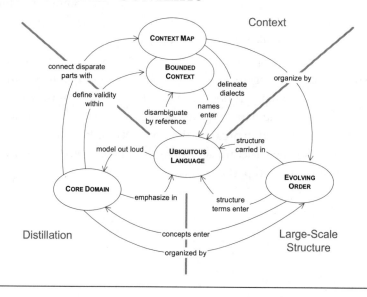

Figure 17.1

The three basic principles of strategic design (context, distillation, and large-scale structure) are not substitutes for each other; they are complementary and interact in many ways. For example, a large-scale structure can exist within one BOUNDED CONTEXT, or it can cut across many of them and organize the CONTEXT MAP.

The previous examples of RESPONSIBILITY LAYERS were confined to one BOUNDED CONTEXT. This is the easiest way to explain the idea, and it's a common use of the pattern. In such a simple scenario, the meanings of layer names are restricted to that CONTEXT, as are the names of model elements or subsystem interfaces that exist within that CONTEXT.

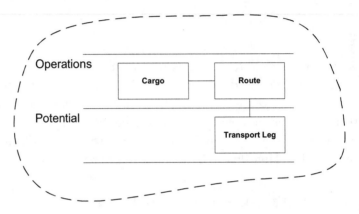

Figure 17.2
Structuring a model within a single
BOUNDED CONTEXT

Such a local structure can be useful in a very complicated but unified model, raising the complexity ceiling on how much can be maintained in a single BOUNDED CONTEXT.

But on many projects, the greater challenge is to understand how disparate parts fit together. They may be partitioned into separate CONTEXTS, but what part does each play in the whole integrated system and how do the parts relate to each other? Then the large-scale structure can be used to organize the CONTEXT MAP. In this case, the terminology of the structure applies to the whole project (or at least some clearly bounded part of it).

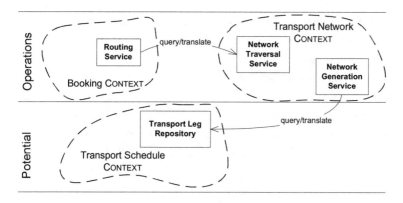

Figure 17.3
Structure imposed on the relationships of components of distinct BOUNDED CONTEXTS

Suppose you want to adopt RESPONSIBILITY LAYERS, but you have a legacy system whose organization is inconsistent with your desired large-scale structure. Do you have to give up your LAYERS? No, but you have to acknowledge the actual place the legacy has within the structure. In fact, it may help to characterize the legacy. The SERVICES the legacy provides may in fact be confined to only a few LAYERS. To be able to say that the legacy system fits within particular RESPONSIBILITY LAYERS concisely describes a key aspect of its scope and role.

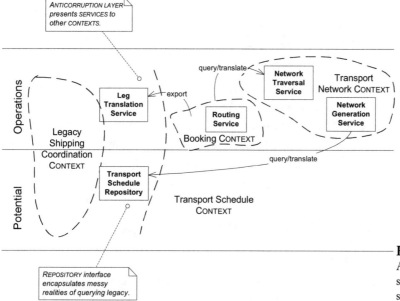

Figure 17.4
A structure that allows some components to span layers

If the legacy subsystem's capabilities are being accessed through a FACADE, you may be able to design each SERVICE offered by the FACADE to fit within one layer.

The interior of the Shipping Coordination application, being a legacy in this example, is presented as an undifferentiated mass. But a team on a project with a well-established large-scale structure spanning the CONTEXT MAP could choose, within their CONTEXT, to order their model by the same familiar LAYERS.

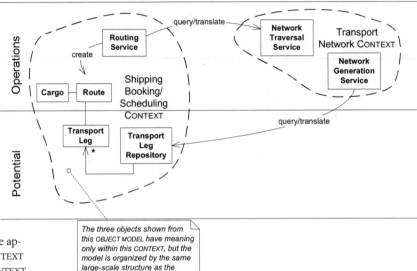

Figure 17.5
The same structure applied within a CONTEXT and across the CONTEXT MAP as a whole

The three objects shown from this OBJECT MODEL have meaning only within this CONTEXT, but the model is organized by the same large-scale structure as the CONTEXT MAP.

Of course, because each BOUNDED CONTEXT is its own name space, one structure could be used to organize the model within one CONTEXT, while another was used in a neighboring CONTEXT, and still another organized the CONTEXT MAP. However, going too far down that path can erode the value of the large-scale structure as a unifying set of concepts for the project.

Combining Large-Scale Structures and Distillation

The concepts of large-scale structure and distillation also complement each other. The large-scale structure can help explain the relationships within the CORE DOMAIN and between GENERIC SUBDOMAINS.

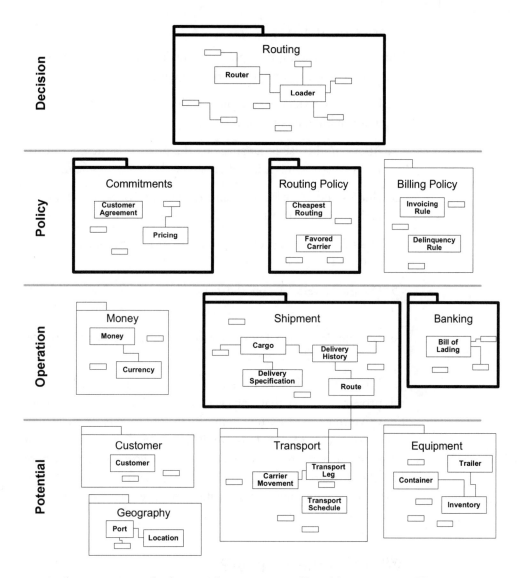

At the same time, *the large-scale structure itself may be an important part of the CORE DOMAIN.* For example, distinguishing the layering of potential, operations, policy, and decision support distills an insight that is fundamental to the business problem addressed by the software. This insight is especially useful if a project is carved up into many BOUNDED CONTEXTS, so that the model objects of the CORE DOMAIN don't have meaning over much of the project.

Figure 17.6
MODULES of the CORE DOMAIN (*in bold*) and GENERIC SUBDOMAINS are clarified by the layers.

Assessment First

When you are tackling strategic design on a project, you need to start from a clear assessment of the current situation.

1. Draw a CONTEXT MAP. Can you draw a consistent one, or are there ambiguous situations?

2. Attend to the use of language on the project. Is there a UBIQUITOUS LANGUAGE? Is it rich enough to help development?

3. Understand what is important. Is the CORE DOMAIN identified? Is there a DOMAIN VISION STATEMENT? Can you write one?

4. Does the technology of the project work for or against a MODEL-DRIVEN DESIGN?

5. Do the developers on the team have the necessary technical skills?

6. Are the developers knowledgeable about the domain? Are they *interested* in the domain?

You won't find perfect answers, of course. You know less about this project right now than you ever will in the future. But these questions give you a solid starting point. By the time you have specific initial answers to these questions, you'll have started getting insight into what most urgently needs to be done. As time goes along, you can refine the answers—especially the CONTEXT MAP, DOMAIN VISION STATEMENT, and any other artifacts you've created—to reflect changed situations and new insights.

Who Sets the Strategy?

Traditionally, architecture is handed down, created before application development begins, by a team that has more power in the organization than the application development team. But it doesn't have to be that way. That way doesn't usually work very well.

Strategic design, by definition, must apply across the project. There are many ways to organize a project, and I don't want to be too prescriptive. However, for any decision-making process to be effective, some fundamentals are required.

First, let's take a quick look at two styles that I've seen provide some value in practice (thus ignoring the old "wisdom-from-on-high" style).

Emergent Structure from Application Development

A self-disciplined team made up of very good communicators can operate without central authority and follow EVOLVING ORDER to arrive at a shared set of principles, so that order grows organically, not by fiat.

This is the typical model for an Extreme Programming team. In theory, the structure may emerge completely spontaneously from the insight of any programming pair. More often, having an individual or a subset of the team with some oversight responsibility for large-scale structure helps keep the structure unified. This approach works well particularly if such an informal leader is a hands-on developer—an arbiter and communicator, and not the sole source of ideas. On the Extreme Programming teams I have seen, such strategic design leadership seems to have emerged spontaneously, often in the person of the coach. Whoever this natural leader is, he or she is still a member of the development team. It follows that the development team must have at least a few people of the caliber to make design decisions that are going to affect the whole project.

When a large-scale structure spans multiple teams, closely affiliated teams may begin to collaborate informally. In such a situation, each application team still makes the discoveries that lead to the idea for a large-scale structure, but then particular options are discussed by the informal committee, made up of representatives of the various teams. After assessing the impact of the design, participants may decide to adopt it, modify it, or leave it on the table. The teams attempt to move together in this loose affiliation. This arrangement can work when there are relatively few teams, when they are all committed to coordinating with each other, when their design capabilities are comparable, and when their structural needs are similar enough to be met by a single large-scale structure.

A Customer-Focused Architecture Team

When a strategy will be shared among several teams, some centralization of decision making does seem attractive. The failed model of the ivory tower architect is not the only possibility. An architecture team can act as a peer with various application teams, helping to coordinate and harmonize their large-scale structures as well as BOUNDED CONTEXT boundaries and other cross-team technical issues. To be useful in this, they must have a mind set that emphasizes application development.

On an organization chart, this team may look just like the traditional architecture team, but it is actually different in every activity. Team members are true collaborators with development, discovering patterns along with the developers, experimenting with various teams to reach distillations, and getting their hands dirty.

I have seen this scenario a couple of times, when a project ends up with a lead architect who does most of the things on the following list.

Six Essentials for Strategic Design Decision Making

Decisions must reach the entire team.

Obviously, if everyone doesn't know the strategy and follow it, it is irrelevant. This requirement leads people to organize around centralized architecture teams with official "authority"—so that the same rules will be applied everywhere. Ironically, ivory tower architects are often ignored or bypassed. Developers have no choice when the architects' lack of feedback from hands-on attempts to apply their own rules to real applications results in impractical schemes.

On a project with very good communication, a strategic design that emerges from the application team may actually reach everyone more effectively. The strategy will be relevant, and it will have the authority that attaches to intelligent community decisions.

Whatever the system, be less concerned with the authority bestowed by management than with the actual relationship the developers have with the strategy.

The decision process must absorb feedback.

Creating an organizing principle, large-scale structure, or distillation of such subtlety requires a really deep understanding of the needs of the project and the concepts of the domain. The only people who have that depth of knowledge are the members of the application development team. This explains why application architectures created by architecture teams are so seldom helpful, despite the undeniable talent of many of the architects.

Unlike technical infrastructure and architectures, strategic design does not itself involve writing a lot of code, although it influences all development. What it does require is involvement with the application development teams. An experienced architect may be able to listen to ideas coming from various teams and facilitate the development of a generalized solution.

One technical architecture team I worked with actually circulated its own members through the various application development teams that were attempting to use its framework. This rotation pulled into the architecture team the hands-on experience of the challenges facing the developers, while it simultaneously transferred the knowledge of how to apply the subtleties of the framework. Strategic design has this same need of a tight feedback loop.

The plan must allow for evolution.

Effective software development is a highly dynamic process. When the highest level of decisions is set in stone, the team has fewer options when it must respond to change. EVOLVING ORDER avoids this trap by emphasizing ongoing change to the large-scale structure in response to deepening insight.

When too many design decisions are preordained, the development team can be hobbled, without the flexibility to solve the problems they are charged with. So, while a harmonizing principle can be valuable, it must grow and change with the ongoing life of the development project, and it must not take too much power away from the application developers, whose job is hard enough as it is.

With strong feedback, innovations emerge as obstacles are encountered in building applications and as unexpected opportunities are discovered.

Architecture teams must not siphon off all the best and brightest.

Design at this level calls for sophistication that is probably in short supply. Managers tend to move the most technically talented developers into architecture teams and infrastructure teams, because they want to leverage the skills of these advanced designers. For their part, the developers are attracted to the opportunity to have a broader impact or to work on "more interesting" problems. And there is prestige attached to being a member of an elite team.

These forces often leave behind only the least technically sophisticated developers to actually build applications. But building good applications takes design skill; this is a setup for failure. Even if a strategy team creates a great strategic design, the application team won't have the design sophistication to follow it.

Conversely, such teams almost never include the developer who perhaps has weaker design skills but who has the most extensive experience in the domain. Strategic design is not a purely technical task; cutting themselves off from developers with deep domain knowledge hobbles the architects' efforts further. And domain experts are needed too.

It is essential to have strong designers on all application teams. It is essential to have domain knowledge on any team attempting strategic design. It may simply be necessary to hire more advanced designers. It may help to keep architecture teams part-time. I'm sure there are many ways that work, but any effective strategy team has to have as a partner an effective application team.

Strategic design requires minimalism and humility.

Distillation and minimalism are essential to any good design work, but minimalism is even more critical for strategic design. Even the slightest ill fit has a terrible potential for getting in the way. Separate architecture teams have to be especially careful because they have less feel for the obstacles they might be placing in front of application teams. At the same time, the architects' enthusiasm for their primary responsibility makes them more likely to get carried away. I've seen this phenomenon many times, and I've even done it. One good idea leads to another, and we end up with an overbuilt architecture that is counterproductive.

Instead, we have to discipline ourselves to produce organizing principles and core models that are pared down to contain nothing that does not significantly improve the clarity of the design. The truth is, almost everything gets in the way of something, so each element had better be worth it. Realizing that your best idea is likely to get in somebody's way takes humility.

Objects are specialists; developers are generalists.

The essence of good object design is to give each object a clear and narrow responsibility and to reduce interdependence to an absolute minimum. Sometimes we try to make interactions on teams as tidy as they should be in our software. A good project has lots of people sticking their nose in other people's business. Developers play with frameworks. Architects write application code. Everyone talks to everyone. It is efficiently chaotic. Make the objects into specialists; let the developers be generalists.

Because I've made the distinction between *strategic design* and other kinds of design to help clarify the tasks involved, I must point out that having two kinds of design activity does not mean having two kinds of people. Creating a supple design based on a deep model is an advanced design activity, but the details are so important that it has to be done by someone working with the code. Strategic design emerges out of application design, yet it requires a big-picture view of activity, possibly spanning multiple teams. People love to find ways to chop up tasks so that design experts don't have to know the business and domain experts don't have to understand technology. There is a limit to how much an individual can learn, but overspecialization takes the steam out of domain-driven design.

The Same Goes for the Technical Frameworks

Technical frameworks can greatly accelerate application development, including the domain layer, by providing an infrastructure layer that frees the application from implementing basic services, and by helping to isolate the domain from other concerns. But there is a risk that an architecture *can interfere with expressive implementations of the domain model and easy change*. This can happen even when the framework designers had no intention of venturing into the domain or application layers.

The same biases that limit the downside of strategic design can help with technical architecture. Evolution, minimalism, and involvement with the application development team can lead to a continuously refined set of services and rules that genuinely help application development without getting in the way. Architectures that don't follow this path will either stifle the creativity of application development or will find their architecture circumvented, leaving application development, for practical purposes, with no architecture at all.

There is one particular attitude that will surely ruin a framework.

Don't write frameworks for dummies.

Team divisions that assume some developers are not smart enough to design are likely to fail because they underestimate the difficulty of application development. If those people are not smart enough to design, they shouldn't be assigned to develop software. If they are smart enough, then the attempts to coddle them will only put up barriers between them and the tools they need.

This attitude also poisons the relationship between teams. I've ended up on arrogant teams like this and found myself apologizing to developers in every conversation, embarrassed by my association. (I've never managed to change such a team, I'm afraid.)

Now, *encapsulating irrelevant technical detail is completely different* from the kind of prepackaging I'm disparaging. A framework can place powerful abstractions and tools in developers' hands and free them from drudgery. It is hard to describe the difference in a generalized way, but you can tell the difference by asking the framework designers what they expect of the person who will be using the tool/framework/components. If the designers seem to have a high level of respect for the user of the framework, then they are probably on the right track.

Beware the Master Plan

A group of architects (the kind who design physical buildings), led by Christopher Alexander, were advocates of piecemeal growth in the realm of architecture and city planning. They explained very nicely why master plans fail.

> Without a planning process of some kind, there is not a chance in the world that the University of Oregon will ever come to possess an order anywhere near as deep and harmonious as the order that underlies the University of Cambridge.

> The master plan has been the conventional way of approaching this difficulty. The master plan attempts to set down enough guidelines to provide for coherence in the environment as a whole—and still leave freedom for individual buildings and open spaces to adapt to local needs.

> . . . and all the various parts of this future university will form a coherent whole, because they were simply plugged into the slots of the design.

> . . . in practice master plans fail—because they create totalitarian order, not organic order. They are too rigid; they cannot easily adapt to the natural and unpredictable changes that inevitably arise in the life of a community. As these changes occur . . . the master plan becomes obsolete, and is no longer followed. And even to the extent that master plans *are* followed . . . they do not specify enough about connections between buildings, human scale, balanced function, etc. to help each local act of building and design become well-related to the environment as a whole.

> . . . The attempt to steer such a course is rather like filling in the colors in a child's coloring book . . . . At best, the order which results from such a process is banal.

> . . . Thus, as a source of organic order, a master plan is both too precise, and not precise enough. The totality is too precise: the details are not precise enough.

> . . . the existence of a master plan alienates the users [because, by definition] the members of the community can have little impact on the future shape of their community because most of the important decisions have already been made.

> —From *The Oregon Experiment*, pp. 16–28 (Alexander et al. 1975)

Alexander and his colleagues advocated instead *a set of principles* for all community members to apply to every act of piecemeal growth, so that "organic order" emerges, well adapted to circumstances.

Conclusion

Epilogues

Although it is very satisfying working on a cutting-edge project and experimenting with interesting ideas and tools, for me it is a hollow experience if the software does not find productive use. In fact, the true test of success is how the software serves over a period of time. I have been able to follow the stories of some of my former projects over the years.

I'll discuss here five of those, each of which made a serious attempt at domain-driven design, though not systematically and not by that name, of course. All of these projects did deliver software: some managed to carry through and produce a model-driven design, while one slipped off that track. Some of the applications continued to grow and change for many years, while one stagnated and one died young.

The PCB design software described in Chapter 1 was a smash hit among beta users in the field. Unfortunately, the start-up company that had initiated the project utterly failed in its marketing function and was eventually euthanized. The software is now used by a handful of PCB engineers who have old copies they kept from the beta program. Like any orphan software, it will continue to work until there is some fatal change to one of the programs with which it is integrated.

The loan software whose story was told in Chapter 9 thrived and evolved along much the same track for three years after the break-through I wrote about. At that point, the project was spun off as an

A Newly Planted Olive Grove

independent company. In the turmoil of this reorganization, the project manager who had led the project from the beginning was ejected, and some of the core developers left with him. The new team had a somewhat different design philosophy, not as fully committed to object modeling. But they retained a distinct domain layer with complex behavior and continued to value domain knowledge on the development team. Seven years after the spin-off, the software continues to be enhanced with new features. It is the leading application in its field and serves an increasing number of client institutions, as well as being the largest revenue stream for the company.

Until the domain-driven approach is more widespread, the interesting software on many projects will be built in a short, highly productive interval. Eventually the project will transform into something more conventional that may not be able to fully exploit, much less enhance, the power of the deep models that were distilled earlier. I could wish for more, but truly those are successes that deliver sustained value to users over many years.

On one project I paired with another developer to write a utility the customer needed to produce its core product. The features were fairly complicated and combined in intricate ways. I enjoyed the project work and we produced a supple design with an ABSTRACT CORE. When this software was handed off, that was the end of involvement for everyone who had initially developed it. Because it was such an

Seven Years Later

abrupt transition, I expected that the design features which supported the combinable elements might be confusing and might get replaced by more typical case logic. This did not initially happen. When we handed off, the package included a thorough test suite and a distillation document. The new team members used that document to guide their explorations, and as they looked into things, they became excited by the possibilities the design presented. When I heard their comments a year later, I realized that the UBIQUITOUS LANGUAGE had sparked across to the other team and stayed alive, continuing to evolve.

Then, another year later, I heard a different story. The team had encountered new requirements that the developers didn't see any way to accomplish within the inherited design. They had been forced to change the design almost beyond recognition. As I probed for more details, I could see that aspects of our model would have made solving those problems awkward. It is precisely during such moments when a breakthrough to a deeper model is often possible, especially when, as in this case, the developers had accumulated deep knowledge and experience in the domain. In fact, they had had a rush of new insights and ended up transforming the model and design based on those insights.

They told me this story carefully, diplomatically, expecting, I suppose, that I would be disappointed by their discarding of so much of my work. I am not that sentimental about my designs. The success of a design is not necessarily marked by its stasis. Take a system people depend on, make it opaque, and it will live forever as untouchable legacy. A deep model allows clear vision that can yield new insight, while a supple design facilitates ongoing change. The model they came up with was deeper, better aligned with the real concerns of the users. Their design solved real problems. It is the nature of software to change, and this program has continued to evolve in the hands of the team that owns it.

The shipping examples scattered through the book are loosely based on a project for a major international container-shipping company. Early on, the leadership of the project was committed to a domain-driven approach, but they never produced a development culture that could fully support it. Several teams with widely different levels of design skill and object experience set out to create modules, loosely coordinated by informal cooperation between team leaders and by a customer-focused architecture team. We did develop a reasonably deep model of the CORE DOMAIN, and there was a viable UBIQUITOUS LANGUAGE.

But the company culture fiercely resisted iterative development, and we waited far too long to push out a working internal release. Therefore, problems were exposed at a late stage, when they were more risky and expensive to fix. At some point, we discovered specific aspects of the model were causing performance problems in the database. A natural part of MODEL-DRIVEN DESIGN is the feedback from implementation problems to changes in the model, but by that time there was a perception that we were too far down the road to change the fundamental model. Instead, changes were made to the code to make it more efficient, and its connection to the model was weakened. The initial release also exposed scaling limitations in the technical infrastructure that threw a scare into management. Expertise was brought in to fix the infrastructure problems, and the project bounced back. But the loop was never closed between implementation and domain modeling.

A few teams delivered fine software with complex capabilities and expressive models. Others delivered stiff software that reduced the model to data structures, though even they retained traces of the UBIQUITOUS LANGUAGE. Perhaps a CONTEXT MAP would have helped us as much as anything, as the relationship between the output of the various teams was haphazard. Yet that CORE model carried in the UBIQUITOUS LANGUAGE did help the teams ultimately to glue together a system.

Although reduced in scope, the project replaced several legacy systems. The whole was held together by a shared set of concepts, though most of the design was not very supple. It has itself largely fossilized into legacy now, years later, but it still serves the global business 24 hours a day. Although the more successful teams' influence gradually spread, time runs out eventually, even in the richest company. The culture of the project never really absorbed MODEL-DRIVEN DESIGN. New development today is on different platforms and is only indirectly influenced by the work we did—as the new developers CONFORM to their legacy.

In some circles, ambitious goals like those the shipping company initially set have been discredited. Better, it seems, to make little applications we know how to deliver. Better to stick to the lowest common denominator of design to do simple things. This conservative approach has its place, and allows for neatly scoped, quick-response projects. But integrated, model-driven systems promise value that those patchworks can't. There is a third way. Domain-driven design allows piecemeal growth of big systems with rich functionality, by building on a deep model and supple design.

I'll close this list with Evant, a company that develops inventory management software, where I played a secondary supporting role and contributed to an already strong design culture. Others have written about this project as a poster child of Extreme Programming, but what is not usually remarked upon is that the project was intensely domain-driven. Ever deeper models were distilled and expressed in ever more supple designs. This project thrived until the "dot com" crash of 2001. Then, starved for investment funds, the company contracted, software development went mostly dormant, and it seemed that the end was near. But in the summer of 2002, Evant was approached by one of the top ten retailers in the world. This potential client liked the product, but it needed design changes to allow the application to scale up for an enormous inventory planning operation. It was Evant's last chance.

Although reduced to four developers, the team had assets. They were skilled, with knowledge of the domain, and one member had expertise in scaling issues. They had a very effective development culture. And they had a code base with a supple design that facilitated change. That summer, those four developers made a heroic development effort resulting in the ability to handle billions of planning elements and hundreds of users. On the strength of those capabilities, Evant won the behemoth client and, soon after, was bought by another company that wanted to leverage their software and their proven ability to accommodate new demands.

The domain-driven design culture (as well as the Extreme Programming culture) survived the transition and was revitalized. Today, the model and design continue to evolve, far richer and suppler two years later than when I made my contribution. And rather than being assimilated into the purchasing company, the members of the Evant team seem to be inspiring the company's existing project teams to follow their lead. This story isn't over yet.

No project will ever employ every technique in this book. Even so, any project committed to domain-driven design will be recognizable in a few ways. The defining characteristic is a priority on understanding the target domain and incorporating that understanding into the software. Everything else flows from that premise. Team members are conscious of the use of language on the project and cultivate its refinement. They are hard to satisfy with the quality of the domain model, because they keep learning more about the domain. They see continuous refinement as an opportunity and an ill-fitting model as a risk. They take design skill seriously because it isn't easy to develop production-quality software that clearly reflects the domain model. They stumble over obstacles, but they hold on to their principles as they pick themselves up and continue forward.

Looking Forward

Weather, ecosystems, and biology used to be considered messy, "soft" fields in contrast to physics or chemistry. Recently, however, people have recognized that the appearance of "messiness" in fact presents a profound technical challenge to discover and understand the order in these very complex phenomena. The field called "complexity" is the vanguard of many sciences. Although purely technological tasks have generally seemed most interesting and challenging to talented software engineers, domain-driven design opens up a new area of challenge that is at least equal. Business software does not have to be a bolted-together mess. Wrestling a complex domain into a comprehensible software design is an exciting challenge for strong technical people.

We are nowhere near the era of laypeople creating complex software that works. Armies of programmers with rudimentary skills can produce certain kinds of software, but not the kind that saves a company in its eleventh hour. What is needed is for tool builders to put their minds to the task of extending the power and productivity of talented software developers. What is needed are sharper ways of exploring domain models and expressing them in working software. I look forward to experimenting with new tools and technologies devised for this purpose.

But though improved tools will be valuable, we mustn't get distracted by them and lose sight of the core fact that creating good software is a learning and thinking activity. Modeling requires imagination and self-discipline. Tools that help us think or avoid distraction are good. Efforts to automate what must be the product of thought are naive and counterproductive.

With the tools and technology we already have, we can build systems much more valuable than most projects do today. We can write software that is a pleasure to use and a pleasure to work on, software that doesn't box us in as it grows but creates new opportunities and continues to add value for its owners.

The Use of Patterns in This Book

My first "nice car," which I was given shortly after college, was an eight-year-old Peugeot. Sometimes called the "French Mercedes," this car was well crafted, was a pleasure to drive, and had been very reliable. But by the time I got it, it was reaching the age when things start to go wrong and more maintenance is required.

Peugeot is an old company, and it has followed its own evolutionary path over many decades. It has its own mechanical terminology, and its designs are idiosyncratic; even the breakdown of functions into parts is sometimes nonstandard. The result is a car that only Peugeot specialists can work on, a potential problem for someone on a grad student income.

On one typical occasion, I took the car to a local mechanic to investigate a fluid leak. He examined the undercarriage and told me that oil was "leaking from a little box about two-thirds of the way back that seems to have something to do with distributing braking power between front and rear." He then refused to touch the car and advised me to go to the dealership, fifty miles away. Anyone can work on a Ford or a Honda; that's why those cars are more convenient and less expensive to own, even though they are equally mechanically complex.

I did love that car, but I will never own a quirky car again. A day came when a particularly expensive problem was diagnosed, and I had had enough of Peugeots. I took it to a local charity that accepted cars as donations. Then I bought a beat-up old Honda Civic for about what the repair would have cost.

Standard design elements are lacking for domain development, and so every domain model and corresponding implementation is quirky and hard to understand. Moreover, every team has to reinvent the wheel (or the gear, or the windshield wiper). In the world of object-oriented design, everything is an object, a reference, or a message—which, of course, is a useful abstraction. But that does not sufficiently constrain the range of domain design choices and does not support an economical discussion of a domain model.

To stop with "Everything is an object" would be like a carpenter or an architect summing up houses by saying "Everything is a room." There would be the big room with high-voltage outlets and a sink, where you might cook. There would be the small room upstairs, where you might sleep. It would take pages to describe an ordinary house. People who build or use houses realize that rooms follow patterns, patterns with special names, such as "kitchen." This language enables economical discussion of house design.

Moreover, not all combinations of functions turn out to be practical. Why not a room where you bathe and sleep? Wouldn't that be convenient. But long experience has precipitated into custom, and we separate our "bedrooms" from our "bathrooms." After all, bathing facilities tend to be shared among more people than bedrooms are, and they require maximum privacy, even from the others who share the same bedroom. And bathrooms have specialized and expensive infrastructure requirements. Bathtubs and toilets typically end up in the same room because both require the same infrastructure (water and drainage) and both are used in private.

Another room that has special infrastructure requirements is that room where you might prepare meals, also known as the "kitchen." In contrast to the bathroom, a kitchen has no special privacy requirements. Because of its expense, there is typically only one, even in relatively large houses. This singularity also facilitates our communal food preparation and eating customs.

When I say that I want a three-bedroom, two-bath house with an open-plan kitchen, I have packed a huge amount of information into a short sentence, and I've avoided a lot of silly mistakes—such as putting a toilet next to the refrigerator.

In every area of design—houses, cars, rowboats, or software—we build on patterns that have been found to work in the past, improvising within established themes. Sometimes we have to invent something completely new. But by basing standard elements on patterns, we avoid wasting our energy on problems with known solutions so that we can focus on our unusual needs. Also, building from conventional patterns helps us avoid a design so idiosyncratic that it is difficult to communicate.

Although software domain design is not as mature as other design fields—and in any case may be too diverse to accommodate patterns as specific as those used for car parts or rooms—there is nonetheless a need to move beyond "Everything is an object" to at least the equivalent of distinguishing bolts from springs.

A form for sharing and standardizing design insight was introduced in the 1970s by a group of architects led by Christopher Alexander (Alexander et al. 1977). Their "pattern language" wove together tried-and-true design solutions to common problems (much more subtly than my "kitchen" example, which has probably caused some readers of Alexander to cringe). The intent was that builders and users would communicate in this language, and they would be guided by the patterns to produce beautiful buildings that worked well and felt good to the people who used them.

Whatever architects might think of the idea, this pattern language has had a big impact on software design. In the 1990s software patterns were applied in many ways with some success, notably in detailed design (Gamma et al. 1995) and technical architectures (Buschmann et al. 1996). More recently, patterns have been used to document basic object-oriented design techniques (Larman 1998) and enterprise architectures (Fowler 2003, Alur et al. 2001). The language of patterns is now a mainstream technique for organizing software design ideas.

The pattern names are meant to become terms in the language of the team, and I've used them that way in this book. When a pattern name appears in a discussion, it is FORMATTED IN SMALL CAPS to call it out.

Here is how I've formatted patterns in this book. There is some variation around this basic plan, as I have favored case-by-case clarity and readability over rigid structure. . . .

Pattern Name

[Illustration of concept. Sometimes a
visual metaphor or evocative text.]

[Context. A brief explanation of how the concept relates to other patterns. In some cases, a brief overview of the pattern.

However, much of the context discussion in this book is in the chapter introductions and other narrative segments, rather than within the patterns.

✳ ✳ ✳]

[Problem discussion.]
Problem summary.
Discussion of the resolution of problem forces into a solution.
Therefore:
Solution summary.
Consequences. Implementation considerations. Examples.

✳ ✳ ✳

Resulting context: A brief explanation of how the pattern leads to later patterns.

[Discussion of implementation challenges. In Alexander's original format, this discussion would have been folded into the section describing the resolution of the problem, and I have often followed Alexander's organization in this book. But some patterns demand lengthier discussions of implementation. To keep the core pattern discussion tight, I have moved such long implementation discussions out, after the pattern.

Also, lengthy examples, particularly those that combine multiple patterns, are often outside the patterns.]

GLOSSARY

Here are brief definitions of selected terms, pattern names, and other concepts used in the book.

AGGREGATE   A cluster of associated objects that are treated as a unit for the purpose of data changes. External references are restricted to one member of the AGGREGATE, designated as the *root*. A set of consistency rules applies within the AGGREGATE's boundaries.

analysis pattern   A group of concepts that represents a common construction in business modeling. It may be relevant to only one domain or may span many domains (Fowler 1997, p. 8).

ASSERTION   A statement of the correct state of a program at some point, independent of how it does it. Typically, an ASSERTION specifies the result of an operation or an invariant of a design element.

BOUNDED CONTEXT   The delimited applicability of a particular model. BOUNDING CONTEXTS gives team members a clear and shared understanding of what has to be consistent and what can develop independently.

client   A program element that is calling the element under design, using its capabilities.

cohesion   Logical agreement and dependence.

command (a.k.a. *modifier*)   An operation that effects some change to the system (for example, setting a variable). An operation that intentionally creates a side effect.

CONCEPTUAL CONTOUR   An underlying consistency of the domain itself, which, if reflected in a model, can help the design accommodate change more naturally.

context   The setting in which a word or statement appears that determines its meaning. See BOUNDED CONTEXT.

CONTEXT MAP   A representation of the BOUNDED CONTEXTS involved in a project and the actual relationships between them and their models.

CORE DOMAIN   The distinctive part of the model, central to the user's goals, that differentiates the application and makes it valuable.

declarative design   A form of programming in which a precise description of properties actually controls the software. An executable specification.

deep model   An incisive expression of the primary concerns of the domain experts and their most relevant knowledge. A deep model sloughs off superficial aspects of the domain and naive interpretations.

design pattern   A description of communicating objects and classes that are customized to solve a general design problem in a particular context. (Gamma et al. 1995, p. 3)

distillation   A process of separating the components of a mixture to extract the essence in a form that makes it more valuable and useful. In software design, the abstraction of key aspects in a model, or the partitioning of a larger system to bring the CORE DOMAIN to the fore.

domain   A sphere of knowledge, influence, or activity.

domain expert   A member of a software project whose field is the domain of the application, rather than software development. Not just any user of the software, the domain expert has deep knowledge of the subject.

domain layer   That portion of the design and implementation responsible for domain logic within a LAYERED ARCHITECTURE. The domain layer is where the software expression of the domain model lives.

ENTITY   An object fundamentally defined not by its attributes, but by a thread of continuity and identity.

FACTORY   A mechanism for encapsulating complex creation logic and abstracting the type of a created object for the sake of a client.

function   An operation that computes and returns a result without observable side effects.

immutable   The property of never changing observable state after creation.

implicit concept   A concept that is necessary to understand the meaning of a model or design but is never mentioned.

INTENTION-REVEALING INTERFACE   A design in which the names of classes, methods, and other elements convey both the original developer's purpose in creating them and their value to a client developer.

invariant An ASSERTION about some design element that must be true at all times, except during specifically transient situations such as the middle of the execution of a method, or the middle of an uncommitted database transaction.

iteration A process in which a program is repeatedly improved in small steps. *Also*, one of those steps.

large-scale structure A set of high-level concepts, rules, or both that establishes a pattern of design for an entire system. A language that allows the system to be discussed and understood in broad strokes.

LAYERED ARCHITECTURE A technique for separating the concerns of a software system, isolating a domain layer, among other things.

life cycle A sequence of states an object can take on between creation and deletion, typically with constraints to ensure integrity when changing from one state to another. May include migration of an ENTITY between systems and different BOUNDED CONTEXTS.

model A system of abstractions that describes selected aspects of a domain and can be used to solve problems related to that domain.

MODEL-DRIVEN DESIGN A design in which some subset of software elements corresponds closely to elements of a model. *Also,* a process of codeveloping a model and an implementation that stay aligned with each other.

modeling paradigm A particular style of carving out concepts in a domain, combined with tools to create software analogs of those concepts (for example, object-oriented programming and logic programming).

REPOSITORY A mechanism for encapsulating storage, retrieval, and search behavior which emulates a collection of objects.

responsibility An obligation to perform a task or know information (Wirfs-Brock et al. 2003, p. 3).

SERVICE An operation offered as an interface that stands alone in the model, with no encapsulated state.

side effect Any observable change of state resulting from an operation, whether intentional or not, even a deliberate update.

SIDE-EFFECT-FREE FUNCTION *See* **function**.

STANDALONE CLASS A class that can be understood and tested without reference to any others, except system primitives and basic libraries.

stateless   The property of a design element that allows a client to use any of its operations without regard to the element's history. A stateless element may use information that is accessible globally and may even change that global information (that is, it may have side effects) but holds no private state that affects its behavior.

strategic design   Modeling and design decisions that apply to large parts of the system. Such decisions affect the entire project and have to be decided at team level.

supple design   A design that puts the power inherent in a deep model into the hands of a client developer to make clear, flexible expressions that give expected results robustly. Equally important, it leverages that *same* deep model to make the design itself easy for the implementer to mold and reshape to accommodate new insight.

UBIQUITOUS LANGUAGE   A language structured around the domain model and used by all team members to connect all the activities of the team with the software.

unification   The internal consistency of a model such that each term is unambiguous and no rules contradict.

VALUE OBJECT   An object that describes some characteristic or attribute but carries no concept of identity.

WHOLE VALUE   An object that models a single, complete concept.

REFERENCES

Alexander, C., M. Silverstein, S. Angel, S. Ishikawa, and D. Abrams. 1975. *The Oregon Experiment.* Oxford University Press.

Alexander, C., S. Ishikawa, and M. Silverstein. 1977. *A Pattern Language: Towns, Buildings, Construction.* Oxford University Press.

Alur, D., J. Crupi, and D. Malks. 2001. *Core J2EE Patterns.* Sun Microsystems Press.

Beck, K. 1997. *Smalltalk Best Practice Patterns.* Prentice Hall PTR.

———. 2000. *Extreme Programming Explained: Embrace Change.* Addison-Wesley.

———. 2003. *Test-Driven Development: By Example.* Addison-Wesley.

Buschmann, F., R. Meunier, H. Rohnert, P. Sommerlad, and M. Stal. 1996. *Pattern-Oriented Software Architecture: A System of Patterns.* Wiley.

Cockburn, A. 1998. *Surviving Object-Oriented Projects: A Manager's Guide.* Addison-Wesley.

Evans, E., and M. Fowler. 1997. "Specifications." Proceedings of PLoP 97 Conference.

Fayad, M., and R. Johnson. 2000. *Domain-Specific Application Frameworks.* Wiley.

Fowler, M. 1997. *Analysis Patterns: Reusable Object Models.* Addison-Wesley.

———. 1999. *Refactoring: Improving the Design of Existing Code.* Addison-Wesley.

———. 2003. *Patterns of Enterprise Application Architecture.* Addison-Wesley.

Gamma, E., R. Helm, R. Johnson, and J. Vlissides. 1995. *Design Patterns.* Addison-Wesley.

Kerievsky, J. 2003. "Continuous Learning," in *Extreme Programming Perspectives,* Michele Marchesi et al. Addison-Wesley.

———. 2003. Web site: http://www.industriallogic.com/xp/refactoring.

Larman, C. 1998. *Applying UML and Patterns: An Introduction to Object-Oriented Analysis and Design.* Prentice Hall PTR.

Merriam-Webster. 1993. *Merriam-Webster's Collegiate Dictionary.* Tenth edition. Merriam-Webster.

Meyer, B. 1988. *Object-oriented Software Construction.* Prentice Hall PTR.

Murray-Rust, P., H. Rzepa, and C. Leach. 1995. *Abstract 40.* Presented as a poster at the 210th ACS Meeting in Chicago on August 21, 1995. http://www.ch.ic.ac.uk/cml/

Pinker, S. 1994. *The Language Instinct: How the Mind Creates Language.* HarperCollins.

Succi, G. J., D. Wells, M. Marchesi, and L. Williams. 2002. *Extreme Programming Perspectives.* Pearson Education.

Warmer, J., and A. Kleppe. 1999. *The Object Constraint Language: Precise Modeling with UML.* Addison-Wesley.

Wirfs-Brock, R., B. Wilkerson, and L. Wiener. 1990. *Designing Object-Oriented Software.* Prentice Hall PTR.

Wirfs-Brock, R., and A. McKean. 2003. *Object Design: Roles, Responsibilities, and Collaborations.* Addison-Wesley.

PHOTO CREDITS

All photographs appearing in this book have been used with permission.

Richard A. Paselk, Humboldt State University
Astrolabe (Chapter 3, page 47)

© Royalty-Free/Corbis
Fingerprint (Chapter 5, page 89), Service Station (Chapter 5, page 104), Auto Factory (Chapter 6, page 136), Librarian (Chapter 6, page 147)

Martine Jousset
Grapes (Chapter 6, page 125), Olive Trees (young and old)(Conclusion, pages 500–501)

Biophoto Associates/Photo Researchers, Inc.
Electron micrograph of Oscillatoria (Chapter 14, page 335)

Ross J. Venables
Rowers (group and single) (Chapter 14, pages 341 and 371)

Photodisc Green/Getty Images
Runners (Chapter 14, page 356), Child (Chapter 14, page 361)

U.S. National Oceanic and Atmospheric Administration
Great Wall of China (Chapter 14, page 364)

© 2003 NAMES Project Foundation, Atlanta, Georgia.
Photographer Paul Margolies. www.aidsquilt.org
AIDS Quilt (Chapter 16, page 439)

INDEX

Business logic, in user interface layer, 77

Business rules, 17, 225

C

Callbacks, 73

Cargo shipping examples. *See* examples, cargo shipping.

Changing the design. *See* refactoring.

Chemical warehouse packer example, 235–241

Chemistry example, 377

Cleese, John, 5

CLOSURE OF OPERATIONS, 268–270

Code as documentation, 40

Code reuse
BOUNDED CONTEXT, 344
GENERIC SUBDOMAINS, 412–413
reusing prior art, 323–324

Cohesion, MODULES, 109–110, 113

COHESIVE MECHANISMS
and declarative style, 426–427
example, 425–427
overview, 422–425
vs. GENERIC SUBDOMAINS, 425

Common language. *See* PUBLISHED LANGUAGE; UBIQUITOUS LANGUAGE.

Communication, speech. *See* UBIQUITOUS LANGUAGE.

Communication, written. *See* documents; UML (Unified Modeling Language); UBIQUITOUS LANGUAGE.

Complexity, reducing. *See* distillation; large-scale structure; LAYERED ARCHITECTURE; supple design.

COMPOSITE pattern, 315–320

Composite SPECIFICATION, 273–282

Concept analysis. *See also* analysis patterns; examples, concept analysis.
awkwardness, 210–216
contradictions, 216–217
explicit constraints, 220–222
language of the domain experts, 206–207
missing concepts, 207–210

processes as domain objects, 222–223
researching existing resources, 217–219
SPECIFICATION, 223
trial and error, 219

CONCEPTUAL CONTOURS, 260–264

Conceptual layers, *See* LAYERED ARCHITECTURE; RESPONSIBILITY LAYERS

Configuring SPECIFICATION, 226–227

CONFORMIST, 361–363, 384–385

Constructors, 141–142, 174–175. *See also* FACTORIES.

CONTEXT MAP. *See also* BOUNDED CONTEXT.
example, 346–351
organizing and documenting, 351–352
overview, 344–346
vs. large-scale structure, 446, 485–488

CONTEXT MAP, choosing a strategy
ANTICORRUPTION LAYER, 384–385
CONFORMIST, 384–385
CUSTOMER/SUPPLIER DEVELOPMENT TEAMS, 356–360
defining BOUNDED CONTEXT, 382
deployment, 387
external systems, 383–385
integration, 384–385
merging OPEN HOST SERVICE and PUBLISHED LANGUAGE, 394–396
merging SEPARATE WAYS and SHARED KERNEL, 389–391
merging SHARED KERNEL and CONTINUOUS INTEGRATION, 391–393
packaging, 387
phasing out legacy systems, 393–394
for a project in progress, 388–389
SEPARATE WAYS, 384–385
SHARED KERNEL, 354–355
specialized terminologies, 386–387
system under design, 385–386
team context, 382
trade-offs, 387
transformations, 389
transforming boundaries, 382–383

Context principle, 328–329. *See also*
    BOUNDED CONTEXT; CONTEXT
    MAP.
CONTINUOUS INTEGRATION, 341–343,
    391–393. *See also* integration.
Continuous learning, 15–16
Contradictions, concept analysis,
    216–217
CORE DOMAIN
    DOMAIN VISION STATEMENT,
        415–416
    flagging key elements, 419–420
    MECHANISMS, 425
    overview, 400–405
Costs of architecture dictated
    MODULES, 114–115
Coupling MODULES, 109–110
Customer-focused teams, 492
CUSTOMER/SUPPLIER, 356–360

D
Database tuning, example, 102
Declarative design, 270–272
Declarative style of design, 273–282,
    426–427
Decoupling from the client, 156
Deep models
    distillation, 436–437
    overview, 20–21
    refactoring, 189–191
Deployment, 387. *See also* MODULES.
Design changes. *See* refactoring.
Design patterns. *See also* analysis
    patterns.
    COMPOSITE, 315–320
    FLYWEIGHT, 320
    overview, 309–310
    STRATEGY, 311–314
    vs. domain patterns, 309
Development teams. *See* teams.
Diagrams. *See* documents; UML
    (Unified Modeling Language).
Discovery, 191–192
Distillation. *See also* examples,
    distillation.
    ABSTRACT CORE, 435–437
    deep models, 436–437

DOMAIN VISION STATEMENT,
    415–416
encapsulation, 422–427
HIGHLIGHTED CORE, 417–421
INTENTION-REVEALING INTERFACES,
    422–427
large-scale structure, 483, 488–489
overview, 397–399
PCB design anecdote, 7–13
polymorphism, 435–437
refactoring targets, 437
role in design, 329
SEGREGATED CORE, 428–434
separating CORE concepts, 428–434
Distillation, COHESIVE MECHANISMS
    and declarative style, 426–427
    overview, 422–425
    vs. GENERIC SUBDOMAINS, 425
Distillation, CORE DOMAIN
    DOMAIN VISION STATEMENT,
        415–416
    flagging key elements, 419–420
    MECHANISMS, 425
    overview, 400–405
Distillation, GENERIC SUBDOMAINS
    adapting a published design, 408
    in-house solution, 409–410
    off-the-shelf solutions, 407
    outsourcing, 408–409
    overview, 406
    reusability, 412–413
    risk management, 413–414
    vs. COHESIVE MECHANISMS, 425
Distillation document, 418–419,
    420–421
Documents
    code as documentation, 40
    distillation document, 418–419,
        420–421
    DOMAIN VISION STATEMENT,
        415–416
    explanatory models, 41–43
    keeping current, 38–40
    in project activities, 39–40
    purpose of, 37–40
    validity of, 38–40
    UBIQUITOUS LANGUAGE, 39–40

PLUGGABLE COMPONENT FRAME-
WORK, 475–479
POLICY pattern. *See* STRATEGY
pattern.
Polymorphism, 435–437
Presentation layer. *See* user interface
layer.
Procedural languages, and MODEL-
DRIVEN DESIGN, 51–54
Processes as domain objects,
222–223
Prototypes, 238–241
PUBLISHED LANGUAGE
elephant and the blind men,
378–381
example, 377
merging with OPEN HOST SERVICE,
394–396
overview, 375–377

Q

Quilt project, 479

R

Reconstitution, 145–146, 148
Refactoring
breakthroughs, 193–200
during a crisis, 325–326
deep models, 189–191
definition, 188
designing for developers, 324
discovery, 191–192
distillation, 437
examples, 177–179, 181–185,
194–200, 247–249
exploration teams, 322–323
initiation, 321–322
large-scale structure, 481
levels of, 188–189
MODULES, 110, 111
to patterns, 188–189
reusing prior art, 323–324
supple design, 191
timing, 324–325
Refactoring targets, 437
Reference objects. *See* ENTITIES.
REPOSITORIES
advantages, 152

architectural frameworks, 156–157
decoupling from the client, 156
designing objects for relational databases, 159–161
encapsulation, 154
example, 172–173
and FACTORIES, 157–159
global searches, 150–151
implementing, 155–156
METADATA MAPPING LAYERS, 149
object access, 149–151
overview, 147–152
persistent objects, 150–151
querying, 152–154
references to preexisting domain
objects, 149
transaction control, 156
transient objects, 149
type abstraction, 155–156
Requirements gathering. *See* concept
analysis; knowledge crunching;
UBIQUITOUS LANGUAGE.
RESPONSIBILITY LAYERS
choosing layers, 460–464
example, 452–460
overview, 450–452
useful characteristics, 461
Reusing code
BOUNDED CONTEXT, 344
GENERIC SUBDOMAINS, 412–413
reusing prior art, 323–324
Risk management, 413–414

S

Scenarios, examples, 173–177
SEGREGATED CORE, 428–434
Selecting objects, 229–234, 269–270
SEPARATE WAYS, 384–385, 389–391
SERVICES. *See also* ENTITIES; VALUE
OBJECTS.
access to, 108
characteristics of, 105–106
granularity, 108
and the isolated domain layer,
106–107
naming, 105
overview, 104–105
partitioning into layers, 107

CONFORMIST, 361–363
CUSTOMER/SUPPLIER, 356–360
  example, 358–360
  SHARED KERNEL, 354–355, 359
  strategic design, 491
Terminology. *See* BOUNDED CONTEXT;
  PUBLISHED LANGUAGE; UBIQUI-
  TOUS LANGUAGE.
Testing boundaries, 351
Transaction control, 156
TRANSACTION SCRIPT, 79
Transformations, 389
Transforming boundaries, 382–383
Transient objects, 149
Translation layers, 374
Tuning a database, example, 102

U

UBIQUITOUS LANGUAGE. *See also*
  PUBLISHED LANGUAGE.
  analysis patterns, 306–307
  cargo router example, 27–30
  consistent use of, 32–35
  designing objects for relational databases, 160–161
  domain-specific language,
  272–273
  language of the domain experts,
  206–207
  overview, 24–27
  refining the model, 30–32
  specialized terminologies, 386–387
  requirements analysis, 25
  speech, role of, 30–32
UML (Unified Modeling Language),
  35–37

Unification, 332. *See also* CONTINU-
  OUS INTEGRATION.
Unified Modeling Language (UML),
  35–37
Updating the design. *See* refactoring.
User interface layer
  business logic, 77
  definition, 70
  separating from application and
  domain, 76–79

V

Validating objects, 227, 228–229
VALUE OBJECTS. *See also* ENTITIES;
  SERVICES.
  associations, 102–103
  bidirectional associations, 102–103
  change management, 101
  clustering. *See* AGGREGATES.
  designing, 99–102
  example, 167–168
  immutability, 100–101
  object assemblages, 98–99
  overview, 97–99
  passing as parameters, 99
  referencing ENTITIES, 98–99
  sharing, 100–101
  tuning a database, example, 102
Vision statement. *See* DOMAIN VISION
  STATEMENT.
Vocabulary. *See* PUBLISHED LAN-
  GUAGE; UBIQUITOUS LANGUAGE.

W

Waterfall design method, 14
Web site bookmark anecdote, 57–59